LAW WITHOUT VALUES

LAW
WITHOUT
VALUES

The Life, Work, and Legacy
of Justice Holmes

ALBERT W. ALSCHULER

The University of Chicago Press
Chicago and London

ALBERT W. ALSCHULER is the Wilson-Dickinson Professor of Law at the University of Chicago Law School. He is a coauthor of *The Privilege against Self-Incrimination: Its Origins and Development* (1997), also published by the University of Chicago Press.

The University of Chicago Press, Chicago 60637
The University of Chicago Press, Ltd., London
© 2000 by The University of Chicago
All rights reserved. Published 2000
Printed in the United States of America
09 08 07 06 05 04 03 02 01   3 4 5

ISBN: 0-226-01520-3 (cloth)

Library of Congress Cataloging-in-Publication Data

Alschuler, Albert W., 1940–
    Law without values : the life, work, and legacy of Justice Holmes / Albert W. Alschuler.
      p.   cm.
    Includes bibliographical references and index.
    ISBN 0-226-01520-3 (cloth)
    1.   Holmes, Oliver Wendell, 1841–1935. 2.   Judges—United States—Biography.
 I.   Title.

  KF8745.H6A4   2000
  347.73'2634—dc21

                                           00-008279

♾ The paper used in this publication meets the minimum requirements of the American National Standard for Information Sciences—Permanence of Paper for Printed Library Materials, ANSI Z39.48-1992.

In memory of Winifred King Alschuler
1914–1998

Contents

Sydney Hyman, David Luban, Andrei Marmor, Winston Nagin, Sheldon Novick, Susan Schwouchau, Brian Simpson, Steven Smith, Geoffrey Stone, Stephen Pepper, Eric Posner, and Richard Posner.

Richard Posner merits special thanks. I may have cast Justice Holmes as the villain of this book, but Judge Posner is the runner-up. I count no fewer than seventeen places in which I cite Posner's writings to criticize them—as well as about seven places in which I cite Posner's writings favorably. Posner and I differ on many things, and our views of Holmes are especially far apart. Our differences simply underscore the gracious-ness of the constructive and insightful help that Posner gave me. Posner is the busiest and most productive person I know. As chief judge of the United States Court of Appeals for the Seventh Circuit, his administrative duties are heavy; he writes thorough and wide-ranging opinions without preliminary drafting assistance from his clerks; he teaches and lectures; and he remains America's most prolific author of first-rate legal scholar-ship. He has a life away from work too. Posner nevertheless finds time to aid my work whenever I ask, and he has given the same patient help to innumerable others. No one offers a better model of academic openness, generosity, and cooperation.

Acknowledgments

The Rockefeller Foundation enabled me to begin this study in 1991 in an idyllic setting, the Foundation's Study Center in Bellagio, Italy. A fellowship from the John Simon Guggenheim Memorial Foundation and support from the University of Chicago Law School enabled me to conclude the project in 1998 in another wonderful environment, Boulder, Colorado. In the summers between 1991 and 1998, I received research support from the Leonard Sorkin Faculty Fund, the Sonnenschein Fund, the Herbert and Marjorie Fried Faculty Research Fund, and the Russell Baker Scholars Fund at the University of Chicago Law School. Support from the Dwight P. Green Sr. Fund permitted revision of the manuscript in the summer of 1999. I am grateful to these mentors and to my patient and supportive dean, Douglas Baird.

I presented parts of this book as lectures or workshops at the University of Arizona, the University of Arkansas (Fayetteville), the Brooklyn Law School, the University of Chicago, the University of Colorado, the University of Denver, the Dickinson School of Law, the University of Florida, the University of Georgia, the McGeorge School of Law, the University of Iowa, and the University of Pittsburgh, and I gathered knowledge and insight at every stop. Portions of this book appeared in Albert W. Alschuler, *The Descending Trail: Holmes' Path of the Law One Hundred Years Later,* 49 Fla L Rev 353 (1997), and these portions are republished here with permission of the *Florida Law Review.*

I profited greatly from the wise and skillful editing of David Bemelmans and from the comments of people who read and criticized parts of the manuscript. They included David Dolinko, Frank Easterbrook, Richard Epstein, Judith Gardiner, John Goldberg, James Gordley, Paul Heald,

Chapter One

Moral Skepticism in Twentieth-Century American Law

The left and the right in American legal thought are more alike than different. They are united in their skepticism, especially concerning values. Oliver Wendell Holmes sounded the principal theme of twentieth-century jurisprudence when he wrote that moral preferences are "more or less arbitrary. . . . Do you like sugar in your coffee or don't you? . . . So as to truth."[1]

This book presents a critical review of the life and work of Justice Holmes, the scholar and jurist who, more than any other individual, shaped the law of the twentieth century. The book is unusual in fitting the pieces of Holmes's philosophy, life experience, personality, and legal work together in a nonchronologial way. Because its primary focus is Holmes's worldview, the book turns after this chapter to a description of that outlook. It then considers how Holmes's skepticism developed and how he manifested it in his personality, judicial opinions, and scholarly writings.

This introductory chapter provides background for the study. It focuses on legal thought after Holmes, describing the current state of American legal scholarship and noting the extent to which post-Holmes visions of law differ from pre-Holmes visions. The chapter argues that the post-Holmes visions of law are the product of a revolt against objective concepts of right and wrong rather than a revolt against formalism, and it suggests that in important respects, the path of the law since Holmes has been downward.

TWO BRANDS OF SKEPTICISM

The value skepticism of recent legal thought has taken two principal forms. The milder form, a murky utilitarian pragmatism, dominated American law schools to the virtual exclusion of other approaches from at least the end of World War II until at least the mid-1970s. Although the consensus of that era has fragmented, utilitarian pragmatism remains the principal style of analysis in American law schools. It is also the dominant style in American courts, especially the Supreme Court of the United States.[2]

The second, more extreme form of skepticism sees law, not as seeking the greatest attainable satisfaction of everyone's wants, but as the self-interested exercise of power. On this view, law is a matter of who gets what—of politics unguided by principle. Champions of both the mild brand of skepticism (utilitarian pragmatism) and the piquant (law as power) are the heirs of Holmes. Which of the two competing skeptical views better captures the prophet's teaching is in fact a matter of dispute: Was Holmes a pragmatist or a utilitarian, or was he a Nietzchean, a social Darwinist, or a nihilist? Although elements of both brands of skepticism appear in Holmes's work, this book maintains that the more thoroughgoing skeptics have by far the stronger claim to his mantle.

BRAKING HALFWAY DOWN: PRAGMATISM AND UTILITARIANISM

Pragmatism is distinctly American in its mistrust of abstraction. This philosophy "is freedom from theory-guilt," says Thomas Grey.[3] It proclaims itself the philosophy of "doing without a philosophy" and of "experimenting," "muddling through," and determining "what works." Pragmatism is consequentialist. It judges the worth of acts and beliefs by what they produce, declaring simply that good acts and good beliefs are those that have good consequences. Cornel West observes that the "common denominator" of pragmatism is "a future-oriented instrumentalism that tries to deploy thought as a weapon to enable more effective action."[4] Although pragmatism is instrumental—concerned about matching means to ends—it is deliberately vague about ends.[5] Richard Rorty, the most prominent exponent of pragmatism today, calls his version of the philosophy "the new fuzziness."[6] Yogi Berra offered Rorty and other pragmatists good advice when he said, "You've got to be careful if you don't know where you're going because you might not get there."[7]

The late-nineteenth-and early-twentieth-century Americans who invented pragmatism[8] were influenced by the Darwinism of their era. They envisioned thought as simply a means by which human beings adapt to their environment, and they judged all thought on the basis of its instrumental or adaptive success without regard to whether it corresponded to external reality. They believed, moreover, that, even without clear objectives or values, random experimentation could generate social progress. In the same way that a mindless process of random selection had created the wonders of the biological world, people could advance toward social success just by "trying things out" and discarding those that failed.

Although pragmatism appears to renounce utilitarianism along with all other systematic philosophies, one cannot know "what works" without a concept of success or what consequences to count as good without a concept of the good.[9] Implicitly or explicitly, pragmatists join everyone else in endorsing objectives—democracy, survival, reproductive success, community, happiness, "flourishing," or something else. Whether under the table or above it, the philosophy of doing without a philosophy always imports a philosophy.[10] For skeptical people, moreover, utilitarianism is likely to seem as good a philosophy as any and better than most, for it approves whatever wants people have without ranking them.

By the time I attended law school in the 1960s, my teachers had law figured out. They were pragmatists, and they favored "the functional approach." Although no one explained what function was served by the functional approach, I sensed what they meant. Law was a matter of balancing interests and of determining which ones "predominated."[11] Interests were what people had or wanted to get, and the goal was to satisfy as many of these interests as possible. Balancing usually meant the greatest good for the greatest number, the maximum satisfaction of wants, and the maximization of happiness. It meant, in a word, utilitarianism.

In the decades after I left law school, law and economics scholars sought to reduce interest balancing to a science, one replete with mathematical formulas. These scholars treated all desires as exogenous (that is, as coming from "outside," as "given," or as the starting point for analysis). Some of the economists' critics objected that this approach was too simple. Desires were socially constructed, and shaping preferences was an appropriate function of law.[12] Observers of the debate between the economists and their critics apparently were left with a choice between "exogenous" (or "just there") values and "socially constructed" values. The notion that values might be right or wrong—that they could promote justice or advance the "true" happiness of human beings—had faded altogether.

In a noted 1979 article, the most prominent of the law and economics scholars, Richard Posner, rejected the common view that law and economics is "applied utilitarianism."[13] Posner maintained that welfare economists seek the maximum satisfaction, not of all human desires, but only of desires backed by wealth. He claimed that by adding a wealth constraint to classical utilitarianism, he had made his moral relativism less troublesome than that of Jeremy Bentham. In Bentham's utilitarian world, a sadist who derived enough pleasure from torture to outweigh his victim's suffering would be justified in tormenting her. Jeremy's joy could excuse Alice's anguish. As Posner described his own vision of justice, however, "[a sadist] would have to *buy* [his or her] victims' consent, and these purchases would soon deplete the wealth of all but the wealthiest sadists."[14]

As Arthur Leff summarized both Posner's bottom line and Bentham's, "each of the Seven Deadly Sins is as licit as any of the others, and as any of the Cardinal virtues."[15] All human desires have become, for economists and many others, equivalent to one another. The pleasure of pulling the wings off flies ranks as high as that of feeding the hungry. As Robert Bork writes,

> [T]here is no principled way to decide that one man's gratifications are more deserving of respect than another's or that one form of gratification is more worthy than another. Why is sexual gratification more worthy than moral gratification? Why is sexual gratification nobler than economic gratification? There is no way of deciding these matters other than by reference to some system of moral or ethical values that has no objective or intrinsic validity of its own and about which men can and do differ.[16]

For economically minded scholars and others, the function of law, the market, and other social institutions is to achieve the maximum satisfaction of human wants regardless of their content (or, if you prefer Posner's variation, to achieve the maximum satisfaction of desires backed by wealth). This viewpoint elides a distinctive and persistent characteristic of human thought—the evaluation of desires on scales other than intensity.

Pragmatism views thought in even its most abstract form as adaptive, problem solving, and want satisfying. Pragmatic reasoning in this sense is shared by human beings and animals. Although Aristotle may have doubted that animals have the capacity to reason,[17] he never met Ron's cat, which refuted the philosopher by placing a paw over the bell on its neck and stalking birds on three legs. Ron's cat was a pragmatist, and although humanity may share more than Aristotle suspected with "dolphinity, beaverishness, and wolfhood,"[18] human thought differs from the reasoning of cats partly because, in James Gustafson's words, people are "valuing animals."[19] They think not only about how to get from here to there but also about the "there's" they want to get to.

People use their mental capacities to reflect about principles, duties, obligations, and ends. They examine critically the objects of their valuation. They sense that some desires are not simply stronger in intensity but more virtuous than others, and they struggle toward a proper ordering of the objects of desire.[20] Treating this activity as a mode of self-interested, cat-like adaptation to the environment, pragmatic thinkers deny or treat as epiphenomenal an important part of the experience of being human. As Ludwig Wittgenstein asked, "Does man think . . . because he has found that thinking pays?—Because he thinks it advantageous to think? (Does he bring up his children because he has found it pays?)"[21]

The skepticism of welfare economists, pragmatists, and utilitarians is only partial. These thinkers attempt, without much success, to put on the brakes halfway down. Their beliefs are vulnerable to the same "sez who?" skepticism that leads them to reject the creeds of others.[22] They are unable to justify even the minimal values they retain.

The core impulse of utilitarianism may seem attractive: "I know nothing of cosmic justice, but I have met many of my fellow human beings. I can see that they have needs and desires just as I do. What is more, I perceive no basis for ranking my own desires more highly than theirs." This ethical position is principled and neutral and often demands altruism. A person who accepted it might unhesitatingly sacrifice her life to save the lives of two strangers (that is, if she considered the interpersonal comparison of utilities impossible, did not have enough time or resources to make the comparison, or discovered that her capacity for future happiness was not in fact as great as the combined capacities of the people she could save). Utilitarianism's principal attraction is its strong sense of equality (a virtue that Richard Posner's wealth-driven version of the creed tosses aside). This theory ranks everyone's happiness as highly as the king's.

One can, however, apply a "sez who?" to utilitarianism as easily as to anything else. Although utilitarianism views all desires as commensurable with all other desires (and although law and economics theorists treat all desires as commensurable with money), utilitarianism remains an *ethical* system. What, then, makes this system just? Despite Jeremy Bentham's insistence that "natural rights are simply nonsense . . . nonsense on stilts,"[23] does even this happiness-focused ethical system require external justification? Can utilitarianism, wealth maximization, or any other ethical system make sense in the absence of "a brooding omnipresence in the sky"?[24] Can one truly brake ethical skepticism halfway down? What's so great about egalitarianism, altruism, neutrality, and human (or hippopotamus)[25] happiness anyway?

In the absence of external justification, the desire that everyone's desires be satisfied is just another desire, and utilitarianism can be no more than a taste. Jeremy Bentham and his followers hoped to maximize happiness; Richard Posner and his followers seek to maximize wealth; and Adolf Hitler and his followers preferred building a master race. Different strokes for different folks.

MORE PIQUANT PLEASE

Richard Posner observes that "the skeptical mood has . . . a distinctive and bracing tone—astringent, irreverent, unsentimental, no nonsense."[26] People drawn to these emotional attributes (the "aftershave" virtues) may find it difficult to brake their skepticism at the pragmatic, utilitarian midpoint.

Justice Holmes did not brake. In his world, nearly every assertion of values beyond personal or, at most, class self-interest was pretense, and just about every ethical question could be reduced to an issue of dominance, power, death, and survival. Holmes saw human rights as no more than what "a given crowd . . . will fight for,"[27] and he remarked that people will fight for their rights just as "[a] dog will fight for his bone."[28]

Holmes's view that rights are the bones over which people fight has found new champions in the academy in recent years. Law and economics scholars make room in their scholarship for both the "mild" and the "piquant" brands of skepticism. As noted above, the economists' own ethical views are mostly "mild." They suggest, moreover, that in areas not governed by legislation (that is, in areas of common law adjudication), courts have sought to maximize "efficiency" in much the same way as the economists themselves.

For many economists, however, legislatures are inviting targets for darker skeptical analysis. These economists view most legislation either as the product of bargains among selfish interest groups or as the product of the capture of the legislature by whatever group "bid highest." On this view, the public purposes asserted for legislation are mostly masks.[29] The economists echo Holmes: "[I]t is no sufficient condemnation of legislation that it favors one class at the expense of another; for much or all legislation does that. . . . [Legislation] is necessarily made a means by which a body, having the power, put burdens which are disagreeable to them on the shoulders of somebody else."[30] Some law and economic scholars propose, in fact, that courts treat the interpretation of statutes as essentially a branch of contract law, construing statutes narrowly in order to carry out, not their asserted public goals, but the interest-group bargains behind them.[31]

A distinct branch of economic analysis called "public choice theory" is devoted to proving that public choice is not what it seems. This branch focuses on legislatures and other public agencies in its efforts to demonstrate that governmental actions serve selfish private ends.[32] Public choice theorists have contended that laws ostensibly designed to prevent securities fraud were the product of bankers' fears of losing savings deposits,[33] that the votes of federal trial judges on the constitutionality of sentencing guidelines were affected by the prospects of the judges' appointment to appellate courts,[34] that nineteenth-century politicians allowed fires to rage out of control to encourage the establishment of fire departments that would give jobs to the politicians' supporters,[35] and that members of Congress have supported the creation of federal bureaucracies in order to enhance their political support by aiding constituents whom these bureaucracies would treat unfairly.[36]

Taxonomies of current legal scholarship place public choice theory together with law and economics on the political right. They place critical legal studies, critical race theory, and feminist jurisprudence on the left. Nearly all of the scholars associated with all of these movements, however—like nearly all of the pragmatists and functionalists in the center—are the heirs of Holmes.

The skepticism of many members of the critical legal studies (CLS) movement is pure salsa piccante.[37] A single CLS motto best conveys the movement's spirit: "Law is politics."[38] In a sense, this motto should be uncontroversial. My dictionary endorses it, saying that all of government is politics.[39] There are good politics, bad politics, interest-group politics, republican politics, mean-spirited politics, noble politics, honest politics, dishonest politics, principled politics, unprincipled politics, traditional politics, revolutionary politics, and countless other kinds. To recite the dictionary, however, is to trifle. The CLS scholars intend no truism. They know what politics is. Politics is who you cheer for. The white male elite who wrote the laws cheered for themselves; CLS cheers for their victims. That is all there is to it. Anything else is mystification, false consciousness, and "mind fuck."[40]

Critical race theorists and radical feminists[41] are the heirs of Holmes too. Many of these scholars deny the possibility of a principled response to the unprincipled subordination of minorities and women. Emphasizing that the rhetoric of neutral principles often has masked subordination, they decline to use this language. Kimberle Crenshaw, a founder of critical race theory, describes this movement as "grounded in a bottom-up commitment to improve the substantive conditions" of minorities. She contrasts this apparent focus on the material bottom line with the older objective of the civil rights movement—resisting "the use of race . . . to interfere with decisions that would otherwise be fair or neutral."[42]

Ann Scales observes, "Feminism does not claim to be objective, because objectivity is the basis of inequality."[43] She adds, "Feminism is result-oriented. . . . [W]hen dealing with social inequality there are no neutral principles."[44] Catharine MacKinnon declares:

> When [sex inequality] is exposed as a naked power question, there is no separable question of what ought to be. . . . In this shift of paradigms, equality propositions become no longer propositions of good and evil, but of power and powerlessness, no more disinterested in their origins or neutral in their arrival at conclusions than are the problems they address.[45]

SLIDING FROM SOCRATES

All of these American scholars have tilted from Socrates on the issue that marks the largest and most persistent divide in all of jurisprudence. In ancient Athens, the philosopher Thrasymachus anticipated Holmes by 2,300 years when he said, "Justice is nothing else than the interest of the stronger."[46] Socrates replied that justice was not the will of the powerful but "the excellence of the soul."[47] He argued that justice was unlike medical treatment (a means to an end) or an amusing game (which had no end beyond itself). Justice was a good of the highest order—an end and a means, a good to be valued for itself and for its consequences.[48] In Rome four hundred years later, Cicero described justice as "right reason in agreement with nature."[49]

As others revisited the issue in the centuries that followed, some gave voice to the harsher and more skeptical position. In 1651, for example, Thomas Hobbes declared that the concepts of good and evil masked personal appetites and desires. These concepts had no meaning apart from the preferences of the people who invoked them:

> [W]hatsoever is the object of any man's appetite or desire, that is it which he for his part calleth *good:* and the object of his hate and aversion, *evil.* . . . For these words of good [and] evil . . . are ever used with relation to the person that useth them: there being nothing simply and absolutely so.[50]

Throughout Western history until the final third of the nineteenth century, however, Socrates' position dominated European and, in later centuries, American law. The views of moral realists like Aristotle, Gratian, Accursius, Bonaventura, Thomas Aquinas, John Duns Scotus, Richard Hooker, Hugo Grotius, Jean Domat, Samuel von Pufendorf, Edward Coke, John Locke, William Blackstone, Thomas Jefferson, and Abraham Lincoln shaped cultural understandings of justice. The past century appears to have given moral relativism its longest sustained run in Western history.

In American law, the beginning of the final third of the nineteenth century marks a surprisingly bright divide. In January 1867, Holmes joined the staff of the *American Law Review* and began publishing case digests and book notices.[51] His first major legal essay appeared in 1870,[52] the same year that Christopher Columbus Langdell became the first dean of the Harvard Law School.[53] The English and American writers who shaped American law prior to the Civil War (or who began publishing earlier although their principal influence came later)[54] generally credited natural law. Among these writers were Locke, Blackstone, Jefferson, Wilson, Madison, Tucker, Marshall, Kent, Story, Lieber, Lincoln, and Pomeroy.[55] With few exceptions, writers who began publishing after the Civil War had little use for natural law. These writers included Holmes, Langdell, Tiedeman, Carter, Beale, and Pound.

The moral realism that shaped American law prior to the final third of the nineteenth century may have contributed to the law's vitality. Even the legal realists, pragmatists, and critical legal scholars of our era have described this earlier period as the "golden age" of American law, the "age of discovery," and the epoch of "the grand style."[56] The Darwinism of post–Civil War America helped to bring this epoch to an end.

Contrary to the currently prevalent myth, Holmes and those who joined him did not bring something bold or new to law by proclaiming that it is evolutionary and adaptive and can further human needs. As this book will show, those ideas were a source of pride for Americans from the beginning. Instead, Holmes and his twentieth-century followers joined the late-nineteenth-century formalists in taking something away from law—the sense that law can further objectives beyond internal coherency, personal tastes, and selfish interests. Holmes was at the forefront of a revolution whose achievements were mostly negative. This revolution was not a "revolt against formalism"[57] but a revolt against objective concepts of right and wrong—a revolt against natural law.

ABOUT THIS BOOK

The first complete biography of Holmes (Sheldon Novick's) appeared in 1989.[58] The past decade has seen two other major biographies (Liva Baker's and G. Edward White's),[59] a shorter profile (Gary Aichele's),[60] and an extraordinary wealth of other writing about Holmes, nearly all of it laudatory.[61] The criticisms of Holmes voiced thirty-five to sixty-five years ago by such writers as Mortimer Adler,[62] H. L. Mencken,[63] Yosal Rogat,[64] Saul Touster,[65] and Edmund Wilson[66] have faded from view, as have those of a group of Catholic scholars who wrote during and shortly after World War II. These scholars saw in Holmes much the same ideology that the Allies resisted in Europe.[67]

The information that writers of the past decade have supplied about Holmes invites a reexamination of his life and work, and many of the writers' own appraisals invite a response. This book reviews the evidence and concludes with the critics that Holmes had a brutal worldview and was indifferent to the welfare of others. Holmes's acknowledgment that he came "devilish near to believing that might makes right" was correct—or perhaps an understatement.[68] Because many of the views expressed in this book are unorthodox and also because Holmes wrote in colorful and memorable ways, the book makes frequent use of verbatim quotations. Endnotes, which my editors complain are too extensive, provide further documentation.

Chapter 2 examines Holmes's power-focused philosophy, particularly as he expressed it in his speeches and letters. These informal writings reveal in a less cautious manner than Holmes's opinions and legal scholarship his worldview and where it led him. This chapter rejects the common claim that Holmes's thought was dualistic, with a good and bad side. Essentially, although Holmes celebrated personal passion and claimed to have convictions, he "sneered" at all political and moral causes except eugenics, which he supported in an especially chilling form by advocating the execution of "everyone below standard."

Chapter 3 examines Holmes's character and personality, emphasizing descriptions by people who knew him well. Like his biographers, these contemporaries noted Holmes's lack of involvement with others (as Holmes sometimes did himself). Although Richard Posner rightly insists that people like Holmes "whose cast of mind is skeptical, Darwinian, and atheistic" need not be "personally bleak and cold,"[69] the extent to which Holmes's worldview, politics, legal work, and personality all matched one another is remarkable. There was a unity to his epistemology (truth is "the majority view of the nation which can lick all others")[70], jurisprudence (rights are "what a given crowd will fight for")[71], and personal ethics ("[I]n the last resort a man rightly prefers his own interest to that of his neighbors").[72] Sometimes the values by which one lives one's life also shape one's understanding of law.

Chapter 4 describes how Holmes's Civil War wounds and the other horrors he experienced during the war apparently contributed to the transformation of his personality and outlook. This chapter notes in addition the social Darwinism that Holmes embraced, emphasizing that this Darwinism fit nicely with Holmes's postwar romanticization of war and struggle.

Three lengthy chapters then examine Holmes's professional work. Chapter 5 focuses on his judicial opinions. It concludes that Holmes's work as a judge was largely but not entirely consistent with his might-makes-right philosophy. When Justice Louis D. Brandeis joined the Supreme Court and Holmes turned seventy-eight, the old soldier did seem to mellow a little.

The next two chapters explore Holmes's most noted scholarly works. Chapter 6 examines his book *The Common Law* and chapter 7 his essay *The Path of the Law*. In one paragraph at the beginning and several toward the end of the initial chapter of *The Common Law*, Holmes presented a noted description of how law develops (including the statement, "The life of the law has not been logic: It has been experience"). This description was eloquent—but not at all the innovation that twentieth-century lawyers have imagined it to be. Moreover, most of Holmes's book consisted of tendentious argument in support of an untenable historical thesis—that the common law had steadily replaced "subjective" (or "internal") standards of liability with "objective" (or "external") standards, becoming ever more willing to sacrifice blameless individuals to accomplish its goals.

The Path of the Law offered Holmes's fullest articulation of his concept of law. He declared, "If you want to know the law and nothing else, you must look at it as a bad man, who cares only for the material consequences which such knowledge enables him to predict."[73] Chapter 7 argues that this concept does not begin to capture what law means in civilized societies. After reviewing some familiar objections to Holmes's vision of law, this chapter criticizes Holmes's good-man, bad-man dichotomy. It emphasizes that this division obscures a reason for law observance that often proves decisive when people are neither entirely selfish nor entirely selfless—a sense of mutual obligation.

Chapter 7 then argues that, although law and morality are distinct in some respects, our thought and language make complete separation of the "is" and the "ought" impossible. After considering a definition of law that is essentially the opposite of Holmes's—law consists of those societal settlements that a good person should regard as obligatory—the chapter turns to Holmes's proposal to purge moral terminology from the law. It argues that Holmes inverted ordinary language for no evident reason, diminishing rather than enhancing the law's ability to accomplish its ends.

Chapter 8 considers why a figure as harsh as Holmes became the most noted oracle of American law. Although many circumstances contributed to Holmes's reputation (including deliberate myth making by some young admirers as well as Holmes's brilliance, literary skill, and prescient opinions in a few areas of constitutional law), a large part of the explanation is simply that Holmes's celebration of power found a receptive audience in post-Darwinian America.

Chapter 9, which ends the book, reviews some objective indicators of America's current social disintegration and malaise. Without attempting the task of causal attribution, it suggests an affinity between the nation's sullen mood and the ethical skepticism that now dominates the academy. Twentieth-century pragmatism failed its own test of truth. A new epistemology, developed primarily by post–World War II writers, now offers a better test. This epistemology focuses, not on the utility of beliefs in shaping future action, but on "coherency," "reflective equilibrium," and the discovery of patterns in present and past experience. By putting first things first and by revealing the nonarbitrary way in which people make and revise ethical judgments, this epistemology exposes the brooding of the skeptics as adolescent and destructive. Recognizing how ethical judgments blend with empirical judgments to enable us to make sense of the world around us could tilt our views of justice back toward Socrates.

Chapter Two

A Power-Focused Philosophy

THE HERO OF AMERICAN LAW

Hymns have been written of Justice Holmes. Benjamin Cardozo called him "the great overlord of the law and its philosophy."[1] Cardozo, who would succeed Holmes on the Supreme Court, added that Holmes "is today for all students . . . of human society the philosopher and the seer, the greatest of our age in the domain of jurisprudence. . . ."[2]

"He is indeed the philosopher become king," declared Felix Frankfurter.[3] "For centuries . . . men who never heard of him 'will be moving to the measure of his thought.'"[4]

"[L]ike the winged victory of Samothrace he is the summit of hundreds of years of civilization," Charles Wyzanski proclaimed.[5] "His was the most distinguished mind of its time," judged Henry Steele Commager.[6]

"[T]he great oracle of American legal thought," said Thomas Grey.[7] "America's most distinguished citizen," said Karl Llewellyn.[8] "The only great American legal thinker," said Morton Horwitz.[9] "[T]he most illustrious figure in the history of American law," said Richard Posner.[10] As Harry Kalven and Hans Zeisel concluded, "[F]or the American lawyer, he is the beau ideal."[11]

Holmes was the only American jurist ever awarded honorary degrees by Harvard, Oxford, and Yale.[12] A 1990 study reported that law reviews mentioned him more frequently than any other judge except a few still on the bench.[13] In the confirmation proceedings for the two most recently appointed Supreme Court justices, Holmes was mentioned repeatedly as the epitome of what a jurist should be.[14]

Holmes may be the ideal of the public as well as the members of his profession. He is the only justice of the Supreme Court to have been the subject of a best-selling historical novel, a hit Broadway play, and a motion picture.[15] A mountain in Alaska bears his name, and when letters could be mailed for 15 cents, he peered from their corners on purple postage stamps.[16] One writer declared, "The automobile industry has Henry Ford; jazz, Louis Armstrong; Hollywood, Marilyn Monroe; and baseball, Babe Ruth. American law has Oliver Wendell Holmes."[17]

DR. JEKYLL AND MR. HYDE

Despite these hosannas to Holmes, a common theme in writing about him is that he was two people—Jekyll-Holmes and Hyde-Holmes. As early as 1869, when Holmes was twenty-eight, William James declared that he was "composed of at least two and a half different people rolled into one, and the way he keeps them together in one tight skin, without quarreling any more than they do, is remarkable."[18] Sixty-two years later, while Holmes was a justice of the Supreme Court, Mortimer Adler said that it was necessary to separate "the greatness of Holmes as a judge and a person" from his "highly questionable jurisprudential doctrines."[19] Shortly after Holmes's retirement, H. L. Mencken wrote, "On at least three days out of four, . . . the learned justice remained the soldier— precise, pedantic, unimaginative, even harsh. But on the fourth day a strange amiability overcame him."[20]

In the 1940s and early 1950s, lay and clerical Catholic lawyers emphasized the darkness of Holmes jurisprudence.[21] Even the critic who titled his article *Hobbes, Holmes and Hitler,* however, announced in his opening sentence, "All Americans . . . are proud of Mr. Justice Holmes."[22] Another writer urged vigilance against the possibility of a Holmesian dictatorship but observed that Holmes's rulings as a judge "seemed to express in epigrams a heart that welled with understanding and deep solicitude for the dignity of the individual and especially for the less fortunate."[23] One wonders which half of that writer's schizophrenic Holmes would have been more likely to make the real Holmes retch.

Mathias Reimann recently praised Holmes at length, declaring that Holmes was "a professed idealist, not scorning the comforts of modern life, but asking for goals far beyond it." A few pages later, Reimann observed, "In the end, a complete picture of Holmes shows a man who was unable to care much about anything but himself."[24]

Daniel Boorstin wrote of Holmes's "elusiveness,"[25] Saul Touster of his "double-facedness,"[26] and G. Edward White of "[t]he capacity of his thought to contain . . . self-opposing points of view."[27] Francis Biddle wrote of his "dualism,"[28] and echoes of Jekyll-Hyde dualism recur in Sheldon Novick's biography. The book's frontispiece quotes Cardozo: "One cannot read [Holmes's] opinions without seeing honor and courage written down on every page."[29] Most of Novick's discussion of Holmes as a judge and scholar is in accord. Novick's preface, however, remarks that Holmes "in personal letters seemed to espouse a kind of fascist ideology."[30] A reader might wonder whether the letter writer and the judge were the same.

RACE, RELIGION, AND GENDER

Richard Posner says that Novick, in his reference to fascist ideology (and also in his description of Holmes as "a violent, combative, womanizing aristocrat"), has "gone overboard."[31] Although Holmes favored eugenics, glorified war, and believed that might made right, Posner rejects the word *fascist* because Holmes was not anti-Semitic[32] and favored democracy and free speech.[33] In addition, Posner claims that "Holmes is the victim . . . of political correctness." Although "it is easy to find many instances in which, particularly on matters of race and sex, [Holmes] failed to display a 1990s sensibility, . . . on the whole his outlook was remarkably tolerant and indeed cosmopolitan by the standards of his generation."[34]

Holmes enjoyed "the impregnable security of belonging to the Boston 'Brahmin' caste" (a term invented by Holmes's father),[35] but unlike many other members of this caste, he welcomed the company of Jews.[36] As a justice of the Supreme Court, he hired Jewish and Irish-American law clerks—all of them, like all but one of his other clerks, white, male, unmarried, high-ranking graduates of the Harvard Law School.[37] Holmes was not, however, entirely free of religious bias. He once remarked that although he would rather "see power in the hands of the Jews than in the Catholics,'" he did not "wish to be run by either."[38]

As Posner indicated, Holmes was more tolerant of Jews and Catholics than others who shared his background, but contrary to Posner's suggestion, Holmes's views concerning gender and race were probably more offensive from today's perspective than the dominant sentiment of his era. For example, Holmes opposed the vote for women at a time when most men approved it,[39] and he once wrote, "[I]f I were sincere and were asked certain *whys* by a woman [I] should reply, 'Because Ma'am I am the bull.'"[40]

Dissenting in *Adkins v Children's Hospital*,[41] Holmes responded to the majority's judgment that gender differences "have now come almost, if not quite, to the vanishing point" by declaring, "It will take more than the Nineteenth Amendment to convince me that there are no differences between men and women."[42] Writing for the Court in *Quong Wing v Kirkendall*,[43] he said that a state could legitimately impose "a lighter burden upon women than upon men" because "the Fourteenth Amendment does not interfere by creating a fictitious equality where there is a real difference." Holmes indicated that the "lighter burden" of which he spoke—an exemption from Montana's occupational tax for launders—would encourage women to choose "an employment that our people commonly regard as more appropriate" for them.[44]

Holmes wrote, "One accepts the union of O[thello] and D[esdemona], black and white, because one has been so accustomed to it. Otherwise it would disgust most of us."[45] He confessed, "[W]hen I was a sophomore, I didn't like the nigger minstrels because they seemed to belittle the race. . . . [Now] I fear you would shudder . . . at the low level of some of my social beliefs."[46] Chapter 5 will discuss Holmes's judicial opinions on issues of racial equality, revealing that he was considerably less supportive of the rights of racial minorities than other members of his segregation-era Court.[47]

LABELING HOLMES

People have applied labels other than fascist to Holmes—positivist, realist, social Darwinist, totalitarian,[48] intellectual radical,[49] liberal, conservative, and many more. Many academic writers have insisted that he was a utilitarian[50] or a pragmatist.[51]

As early as 1873, however, Holmes turned his skeptical cannon toward utilitarianism and fired a Darwinist "sez who?" (one that later racebuilders would have approved): "Why should the greatest *number* be preferred? Why not the greatest good of the most intelligent and most highly developed?"[52] Holmes declared in the same essay, "[I]n the last resort a man rightly prefers his own interest to that of his neighbors."[53] Holmes biographer Sheldon Novick observes, "It is curious that despite Holmes's explicit and repeated rejection of Utilitarianism, some modern writers continue to describe him as in some degree its follower."[54] As Novick remarks, "[Holmes] energetically denied the principle of utility. . . . There was no overall good of the community but only the conflicting interests of competing groups."[55]

Richard Posner adds:

What is distinctive about utilitarianism is, precisely, the belief that the proper goal . . . is to maximize the amount of happiness in the society. . . . Holmes was not a utilitarian in this sense. . . . [He] was a social and biological Darwinian, and hence a skeptic who believed that the good and true, in any sense that people could recognize, was whatever emerged from the struggles of warring species, nations, classes, and ideas.[56]

Holmes equally rejected the principal alternative to utilitarianism, the philosophy of Immanuel Kant. He said of Kant's injunction to view every person as an end, not a means,[57] "I confess that I rebel at once."[58] Holmes explicitly rejected pragmatism, too, repeatedly calling this philosophy "an amusing humbug."[59] He identified pragmatism's main thesis as the claim that "the truthfulness of our ideas consists in the fact that they will work," and he suggested that William James had advanced this vision of truth in order to make a "warm God . . . that loves and admires us" seem more plausible than an "automatic universe."[60] According to Holmes, James's pragmatism resembled "the spiritualist's promise of a miracle if you will turn down the gas."[61] Holmes "never could make anything out of" it except, perhaps, "that by yearning we can modify the multiplication table."[62]

The word *pragmatism* appears to be used in different senses by philosophers and lawyers,[63] but neither sense appropriately characterizes Holmes's thought. Holmes was not a philosophical pragmatist, for he "was firmly committed to the existence of a mind-independent reality."[64] It was this commitment that led him to ridicule pragmatism's antirealism.[65] Moreover, for the same reason that Holmes was not a utilitarian, he was not a pragmatist in the style of the law schools: He was indifferent to the "flourishing" of everyone in society.[66]

The judgment that Holmes was a utilitarian or pragmatist stems primarily from his focus on the law in action. Like utilitarians, and like both philosophical and lawyer pragmatists, Holmes was a consequentialist. He wrote, for example, "[T]he justification of a law . . . must be found in some help the law brings toward reaching a social end which the governing power of the community has made up its mind that it wants."[67] Holmes, however, emphasized law's practical consequences and the possibility that ancient law might no longer serve its purposes because he believed that winners in the struggle for dominance should accomplish

their objectives without self-delusion and waste. His emphasis on consequences was not directed toward advancing the welfare of society in
general.[68]

Perhaps because the word was not current during Holmes's lifetime,
few scholars have used a label that comes closer to capturing his viewpoint than the ones most commonly applied to him. Existentialism can
be regarded as the belief that human life is meaningless except insofar as
it is invested with meaning through personal acts of will. Only an "existential leap" can overcome "existential doubt," "existential despair," and
"existential nausea."[69] On this understanding of the concept, Oliver Wendell Holmes was an existentialist.[70]

J. W. Burrow, Richard Posner, and David Luban have suggested another label that may be even more apt. In Burrow's words, "[O]ne want[s]
to murmur 'Nietzschean' . . . about Holmes's celebrations of war, intensity of life, heroism, and will."[71] As Luban observes, both Holmes and
Nietzche believed that the solution "to the problem [of nihilism] lies in
the affirmation of the very contingency and goallessness of the universe
that provokes us to nihilism in the first place."[72]

Holmes and Nietzche were born three years apart and had much in
common. Both viewed life as a struggle for power; both were antireli-
gious (though Holmes focused less on the issue and was less virulent
about it); both saw ethics as lacking any external foundation; both could
fairly be regarded as existentialists; both saw the suffering and exploitation of some as necessary to the creative work of others; both were personally ambitious and had a strong work ethic (possibly reflecting their
Protestant heritage); both had a strong sense of personal destiny; both
viewed the disciplined, creative life as an ideal; both often seemed indifferent to the feelings of those around them; both found in their wartime experiences a metaphor for the universe at large; and both had
military-style moustaches.[73]

Luban notes two significant differences. First, Holmes believed that
external reality existed without regard to his thoughts about it ("I am in
the universe, not it in me")[74] while Nietzsche was an extreme idealist.[75]
Second, Holmes proposed overcoming nihilism and despair by narrowing
our focus to particular tasks and, in Luban's words, "wreaking ourselves
on life while insisting that we know nothing whatever of the point of our
doing so." Nietzsche, by contrast, proposed broadening our focus to the
point of all-inclusiveness.[76] Luban nevertheless concludes, "Holmes's
philosophical views were . . . strikingly similar to those of Nietzsche."[77]

When one abandons efforts to transform Holmes into a utilitarian or pragmatist and sees him as an existentialist, social Darwinist,[78] Thrasymachian,[79] and Nietzschean, he no longer appears complex, contradictory, or dualistic. Instead, his personality, intellectual stance, and legal judgments seem remarkably consistent. Jeckyll-Holmes, Hyde-Holmes becomes just Holmes.

NOBLE NIHILISM

A letter from Holmes to Lady Castletown, an English peeress who may have been his lover,[80] offered a one-sentence statement of his creed: "Nothing could be more enchanting than to see a man nearly killing himself for an end which derives its worth simply from his having affirmed it."[81] In true postmodern fashion, Holmes called this style of commitment "nonsensical and sublime."[82] His frequent glorification of the death of soldiers committed to causes they do not understand bespoke the same perspective.[83] He wrote of the person "able to lift himself by the might of his own soul, unaided, able to face annihilation for a blind belief."[84] Earlier, Holmes had written of "the divine folly of honor which has no value but what [one's] own heart gives it"[85] and of "man's most peculiar power—the power to deny the actual and to perish."[86]

In an address in 1900, Holmes observed, "[F]rom the point of view of the world the end of life is life. Life is action, the use of one's powers. As to use them to their height is our joy and our duty, so it is the one end that justifies itself."[87] In his remarks, Holmes even read Scripture as though the important part had been drafted by Nietzsche: "I think 'Whatsoever thy hand findeth to do, do it with thy might,' infinitely more important than the vain attempt to love thy neighbor as thyself."[88] Holmes's concluding paragraph declared, "We are all very near despair . . . ; but these thoughts have carried me . . . through long years of doubt, self-distrust and solitude."[89] He described his nearness to despair by quoting what he called "the words of a touching negro song: 'Sometime's I's up, sometimes I's down, Sometimes I's almost to the groun'."[90] Mrs. Holmes is reported to have said, "Wendell's latest plaything is Despair."[91]

Although Holmes wrote that "the end of life is life," he also wrote of "suicide as the ideal expression of that illusory personal spontaneity or independence which exhibits itself in less marked forms as consideration for the weak, charity to the poor, drunkenness, going to the play, painting pictures, etc., in short, uneconomic expenditure of force. . . ."[92]

Thomas Grey has noted that Holmes's speeches on ceremonial occasions never described law as a force for good. Law in his rhetoric was neither "the bulwark of liberty, the refuge of the oppressed, the source of order and stability, [n]or the guarantor of prosperity."[93] Holmes's speeches emphasized instead the intrinsic joy of legal work. He said on one occasion, "I say . . . that a man may live greatly in the law as elsewhere; that there as well as elsewhere he may wreak himself upon life, may drink the bitter cup of heroism, may wear his heart out after the unattainable."[94]

On Holmes's ninetieth birthday, he responded to a series of tributes in a memorable radio address:

> The riders in a race do not stop short when they reach the goal. There is a little finishing cantor before coming to a standstill. There is time to hear the kind voice of friends and to say to one's self: "The work is done." But just as one says that, the answer comes: "The race is over, but the work is never done when the power to work remains." The canter that brings you to a standstill need not be only coming to rest. It cannot be while still you live. For to live is to function. That is all there is to living.[95]

Viewing life as a race or contest—an occasion for functioning and nothing more—was a basic Holmesian theme. When Yale University awarded Holmes an honorary degree in 1886, he responded: "I never heard anyone profess indifference to a boat race. Why should you row a boat race? Why endure long months of pain in preparation for a fierce half-hour that will leave you all but dead? Does any one ask the question? . . . Is life less than a boat race?"[96]

At a law school dedication in 1902, Holmes observed, "Art, philosophy, charity, the search for the north pole, the delirium of every great moment in man's experience—all alike mean uneconomic expenditure—mean waste—mean a step toward death."[97] He then remarked an explorer's "account of his search for the pole rather loses than gains in ideal satisfaction by the pretence of a few trifling acquisitions for science."[98]

Holmes once recalled:

> I . . . spent a summer at Niagara Falls and on the fourth of July I went down to see a man go through the rapids on a boat of his own construction. I got there a little late and the man had drowned before I arrived. Afterwards a lady talking of the accident said that if the attempt had promised any possible good to his fellow men the case would have

been different, but that under the circumstances she could not see any justification for a pure waste of life. I replied, Madam, on the contrary precisely because it was not useful it was a perfect expression of the male contribution to our common stock of morality. . . . This uselessness is the highest kind of use. It is kindling and feeding the ideal spark without which life is not worth living.[99]

As Holmes summarized his position twenty-three years later, "The useless is the ideal expression of man."[100]

In a noted commemorative address, *The Soldier's Faith,*[101] Holmes suggested that athletics sometimes had an instrumental objective. The goal of these contests was eugenic—breeding tougher, stronger, and better human beings:

> I rejoice at every dangerous sport which I see pursued. The students at Heidelberg, with their sword-slashed faces, inspire me with sincere respect. I gaze with delight upon our polo-players. If once in a while in our rough riding a neck is broken, I regard it, not as a waste, but as a price well paid for the breeding of a race fit for headship and command.[102]

A turn-of-the-century traveler described the German duels of which Holmes spoke:

> The whole interest is centered in watching the wounds. . . . Sometimes a portion of hairy scalp or section of cheek flies up into the air, to be carefully preserved in an envelope by its proud possessor, or, strictly speaking, its proud former possessor, and shown round on convivial evenings. . . . [Blood] sprinkles ceilings and walls; it saturates the fighters, and makes pools for itself in the sawdust. . . . Now and then you see a man's teeth laid bare almost to the ear, so that for the rest of the duel he appears to be grinning at one half of the spectators, his other side remaining serious; and sometimes a man's nose gets slit, which gives to him as he fights a singularly supercilious air.[103]

For Holmes, life was a horse race, a boat race, a trek to the North Pole, a plunge over Niagara Falls, a duel with swords, and a neck-risking game of polo. It might even be a game of cards: "Why do I desire to win my game of solitaire? A foolish question, to which the only answer is that you are up against it. Accept the inevitable and do your damnedest."[104]

Leo Strauss once said of Max Weber that he transformed the com-

mand "Thou shalt have ideals" into the command "Thou shalt live passionately." Strauss wrote, "One may call the nihilism to which Weber's thesis
leads 'noble nihilism.'"[105] Strauss might equally have been writing about
Holmes. Edmund Wilson wrote of Holmes's "dedication to an ideal of
excellence which is not to save others but to justify oneself."[106]

William James offered this comment:

> I'm disappointed in O.W.H. for being unable to make any other than
> that one set speech which comes out on every occasion. It's all right
> for once, in the exuberance of youth, to celebrate mere vital excite-
> ment, *la joie de vivre,* as a protest against humdrum solemnity. But to
> make it systematic, and oppose it, as an ideal and a duty to the ordi-
> narily recognized duties, is to pervert it altogether. . . . Mere excite-
> ment is an immature ideal, unworthy of the Supreme Court's official
> endorsement.[107]

Perhaps the greatest paradox of Holmes's thought was this: Although
he described judging in terms of "weighing considerations of social advantage,"[108] Holmes valued personal action mostly for its expressive and
not its instrumental qualities. Individual action was admirable to the extent that it was "uneconomic." The less functional an action, the more it
became "sublime." Blind commitment alone gave meaning to life. It did
not matter whether this commitment found expression in art, charity,
exploration of the arctic, a legal career, a boat race, a plunge over dangerous falls, a game of solitaire, death on the battlefield, or suicide.

CAN'T HELP WHAT?

The ability to affirm a game-like end, to make it one's own, and to function could make life worthwhile, but apart from the power to sense one's
existence fully, life for Holmes was apparently a void:

> [M]y bet is that we have not the kind of cosmic importance that the
> parsons and philosophers teach. I doubt if a shudder would go through
> the spheres if the whole ant heap were kerosened.[109]

> I see no reason for attributing to a man a significance different in kind
> from that which belongs to a baboon or to a grain of sand.[110]

> I wonder if cosmically an idea is any more important than the
> bowels.[111]

I think that the sacredness of human life is a purely municipal ideal of no validity outside the jurisdiction. I believe that force, mitigated so far as may be by good manners, is the *ultima ratio*. . . . [E]very society rests on the death of men. . . .[112]

Holmes had values, or said he did. He called these values his "can't helps":

As I probably have said many times before, all I mean by truth is what I can't help believing—I don't know why I should assume except for practical purposes of conduct that [my] *can't help* has more cosmic worth than any other—I can't help preferring port to ditch-water, but I see no ground for supposing that the cosmos shares my weakness. . . . [I] demand of my philosophy simply to show that I am not a fool for putting my heart into my job.[113]

Holmes compared "moral and aesthetic preferences" to a taste for sugar.[114] He declared, "Our tastes are finalities."[115]

Port over ditch-water and sweet coffee over bitter, Holmes had his "can't helps." Apart from his personal passion, his *joie de vivre,* and his celebration of war and struggle, however, it was difficult to determine what they were. Arthur Sutherland, one of his law clerks, attributed "much of the greatness of Justice Holmes" to "an aristocracy so complete that he disdained ordinary emotional partisanship."[116]

Holmes's "can't helps" included few charitable or political causes.[117] Blackstone, whose view of natural rights has contributed to his current disfavor, contended that everyone had a right to life, including a right to "a sufficient supply for all the necessities of life."[118] Holmes maintained, "As to the *right* of citizens to support and education I don't see it. It may be a desirable ideal to aim at, but I see no right in my neighbor to share my bread. I mean moral right of course—there is no pretense of any other, except so far as he in combination has power to take it."[119]

Holmes, committed to living passionately, disparaged most passionate commitments:

[John Dewey] talks of the exploitation of man by man—which always rather gets my hair up. . . . [A]ll society rests on the death of men.[120]

[W]hen my [law clerk] talks of more rational methods [of resolving international disputes] I get the blood in my eye and say that war is the ultimate rationality.[121]

I never read a Socialist yet from Karl Marx down . . . that I don't think talked drool.[122]

The notion that we can secure an economic paradise by changes in property alone seems to me twaddle.[123]

[I]f you think that I am going to bother myself again before I die about social improvement or read any of those stinking onward and upward-ers—you err. I mean to have some good out of being old.[124]

Holmes apparently could not envision any basis for political, social, or personal action other than self-interest or devotion to an arbitrary, uncomprehended goal. He wrote, "[T]he condition of others is primarily their business and certainly is beyond our power. Whence the futility of the command to love one's brother as oneself."[125] He also observed:

I don't see why we mightn't as well invert the Christian saying and hate the sinner but not the sin. Hate . . . imports no judgment. Disgust is ultimate and therefore as irrational as reason itself—a dogmatic da-tum. The world has produced the rattlesnake as well as me, but I kill it if I get a chance, as also mosquitos, cockroaches, murderers, and flies. My only judgment is that they are incongruous with the world I want; the kind of world we all try to make according to our power.[126]

Similarly, Holmes's "can't helps" did not include religious belief. His dismissal of pragmatism was abrupt: "I now see . . . that the aim and end of the whole business is religious."[127] Pragmatism would permit believers to "bully *nous autres*" from a new "dogmatic foothold."[128] Moral principles as an "end in themselves," moreover, had no firmer grounding than re-ligion:

I said to a lady at dinner the other night that morals were a contrivance of man to take himself seriously, which means that the philosophers . . . make them an end in themselves, an absolute matter, and so an excuse for their pretention to be on the ground floor and personal friends of God.[129]

For Christians, a touching passage of Scripture tells of an old man named Simeon, who has been promised that he will see the Messiah. When Simeon, apparently near death, holds an infant named Jesus, he prays, "Lord, now lettest thou thy servant depart in peace, according to thy word: For mine eyes have seen thy salvation, Which thou has prepared before the face of all people; A light to lighten the Gentiles, and the glory of thy people Israel."[130] At the age of eighty-eight, Oliver Wendell Holmes revealed that he had lost neither his toughness nor his sense of humor. Remarking that his wife's recent death "not only takes away a half of my life but gives me notice," he recalled Simeon's prayer and wrote, "O Cosmos—Now lettest thou thy ganglion dissolve in peace."[131]

Holmes's "can't helps" did not include a belief in natural justice or innate human rights. "I take no stock in abstract rights," he said, and "equally fail to respect the passion for equality."[132] He observed that "the passion for equality . . . seems to me merely idealizing envy,"[133] and he wrote to one of his correspondents, "You respect the rights of man—I don't, except those things a given crowd will fight for. . . ."[134] On another occasion, Holmes observed, "All my life I have sneered at the natural rights of man."[135]

While a justice of the Supreme Court, Holmes wrote an article on natural law in the *Harvard Law Review*. Asserting that a right was natural or innate, he said, was like insisting that one's lady was the fairest rather than simply a nice girl.[136] A right, in Holmes's view, was "only the hypostasis of a prophecy—the imagination of a substance supporting the fact that public force will be brought to bear on those who do things said to contravene it."[137] Holmes had earlier observed, "[A]ll law means I will kill you if necessary to make you conform to my requirements."[138]

The first "unalienable" right articulated by the Declaration of Independence was life, but the Founders' self-evident truths were not among Holmes's "can't helps." In 1929, Holmes dissented from the Supreme Court's ruling that Rosika Schwimmer, a well-known pacifist, could not be a citizen of the United States. Schwimmer had refused to swear that she would bear arms in case of war. As a letter by Holmes recounted her lawyer's argument, Schwimmer "wouldn't do what the law wouldn't let her do."[139] A federal statute demanded a pledge to "support and defend the Constitution . . . against all enemies, foreign and domestic," and the Court's majority read this statute to preclude Schwimmer's naturalization.

Holmes's dissent spoke eloquently of "freedom for the thought we hate."[140] Then, commenting on Schwimmer's pacifism in a letter, Holmes revealed how much he did hate the thought: "What damned fools people are who believe things. . . . All 'isms seem to me silly—but this hyperaethereal respect for human life seems perhaps the silliest of all."[141]

Holmes had addressed the same subject in a letter to Dean Wigmore:

Doesn't this squashy sentimentality of a big minority of our people about human life make you puke? [That minority includes] people who believe there is an onward and upward—who talk of uplift—who think that something in particular has happened and that the universe is no longer predatory. Oh bring in a basin.[142]

Someone who adopts a skeptical posture may find it difficult to affirm a belief in any cause. Confronting the plausible "sez who's?" of others diminishes the ability to fire "sez who's?" oneself, and Holmes eliminated the obvious candidates from his list of "can't helps." Still, Holmes's list was not empty. He stood squarely for an expressive rather than instrumental jobism and for the glory of struggle and war. "[W]hen men differ in taste as to the kind of world they want the only thing to do is to go to work killing," he said.[143] He wrote on another occasion, "[U]ntil the world has got further along, war not only is not absurd but is inevitable and rational."[144]

EXTERMINATING THE INADEQUATE

Holmes had one more cause or "can't help"—his "starting point for an ideal for the law":

I believe that the wholesale social regeneration which so many now seem to expect, if it can be helped by conscious, coordinated human effort, cannot be affected appreciably by tinkering with the institution of property, but only by taking in hand life and trying to build a race. That would be my starting point for an ideal for the law.[145]

Many of Holmes's statements on race engineering seem chilling, especially in light of later history. He wrote of "substitut[ing] artificial selection for natural by putting to death the inadequate"[146] and of his "contempt" for "socialisms not prepared . . . to kill everyone below standard."[147] Holmes declared in *The Soldier's Faith,* "I can imagine a future in which science shall have passed from the combative to the dogmatic stage, and shall have gained such catholic acceptance that it shall take control of life, and condemn at once with instant execution what now is left for nature to destroy."[148] He spoke of the possibility of a future civilization "with smaller numbers, but perhaps also bred to greatness and splendor by science,"[149] and he wrote, "I can understand saying, whatever the cost, so far as may be, we will keep certain strains out of our blood."[150]

In a letter to Felix Frankfurter, Holmes expressed irritation with Francis Philbrick, a reviewer of his *Collected Legal Papers:*

> He says, "whatever that may mean" when I say that I don't think you can do much by tinkering with property without taking in hand life. I meant what I suppose he would think horrible—restricting propagation by the undesirables and putting to death infants that didn't pass the examination, etc., etc.[151]

Holmes then grumbled, "I suspect that Mr. Philbrick believes in some ism. . . ."[152]

In 1941, Father Francis E. Lucey noted one of Holmes's statements concerning eugenics—"I shall think socialism begins to be entitled to serious treatment when and not before it takes life in hand and prevents continuance of the unfit."[153] Lucey remarked that "if recent reports are true" the socialist state in Germany appeared to satisfy Holmes's standard for serious treatment.[154]

Richard Posner has noted that "belief in human eugenics was a staple of progressive thought in Holmes's lifetime." Posner added that although people now consider Holmes's eugenic enthusiasms shocking, "with the renewed interest . . . in euthanasia, and with the rise of genetic engineering, we may yet find those enthusiasms prescient rather than depraved."[155] As Sheldon Novick has observed, however, Holmes's position went "well beyond the conventional views on eugenics of his day."[156]

Some members of the twentieth-century eugenics movement confined their goals to "positive" eugenics—encouraging reproduction of the "fit" through early marriages and healthy child rearing. Others endorsed "negative" eugenics as well; they hoped to limit or discourage reproduction of the "unfit." Even among this second group, however, voluntary birth control was controversial,[157] and requiring a medical certificate of fitness prior to marriage was described as "crude," "impractical," and lacking any "serious advocates."[158]

The Supreme Court, in an infamous 1927 opinion by Holmes, upheld legislation requiring the sterilization of "imbeciles."[159] Thirty states ultimately approved legislation of this sort,[160] and more than eighteen thousand people in the United States were sterilized involuntarily following the Court's decision. Because state courts generally had held involuntary sterilization legislation unconstitutional, relatively few had been sterilized earlier.[161] Support for forced sterilization marked the outer limits of the eugenics movement in America—apart, that is, from the remarks of Justice Holmes and a very few others. As one eugenics enthusiast declared, "Beyond preventing the perpetuation of the feeble-minded, the insane, and the bearers of some other grave hereditary defects, no sensible eugenist proposes to enforce any arbitrary restrictions upon the reproduction of any class of the population."[162]

One discovers many familiar names on the list of twentieth-century English and American eugenists, including H. G. Wells, Theodore Roosevelt, Beatrice and Sidney Webb, Margaret Sanger, Havelock Ellis, George Bernard Shaw, and Harold Laski.[163] No one of note, however, joined Holmes in writing approvingly of killing "everyone below standard" and "putting to death infants that didn't pass the examination."[164] Eugenics, moreover, was the *only* progressive movement Holmes favored.[165]

THE MEANINGFUL MYSTERY OF EMPTINESS

Holmes's speeches sometimes sounded noble themes that may seem incompatible with his skepticism. He wrote, for example, "[O]ur only but wholly adequate significance is as parts of the unimaginable whole. . . . [E]ven while we think that we are egotists we are living to ends outside ourselves."[166] He added, "Life is a roar of bargain and battle, but in the very heart of it there rises a mystic spiritual tone that gives meaning to the whole."[167] In assessing statements like these, recall that Holmes proclaimed the message of war "divine"[168] and insisted that a fatal plunge over Niagara Falls in a homemade boat was "kindling and feeding that ideal spark without which life is not worth living."[169] People who call Holmes a romantic tend to overlook what he romanticized.[170] For the most part, Holmes's statements about the cosmos and the infinite appear to declare his reverence for what he regarded as the order of the universe—struggle, violence, death, and the unknown.[171]

The chapters that follow consider how Holmes's war experience and social Darwinism helped generate his skeptical views, and they examine the extent to which Holmes's skepticism found expression in his personality, opinions, and scholarly writings. At this point, two observations concerning his skepticism seem appropriate. First, Holmes hardly ever offered arguments or analysis to support his skeptical stands. When he said that he sneered at the rights of man, he described both his method and his position. Skeptics are as likely as believers to rely on assertion; a person's convictions concerning the most important issues of life often seem to hang by a thread. They appear to depend on the believer's or skeptic's mood, perhaps, or on her allocation of the lawyer's burden of proof.

Second, Holmes revealed that a skeptic who tries to avoid the precipice can make an existential leap to the right as readily as to the left. Moreover, Holmes saw more clearly than later skeptics the implications of his position. He did not claim to believe in much; for the most part, his existential leaps were short. Unlike successor skeptics, Holmes did not insist that he had deconstructed all extant categories of thought while still believing somehow in redistribution, participatory democracy, and the intersubjective zap. "[T]o live is to function," he said. "That is all there is to living." It was enough for Holmes to have done a job; then he could make fun of the onward and upwarders. Unlike many of his intellectual heirs later in the century, Holmes had the courage of his nonconvictions.

Chapter Three

Would You Have Wanted
Justice Holmes as a Friend?

HOLMES AND HIS BIOGRAPHERS

In light of the reverence that Holmes has inspired, it seems surprising that
the first complete biography of the justice appeared only in 1989, more
than a half century after his death.[1] Shortly after the book's appearance,
my colleague Gerhard Casper asked its author, Sheldon Novick, a question that every biographer should be asked about his subject: "Would you
have wanted Holmes as a friend?" Novick hesitantly answered no. He
added that, as a mature adult, Holmes was always surrounded by young
admirers[2] but apart from his wife had no close friends.

In explaining his answer to Casper's question, Novick noted that, as
Holmes's biographer, he had in effect lived with Holmes for an extended
period. One reason why no complete biography appeared before 1989
may have been the difficulty of living with Holmes in this fashion. Upon
the death of the second of the justice's authorized biographers (Mark De-
Wolfe Howe, Jr.), the biographer's widow and the Harvard Law School
(the literary executor of Holmes's estate) selected Grant Gilmore as the
third. Gilmore labored at his biography for fifteen years but never published any part of it.[3] After he had been at work on the project for ten
years, Gilmore offered this assessment in his Storrs Lectures at Yale:

> Put out of your mind the picture of the tolerant aristocrat, the great
> liberal, the eloquent defender of our liberties, the Yankee from Olym-
> pus. All that was a myth, concocted principally by Harold Laski and
> Felix Frankfurter, about the time of World War I. The real Holmes
> was savage, harsh, and cruel, a bitter and lifelong pessimist who saw

in the course of human life nothing but a continuing struggle in which the rich and powerful impose their will on the poor and weak.[4]

When the Harvard Law School prepared an exhibit to mark the fortieth anniversary of Holmes's death, Gilmore's essay for the catalogue was so critical of Justice Holmes that the school refused to publish it.[5] Like Novick, Gilmore apparently would not have wanted Holmes as a friend. Novick suggests that Mark DeWolfe Howe found his work on Holmes distasteful and difficult as well.[6] Novick notes, "Overtaxed as he was and discouraged by what seemed to him the bleakness of Holmes' character, Professor Howe left the biography of Holmes unfinished. . . ."[7]

Although the appearance of a full Holmes biography may have been delayed by the authorized biographers' disillusionment with their subject, it also was hindered by the burdens they and others imposed on "unauthorized" scholars. The Harvard Law School restricted access to Holmes's papers, refusing, for example, to allow Catherine Drinker Bowen to use them. Abandoning her plan to write a biography of Holmes, Bowen relied on the personal reminiscences of relatives and law clerks to write a flattering, fictionalized bestseller.[8] Felix Frankfurter, Holmes's first authorized biographer,[9] prevented Alpheus T. Mason from consulting relevant judicial papers. Mark DeWolfe Howe, after turning down the project himself, delayed the efforts of James Peabody to edit the correspondence between Holmes and Lewis Einstein. Grant Gilmore denied Liva Baker access to the Holmes papers on the ground that she was not a member of a university faculty and therefore not a professional scholar.[10]

Gilmore's death in 1982 marked the end of the plan to prepare an authorized biography, and the Harvard Law School made Holmes's papers more accessible. Although the biographers of the past decade have uniformly praised Holmes's scholarship and judicial opinions, they have been less enamored with his personality. Novick, for example, comments:

> Holmes lived intensely, and seen inwardly, two strong impulses dominated his life. The first was the kind of limitless ambition that is born of violent rivalry: he wanted not to be good, but to be the best. Even sexual passion was for him a mode of achievement, and his thought was fundamentally combative. He wished, intensely, to be remembered as the greatest legal thinker who had ever lived—sometimes he omitted the qualifying "legal." . . . Set against this ambition was an equally stern devotion to duty.[11]

Biographer G. Edward White observes:

For his entire career, [Holmes] was remarkably detached, not only from those whose lives his decisions affected, but from the judges who joined those decisions, the lower courts who sought guidance from his opinions, the lawyers who argued the cases, and the public who reacted to the issues he resolved. . . .

It is one of the ironies of Holmes' career that although he cared so much for recognition, and although so many persons, over the years, have made an investment in his ideas or in his work or his life, he gave so little of himself to the persons around him. . . .[12]

White also observes:

When one seeks to sum up Holmes' central personal characteristics, the quality that first comes to mind is his vast and driving ambition. . . . Ambition . . . fostered Holmes' singular competitiveness, his extreme sensitivity to criticism, his thirst for recognition, even the perverse glumness with which he accepted praise and his insatiable desire for an even higher level of accomplishment.[13]

As the remainder of this chapter will reveal, people who knew Holmes well formed similar judgments.

HOLMES IN THE EYES OF THOSE WHO KNEW HIM

Among the contemporaries of Holmes who noted his detachment and indifference to others was his father. Oliver Wendell Holmes, Sr., an innovative physician and a vivid essayist, poet, and journalist, had helped found and had named the *Atlantic Monthly*. In 1872, he began a series in that magazine called "The Poet at the Breakfast Table." Holmes modeled one character, the Young Astronomer, after his son. On one occasion, Holmes, Sr. even revised and published poetry that Holmes, Jr. had written, attributing this poetry to the Young Astronomer.[14] The son was then thirty-one years old. He had returned from military service in the Civil War, completed law school, and traveled to Europe. He was practicing law, had begun writing jurisprudential papers, and still lived with his parents.[15]

The Poet described the Young Astronomer as "[a] strange unearthly being; lonely, dwelling far apart from the thoughts and cares of the planet on which he lives,"[16] adding, "I fear that he is too much given . . . to looking at life as at a solemn show where he is only a spectator."[17] The senior Holmes also wrote, "[O]ur young man seems further away from life than any student whose head is bent downwards over his books. His eyes are turned away from all human things."[18]

The Young Astronomer's lack of involvement may have been deliberate, self-imposed, and partly the product of personal and intellectual ambition. The younger Holmes later wrote that a necessary condition of original thought was "a black gulf of solitude more isolating than that which surrounds the dying man."[19]

Long after Holmes Sr. expressed concern about his son's disinterest in human things, the son, then fifty-seven, described himself as a "recluse." He added, "Most of my old friends are dead . . . and I do not make new ones, unless very rarely as I do not give myself the chance."[20] Holmes's reference to friends who had predeceased him was mostly to comrades killed during the Civil War thirty-five years earlier. At the time of his remarks, Holmes had returned from one of his visits to England. Although he visited England no more frequently than every second or third year, he noted, "I have almost more friends [in England] whom I love, than I have here."[21]

On the day in 1872 that Oliver Wendell Holmes married Fanny Dixwell, he wrote in his journal, "Married. Sole editor of Law Rev."[22] The couple took no honeymoon.[23] Mark DeWolfe Howe, who completed two volumes of his contemplated biography of Holmes,[24] noted that Mrs. Holmes probably realized from the outset that her husband "would not permit the conventional burdens of marriage to distract him from his search for the goals of achievement."[25]

Prior to his marriage, Holmes had told a distant cousin that his goal was to become chief justice of Massachusetts and "eventually impossible as it might seem" to become a justice of the U.S. Supreme Court.[26] Following his appointment to the Supreme Court thirty years later, Holmes wrote of the pleasure he took in "feeling a vast world vibrate to one's determinations. . . . At bottom I am profoundly happy."[27] After Holmes had been on the Supreme Court ten years, he confessed, "I should like to be admitted to be the greatest jurist in the world."[28]

Mrs. Holmes differed sharply from her husband. She "was not an intellectual,"[29] and her diary entries during a European journey were "girlish, clumsy, [and] misspelled."[30] Artistically inclined, she labored at embroidery, which she exhibited to acclaim.[31] Fanny Holmes abandoned her needlework, however, and "for reasons known only to herself" destroyed most of what she had done.[32]

Liva Baker reports:

> It was said by some who knew [Mrs. Holmes] that she had no close friends and "hated" most of her sisters. . . . As she grew older, her inclination to solitude became more pronounced, and in time she became a virtual recluse and a symbol of unsociability for other Bostonians. . . . The philanthropic social service organizations and women's clubs that were springing up in the second half of the nineteenth century . . . did not seem to interest [her].[33]

Although an able and intelligent conversationalist,[34] Fanny Holmes often remained at home when Holmes went out. She did not accompany him on several European journeys.[35] Holmes described his wife as "a very solitary bird, [who], if her notion of duty did not compel her to do otherwise, . . . would be an absolute recluse."[36] After her death, Holmes recalled that she had "shocked Gifford Pinchot once by saying 'I have no friends'; and it was true that there was no one except me with whom she was very intimate."[37] In later life, Mrs. Holmes reportedly took no interest in her appearance.[38]

Mrs. Holmes was beset by rheumatic fever twice during her marriage. Particularly during the three years following the disease's recurrence, both her manner and her tastes were eccentric. "Some of her birds were allowed to fly freely, marmosets and squirrels ran uncaged in the bedroom. Fanny spoke to the animals, . . . talked somewhat oddly to the servants, . . . [and] wrote angry, disoriented messages to Holmes."[39]

The marriage continued for fifty-six years until Fanny's death, and at least in the later years, there was evident affection between the couple. Novick describes Mrs. Holmes's practice of reading to Holmes while he played solitaire, the elaborate surprise parties she arranged for his seventy-fifth and eightieth birthdays, his deep regret at leaving on a European trip without her, a love letter she wrote him while he was abroad ("My dearest, dearest, Dearest"), and some playfulness between the couple (kicking each other under the lap robe while riding in an open-topped car).[40] On Fanny Holmes's death, her husband wrote, "For sixty years she made life poetry for me."[41] Thereafter Oliver Wendell Holmes visited Fanny Dixwell Holmes's grave about once each month, running his fingers over her memorial stone without comment.[42]

Perhaps because of Mrs. Holmes's ill health, the pair did not have children. Holmes once wrote, "I am so far abnormal that I am glad that I have [no children]."[43] He added, "Of course, if I should break down before I die it would be awkward as there is no one to look after me as a child would—but I daresay my nephew and friends would cook up something."[44] Judge Learned Hand once asked, "Mr. Justice, have you ever been sorry that you never had any children?" Holmes replied, "This is not the kind of world I want to bring anyone else into."[45]

Holmes's relationship with his mother was apparently affectionate, but his relationship with his father was strained.[46] Holmes, Sr. once asked Henry James, Sr. whether he did not find that his sons despised him,[47] and Holmes, Jr. noted that after assembling his father's papers following the latter's death he felt "a sort of filial duty performed . . . , I not spending my time adoring him when he was alive."[48] Concerning the other members of Holmes's family, Howe observed, "[T]here are no indications that Holmes and his sister were close to one another, or that Holmes followed with any special sympathy the misfortunes of his younger brother. . . ."[49]

The philosopher and psychologist William James was one of Holmes's closest friends in the period after the Civil War. They engaged in late-night conversation and adopted a fancy style in their correspondence. At the age of twenty-six, Holmes addressed James in a letter as "Oh! Bill, my beloved" and proclaimed, "[H]ow I have yearned after thee all this long time."[50] In response, James called Holmes "my Wendly boy."[51] Four months later, James objected that Holmes's "logical and orderly mode of thinking" made it uncomfortable to be in his presence. "I put myself involuntarily into a position of self-defense, as if you threatened to overrun my territory. . . ."[52] A year after this complaint, James wrote his brother Henry of the "cold-blooded, conscious egotism and conceit" by which "[a]ll the noble qualities of Wendell Holmes . . . are poisoned."[53] Several years later, James described Holmes as "a powerful battery, formed like a planing machine to gouge a deep self-beneficial groove through life."[54] Holmes and James maintained contact throughout their lifetimes but never recovered their friendship.[55] When James died in 1910, Holmes wrote that his "demi spiritualism and pragmatism" had driven them apart.[56]

James Bradley Thayer was one of Holmes's principal mentors. A partner in the law firm where Holmes began his professional career and later a member of the Harvard Law School Faculty, Thayer hired Holmes to assist in preparing a new edition of James Kent's *Commentaries.* When Holmes undertook a more ambitious project than the one Thayer had been commissioned by Kent's grandson to prepare, Thayer agreed to step aside and to allow Holmes to become the sole editor.

Mary James, the mother of William, Henry, and Alice, noted Holmes's devotion to his scholarly project:

He carries about his manuscript in his green bag and never loses sight
of it for a moment. He started to go to Will's room and wash his hands,
but came back for his bag, and when we went to dinner, Will said,
"Don't you want to take your bag with you?" He said, "Yes, I always do
at home." His pallid face, and this fearful grip on his work, make him
a melancholy sight.[57]

Holmes in fact subjected the members of his household to "a monthly
fire drill designed to instill in each [of them] the duty to rescue" his manuscript first of all.[58]

Thayer once submitted Holmes's name for appointment to the Supreme Judicial Court of Massachusetts.[59] He was also the principal sup-
porter of Holmes's appointment to the Harvard Law School faculty[60] and
undertook the job of raising the funds needed to endow Holmes's chair
at Harvard.[61] Early in this undertaking, Thayer consulted Louis D. Brandeis, a Harvard Law School graduate who had begun practicing law in
Boston, and Brandeis suggested that he contact William F. Weld, Jr. Weld
had attended the Harvard Law School but, apparently after failing
Thayer's course, had been denied a degree. Weld agreed to fund Holmes's
chair from the $3 million that he had recently inherited from his father,
who had once owned the largest shipping company in America. Weld
proposed, however, that his contribution remain confidential. He was interested in taking his law school degree the following spring and suggested that "neither the college nor he should wish to have it supposed
that he bid for a degree." Thayer promised to keep Weld's role confidential until "after the degree matter was over." "As to the degree itself,"
Thayer said, "you may rely on our dealing with you with absolute impar-
tiality." Weld never received a Harvard Law School degree.[62]

Holmes conditioned his acceptance of the position at Harvard by noting that he would still consider a judgeship if one were offered.[63] He in
fact accepted appointment to the Supreme Judicial Court of Massachusetts on December 8, 1882, after only about two months of teaching.
Holmes not only resigned from the faculty in the middle of the term; he
also failed to consult or inform any of his colleagues. The dean and faculty
(there were only four besides Holmes) learned of his appointment from
the newspapers.[64] Thayer noted in his diary that although Holmes had
been teaching only a short time, he had been on the Harvard payroll for
nine or ten months—"since Feb. 1, I think—March 1st at any rate; the
year at the school had only begun; [and] students were here who had been
mainly induced to come by his being here."[65] Holmes seemed not "to have

conceived . . . that it should not have been possible for him to accept without a conference with Eliot [Harvard's president]."[66] Thayer's diary entry concluded that Holmes was "wanting sadly in the noblest region of human character." Despite his "attractive qualities and his solid merits," Holmes was "selfish, vain, thoughtless of others."[67] Holmes later consulted a lawyer about whether to return part of the salary that he had received from Harvard, but he evidently decided not to.[68]

Holmes, who once described "lov[ing] thy neighbor as thyself" as "the test of the meddling missionary,"[69] rarely supported charities or political causes, and neither he nor his law firm seem to have provided services *pro bono publico*.[70] Borrowing the sentiment from an acquaintance of Holmes, Edmund Wilson described him as "[h]aving rarely, so far as is known, given a penny to a cause or charity, indifferent to the improvement of others while preoccupied with the improvement of himself."[71] Perhaps facetiously, Holmes once complained to a law clerk about the endowment of a public library by Andrew Carnegie. By donating his wealth to "a non-productive enterprise," Carnegie had failed "to fulfill his public function" and so had prompted Holmes's first doubts about a system of private property.[72] In his own most notable charitable act, Holmes on his death left $263,000, the bulk of his estate, to the federal government without explanation.[73]

In searching for a beneficent side of Holmes, one can note his unfailing graciousness to admirers and several acts of kindness of a sort that a gentleman might have sensed a duty to perform. For example, he and his wife cared for Holmes's widowed father during his final years.[74] Holmes described living with his father following his mother's death as "the only practicable or possible thing," adding that "Mrs. Holmes wants me to go abroad this summer prophesying that it will make the first summer easier for my father."[75]

Only one apparent act of kindness beyond duty stands out— Holmes's generosity to John Jay Chapman. Chapman would later abandon the practice of law and become a noted writer, but in 1887 he was a handsome, brilliant, mentally disturbed Harvard law student. Holmes, a justice of the Massachusetts Supreme Judicial Court, was a frequent dinner guest of Chapman and his housemates. Chapman came to imagine that another youth had seduced Minna Timmins, whom he loved; and after a party one evening, Chapman followed the object of his jealous delusion outside and beat him with a cane. Two days later, Chapman plunged his own left hand into a fire and held it there with his right hand for two minutes. The burned hand was amputated, and Holmes visited Chapman repeatedly in the hospital. He and Fanny then took Chapman into their home. Because Minna Timmins was not permitted to see Chapman, Holmes carried messages between them.[76] Chapman and Timmins were married two years later.[77]

Following his convalescence, Chapman turned against his benefactor and contemplated killing Holmes and himself. He described Holmes as "polluted in his body and soul" and reported that he "always touched the thing with a touch that was cold and had sex in it."[78] Liva Baker speculated that "the thing" to which Chapman referred was his stump.[79] Holmes might have been as kind to Chapman if the young man had suffered a less grotesque malady—say, pneumonia—but one wonders.[80]

Holmes was lively, witty, and brilliant. Richard Rovere remarked that during his long life (he died just short of his ninety-fourth birthday), he knew everyone from John Quincy Adams through Alger Hiss.[81] Holmes's acquaintances included nearly every significant figure in law, letters, philosophy, and politics in both America and England (including Hiss, his law clerk in 1929 and 1930,[82] and *perhaps* including Adams, the sixth president of the United States[83]). During Holmes's Civil War service, he was on the battlefield at Fort Stevens with the sixteenth president, Abraham Lincoln. (Holmes's claim to have been the soldier who shouted to Lincoln, "Get down, you damned fool!," however, was probably a fabrication.)[84] In 1902, when Holmes was sixty-one and had been a member of the Massachusetts Supreme Judicial Court for twenty years (both as justice and as chief justice), the twenty-sixth president, Theodore Roosevelt, appointed him to the Supreme Court. Twenty-nine years later, another President Roosevelt called on Holmes; it was two months after Holmes's retirement from the Court and four days after FDR's inauguration.[85] The thirty-second president's visit came on Holmes's ninety-first birthday.

One could not have hoped for a more interesting and stimulating companion or correspondent than Holmes, and his correspondence was extensive. It is estimated that he wrote more than ten thousand letters in his lifetime.[86] His correspondence with Sir Frederick Pollock, which extended over fifty-eight years and fills two volumes, is particularly notable for both its quantity and intellectual quality.[87] Holmes and Pollock lived on opposite sides of the Atlantic, however, and met infrequently. When Sheldon Novick remarked on Holmes's lack of friends, he evidently spoke of more intimate relationships than those evidenced by the banter and book notes that comprise most of Holmes's letters. Commenting on a lifetime of these letters, Edmund Wilson noted Holmes's "almost complete lack of interest in other people as individuals."[88] G. Edward White reported, "Holmes's correspondence ultimately reveals his profound self-absorption. . . ."[89]

One may speculate that although Holmes's life was intense, it was not particularly satisfying. He lacked (and resisted) familiar forms of love and support and took no comfort in ordinary pieties. He believed it his duty to make something of himself, yet he sometimes seemed to value only unattainable cosmic achievement. Functionless acts of will and exertion were, he apparently concluded, the nearest available substitutes. With these convictions, Holmes might have seen life as a trap.[90] How he developed his view of the world and of human relationships—a view that might have made him more attractive as a dinner companion than a friend—is the subject of the chapter that follows.

Chapter Four

The Battlefield Conversion of Oliver Wendell Holmes

THE PREWAR HOLMES

At Harvard College just before the Civil War, Oliver Wendell Holmes showed few signs of the ethical skepticism that characterized his outlook in the decades following his military service.[1] His first published work, an anonymous essay on *Books,* appeared during his sophomore year. It declared that "[t]he highest conversation" must address "great questions of right and wrong, and . . . the relations of man to God."[2]

In his senior year, Holmes won twenty dollars for the best undergraduate essay published in the *University Quarterly.* This essay criticized Plato, arguing that his "fundamental classification of . . . ideas was loose and unscientific" and that his "conception of the true method of investigating their nature was vague and incorrect."[3] When Holmes showed the essay to Ralph Waldo Emerson, Emerson returned it with the comment, "When you strike at a king, you must *kill* him."[4] As Mark DeWolfe Howe observed, the mood of Holmes's essay was reverent.[5] Sounding much like a natural lawyer, Holmes distinguished the "necessary ideas" that exist permanently "in the mind of the Creator" from "conceptions . . . which are evidently mere arbitrary combinations effected by man."[6] Holmes asserted that "our intuitive faculty" enabled us to recognize the "necessary ideas." He spoke of Plato's vision of "the higher beauty of the soul" and of his notion that "Love is the faculty by which we immediately apprehend the Good."[7]

A third published essay, *Notes on Albert Durer,* declared, "[H]igher than anything connected with the individual is the conception of the harmonious whole of a great work, and this again is great, just as its idea partakes of what is eternal. And this striving to look on types and eternal ideas, is that highest gift of the artist. . . ."[8]

During his sophomore year, Holmes joined the Christian Union, a group whose membership was open to "all students of good moral character, without distinction of sect, claiming to believe in the truths of Christianity."[9] Although Holmes was not an active member, he explained at the end of his college career that he had retained his affiliation "because I wanted to bear testimony in favor of a Religious society founded on liberal principles in distinction to the more 'orthodox' and sectarian platform of the 'Xtian Brethren.'"[10]

Prior to the war, Holmes participated in a moral crusade. He was, as he wrote seventy years later, "deeply moved by the Abolition cause."[11] Holmes's mother, Amelia Jackson Holmes, apparently shared his abolitionist sympathies,[12] but his father did not. Oliver Wendell Holmes, Sr.'s declaration that antislavery extremists had done "great mischief . . . by violence and vituperation" and his calls for compromise with the South led Horace Greeley's *New York Tribune* to declare that he should have been lynched.[13]

A financial contribution by the younger Holmes to the abolitionist cause was noted in the *Liberator*—twenty-five cents.[14] At the 1861 annual meeting of the Massachusetts Anti-Slavery Society, Holmes was one of a group of young men who served as bodyguards to Wendell Phillips (a "pestilent abolitionist," according to Holmes's father,[15] and a distant cousin of the Holmeses).[16] When war came in April 1861, Holmes, then twenty, abandoned the final two months of his college studies and enlisted in the Massachusetts Militia.[17] Mark DeWolfe Howe commented, "Doubtless the conviction that slavery was an intolerable evil in a civilized society played its crucial part in Holmes's decision."[18] By enlisting Holmes risked losing his degree, but on June 10, the Harvard faculty voted "that Hallowell and Holmes, Seniors, be informed that they must return to College and pass the usual examination of their class as a condition of receiving their degrees." The two officers did return and graduated with their class. Holmes delivered the Class Poem, and his friend Pen Hallowell gave the Class Oration.[19]

THE WAR YEARS: WAVERING FAITH

The three-year period that followed shaped Holmes's jurisprudence and his personal qualities more than any other. It was not a period during which law was much on his mind.

Three months after his enlistment, Holmes was commissioned a lieutenant in the Twentieth Massachusetts Regiment, and three months after that, he was seriously wounded in the chest at Ball's Bluff during his first intense combat.[20] Bleeding freely from the mouth and expecting to die, he thought briefly of taking the laudanum his father had given him for use if the pain became unbearable.[21] Two days later, he wrote his mother that he was "very happy in the conviction I did my duty handsomely."[22]

Within a year, Holmes was wounded a second time. A bullet through his neck at Antietam Creek created a gaping hole, but the harm was less serious than it seemed. Learning of the wound, Holmes's father went in search of him. He took two weeks and interviewed a number of people in the process.[23] Published in the *Atlantic Monthly,* the father's article *My Hunt after "the Captain"* brought the younger Holmes to national attention.[24] Holmes Sr. had gained national attention at the same age with his poem "Old Ironsides"—a verse that rescued the frigate *Constitution* from scheduled destruction.

Within another year, there was a third wound—a ball into the heel at Chancellorsville. To Holmes's disappointment, his foot was not amputated; amputation would have rescued him from further fighting.[25]

Holmes's letters and war diary described bouts of dysentery and scurvy, grueling labor, harsh physical conditions, long periods of boredom, senseless orders, and the horror of war:

> I remember . . . a red blanket with an arm lying on it in a pool of blood—it seems as if instinct told me it was John Putnam's . . .—and near the entrance a surgeon calmly grasping a man's finger and cutting it off.[26]

> It is singular with what indifference one gets to look on the dead bodies in gray clothes wh[ich] lie around. . . . As you go through the woods you stumble constantly, and, if after dark, as last night on picket, perhaps tread on the swollen bodies already fly blown and decaying, of men shot in the head back or bowels—Many of the wounds are terrible to look at—Well we licked 'em. . . .[27]

> [I]t's odd how indifferent one gets to the sight of death—perhaps, because one gets aristocratic and don't value much a common life—Then they are apt to be so dirty it seems natural—'Dust to dust'—I would do anything that lay in my power but it doesn't much affect my feelings.[28]

[F]ound woods afire & bodies of Rebs & our men just killed and scortching.[29]

Today is the 7th day we have fought . . . averaging a loss I guess of 3000 (three thousand) a day at least.[30]

In the corner of the woods . . . the dead of both sides lay piled in the trenches 5 or 6 deep—wounded often writhing under superincumbent dead. . . .[31]

Before you get this you will know how immense the butchers bill has been. . . . I have not been & am not likely to be in the mood for writing details. . . . . Enough that these nearly two weeks have contained all of fatigue & horror that war can furnish. . . .[32]

[N]early every Regimental off[icer] I knew or cared for is dead or wounded. . . .[33]

The whole ground stunk horribly with dead men & horses. . . .[34]

At the midpoint of Holmes's three-year enlistment, slightly more than a year after his wounding at Ball's Bluff and two months after his wounding at Antietam, he voiced his disillusionment:

I've pretty much made up my mind that the South have achieved their independence & I am almost ready to hope spring will see an end— . . . [B]elieve me, we never shall lick 'em—The Army is tired with its hard, & its terrible experience & still more with its mismanagement & I think before long the majority will say that we are vainly working to effect what never happens—the subjugation (for that is it) of a great civilized nation. We shan't do it—at least the Army can't. . . .[35]

A few months later, Holmes received a letter that seemed to test his commitment to the abolitionist cause. Its author was Holmes's closest friend in college, Pen Hallowell.[36] Hallowell, a Philadelphia Quaker who hated slavery more than he did war, had left Harvard to enlist when Holmes did. When other Quakers criticized him for serving in the military, Hallowell reminded them of George Fox's admonition to "Mind the Inner light."[37] The two classmates served together as officers of the Twentieth Massachusetts Regiment.

Holmes's letters and diary note that when his life hung in the balance at Ball's Bluff Hallowell appeared and kissed him, that Hallowell "fought like a brick" in that engagement, that serving in the company Hallowell commanded made "all the difference in the world," and that Holmes was "awfully frightened" when Hallowell received a cut in the Seven Days

Battle.[38] A letter by Holmes included his sketch of the two comrades-in-arms smoking pipes under Holmes's rain gear while on picket during a storm.[39] Another reported that the two officers spent hours waiting together for medical attention in a house that once fell behind enemy lines after both were wounded at Antietam.[40]

The letter that Hallowell sent Holmes in February 1863 concerned the formation of the Fifty-fourth Massachusetts Regiment—a regiment of black soldiers commanded by white officers whose history the 1991 motion picture *Glory* retold. The governor of Massachusetts was recruiting officers from among "young men of military experience [and] firm anti-slavery principles."[41] Hallowell wrote Holmes:[42]

> Dear O. W.
>
> By a power as irresistible as fate I am drawn into the colored regiment (54th) as Lt. Col. Would you take the majority? not that it would be offered to you certainly, but your name would command attention. Bob Shaw has accepted the Colonelcy.
>
> Difficulties of every kind rise up. One by one they will be overcome. . . .
>
> Thine affectionately
> N. P. Hallowell

Holmes's response to Hallowell has not survived, and any reference that he might have made to Hallowell's overture in letters to his family vanished when Holmes edited his Civil War letters and destroyed many of them.[43] Nevertheless, as Mark DeWolfe Howe concluded, "it is probable that it was by his own choice that Holmes remained with the Twentieth."[44]

Hallowell may have approached Holmes once more. In July 1863, the Fifty-fourth Massachusetts and a newer regiment of black soldiers—the Fifty-fifth, commanded by Hallowell—suffered overwhelming casualties in an unsuccessful assault on Fort Wagner. W. E. B. Du Bois would later observe that only the death of thirty-seven thousand black American troops during the Civil War permitted black men to gain the vote after the war ended.[45] Attempting to fill the decimated ranks of officers of the two regiments, Hallowell again may have asked Holmes to join him. Holmes at the time was at home recuperating from his third war wound and reading, among other things, Spencer's *Social Statics*.[46] A letter to Holmes from another of his close friends, Henry "Little" Abbott, provides the principal evidence that Holmes again declined Hallowell's proposal.

Abbott was a hero of the Battle of Fredericksburg who soon would receive a fatal wound in the Battle of the Wilderness.[47] Although his politics differed from Hallowell's and Holmes's, they fit comfortably with those of most other officers of the Twentieth Massachusetts Regiment, which was known as the Copperhead Regiment. Abbott's letter in October 1863 complimented Holmes on his decision to return to the Twentieth: "I believe you have done not only what is agreeable to yourself and us, but what is thoroughly right & proper, instead of absurdly wasting yourself before the shrine of the great nigger."[48]

Within another year, Holmes declined reenlistment. His regiment's losses had been greater than its original strength,[49] and he wrote home, "I cannot now endure the labors & hardship of the line."[50]

THE POSTWAR HOLMES

The passion that Holmes had felt for the abolition of slavery before the Civil War faded during his ordeal and turned to disdain after the war ended. In a letter to Harold Laski in 1930, Holmes wrote of Bertrand Russell that "[h]e seems to me in the emotional state not unlike that of the abolitionists in former days, which then I shared and now much dislike. . . ."[51] Earlier he had written to Laski, "You put your ideals or prophecies with the slight superior smile of the man who is sure he has the future——(I have seen it before in the past from the abolitionists to Christian Science). . . ."[52] Of Leon Trotsky's autobiography, Holmes wrote, "I feel the tone that I became familiar with in my youth among the abolitionists."[53] He wrote that an "account of the Communists shows in the most extreme form what I came to loathe in the Abolitionists—the conviction that anyone who did not agree with them was a knave or a fool. You see the same in some Catholics and some of the 'Drys' apropos of the 18th amendment."[54] In other letters, Holmes compared abolitionists to John Calvin on Catholics, Catholics on John Calvin, and Emma Goldman.[55]

Despite the triumph of a cause that had moved him deeply, Holmes came to regard passionate belief in that cause as vanity. In effect, the postwar Holmes mocked the prewar Holmes, a twenty-year-old foolish enough to have causes. In 1864, explaining his decision not to reenlist, Holmes wrote to his parents, "I am not the same man,"[56] and he truly was not.

After the war, Holmes for a time seemed disillusioned and detached,[57] but when he began, twenty years after leaving the army, to give speeches about his war experience, he appeared to have experienced an odd inversion of values.[58] He had reinterpreted the war experience as positive.[59] In his memory, the mud-black, blood-red fields were transformed to white and gold. Holmes wrote, "Through our great good fortune, in our youth our hearts were touched with fire. . . . [W]e have seen with our own eyes, beyond and above the gold fields, the snowy heights of honor, and it is for us to bear the report to those who come after us."[60] In war, Holmes had "touched the blue steel edge of actuality for half an hour" and "come down to truth."[61] He declared that "life is war, and the part of man in it is to be strong."[62] Holmes's correspondence offered such comments as, "It did those chaps a lot of good to live expecting some day to die by the sword."[63] He concluded that he had experienced life most fully in the years that he risked death. Peril, exertion, violent struggle, and commitment in the teeth of danger gave life its intensity and made it worthwhile.

An address by Holmes in 1895, "The Soldier's Faith," brought congratulations from the man who later would appoint him to the Supreme Court. Theodore Roosevelt recalled the address when he considered whether to nominate Holmes to fill the vacancy left by Horace Gray's resignation in 1902. The president told Senator Henry Cabot Lodge that Holmes's address had reassured him on a critical issue. With Gray's departure, the Supreme Court was divided four to four on the constitutionality of taxing the people of Puerto Rico and the Philippines. This issue would determine the applicability of the Constitution to the territories and the constitutionality of American imperialism.[64] Lodge agreed with the president that he would not appoint even his "best beloved" to the Court unless he were confident that the appointee would vote to uphold the power to tax. Although President Roosevelt remarked that he admired the "mental attitude" shown in Holmes's 1895 address, he also requested and apparently received assurances from Holmes himself—first indirectly (Lodge wrote the president, "I can put it to Holmes with absolute frankness & shall")[65] and then through a secret meeting with Holmes.[66] At the time of his appointment, Holmes lied to the press about this meeting.[67]

The 1895 address romanticized the war experience that Holmes could not endure when he declined reenlistment in 1864 and that he would have sacrificed a foot to avoid in 1863. Holmes recognized his change in attitude. "War when you are at it," he said, "is horrible and dull.

It is only when time has passed that you see that its message was divine."[68] He proclaimed, "We have shared the incommunicable experience of war; we have felt, we still feel, the passion of life to its top."[69] Two years later, at a reunion of his regiment, Holmes invoked some ancient rhetoric and declared, "Those who died [in battle] died . . . with a bird singing in their breast."[70]

"The Soldier's Faith" had a Darwinian cast: "Moralists and philosophers . . . declare that war is wicked, foolish, and soon to disappear. . . . For my own part, I believe that the struggle for life is the order of the world at which it is vain to repine. . . . The ideals of the past for men have been drawn from war, as those for women have been drawn from motherhood."[71] The most noted passage of the address—the one that may have touched Roosevelt most deeply—revealed Holmes's glorification not only of war but also of blind commitment:

> [I]n the midst of doubt, in the collapse of creeds, there is one thing I do not doubt, that no man who lives in the same world with most of us can doubt, and that is that the faith is true and adorable which leads a soldier to throw away his life in obedience to a blindly accepted duty, in a cause which he little understands, in a plan of campaign of which he has no notion, under tactics of which he does not see the use.[72]

Roosevelt wrote Senator Lodge, "By Jove, that speech of Holmes was fine."[73]

The president judged Holmes's military sentiments correctly. Following the Senate's confirmation of his nomination, Holmes spoke to the Middlesex Bar Association of the challenge of his new position: "To have the chance to do one's share in shaping the laws of the whole country spreads over one the hush that one used to feel when one was awaiting the beginning of a battle." He concluded, "We will not falter, we will not fail. We will reach the earthworks if we live, and if we fail we will leave our spirit in those who follow. . . . All is ready. Bugler, blow the charge."[74] Some members of the audience snickered.[75]

Holmes ultimately lost Roosevelt's confidence. Two years after his appointment, he alienated the president by revealing his low opinion of antitrust legislation and, in particular, by dissenting in *Northern Securities Co v United States*.[76] Henry Adams said of Holmes's dissent, "Theodore went wild about it."[77] The following year, although Holmes did not question the constitutionality of taxing the people of the Philippines, he wrote an opinion striking some taxes down. He concluded that the governor of the Philippines, William Howard Taft, had imposed these taxes without sufficient congressional authorization.[78] Holmes's opinion incurred Taft's fury and probably Roosevelt's as well.[79] Roosevelt later wrote Lodge, "Holmes should have been an ideal man on the bench. As a matter of fact he has been a bitter disappointment."[80] Holmes's bottom line on Roosevelt was: "He played all his cards—if not more. *R.i.p.*"[81]

Holmes once recalled that Charles Darwin's *On the Origin of the Species*[82] had been published when he was in college and that Herbert Spencer's *Social Statics*[83] had appeared earlier. Spencer's work is the classic exposition of what probably will forever be called "social Darwinism," although the doctrine preceded Darwin's work.[84] Social Darwinism maintains that poverty, suffering, starvation, and warfare are nature's way of eliminating the unfit. Attempted social reforms cannot significantly improve society and may harm it by altering or slowing natural evolution.[85] Spencer, not Darwin, coined the phrase "survival of the fittest."[86]

Holmes described his college acquaintance with Spencer's and Darwin's books by saying, "I hadn't read either of them, to be sure, but . . . it was in the air."[87] Within a few years, Holmes did read Spencer while recuperating from his Chancellorsville wound,[88] and thirty-five years after his college graduation he wrote, "I doubt if any writer of English except Darwin has done so much to affect our whole way of thinking about the universe."[89] A glorification of war, power, and struggle became the centerpiece of Holmes's approach to just about everything.

Liva Baker commented that "Holmes went on illustrating his points with images of war long after most men had stopped talking about it. . . ."[90] Edmund Wilson noted:

> [I]n writing to correspondents, even to those whom he does not know well . . . , he rarely fails to signalize the dates of the Battles of Ball's Bluff and Antietam, at both of which he had been wounded, by some such note as "31 years and one day after Antietam," "Antietam was 65 years ago yesterday," "We are celebrating Antietam, where if a bullet had gone one eighth of an inch differently the chances are that I should not be writing to you."[91]

As Wilson noted, the postwar Holmes seemed to approve of all wars— "at least those in which the English-speaking peoples [took] part."[92]

Holmes's attraction to morbidity was occasionally evidenced by more than his rhetoric. Sheldon Novick noted that Holmes's scrapbook of the war included a page of pictures cut from the newspapers—"hideous drawings of men whose feet had been cut off."[93] Liva Baker reported that during his years in Boston Holmes followed the fire engines whenever the fire bells rang.[94] Holmes himself noted that as a young man he had taken pleasure in seeing "the last quid of tobacco, chewed by some well-known criminal before execution," adding that the same fascination with the macabre had led him to save a letter written to him by Leo Frank shortly before Frank was lynched.[95]

Young men sent to war may return damaged in body and spirit, and the beneficiaries of their service may contrive not to notice the spiritual wounds. As a thought experiment, imagine that your Uncle Bob is a postal clerk whose career has never been interrupted by military service, and imagine that Bob begins one day to voice the thoughts once voiced by Oliver Wendell Holmes. For example, at the dinner table one evening, Bob announces, "[W]hen men differ in taste as to the kind of world they want the only thing to do is to go to work killing."[96] The next day, Bob praises suicide as a more "uneconomic" form of expression than charity to the poor.[97] You and other family members are likely to consider whether Bob needs help.

If Bob were a war hero, however, your response might be somewhat different. The crusty talk of soldiers is part of their charm. This talk may be a way of reminding an audience of an old soldier's history without quite boasting. Perhaps Oliver Wendell Holmes had a license to speak in ways that Uncle Bob would not—or perhaps a license to *think* in ways that would make people who had not endured the hardships of war seem troubled.

The observation that Holmes's war experience transformed his intellect and outlook now seems conventional. Saul Touster called this experience "the source[ ] of Holmes' world-view" and of "the attitudes and feelings that came to dominate his life."[98] Edmund Wilson wrote of "the paralyzing stroke to [Holmes's] idealism administered by the Civil War."[99] Robert Gordon notes:

> The war experience may have laid the foundations of Holmes's aloof detachment, his disengagement from causes and distrust of enthusiasms, and the bleakly skeptical foundations of his general outlook, according to which law and rights were only the systems imposed by force by whatever social groups emerged as dominant in the struggle for existence. From his war service on, he would repeatedly speak of personal and social life in military terms, as a fight carried on by soldiers blindly following incomprehensible orders.[100]

In remarks throughout his life, Holmes gave the lie to the statement of his comrade-in-arms, General William T. Sherman: "It is only those who have neither fired a shot nor heard the shrieks and groans of the wounded who cry aloud for blood, more vengeance, more desolation. War is hell."[101] For Holmes, war was not life gone awry. It was life at its most meaningful.[102]

Chapter Five

Holmes's Opinions

As a justice of the Supreme Court, Holmes wrote many great opinions. The positions that he took in a number of dissents have prevailed, and the positions that he took in majority opinions often have persisted. Holmes frequently argued elegantly for what now appear to be the correct rulings and offered what appear to be the correct reasons for them.

|Holmes also wrote many unfortunate opinions.) History mercifully has not vindicated all of his stands. In opinions both good and bad, Holmes expressed his ethical skepticism and his veneration of power and struggle.

This chapter reviews Holmes's opinions, emphasizing the consistency of his Darwinian outlook. It begins with a brief examination of opinions in six areas in which his work has not stood the test of time—unconstitutional conditions, sovereign immunity, state action, personal jurisdiction, the taxing power of the states, and racial equality. The chapter then examines at greater length Holmes's concept of judicial restraint and, after that, his opinions in the five doctrinal areas primarily responsible for his reputation for greatness as a justice—the judicial review of social welfare statutes and other legislation, the right of workers to organize, the substantive law applicable to federal court diversity cases, freedom of expression, and criminal justice. The chapter that follows this one considers some of Holmes's opinions on common law issues.

This chapter offers two qualifications to its claim that Holmes remained consistent. First, as he approached eighty, the tenor of his First Amendment opinions changed, and he qualified one Darwinian metaphor (survival of the fittest in the political process) with another more protective of freedom of expression (survival of the fittest in the marketplace of ideas). Second, the justice's later opinions on criminal procedure often departed from the skeptical themes that generally characterized his work. With these exceptions, influenced by developments late in life and apparently by Justice Brandeis, Holmes was constant. The language of his opinions was less colorful than that of his speeches and letters, but Holmes was not Jeckyll-Holmes, Hyde-Holmes. There was only one of him.

Someone who criticizes a historic figure like Holmes risks the charge of measuring him against the standards of a later age.[1] Just as other chapters note the extent to which Holmes's contemporaries shared or rejected his positions on social issues, this chapter emphasizes the extent to which other members of his Court shared or rejected his legal positions. When one or more justices (and especially when a majority of the Supreme Court) disagreed with Holmes, he cannot fairly be viewed as a passive mirror of his times. His choices were at least disputable at the time he made them.

EXTINCT DARWINIAN METAPHORS

Unconstitutional Conditions

When lawyers and judges speak of the doctrine of unconstitutional conditions, they mean that the government can violate the Constitution with carrots as well as with sticks. The doctrine of unconstitutional conditions says that the government may not "buy up" rights guaranteed by the Constitution. At least the government must have a better reason for inducing the waiver of a right than that it wishes to discourage the exercise of this right. The government may not provide a job, a research grant, a welfare check, or a parade permit on the condition that the recipient abandon her right to be an atheist or to be free of unreasonable searches and seizures.

The doctrine of unconstitutional conditions seems to reflect the triumph of realism over formalism. Law teachers tell students that in the bad old days judges invoked "the right–privilege distinction." These judges believed that the life of the law was logic rather than experience. They contended that the greater included the lesser and that the government could offer a "privilege" on any condition that it chose. Realist or Holmesian jurisprudence turned this around. Judges today look beyond form to function. They consider the motivation and effect of governmental actions "realistically," and they balance an action's "chilling effect" against the "legitimate governmental purposes" that it serves.

This story has hardly any element of truth. The Supreme Court had developed the doctrine of unconstitutional conditions long before Oliver Wendell Holmes joined it,[2] and although Holmes was not the first justice to oppose this doctrine and to insist on the right–privilege distinction, he was his era's most insistent champion of the government's power to condition a privilege upon the abandonment of constitutional rights. On one occasion when the Court held a state's condition on doing business within the state unconstitutional, Holmes wrote in dissent, "I confess my inability to understand how a condition can be unconstitutional when attached to a matter over which a state has absolute arbitrary power."[3] Holmes said earlier in this opinion, "Even in law the whole generally includes its parts. If the State may prohibit, it may prohibit with the privilege of avoiding the prohibition in a certain way."[4]

As a justice of the Supreme Judicial Court of Massachusetts, Holmes used the same language in an opinion that declared, "The Petitioner may have a constitutional right to talk politics, but he has no constitutional right to be a policeman."[5] He added, "The servant cannot complain, as he takes the employment on the terms which are offered him."[6] Another Holmes opinion concluded that because the Massachusetts legislature had no constitutional duty to provide parks, a person could have no constitutional right to make a speech on Boston Common.[7] Holmes wrote, "For the legislature absolutely or conditionally to forbid public speaking in a highway or public park is no more an infringement of the rights of a member of the public than for the owner of a private house to forbid it in his house."[8]

Sovereign Immunity

Captivated by concepts of power, Holmes became "the chief . . . proponent of sovereign immunity [in modern times]."[9] In his view, "there is no such thing as a right created by law, as against the sovereign who makes the law by which the right is to be created."[10] Holmes wrote, "[T]he authority that makes the law is itself superior to it. . . . Sovereignty is a question of power. . . ."[11]

State Action

With rare exceptions, the Constitution limits only the actions of government. In 1907, the Supreme Court held that the act of a state official could qualify as "state action" and could violate the Constitution although this act also violated state law. Holmes dissented. He argued that because the official's act had violated "the authentic command of the state," it could not be considered state action. Someone injured by a state officer's action could secure a remedy under the federal Constitution only if the state had failed to provide one.[12]

Jurisdiction in Personam

No area of federal constitutional law more clearly requires judges to address issues of political theory than that of jurisdiction over the person. The principal question in this area is: When, under the Fourteenth Amendment's due process clause, may one state require a resident of another state to defend a civil lawsuit in its courts? The Supreme Court has considered what "contacts" between the nonresident defendant and the "forum state" are sufficient—driving on the state's highways, shipping goods from outside the state for sale inside it, or perhaps being handed a summons by a process server while far above the state on an airliner headed toward Cleveland.

For Justice Holmes, the issue of personal jurisdiction was simple: "The foundation of jurisdiction is physical power. . . ."[13] If a nonresident were present in a state so that the state could seize her and bring her into court, the state would have jurisdiction over her. Without this physical power the state would lack jurisdiction. The question of personal jurisdiction was not a question of justice. It was a question of brute force.

Especially in the context of the American federal system, Holmes's view of personal jurisdiction was quirky. Like his views of state action, sovereign immunity, and the right–privilege distinction, this position has few adherents today. Under the federal Constitution, the decisions of a state court with jurisdiction are entitled to full faith and credit in the courts of other states. Both in theory and in practice, Supreme Court rulings on jurisdiction determine a state's power rather than the other way around.

Under the Fourteenth Amendment, the Supreme Court's task in cases of asserted personal jurisdiction is to determine what process is due, not to determine what physical power the state already has. Only someone who believed that might makes right could have considered the two questions equivalent. Before Holmes's service on the Supreme Court, the law of personal jurisdiction in England and America had focused on normative questions, not simply on issues of power.[14] Holmes, captivated by physical images, took a "realistic" position that ignored the reality of the American federal system.

Taxing Power of the States

Echoing his position on jurisdiction *in personam,* Holmes concluded that as long as a state had physical power over any of the parties to a business transaction, it could tax the transaction.[15] His opinion endorsing this position produced a haphazard regime of multiple taxation. Over Holmes's conceptual and sometimes bitter dissents, the Court recognized considerations of social advantage. It narrowed Holmes's ruling, then abandoned it.[16]

Racial Equality

Prior to Holmes's appointment to the Supreme Court, *Plessy v Ferguson*[17] had upheld the constitutionality of state-imposed racial segregation. With Holmes's concurrence, the Court extended *Plessy* by permitting a state to require a private college to segregate, at least so long as the college enjoyed the "privilege" of operating as a corporation.[18] Similarly, Holmes joined the Court's decision that an interstate railroad could segregate in the absence of congressional restriction.[19] Justice Harlan, who had been a slaveowner before becoming one of the foremost champions of civil rights in the Supreme Court's history, dissented from these rulings, as he had dissented in *Plessy.* Holmes once remarked that Harlan had a mind like "a powerful vise, the jaws of which couldn't be got nearer than two inches to each other."[20]

The plaintiffs in *McCabe v Atchison, T & SF Ry,*[21] challenged an Oklahoma law that authorized railroads to provide sleeping cars for white passengers while not providing them for blacks. Although the Court agreed unanimously that, for technical reasons, the plaintiffs had not established their right to an injunction, Justice Charles Evans Hughes's opinion for the Court made clear that the smaller volume of travel by black passengers would not justify the law. The right to equal (albeit separate but equal) accommodations was the right of every traveler; it could not be limited merely by showing some rational economic basis for distinguishing aggregate racial groups.[22]

Holmes was one of four justices who declined to join the Hughes opinion. He sent Hughes a memorandum saying that requiring railroads to provide sleeping cars for blacks only when the volume of travel by blacks had made these cars economically remunerative was "logically exact" equality. Hughes replied that requiring a black passenger to sit up all night while a white passenger enjoyed a sleeping berth was not "exact" equality in his view. It was "a bald, wholly unjustified discrimination against a passenger solely on account of race."[23]

The Thirteenth Amendment to the federal Constitution forbids slavery, but during the early twentieth century, the Alabama legislature worked to keep blacks as near to that condition as it could. When a federal court held one of its efforts unconstitutional in the *Peonage Cases* in 1903,[24] the legislature tried again. It declared that, whenever a laborer was indebted to his employer, the laborer's refusal without just cause to perform work required by a written contract would create a presumption that the laborer had entered into the contract fraudulently—that is, without an intent to perform it. The laborer thus would be guilty of a crime. Moreover, local rules of evidence prevented the laborer from testifying that he in fact lacked a fraudulent intent. With pre-legal-realism realism, the Supreme Court held in *Bailey v Alabama*[25] that this scheme reestablished involuntary servitude and violated the Thirteenth Amendment. Justice Hughes wrote for the Court that the Amendment forbade any attempt "to enforce the 'service of labor of persons' . . . in liquidation of any debt or obligation or otherwise."[26] Justice Holmes dissented. He said that he saw nothing in the Constitution that limited Alabama's ability to punish breach of contract by sentencing a defaulting worker to imprisonment at hard labor.[27]

Holmes did concur in a later decision holding another Alabama peonage law invalid. He reiterated his view that "nothing in the Thirteenth Amendment . . . prevents a State from making a breach of contract a crime and punishing it as such."[28] Without mentioning *Bailey* or explaining how this observation justified a different result from the one he had favored earlier, he added, "But impulsive people with little intelligence or foresight may be expected to lay hold of anything that affords a relief from present pain even though it will cause greater trouble by and by."[29]

In *Giles v Harris*,[30] the plaintiff alleged that Alabama's scheme of voter registration had been designed and administered to exclude him and virtually all other blacks from voting. The Court held that even if the plaintiff's allegations were true, it could not order Alabama officials to register him. Holmes's opinion for the Court said that holding the Alabama registration scheme a fraud on the Constitution and then ordering the plaintiff's registration under that scheme would be contradictory. One scholar appropriately called this ground of decision "whimsical."[31] Holmes did write for a unanimous Court in *Nixon v Herndon*,[32] holding a Texas white primary law unconstitutional.

Summarizing Holmes's opinions in racial equality cases, Robert Gordon observed:

In most race cases the lessons of "experience" were, apparently, that if the white South as the "de facto dominant power in the community" wanted to subordinate its black citizens under the thinnest cover of formal-legal equal treatment, there was nothing the federal courts could or should do about it.[33]

SURVIVING DARWINIAN METAPHORS

Darwinian Detachment and Judicial Review

Clearing the Road to Hell.   Holmes's skepticism concerning "abstract rights" and his view that rights could not be more than "what a given crowd will fight for" led to a broad toleration of legislative struggles and their outcomes. During twenty years' service on the Supreme Judicial Court of Massachusetts, he wrote only one opinion declaring Massachusetts legislation unconstitutional.[34] Although Holmes viewed the legislature as an unprincipled battlefield, he believed that judges should not deprive the victors of their spoils.

During his Civil War years, Holmes had written that he "loathe[d] the thick-fingered clowns we call the people—especially as the beasts are represented at the political centers—vulgar, selfish, and base,"[35] yet he rarely blocked the people's way. An article that he wrote in 1873 took a position he never abandoned:

> [L]egislation should easily and quickly, yet not too quickly, modify itself in accordance with the will of the de facto supreme power in the community. . . . The more powerful interests must be more or less reflected in legislation, which, like every other device of man or beast, must tend in the long run to aid the survival of the fittest. . . . [I]t is no sufficient condemnation of legislation that it favors one class at the expense of another; for much or all legislation does that. . . . [Legislation] is necessarily made a means by which a body, having the power, put burdens which are disagreeable to them on the shoulders of somebody else.[36]

Forty years later, Holmes reiterated, "[I still] regard most statutes that are called good as simply shifting the place where the strain or rub comes."[37] He spoke of legislation as "shift[ing] disagreeable burdens from the shoulders of the stronger to those of the weaker" and declared, "The social reformers of today seem to me . . . to forget that we no more can get something for nothing by legislation than we can by mechanics. . . ."[38]

Despite Holmes's pessimistic view of the legislative process, he almost invariably deferred to it. In his view, political might could make right even when it led to destruction:

> What proximate test of excellence can be found except correspondence to the actual equilibrium of force in the community—that is, conformity to the wish of the dominant power? Of course, such conformity may lead to destruction, and it is desirable that the dominant power should be wise. But wise or not, the proximate test of a good government is that the dominant power has its way.[39]

Holmes wrote to Felix Frankfurter, "I quite agree that a law should be called good if it reflects the will of the dominant forces of the community even if it will take us to hell."[40] He said of the judicial review of legislation, "[I]f you can pay for your ticket and are sure you want to go, I have nothing to say."[41]

Holmes acknowledged that his personal lack of conviction contributed to his view of the judicial role: "I am so skeptical as to our knowledge about the goodness or badness of laws that I have no practical criticism except what the crowd wants."[42] One week before taking his seat on the U.S. Supreme Court, he reviewed his service on the Supreme Judicial Court of Massachusetts:

> I have considered the present tendencies and desires of society and have tried to realize that its different portions want different things, and that my business was not to express my personal wish, but the resultant, as near as I could guess, of the pressure of the past and the conflicting wills of the present.[43]

The Incoherency of Holmes's Justification for Judicial Restraint.   In the dialogues of Plato, Socrates debated two opponents who agreed that might made right but differed on the implications of this position. Thrasymachus in the *Republic*[44] and Callicles in *Gorgias*[45] both argued that virtue lay in strength. Callicles observed, however, that the laws of a community might be dictated by the weak to prevent the strong from acquiring what was theirs by nature. Thrasymachus apparently did not consider this effect of popular legislation unjust. He observed that when the weak enacted legislation to deprive the strong of their gains, *they* became the strong: "[I]n all states [democratical, aristocratical, and tyrannical] there is the same principle of justice, which is the interest of the government."[46]

Socrates rejected both positions. He argued that although physicians receive fees for medical services, true physicians act in the interests of their patients. Similarly, rulers—if true to the art of government—act in the interests of the governed. Thrasymachus scoffed at this response. He suggested that rulers should be compared, not to physicians, but to shepherds who tend their flocks to benefit themselves.[47]

Social Darwinists of the late nineteenth and early twentieth centuries often followed Callicles, resisting legislation that they believed deprived the strong of what was naturally theirs. Holmes followed Thrasymachus. The triumph of a group in the political process itself marked this group as strong. Holmes's power-centered view of legislation was, however, ambiguous. It failed to specify how the supreme or dominant power was supreme or dominant. Neither of the hypotheses that Holmes might have advanced is at all persuasive.

First, Holmes might have referred to the majority's physical strength or to some other "natural" or "inherent" power—a power that the majority would continue to possess if current political arrangements were altered. If Holmes spoke of a natural, prepolitical, residual, or inherent power of the majority, however, he was in error. A majority typically has less power to "lick all the others" than a minority, especially when the minority has the guns. A glance at human history reveals that majorities rarely have been dominant.[48] As Bernard Williams observed of Thrasymachus, "[To speak] as if political or social power were not itself a matter of convention is a view barely adequate to the school playground."[49] If Holmes meant to offer concepts of physical power as the cornerstone of democracy, he was off base. Many things can be said in favor of democracy, but "might makes right" is not one of them.

Holmes might have referred, however, not to physical power or to some other prepolitical strength, but to whatever forces current political arrangements have made dominant. If that was Holmes's intention, however, his position was equally off base. For the dominant power always prevails. To prevail is what it means to be dominant. Being a dominant power would be no fun (as well as impossible) if the dominant power did not have its way. From a positivistic perspective, a Supreme Court justice can never reasonably argue that his dissenting position reflects the will of the dominant forces in the community. Even without his vote, the dominant forces obtained the approval of a majority of the Court and so remained (or became) the dominant forces. Holmes's position was tautological. If "the proximate test of a good government is that the dominant power has its way," every government is good until it is ousted.[50]

A social Darwinist might say with Vince Lombardi, "Winning is not everything; it's the only thing."[51] From the Darwinist-Thrasymachian-Vincian-Lombardian perspective, whatever survives or prevails is right.[52] To maintain that the dominant power should prevail and still to criticize existing arrangements, one must take a step away from Darwinism and positivism. With Callicles, one must envision power as it would exist in a counterfactual situation—a state of nature, perhaps, or a state in which the government's role was limited in some specified way, or (begging the question that Holmes seemed to answer) a state in which the majority always triumphed. Only a step away from the "is" can provide an Archimedian point—a fulcrum on which to rest a lever of criticism. The specification of any Archimedian point, however, would require explanation. It would lead where Holmes struggled not to go—from the world of description to the world of values.

The point can be made less abstractly. The power of a majority of the American people stems largely from law—in particular, from a Constitution that establishes a predominantly democratic form of government. Constitutional restraints on the exercise of legislative power and the institution of judicial review, however, are as much parts of the system of government that the dominant power has established as the power to legislate. A true positivist, like a true Darwinist, must swallow an existing system whole. If legislation, "like every other device of man or beast, must tend in the long run to aid the survival of the fittest," so also judicial review. For Holmes to treat the legislature and not the rest of government as manifesting "the de facto supreme power in the community" was incoherent.[53]

Perhaps, when Holmes spoke of "the actual equilibrium of force in the community," he meant something else—the actual equilibrium of preferences or desires.[54] Perhaps, when he spoke of the dominant power, he meant the dominant sentiment. Perhaps, despite Holmes's explicit rejection of utilitarianism,[55] he was secretly a utilitarian rather than a positivist or a social Darwinist.[56] Or perhaps his metaphors were nothing more than imprecise ways of saying "the majority." One wishes that the great oracle of American law had spoken more clearly. Holmes may have been a noted champion of democracy and of judicial restraint, but his defense of them was a muddle.

This defense was especially muddled in the context of the American political system. In a government designed to balance powers against one another, insisting that might makes right could not take Holmes very far. He struggled to substitute power metaphors for normative analysis and read the Constitution as though it contained only one tautological provision, "Winners win." Perhaps because most lawyers and legal scholars shared his skepticism, they did not notice how farfetched his metaphors were. David Luban comments:

> [A] more eccentric foundation for judicial self-restraint than Holmes's would be hard to find. A form of judicial review based on atheism and cosmic indifference to human aspiration, on the arbitrariness of all value judgments, on the contemptibility of attempting to relieve human suffering through public policy, and on judicial "obedience to a blindly accepted duty" to speed one's fellow citizens on their self-appointed path to Hell could not survive the test of full publicity.[57]

Darwinian Judicial Restraint in Practice

Fortunately for Holmes's historic reputation, the progressive movement achieved considerable political success during and just before his service on the Supreme Court. Throughout his years in Washington, the constitutionality of legislation regulating laborers' ages, wages, hours, and working conditions divided the justices. Sometimes (although not invariably) the Court held this legislation unconstitutional, saying that it violated a right to freedom of contract implicit in the due process clause.[58] Forty or so of the 873 opinions Holmes wrote as a Supreme Court justice were dissents from the Court's invalidation of regulatory legislation.[59]

In *Lochner v New York,*[60] in which the Court guaranteed New York bakers the liberty to work more than ten hours per day, Holmes wrote his most famous dissent.[61] He argued that "the natural outcome of a dominant opinion" should prevail, adding that "[t]he Fourteenth Amendment does not enact Mr. Herbert Spencer's *Social Statics.*"[62] As J. F. Wall has noted, however, the only real social Darwinist on the Court that decided *Lochner* was Holmes.[63]

Some legal scholars have criticized Holmes's dissent. Morton Horwitz, a legal historian and prominent member of the critical legal studies movement, has written of *Lochner,* "I do not believe that the . . . argument for judicial restraint ever made sense. It was an ideology designed for the particular purpose of restraining conservative judges who were interfering too much with a long overdue program of social reform."[64] Despite this disagreement on the left and some criticism on the right by scholars who still consider the majority's position correct,[65] the prevailing view is that Holmes's dissent urged the correct resolution of the most significant constitutional issue of his time. The majority had presumed to resolve a social question that the Constitution had not entrusted to it.[66]

Skeptics tend to view any profession of judicial restraint as posturing; law is politics, and judges and lawyers favor restraint only when it produces outcomes they like. Holmes's skepticism, however, refutes the skepticism of his heirs. Contrary to the suggestion by Morton Horwitz, Holmes's "ideology" was not "designed for the particular purpose" of promoting "a long overdue program of social reform." When Holmes said, "I loathed most of the things I decided in favor of,"[67] he meant it. "I should like to see the truth told," he wrote, "that legislation can't cure things, that the crowd now has substantially all there is, that the sooner they make up their mind to it the better, and that fights against capital are simply fights between the different brands of producers. . . ."[68] According to Holmes, "the crowd if it knew more wouldn't want what it does—but that is immaterial."[69]

Holmes suggested that his epitaph should read, "Here lies the supple tool of power,"[70] and he wrote, "[I]f my fellow citizens want to go to Hell I will help them. It's my job."[71] He viewed democracy as Darwinian struggle and, perhaps, as spectator sport.

Shortly after Holmes's retirement, H. L. Mencken observed:

> [Frantic liberals of the 1920s] concluded that [Holmes] was a sworn advocate of the rights of man. But . . . he was actually no more than an advocate of the rights of lawmakers. . . . He believed that the law-making bodies should be free to experiment almost *ad libitum*. . . . If this is Liberalism, then all I can say is that Liberalism is not what it was when I was young.[72]

As Morton Horwitz suggested, Holmes's restraint may have included an element of politics, but his politics were not progressive. His perspective was more that of a Pyrrhonian philosopher waiting to discover whether the thick-fingered clowns would kerosene the ant heap.[73] The Young Astronomer had become the Yankee from Olympus, still far above the battle.

By voting to uphold the constitutionality of progressive legislation, Holmes gained a reputation as a progressive. An even-handed skeptic, however, he was equally inclined to uphold repressive legislation. An example noted earlier was his dissent from the Supreme Court's ruling in *Bailey v Alabama*[74] that an Alabama peonage law violated the Thirteenth Amendment.

For a nonviolent, white-collar theft of about two hundred dollars, the defendant in *Weems v United States*[75] was sentenced under Philippines law to fifteen years at "hard and painful labor" with "a chain suspended from wrist to ankle."[76] The defendant was also perpetually deprived of various civil and political rights. The Supreme Court held the statute under which the defendant had been sentenced invalid, declaring that so severe a sentence for so minor a crime violated the cruel and unusual punishment clause of the Eighth Amendment.[77] The Court apparently recognized that the principal goal of the cruel and unusual punishment clause had been to prohibit inhuman methods of punishment, not to ensure proportionality between a criminal's punishment and his crime. In the prerealist year of 1910, however, Justice McKenna's opinion for the Court declared:

> Time works changes, brings into existence new conditions and purposes. Therefore a principle to be vital must be capable of wider application than the mischief which gave it birth. This is particularly true of constitutions. . . . [In interpreting] a constitution, therefore, our contemplation cannot be only of what has been but of what may be.[78]

Weems is a landmark, still cited both on the meaning of the cruel and unusual punishment clause and on the appropriateness of "nonoriginalist" interpretation of the Constitution. Justice Holmes dissented.[79]

Following World War I, a number of states prohibited public and private grade schools from teaching modern languages other than English. The Supreme Court held these statutes unconstitutional in *Meyer v Nebraska*.[80] Again Justice Holmes dissented, arguing that the statutes might be regarded "as a reasonable or even necessary method" of encouraging "a common tongue."[81]

As Yosal Rogat demonstrated, Holmes was unsympathetic to the claims of aliens, whether these claims concerned the validity of substantive governmental regulations or procedures for determining issues of exclusion, deportation, and citizenship.[82] The extent of Holmes's deference to legislative judgments was especially evident in *Patsone v Pennsylvania*.[83] A Pennsylvania statute prohibited resident aliens from owning or possessing shotguns or rifles, and Holmes's opinion for the Court said that the legislature might have judged aliens more likely than citizens to use these guns to kill wild birds and animals. The opinion concluded, "[T]his court has no such knowledge of local conditions as to be able to say that [the legislature] was manifestly wrong."[84] As Rogat noted, however, the Pennsylvania legislature was much more concerned with wild aliens than with wild birds: "[The] law . . . was passed at the end of a decade marked by labor unrest and violence, and one month after the local mine worker's contract expired. . . . The number of foreign-born miners in Pennsylvania was very high."[85]

Holmes's most notorious opinion was one in which a nearly unanimous Court joined him. In *Buck v Bell*,[86] the Court upheld a Virginia statute that, in Holmes's description, authorized the superintendent of a mental institution to sterilize "any patient afflicted with hereditary forms of insanity [or] imbecility." The statute gave the superintendent discretion to determine whether sterilization would serve "the best interests of patients and society," and "very careful provisions . . . protect[ed] the patients from possible abuse."[87] Justice Pierce Butler dissented without opinion. Butler, generally regarded as the Supreme Court's most conservative justice, was also the only Catholic member of the Court.

Early in his opinion, Holmes described the petitioner, Carrie Buck, as "a feeble minded white woman[,] . . . the daughter of a feeble minded mother . . . , and the mother of an illegitimate feeble minded child." His resounding conclusion toward the end of the opinion was, "Three generations of imbeciles are enough."[88] Holmes could not have known it, but his characterization was mistaken. Neither Carrie Buck nor her daughter was mentally defective, at least not by today's standards.[89] The daughter, who died of measles after completing the second grade, was in fact reported to have been "very bright."[90] She was listed on her school's honor roll.[91]

Holmes might have noted that the record contained no evidence of the daughter's mental condition. One deposition, by a eugenics "expert" who had diagnosed Carrie Buck as a "low-grade moron" without examining her, did say that the daughter was "supposed to be a mental defective."[92] Without evidentiary support, a lower court opinion also had described the daughter as "apparently feeble minded."[93]

Just as Holmes could not have known the mental condition of Carrie Buck and her daughter, he could not have known that two eugenics enthusiasts, the author of the Virginia sterilization law and the superintendent of the State Colony for Epileptics and Feebleminded, had chosen Buck as a bit player in a test case that they had devised. These supporters of the law had asked Buck's guardian to challenge it. Holmes also could not have known that a friend of the law's author had agreed to serve as Buck's counsel. He conceivably might have noticed that this lawyer had neither challenged the state's eugenic evidence nor presented any eugenic evidence of his own, but a Supreme Court justice cannot do much to correct this sort of deficiency in the record.[94]

Holmes could not have known that "the very careful provisions by which the act protects patients from possible abuse" would be disregarded in later cases—including that of Carrie Buck's sister, who was sterilized without her knowledge after being told that she needed an appendectomy.[95] Moreover, Holmes could not have known that later research would discredit both the concepts of mental disability and the genetic assumptions on which the Virginia statute rested.[96]

Holmes certainly could not have known that Carrie Buck had become pregnant involuntarily after being raped by her foster mother's nephew.[97] He might, however, have noted the clear indication in the record that one purpose of Virginia's sterilization law was to enable the state to recoup the costs of institutionalization by permitting it to place patients as domestic laborers without risking the patients' pregnancy.[98]

Despite these limitations of his knowledge, Holmes's opinion merits its reputation for brutality. He did not say of the Virginia statute what he had said of the Pennsylvania statute challenged in *Patsone:* "[T]his court has no such knowledge of local conditions as to be able to say that [the legislature] was manifestly wrong." He wrote instead of the danger of "being swamped with incompetence" and declared, "It is better for all the world, if instead of waiting to execute degenerate offspring for crime, or to let them starve for their imbecility, society can prevent those who are manifestly unfit from continuing their kind."[99] According to Saul Touster, Holmes's language "was already modified, at the insistence of his brethren, from an even more brutal original draft,"[100] but the earlier draft has not survived.

Buck's counsel had argued that, by subjecting people in mental institutions to sterilization while exempting equally defective people outside, the Virginia statute violated the equal protection clause. Describing this contention as "the usual last resort of constitutional arguments," Holmes responded, "Of course so far as the operations enable those who otherwise must be kept confined to be returned to the world, and thus open the asylum to others, the equality aimed at will be nearly reached."[101]

Holmes's amalgam of pseudoscience in *Buck v Bell* seemed contradictory. If "imbeciles" were likely to starve and to commit crimes warranting their execution, it was doubtful that, once sterilized, they could be released so that Virginia could process the rest batch-by-batch.

Although Holmes loathed most of the things he decided in favor of, he did not loathe the Virginia sterilization statute. He said in a letter to Harold Laski, "I wrote and delivered a decision upholding the constitutionality of a state law for sterilizing imbeciles the other day—and felt that I was getting near the first principle of real reform."[102] He wrote to Lewis Einstein, "[E]stablishing the constitutionality of a law permitting the sterilization of imbeciles . . . gave me pleasure."[103]

Labor Law

Even before Holmes's dissents in *Lochner* and other Supreme Court decisions invalidating social welfare legislation, some people—including the president of the United States—mistook his reverence for struggle with sympathy for progressive causes. While a justice of the Supreme Judicial Court of Massachusetts, Holmes declared his approval of collective bargaining by workers in two dissenting opinions. These dissents led Theodore Roosevelt to remark shortly before appointing Holmes to the Supreme Court that he had expressed "sympathy for the class from which he has not drawn his clients."[104] Holmes's opinions in labor cases, however, revealed no sympathy whatever for the laboring class. They revealed only his fondness for the battle. Although, as he saw it, unions could accomplish nothing for workers as a group, that was no reason not to have a good fight.

Holmes's dissenting opinion in *Plant v Woods*[105] declared:

> While I think the strike a lawful instrument in the universal struggle of life, I think it pure phantasy to suppose that there is a body of capital of which labor as a whole secures a larger share by that means. . . . Organization and strikes may get a larger share for the members of an organization, but, if they do, they get it at the expense of the less organized and less powerful portion of the laboring mass. . . . [S]ubject to the qualifications which I have expressed, I think it lawful for a body of workmen to try by combination to get more than they are now getting, although they do it at the expense of their fellows, and to that end to strengthen their union by the boycott and the strike.

In his dissent in *Vegelahn v Guntner,*[106] Holmes wrote, "If the policy on which our law is founded is too narrowly expressed in the term free competition, we may substitute free struggle for life."[107] He added that "free competition means combination," and that "[w]hether beneficial . . . or detrimental, [competition] is inevitable, unless the fundamental axioms of society, and even the fundamental conditions of life, are to be changed."[108] In Holmes's view, "the policy of allowing free competition justifies the intentional infliction of temporal damage . . . when the damage is done not for its own sake, but as an instrumentality in reaching the end of victory in the battle of the trade."[109]

Competition among sellers generally benefits consumers by reducing prices, but the competition that Holmes endorsed was, as he saw it, a zero-sum battle between union workers and "the less organized and less powerful portion of the laboring mass." As he described this competition, it promoted neither efficiency in the distribution of goods nor socially desirable redistribution. For Holmes, the "inevitability" of the struggle was enough. Following his nomination to the Supreme Court, newspapers reported that his dissents in *Plant v Woods* and *Vegelahn v Guntner* had taken the side of labor. Holmes wrote of his "unreasoning—rage I was going to say—dissatisfaction is nearer" at this misinterpretation of his position.[110]

The Law Applicable to Diversity Cases

Lawyers today generally admire Holmes's dissent in *Brown & White Taxicab & Transfer Co v Brown & Yellow Taxicab & Transfer Co.*[111] This dissent criticized the 1842 ruling in *Swift v Tyson*[112] that federal courts hearing diversity cases (cases between citizens of different states) could appropriately decide substantive common law issues without following the decisions of state courts on these issues. Six years after Holmes retired from the Supreme Court, the Court overruled *Swift* in *Erie RR Co v Tompkins.*[113] Justice Brandeis's opinion for the Court cited approvingly Holmes's dissent in *Brown & White Taxicab.*

This dissent and similar dissents by Holmes in other cases[114] were consistent with his power-focused jurisprudence. Unlike Justice Brandeis's opinion in *Erie,* Holmes's dissent did not discuss the failure of *Swift v Tyson* to promote uniformity, the forum-shopping and other strategic maneuvers that this decision encouraged, or any other unfortunate practical consequences of this decision. Instead, his argument against *Swift* was conceptual and Austinian.[115] As he saw it, any idea of a common law that could exist independently of the power of a particular government to enforce it was gibberish—a conceptual impossibility. The common law depended on state power. A state might refuse to follow this body of law altogether (as one state, Louisiana, had). It followed that determining the content of the common law was a matter of state sovereignty. In judging where sovereignty resided, Justice Story, the author of the opinion in

Swift v Tyson, had done his sums wrong.[116] As G. Edward White observed, "[E]verywhere in his exploration of jurisprudential issues Holmes saw the 'fact' of sovereignty."[117]

In fact, although Justice Story's 1842 opinion did not say so, his position in *Swift* might have rested on the view that the Constitution's grant of authority to the federal courts to decide "[c]ontroversies . . . between Citizens of different States" included the authority to resolve substantive common law issues. It also might have rested on the empirical proposition that the Supreme Court's independent rulings on the common law, which most state judges were likely to follow, offered the best hope of producing a uniform commercial law—a *common* law to which both state and federal judges sought to adhere.[118]

Indeed, the ruling in *Swift* worked essentially as Justice Story thought it would—without complaint and with state-court approval—until after the Civil War. Then tort law began to eclipse commercial law in importance; Supreme Court decisions tilted toward creditors and employers; some state courts balked at following the federal lead; and scholars like Holmes's compatriot John Chipman Gray began to attribute the ruling in *Swift* to Justice Story's advanced age and "restless vanity."[119]

Survival in the Marketplace of Ideas: The Freedom of Speech

Holmes's reputation for greatness as a justice probably rests as much on his role in shaping the law of the First Amendment as on his resistance to invalidating social welfare legislation. In *Schenck v United States,*[120] he advanced a constitutional standard that, as interpreted and revised in later cases, permitted broad freedom of expression: "The question in every case is whether the words used are used in such circumstances and are of such a nature as to create a clear and present danger that they will bring about substantive evils that Congress has a right to prevent."[121] In a dissenting opinion in *Abrams v United States,*[122] he offered a classic metaphor to explain and justify the Constitution's demand for toleration: "[T]he best test of truth is the power of the thought to get itself accepted in the competition of the market. . . ."[123]

Holmes's Initial View of the Freedom of Speech.   Holmes's view of the protection afforded speech changed over time. As noted above, his opinions for the Supreme Judicial Court of Massachusetts declared that people had no right to talk politics if they wished to remain police officers, and no right to give speeches in public parks.[124] In addition, in a libel case, Holmes concluded that a newspaper's common law privilege of fair criticism on matters of public interest was less extensive than an employer's privilege of criticizing an employee when a prospective employer asked for a reference. False statements by an employer often were privileged, but false statements by a newspaper could not be.[125]

In another libel case, a lawyer sued a newspaper because it had described the contents of a petition for his removal from the bar. Without advancing any constitutional defense, the newspaper claimed that its accurate reports of the contents of these legal pleadings were privileged. Holmes rejected this contention, declaring that libelous allegations of misconduct were privileged only if made in the course of the legal proceedings themselves.[126]

Holmes's first opinion for the U.S. Supreme Court on issues of freedom of expression revealed a similarly narrow conception of this freedom. The defendant in *Patterson v Colorado*[127] had published articles and a cartoon critical of the Colorado Supreme Court. The Colorado court concluded that the defendant had sought to influence it in matters still pending and held him in contempt. On appeal, the defendant maintained that he should have been permitted to show the truth of his publication. The Supreme Court rejected this contention and affirmed the defendant's contempt citation.

Writing for the Court, Holmes left open the question whether the Constitution protected the freedoms of speech and of the press against abridgment by the states.[128] Even if it did, the "main purpose" of these freedoms was to protect against "*previous restraint* upon publications."[129] Freedom of the press did "not prevent the subsequent punishment of such as may be deemed contrary to the public welfare."[130] In Holmes's view, "The . . . freedom [from prior restraint] extends as well to the false as to the true; the subsequent punishment may extend as well to the true as to the false."[131] Justice Harlan alone dissented from the Court's judgment "that the legislature may impair or abridge the rights of a free press and of free speech whenever it thinks that the public welfare requires that to be done."[132]

Holmes's second opinion for the Court concerning free expression again revealed little sympathy for dissent. The defendant in *Fox v Washington*[133] had urged a boycott of people he claimed were persecuting his fellow nudists. He was prosecuted for violating a Washington statute outlawing the publication of any material encouraging disrespect for law, and Holmes wrote an opinion upholding the constitutionality of the statute. Devoting no attention to the threatened boycott, the opinion contended that the defendant had encouraged violation of the law against indecent exposure. Any encouragement, however, had come only from the defendant's approval of nudism, not from his advocacy or incitement of any imminent or specific act.

A letter to Felix Frankfurter two years after the decision in *Fox* indicated Holmes's enthusiastic support for the suppression of dissent:

> Patriotism is the demand of the territorial club for priority, and as much priority as it needs for vital purposes, over such tribal groups as the churches and trade unions. I go whole hog for the territorial club and I don't care a damn if it interferes with some of the spontaneities of the other groups. I think the Puritans were quite right when they whipped the Quakers and if it were conceivable—as every brutality is—that we should go back a century or two, the Catholics would be quite right, if they got the power, to make you and me shut our mouth. Which, being so, I think any nation perfectly justified in thinking whether it will have them or not in its territory.[134]

Schenck, Frohwerk, **and** *Debs.* Three prosecutions for violation of the Espionage Act of 1917 during World War I—*Schenck v United States,*[135] *Frohwerk v United States,*[136] and *Debs v United States*[137]—commonly are seen as marking the beginning of modern First Amendment jurisprudence.[138] The Espionage Act proscribed among other things willfully obstructing military recruitment and enlistment during wartime, causing insubordination in the armed forces, and attempting to do so. Juries convicted the defendants in these three cases of various offenses under the Act, and Holmes wrote opinions affirming the convictions.

In the speeches and literature that led to their convictions, the defendants had not directly advocated the violation of draft laws or other laws affecting the military. The issue was whether they had done so obliquely (or, more precisely, whether juries could find that they had) and, if so, whether the Act permitted conviction for their veiled advocacy.

Addressing an issue of statutory construction like the one that confronted the Supreme Court, Judge Learned Hand earlier had concluded in *Masses Publishing Co v Patten*[139] that juries should be permitted to convict only when a defendant's words could fairly be understood as urging violation of the law. Although the advocacy of unlawful acts "may be accomplished as well by indirection as expressly,"[140] permitting juries to speculate about a speaker's tendencies and unexpressed goals invited the punishment of "every political agitation . . . apt to create a seditious temper."[141] Hand concluded, "If one stops short of urging upon others that it is their duty or their interest to resist the law, it seems to me one should not be held to have attempted to cause its violation."[142]

Although urged by counsel to adopt Hand's position, the Supreme Court did not do so. It concluded that, on the evidence, juries could have found that the defendants had intentionally promoted law violation, and it held that their indirect advocacy was sufficient. The weakest of the three cases for the government was probably the one that led to Eugene V. Debs's conviction and ten-year prison sentence.

Debs had spoken, not to draftees or to soldiers, but to a convention of socialists. Holmes noted that the speech included "the usual contrasts between capitalists and laboring men, sneers at the advice to cultivate war gardens, attribution to plutocrats of the high price of coal, &c."[143] He also observed that Debs's speech included "a glorification of minorities."[144] Holmes's recitation of the facts thus revealed that he was every bit as fine a sneerer as Debs. In the course of Debs's remarks, he had called war the "supreme curse of capitalism" and had said that "the working class, who furnish the corpses, have never yet had a voice in declaring war." He also voiced his approval of several people who had been convicted of crimes as a result of their antiwar activities. Holmes concluded that the jury might have found "that one purpose of the speech, whether incidental or not does not matter, was to oppose not only war in general, but this war, and that the opposition was so expressed that its natural and intended effect would be to obstruct recruiting. If that was intended, and if . . . that would be its probable effect, it would not be protected. . . ."[145]

In *Schenck v United States,*[146] a decision affirming another of the Espionage Act convictions, Holmes introduced the phrase "clear and present danger." *Debs* illustrated how little this language meant to him. As Vincent Blasi observes, Holmes "gave no indication that he meant the phrase to embody a harm principle fundamentally different from that which informed the traditional 'bad tendency' test."[147] Not only had Holmes spoken simply of the "natural" and "probable" effect of Debs's speech, but the trial court's instructions to the jury had required merely a finding that Debs's words would have the "natural tendency and reasonably probable effect" of obstructing recruiting.[148] From today's perspective, the clear and present danger standard seems to mark a line between advocacy and incitement. If Holmes and the Supreme Court had meant to draw this line, however, the Court would have been required to place all three Espionage Act cases on the "advocacy" side of the divide.[149]

Briefs on both sides of the Espionage Act cases had disputed the continuing validity of the bad tendency test, with those supporting the defendants noting scholarly opposition to this test.[150] Holmes clearly rejected the defendants' challenge. His opinion in *Schenck* first noted the argument: "But it is said, suppose that [obstruction of the draft] was the tendency of this circular, it is [nevertheless] protected by the First Amendment to the Constitution."[151] The opinion then observed, "The most stringent protection of free speech would not protect a man in falsely shouting fire in a theatre and causing a panic." Following this most memorable of the fire images in Holmes's writings, the opinion introduced the clear and present danger language.[152] The opinion then declared, "If the act, (speaking, or circulating a paper,) its tendency and the intent with which it is done are the same, we perceive no ground for saying that success alone warrants making the act a crime."[153] The opinions in *Schenck, Frohwerk,* and *Debs* were consistent with the view that Holmes offered Learned Hand after Hand's decision in *Masses:* "[F]ree speech stands no differently than freedom from vaccination."[154]

After voting to affirm Debs's conviction, Holmes wrote in a letter, "Now I hope the President will pardon him and some other poor devils with whom I have more sympathy."[155] After Debs had been imprisoned nearly three years, President Harding did commute his sentence. (In 1920, Debs, the nominee of the Socialist Party for president, received more than nine hundred thousand votes while serving this sentence.)[156] Riding to the train station with the farewell cheers of thousands of his fellow inmates in his ears,[157] Debs took from his wallet the five-dollar bill given to him on his release. He sent this bill with a note to the committee working to free Sacco and Vanzetti.[158]

The night before Sacco and Vanzetti were executed, Holmes denied a petition for habeas corpus on their behalf. He previously had denied another habeas corpus petition and a motion for an extension of time for their lawyers to apply for a writ of certiorari.[159] Saul Touster observes:

> [Harold Laski] was patently falsifying when he wrote of the "agony of mind" Holmes suffered in coming to his "ultimate refusal to interfere in the last tragic hour of Sacco and Vanzetti." There isn't a shred of evidence that Holmes suffered any agony at all in this or any other case we know of. He thought their last minute petition had "no shadow of a ground" for intervention. "I could not feel a doubt," wrote Holmes to Laski. "I wrote an opinion on the spot. . . ."[160]

Liva Baker reports that Holmes "was agitated, not by the issues of the [Sacco and Vanzetti] case, but by the 'shriekers' who had elevated the defendants to the status of 'heroes.' . . . [Holmes] thought [the case] only had given 'the reds a chance to howl.'"[161]

Abrams.   The Term of Court following *Schenck* saw the first of several cases in which Holmes dissented from the affirmance of criminal convictions based on speech or publication. The facts of *Abrams v United States*[162] seemed in some respects stronger for the government than those of the cases in which Holmes had written majority opinions affirming convictions eight months earlier. The defendants, supporters of the Russian Revolution, had prepared a leaflet that they distributed partly by throwing copies from the windows of a New York City building. The leaflet declared in Yiddish, "Workers in the ammunition factories, you are producing bullets, bayonets, cannon, to murder not only the Germans, but also your dearest, best, who are in Russia and are fighting for freedom." The leaflet explicitly urged a general strike.

The Supreme Court observed that the "defendant alien anarchists"[163] had argued "somewhat faintly, that [their] acts . . . were not unlawful because within the protection of th[e] freedom of speech and of the press . . . and that the entire Espionage Act is unconstitutional because in conflict with [the First] Amendment."[164] Rejecting these arguments as well as the defendants' claim that the evidence was insufficient to support their convictions, the Court affirmed the defendants' convictions and their twenty-year sentences for violating the Espionage Act.

Joined by Justice Brandeis, Holmes dissented. His opinion offered the marketplace metaphor and said, "[W]e should be eternally vigilant against attempts to check the expression of opinions that we loathe and believe to be fraught with death."[165] Holmes's dissent in *Abrams* has been called "the greatest utterance on intellectual freedom by an American, ranking in the English tongue with Milton and Mill."[166]

Scholars have disputed whether Holmes's view of the constitutional protection afforded speech changed during the period between his majority opinions in *Schenck, Frohwerk,* and *Debs* and his dissenting opinion in *Abrams.* Labeling the claim that Holmes changed his position "revisionist" (while attributing this revisionist view to a near army of respected scholars—David Currie, Gerald Gunther, David Rabban, Fred Ragan, and Laurence Tribe), Sheldon Novick insists that Holmes's position remained "stubbornly consistent."[167] According to Novick, the principal issue that divided Holmes from the majority in *Abrams* was not an issue of proximity—of clear and present danger or of how near a defendant's speech must have come to producing a forbidden result. It was an issue of what mental state was needed to support the defendants' convictions. The *Abrams* majority declared, "Men must be held to have intended, and to be accountable for, the effects which their acts were likely to produce."[168] Holmes replied, "[A] deed is not done with intent to produce a consequence unless that consequence is the aim of the deed."[169]

Holmes's advocacy of a subjective standard in *Abrams* and other free speech cases was ironic. Almost forty years earlier, Holmes's book *The Common Law* had argued that objective standards of liability had displaced subjective standards in nearly every area of law. He saw the disappearance of subjective standards as a mark of the law's progress and maturity.[170] Moreover, Holmes's penchant for objective standards had greatly influenced his rulings on criminal law.[171] It therefore seems surprising that in free expression cases he would insist upon proof of subjective wrongdoing while a majority of his Court did not.

In *Abrams,* Holmes reiterated that subjective standards of responsibility were a departure from "the general principle of civil and criminal liability":

> I am aware of course that the word intent as vaguely used in ordinary legal discussion means no more than knowledge at the time of the act that the consequences said to be intended will ensue. Even less than that will satisfy the general principle of civil and criminal liability. A man may have to pay damages, may be sent to prison, at common law might be hanged, if at the time of his act he knew facts from which common experience showed that the consequences would follow, whether he individually could foresee them or not. But, when words are used exactly, a deed is not done with intent to produce a consequence unless that consequence is the aim of the deed.[172]

The issue that most obviously divided Holmes and the *Abrams* majority was an issue of statutory construction. The Espionage Act used words like "willfully" and "with intent," and the simplest explanation of Holmes's endorsement of a subjective standard is that he was better at reading English than his brethren.[173]

As Sheldon Novick suggests, Holmes's view of the mental state required to support a conviction under the Espionage Act did not change between *Schenck* and *Abrams,* and Holmes was equally consistent on another issue that apparently separated him from other members of his Court. Novick discovered that before Holmes wrote his majority opinion in *Schenck,* he had prepared a dissenting opinion in another Espionage Act prosecution. The defendants in *Baltzer v United States*[174] had written antiwar letters to a governor and to other public officials demanding changes in the Selective Service System, and the Supreme Court voted to affirm their convictions for obstructing military recruitment. The defendants had not circulated their letters publicly, however, and Holmes's dissent (which a note from Justice Brandeis had said he would join) emphasized that unpublished letters to officials posed no risk of obstructing recruitment.[175] Holmes never issued his dissent, however. The government sensibly confessed error. Novick argues that the unpublished *Baltzer* dissent should put to rest any doubt that Holmes changed his mind on issues of free expression.[176]

Yet Holmes did change his mind. His views on the dangers posed by unpublished letters and on the applicability of a subjective standard may have been consistent from one case to the next, but Holmes's consistency on these issues does not speak at all to the claim made by the supposedly revisionist scholars. These scholars contended that Holmes changed his position on the meaning of clear and present danger, the phrase now remembered as one of his principal contributions to First Amendment doctrine. As Gerald Gunther put it, "The *Schenck* standard was not truly speech-protective; and . . . it was not until the fall of 1919, with his famous dissent in [*Abrams*], that Holmes put some teeth in the clear and present danger formula."[177]

Apart from *Schenck's* single use of the word *present,* the opinions in *Schenck, Frohwerk,* and *Debs* did not distinguish incitement from advocacy or immediate from long-term danger. The language of Holmes's dissent in *Abrams* had a very different tone:

> The United States constitutionally may punish speech that produces or is intended to produce a clear and *imminent* danger that it will bring about *forthwith* certain substantive evils. . . .[178]

> It is only the *present* danger of *immediate* evil or an intent to bring it about that warrants Congress in setting a limit to the expression of opinion. . . .[179]

> [W]e should be eternally vigilant against attempts to check the expression of opinions that we loathe and believe to be fraught with death, unless they so *imminently* threaten *immediate* interference with the lawful and pressing purposes of the law that an *immediate* check is required to save the country.[180]

> Only the *emergency* that makes it *immediately* dangerous to leave the correction of evil counsels to time warrants making any exception to

the sweeping command, "Congress shall make no law . . . abridging the freedom of speech."[181]

In a number of cases following *Abrams*, Holmes concluded that expression was protected by the Constitution partly because it did not pose a sufficiently imminent risk of harm.[182]

Why Holmes Switched.   Several voices may have contributed to the change in Holmes's position.[183] Shortly after the decisions in *Schenck, Frohwerk,* and *Debs,* Zechariah Chafee published a landmark article, *Freedom of Speech in Wartime.*[184] Although critical of the ruling in *Debs,* the article praised Holmes and declared that his pronouncement in *Schenck* concerning clear and present danger would make "the punishment of words for their bad tendency impossible."[185] As David Rabban observed, Chafee's statement was "entirely unsupportable."[186] Holmes had relied on the "bad tendency" test in his earliest freedom-of-expression decisions for the Supreme Court; he had rejected challenges to this traditional test in *Schenck* and *Debs;* the convictions in *Schenck, Frohwerk,* and *Debs* were sustainable only on a "bad tendency" theory; and a unanimous Court certainly would not have joined Holmes if its members had viewed his statement concerning clear and present danger as the revolutionary pronouncement Chafee perceived it to be.

Holmes, however, read Chafee's article and judged it "first rate."[187] Harold Laski arranged for Chafee and Holmes to meet briefly in the summer of 1919, and Holmes found Chafee "unusually pleasant and intelligent."[188] Holmes's dissent in *Abrams* the following fall mirrored Chafee's article in several respects,[189] and Chafee's wish may have been one of many parents of Holmes's deed.

Judge Learned Hand wrote a letter criticizing Holmes's Espionage Act opinions, promising that "this is positively my last appearance in the role of liberator." Hand declared (probably disingenuously) that he approved the result in *Debs,* but he protested that neither the foreseeability of a harmful result nor a jury's willingness to find a bad motive should deprive a speaker of protection.[190]

A few years before the first Espionage Act cases (and substantially after Holmes's early opinions on free expression), Louis D. Brandeis joined the Supreme Court. At the time of his nomination, Holmes expected Brandeis to "make a good judge," but because of the intense controversy surrounding the progressive Jewish lawyer, Holmes considered his nomination "a misfortune for the Court."[191] Brandeis, a Boston lawyer, had known Holmes for decades.[192] Chief Justice Taft later would complain that Holmes was "so completely under the control of Brother Brandeis that it gives to Brandeis two votes instead of one."[193] Holmes was eighty-seven when Taft made this remark, and the remark was unfair then. Holmes was merely seventy-eight in the summer between *Schenck* and *Abrams*. Although he was not under Brandeis's control, he might have been somewhat more receptive to suggestion than he would have been at seventy.[194]

Prior to Brandeis's appointment, Holmes had dissented from a number of Supreme Court decisions sustaining claims of individual constitutional rights.[195] So far as I am aware, he had dissented in support of an assertion of individual rights only once.[196] According to G. Edward White, "[Holmes] was no friend of civil liberties or of the rights of minorities in his first thirteen years on the Supreme Court. . . . [H]e had not only voted consistently against claimants alleging that their civil liberties had been violated, he had been less sympathetic to those claimants than justices typically identified as among the most 'conservative' on the Court."[197]

Following Brandeis's appointment, this pattern was reversed. Holmes's dissents from majority decisions sustaining claims of personal constitutional rights came to an end,[198] and his dissents from decisions rejecting individual-rights claims began.[199] Even Sheldon Novick, who maintains that Holmes's views on free speech were "stubbornly consistent,"[200] notes in his biography of Holmes that "[i]n response to Brandeis's urging" Holmes began to dissent in the 1920s from decisions permitting censorship of the mails—a practice "which for twenty years he had allowed to pass without objection."[201]

At the time of his *Abrams* dissent, Holmes enjoyed the company of admirers more than forty years younger than he. Among them were Felix Frankfurter, Harold Laski, Morris Cohen, Herbert Croly, Walter Lippmann, and Lewis Einstein.[202] These admirers may not have pressed Holmes to strengthen the clear and present danger standard, and although Harold Laski took a very different position in a letter to Zechariah Chafee, he wrote to Holmes that the opinions in *Schenck, Frohwerk,* and *Debs* were "very convincing."[203] If Holmes's acolytes influenced him at all,[204] however, it was toward becoming the liberal hero that legend (grounded on his dissent in *Lochner*) had begun to make him.[205]

Certainly if Holmes was interested in encouraging further flattery from this group, his *Abrams* dissent succeeded. Laski wrote that "amongst the many opinions of yours I have read, none seems to me superior either in nobility or outlook, in dignity or phrasing, and in that quality the French call *justesse*." Frankfurter wrote of "the gratitude and . . . the pride I have in your dissent," adding that Holmes had provided "education in the obvious." Chafee wrote in a law review of "Justice Holmes's magnificent exposition of the philosophic basis" of the First Amendment. He proclaimed that because of "the enduring qualities of the reasoning of Justice Holmes," the effect of the majority's decision "should be temporary."[206]

Darwinism, Skepticism, and the Marketplace. ⌐Whatever the forces of flattery and persuasion that shaped them, Holmes's later opinions on issues of free expression merit the respect they have engendered. As he had in his opinions on the validity of social welfare legislation, Holmes argued elegantly for positions that now have demonstrated their "power to get themselves accepted in the competition of the market."⌐

These opinions do not, however, indicate limits to Holmes's veneration of struggle. Long before he advanced the marketplace metaphor in *Abrams,* his writings offered Darwinian and militaristic images of clashing ideas. In 1899, for example, Holmes wrote of "the struggle for life among competing ideas, and of the ultimate victory and survival of the strongest."[207] In 1906 he referred to "the struggle for life carried on among ideas; to the result that some perish and others put on the livery of the conqueror."[208] For Holmes, the marketplace of ideas was one arena of struggle; the political process, another. He rarely addressed the question of which arena should control the other. By concluding that the legislature had been tolerant, he typically avoided the issue.

In both federal and state cases, Holmes's opinions proclaimed the defendant's *conduct* protected by the First Amendment. In federal cases, however, he also announced that this conduct did not violate the relevant statutes. In state cases, moreover, although his opinions implicitly declared state statutes unconstitutional "as applied," he only once declared state legislation unconstitutional "on its face."[209] G. Edward White appropriately concludes, "[T]he assumption that Holmes' free speech decisions represent a dramatic departure from his habitual stance toward judicial review of the constitutionality of legislation is largely misplaced."[210]

Although Holmes's later opinions on the freedom of expression are compatible with a progressive, republican vision of society, they are also compatible with his skepticism.[211] Disarming one side brings struggle to an end, and even if all societies rest on the death of men, they need not rest on the death of ideas.[212] The battle between port and ditch-water, warriors and pacifists, nihilists and onwarders can continue *ad infinitum.*

Holmes took a skeptical view of moral truth.[213] He once wrote, "All I mean by truth is the path I have to travel,"[214] and he defined truth on various occasions as "what I can't help believing,"[215] "the prevailing can't help of the majority,"[216] "the unanimous consent of mankind to a system of propositions,"[217] and "the majority vote of that nation that could lick all others."[218] These definitions—truth is what I believe, what everyone believes, what most people believe, and what the strong believe—were inconsistent, yet all were subjective. All of them departed from the dictionary's declaration that "[t]ruth is most commonly used to mean correspondence with facts or with what actually occurred."[219]

When, however, Holmes said for the Supreme Court that the best test of truth was the power of a thought to find acceptance in the marketplace, his language was ambiguous. Acceptance in the marketplace might be all there was to truth, or it might be the best available indicator of external reality. A year before his dissent in *Abrams,* Holmes indicated how sensible people might look partly to the conclusions of others in judging reality:

> If I think that I am sitting at a table I find that the other persons present agree with me; so if I say that the sum of the angles of a triangle is equal to two right angles. If I am in a minority of one they send for a doctor or lock me up; and I am so far able to transcend the to me convincing testimony of my senses or my reason as to recognize that if I am alone probably something is wrong with my works.[220]

The marketplace metaphor was broad enough to encompass Holmes's skeptical vision of truth and more objective visions as well. He did not say that acceptance by the market defined truth. He said only that acceptance by the market was the best test of truth a society was likely to have. Sanford Levinson therefore seems wrong when he characterizes Holmes's metaphor as a "fully pragmatic" test of truth,[221] and Richard Posner seems equally wrong when he says that the metaphor "rests on skepticism about the possibility of settling intellectual disputes by reason."[222]

David Luban observes:

> [R]egardless of his own quirky epistemology, Holmes offered a formula that is compatible with any view of the nature of truth. Correspondence theorists, coherence theorists, pragmatists, and redundancy theorists can haggle to their hearts' content about the definition of

truth while still agreeing that the competition of the market provides its best test.[223]

Holmes's umbrella, however, has not proven large enough for everyone. In recent years, legal scholars of the left have challenged his vision, arguing that a *laissez-faire* approach to the marketplace of ideas effectively favors the status quo. These scholars doubt that competition in a market shaped by current values can correct harmful and deeply ingrained social attitudes—for example, attitudes condoning the sexual subordination of women. They favor governmental participation in a program of resocialization.[224]

The apparent alternative to governmental programs of resocialization is a Holmesian or Darwinian market—"survival of the fittest" in a world of competing ideas. This metaphor accords with classic liberal sentiments and with the concept of free inquiry and expression that informs the First Amendment. Images of struggle may have led Holmes to sound First Amendment law. Turning his Olympian gaze toward the freedom of speech, Holmes once said of it what he had said of other things: "Little as I believe in it as a theory I hope I would die for it."[225]

Criminal Justice

Holmes's indifference to issues of personal culpability and his preference for external or objective standards of responsibility gave a harsh cast to his opinions on substantive criminal law. He wrote for the Supreme Court, "[T]he law is full of instances where a man's fate depends on his estimating rightly, that is as the jury subsequently estimates it, some matter of degree. If his judgment is wrong, not only may he incur a fine or . . . imprisonment . . . ; he may incur the penalty of death."[226] Holmes's opinions for the Massachusetts Supreme Judicial Court had endorsed the same proposition.[227]

Holmes was sympathetic, however, when a defendant met force with force and killed an attacker. His opinion for a divided Supreme Court rejected the common law rule that a person may not kill in self-defense when he knows that he can avoid all danger by retreating.[228]

As this chapter has noted, Holmes dissented from the Supreme Court's landmark interpretation of the cruel and unusual punishment clause in *Weems v United States,*[229] and he also dissented from the Supreme Court's ruling that the double jeopardy clause precludes the retrial of a defendant who has been acquitted. If a trial error might have contributed to the defendant's acquittal, Holmes would have permitted reversal of the acquittal on appeal and a new trial. He declared, "[I]t seems to me that logically and rationally a man cannot be said to be more than once in jeopardy in the same cause, however often he may be tried."[230]

Some of Holmes's majority opinions on issues of criminal procedure similarly exhibited little sympathy for the claims of defendants. In *Moyer v Peabody*,[231] the Court denied habeas corpus relief to a labor leader whom a state governor had ordered arrested and detained without probable cause. Holmes declared that the governor's personal belief that his action would aid in suppressing an insurrection satisfied all due process requirements. His opinion in *Holt v United States*[232] held that a defendant could be required to aid the prosecution by trying on a shirt. The opinion declared that the privilege against self-incrimination protects only against the forced production of "communicative" evidence. In *Hester v United States*,[233] Holmes's opinion for the Court held that the Fourth Amendment did not limit the ability of police officers to trespass on "open fields" to conduct searches. His final opinion for the Supreme Court—*Dunn v United States*[234]—upheld a defendant's conviction by a jury although the jury's findings on other charges were incompatible with his guilt.

Despite the harshness of some of Holmes's criminal justice opinions, others may be the most difficult of all his opinions to reconcile with his skeptical outlook. With one exception,[235] these other opinions followed Holmes's seventy-eighth birthday and Justice Brandeis's appointment to the Supreme Court.

Holmes argued in favor of making federal remedies more widely available to state prisoners through use of the writ of habeas corpus,[236] and he supported the judicial exclusion of evidence obtained in violation of the Fourth Amendment. Unlike Justice Cardozo, who disparaged the exclusionary rule by saying, "The criminal is to go free because the constable has blundered,"[237] Holmes maintained, "I think it a less evil that some criminals should escape than that the Government should play an ignoble part."[238] Holmes also wrote the opinion extending the exclusionary rule beyond illegally seized evidence to evidence derived from the use of this evidence—what the Court later would call "fruit of the poisonous tree."[239]

In *Olmstead v United States*[240] in 1928, Holmes dissented from the Supreme Court's ruling that the Fourth Amendment's prohibition of unreasonable searches and seizures did not limit governmental wiretapping at all.[241] He initially had voted with the majority in *Olmstead*, but Chief Justice Taft maintained that "Brandeis got after him and induced him to change."[242] Without attributing his revised position on the constitutionality of electronic surveillance to Brandeis, Holmes himself noted that he would not have written a separate dissent in *Olmstead* if Brandeis had not asked him to do so.[243]

None of Holmes's opinions on criminal procedure required him to declare legislation unconstitutional. Like his later opinions in freedom of expression cases, however, they revealed his sympathy for civil liberties. Uncharacteristically, these opinions confirmed that, in the American system of government, individuals may prevail over seemingly dominant forces and that there is more to life than survival of the fittest.

Holmes's later opinions on criminal justice do not make him Jekyll-Holmes, Hyde-Holmes. All of us falter, and the outlook expressed in almost all of Holmes's judicial work was consistent with the power-centered view expressed in other aspects of his life. Nevertheless, H. L. Mencken may have been correct: After Holmes reached the age of seventy-eight, a strange amiability sometimes overcame him.[244]

Chapter Six

Judging the Common Law

In 1881, five days before Holmes turned forty, he opened a bottle of champagne to celebrate the publication of his book *The Common Law*.[1] Holmes was at the time a dissatisfied lawyer with hopes of becoming a professor or, better, a judge.[2] He based his book on a series of lectures delivered the previous year at the Lowell Institute,[3] and he based his lectures on articles he had published in the *American Law Review*.

The Common Law is remembered today primarily for one paragraph, the paragraph that starts the book. It presents a classic description of how law develops and includes Holmes's most noted statement, "The life of the law has not been logic: It has been experience."[4] Near the end of Holmes's introductory lecture, he offered four additional paragraphs on the same theme.[5] These paragraphs, like the first, are insightful and elegant. Most of the remainder of the book isn't.

This chapter begins by considering Holmes's five classic paragraphs. It contends that they were far less pathbreaking than later lawyers and scholars have claimed. The chapter then examines the theory of liability and the historical thesis to which Holmes devoted the bulk of his book, reviewing Holmes's treatment of criminal law, torts, and contracts. A final section examines Holmes's decisions as a common law judge, decisions that even his most enthusiastic admirers regard as undistinguished.

Assessments of *The Common Law* have varied. Richard Posner observed that it is "widely considered the best book on law ever written by an American."[6] G. Edward White called it "arguably [America's] most original work of legal scholarship."[7] Andrew Kaufman described its publication as "a landmark in intellectual history."[8] P. S. Atiyah remarked, however, "[N]ot much can be said [about *The Common Law*'s theory of liability] that is likely to add to Holmes' reputation."⁹ Saul Touster proclaimed the book a "clear failure."¹⁰

Within a single work, Sheldon Novick offered a seemingly schizophrenic assortment of evaluations:

> *The Common Law* has been called the greatest work of American legal scholarship. It became one of the founding documents of the sociological and then the realist schools of jurisprudence, and more recently of legal pragmatism and the study of the economic basis of the law.¹¹

> Holmes' idea that the common law was the result rather than the cause of judicial decisions was epochal; in law it was comparable (and in some ways similar) to the impact of relativity on physics.¹²

> Holmes's extrajudicial writings plainly have very little to do with his modern reputation. *The Common Law,* because of the obscurity of its argument, was nearly forgotten in his lifetime and would be entirely forgotten now, I venture to say . . . if it were not for [Holmes's] celebrity as a judge. The book itself now has little reputation of its own, except as a seminal work in the law of torts.¹³

> *The Common Law* . . . is now a museum piece of Victorian scientism.¹⁴

Novick's initial praise of *The Common Law* was extravagant, but his statement that "Holmes's extrajudicial writings plainly have very little to do with his modern reputation" erred in the opposite direction. The adulation showered upon Holmes by the legal realists, the reverence currently accorded him by writers associated with movements as diverse as critical legal studies and law and economics, and the inclusion of his name on nearly every list of the founders of pragmatism have stemmed more from Holmes's scholarly writings than from his judicial opinions.

No doubt Holmes's scholarly works would have received less attention had he not been a noted jurist, and most Americans probably would not list legal scholarship first among Holmes's achievements. Nevertheless, whether his opinions or his extrajudicial writings have contributed more to his long-term influence and reputation is a close question. The extrajudicial writings—particularly *The Common Law*'s five great paragraphs and *The Path of the Law*—have influenced, directly and indirectly, the way in which virtually all American lawyers now think about law.

THE LIFE OF THE LAW HAS NOT BEEN LOGIC

Historicism in the Scholarship of Oliver Wendell Holmes and Christopher Columbus Langdell

As noted in this book's first chapter, American legal writers who began publishing after the Civil War (including both Holmes and Dean Christopher Columbus Langdell of the Harvard Law School) abandoned the concept of natural law that had guided and inspired earlier writers like Blackstone and Lincoln.[15] Scholars of the period divided post–Civil War legal scholarship into two schools, the "analytic" and the "historicist," and this demarcation remains conventional today. The work of the English legal scholar John Austin provided the principal model for the analytic school. Austin defined law as the command of a sovereign,[16] and analytic jurisprudence was concerned with defining legal concepts and working out their implications.

The historicists took their lead from the work of the German scholar Friedrich Karl von Savigny.[17] They saw law as evolutionary, as developing from the ground up, and as manifesting simply the customs of a people. The historicists believed, moreover, that as law grew increasingly complex, "legal scientists" had a special role—tracing the history of legal doctrines, inferring the principles that lay behind them, and describing these principles in an orderly form.

The historicist and analytic methodologies were distinct, and the historicists sometimes criticized the Austinians for being insufficiently Darwinian and empirical. The two approaches were enough alike, however, that Holmes, Langdell, and many others could employ both without contradiction. The two schools did not differ in the most important respect. They stood together in the revolt against natural law.

As early as 1871, Holmes declared, "A treatise on the sources of law which shall strike half way between . . . Savigny and . . . Austin, will form a chapter of jurisprudence which is not yet written, and which is worthy of the ambition of an aspiring mind to write."[18] The chapter that follows this one—on *The Path of the Law*—will consider Holmes's analytic concept of law ("a statement of the circumstances in which the public force will be brought to bear upon men through the courts").[19] This chapter focuses primarily on Holmes's historicist scholarship.

Both Holmes's analytic concept of law and his constitutional decisions unmistakably manifested his skepticism. As noted in the preceding chapter, Holmes often sought to substitute power metaphors for analysis, and his guiding principle in constitutional adjudication often appeared to be the Darwinian truism, "Winners win." The common law, however, was judge-made law. Its issues could not be resolved by envisioning the legislature as a battlefield and declaring that judges should not deprive the victors of their spoils.

Historicism offered the nearest alternative. Under Savigny's banner, Holmes and most other scholars of his era abandoned the world of normativity and worked (or tried to) primarily within the world of description and synthesis.[20] Judge-made law, like legislation, reflected the will of historically dominant forces, and the function of legal scholars was to capture and articulate its underlying principles. Although Holmes's historicist scholarship may not have expressed his skepticism as sharply as his constitutional decisions and analytic scholarship, it reflected the same viewpoint.

The affinity between historicism and Darwinian natural selection was unmistakable. Mathias Reimann observed, "If the law shared the nature of the world and of life in society, if its warlike and evolutionary character meant that the winner took all, including the definition of right and wrong, then observation of the real facts of life was all that really counted."[21] In 1890, a legal scholar described "wanting historical mindedness" as "a graver charge in these days when evolution is in the very air . . . than heresy or even petty larceny."[22] "Today," Stephen Siegel writes, "historism[[23]] is a discredited and largely forgotten mode of thought."[24] Most of its American practitioners are regarded as formalists.[25]

Joseph Henry Beale, a Harvard professor and, briefly, the University of Chicago Law School's first dean, ranks second only to Dean Langdell on the conventional list of America's dreariest formalists.[26] One reason for this ranking was Beale's conceptual scholarship, but another was his resonant last name, which permitted Jerome Frank to contrast legal realism with Bealism, allowed Thomas Reed Powell to invent adjectives like "Bealy-mouthed" and "ibealistic," and encouraged Thurman Arnold to write poetry that began, "Beale, Beale, marvelous Beale/Only in verse can we tell how we feel."[27] Beale wrote in 1905:

> [T]he impulse given to legal study by the work of Savigny and his school has in the last generation spread over the civilized world and profoundly influenced its legal thought. . . . [I]n the United States it has obtained a powerful hold. . . . We have abandoned the subjective and deductive philosophy of the middle ages, and we learn from scientific

observation and from historical discovery. The newly accepted principles of observation and induction, applied to the law, have given us a generation of legal scholars for the first time since the modern world began, and the work of these scholars has at last made possible the intelligent statement of the principles of law.[28]

Beale declared that the "fundamental principles" of the historical school were "[t]he unity of the past and present, and the need of conforming the law of a people to its needs."[29]

American historicists of the late nineteenth and early twentieth centuries included such figures as Beale, James Coolidge Carter, Christopher Gustavus Tiedeman, Thomas McIntyre Cooley, William Gardiner Hammond, James Barr Ames, John Chipman Gray, and Christopher Columbus Langdell. They also included Oliver Wendell Holmes.

The principal goal of Holmes's early scholarship was "a sound classification of the law,"[30] and some of his writings presented charts offering new conceptual arrangements of legal duties.[31] Holmes's first major article declared, "It is only after a series of determinations on the same subject-matter, that it becomes necessary . . . by a true induction to state the principle which has until then been obscurely felt."[32] *The Common Law* was, in form, almost entirely an effort to extract general principles from past decisions. Holmes explained in that book, "The business of the jurist is to make known the content of the law; that is, to work upon it from within, or logically, arranging and distributing it, in order, from its *summum genus* to its *infima species,* so far as practicable."[33] Holmes emphasized the role of the jurist in order to explain why he would not address such questions as the relationship of legal duties to "moral rights if there are any." "These," he said, "are for the philosopher. . . ."[34]

Dean Langdell had said much the same thing when he was asked to be the secretary of a committee on jurisprudence. Jurisprudence was not a special concern of lawyers, he said; this subject might in fact be of greater interest to public officials and journalists. "The chief business of a lawyer," he declared, "is and must be to learn and administer the law *as it is;* while I suppose the great object in studying jurisprudence should be to ascertain what the law *ought to be;* and although these two pursuits may seem to be of a very kindred nature, I think experience shows that devotion to one is apt to give more or less distaste for the other."[35] Langdell added that jurisprudence should not be taught by "lawyers, whether on or off the Bench, not even professors in Law Schools."[36] As James Herget has observed, "By the last quarter of the nineteenth century, the leading jurists had practically turned all responsibility for questions of morality over to the nonlawyers. . . . Moralists were not interested in law, lawyers were not interested in morality."[37]

As early as 1867, Holmes objected to an author's "habit of moralizing, which is notably out of place among the rules and precedents of courts. . . . When the learned editor calls in the authority of religion . . . he only renders the want of legal authority more conspicuous."[38] Sixty-two years later, as a Supreme Court justice, Holmes wrote a correspondent, "I have said to my brethren many times that I hate justice, which means that I know that if a man begins to talk about that, for one reason or another he is shirking thinking in legal terms."[39]

A passage of Holmes's 1897 essay *The Path of the Law* resembled one that Langdell had written a quarter century earlier—an excerpt from the introduction to Langdell's contracts casebook that is rarely quoted except to deride it. In this passage, which is almost invariably taken as proof of Langdell's "conceptualism," he wrote:

> Law, considered as a science, consists of certain principles or doctrines. . . . Each of these doctrines has arrived at its present state by slow degrees; in other words, it is a growth extending in many cases through centuries. This growth is to be traced in the main through a series of cases; and much the shortest and best, if not the only way of mastering the doctrine effectually is by studying the cases in which it is embodied. . . . Moreover, the number of fundamental legal doctrines is much less than is commonly supposed; the many different guises in which the same doctrine is constantly making its appearance . . . being the cause of much misapprehension. If these doctrines could be so classified and arranged that each should be found in its proper place, and nowhere else, they would cease to be formidable from their number.[40]

Holmes echoed:

> The means of the study [of law] are a body of reports, of treatises, and of statutes, in this country and in England, extending back for six hundred years. . . . In these sibylline leaves are gathered the scattered prophecies of the past upon the cases in which the axe will fall. . . . Far the most important and pretty nearly the whole meaning of every new effort of legal thought is to make these prophecies more precise, and to generalize them into a thoroughly connected system. . . .
>
> The number of our predictions when generalized and reduced to

a system is not unmanageably large. They present themselves as a finite body of dogma which may be mastered within a reasonable time.[41]

Although Holmes and Langdell shared the historicist orientation of their time, they differed in significant respects. Langdell once carried his insistence on following the principles of past decisions to the point of declaring both "substantial justice" and the "interests of the parties" irrelevant to the resolution of a legal issue.[42] In this statement, one of the great legal howlers of all time, Langdell may have become the only figure in the history of legal thought ever to have declared substantial justice and the interests of the parties irrelevant to legal issues.[43] His position departed not only from Holmes's but also from that of nearly every other writer of his era. Samuel Williston, who today is lumped with Langdell as a formalist, objected that Langdell's jurisprudence did not "sufficiently take account of changes in law as a constant and necessary process. . . ."[44]

Although Langdell's "scientific" methodology seemed to leave little room for further development of the law, most late-nineteenth-century historicists insisted that the law's growth had not ceased. They resisted the codification movement led by David Dudley Field precisely on the ground that attempting to capture principles in a code would inhibit the law's ability to adapt to new circumstances.[45] James Coolidge Carter observed that "perhaps the greatest mischief with which codification is pregnant" is "the arrest of the self-development of private law—its true method of growth."[46] Joseph Beale declared, "The chief argument against a Code is . . . [that] if the law has got to grow with the needs of the people, codifying it hardens its shell and it cannot grow."[47]

Despite the historicist bent of Holmes's legal scholarship, he did not romanticize the past in the way Savigny and many American historicists did. Holmes noted in *The Common Law* that one could ask too much as well as too little of history,[48] and he later wrote that continuity with the past is not a duty but merely a necessity.[49] In *The Path of the Law*, he declared, "It is revolting to have no better reason for a rule of law than that so it was laid down in the time of Henry IV."[50]

Positioning himself at the less extreme end of the historicist spectrum,[51] Holmes objected to Langdell's rigidity. In an anonymous book review, he noted the dean's statement about the irrelevance of justice and human interests and called Langdell both our "greatest living legal theologian" and "a Hegelian in disguise, so entirely is he interested in the formal connection of things."[52] Holmes then added, "The Life of the law has not been logic; it has been experience."[53]

Whose Formalism?

Holmes repeated this sentence in the paragraph that opens *The Common Law,* a passage with unmistakable historicist overtones:

> The object of this book is to present a general view of the Common Law. To accomplish the task, other tools are needed besides logic. It is something to show that the consistency of a system requires a particular result, but it is not all. The life of the law has not been logic: It has been experience. The felt necessities of the time, the prevalent moral and political theories, intuitions of public policy, avowed or unconscious, even the prejudices which judges share with their fellow-men, have had a good deal more to do than the syllogism in determining the rules by which men have been governed. The law embodies the story of a nation's development through many centuries, and it cannot be dealt with as if it contained only the axioms and corollaries of a book of mathematics. In order to know what it is, we must know what it has been, and what it tends to become. We must alternately consult history and existing theories of legislation. But the most difficult labor will be to understand the combination of the two into new products at every stage. The substance of the law at any given time pretty nearly corresponds, so far as it goes, with what is then understood to be convenient; but its form and machinery, and the degree to which it is able to work out desired results, depend very much upon its past.[54]

The four paragraphs on the development of law that appear toward the end of Holmes's initial lecture are almost as eloquent as this introductory paragraph. They are Holmes at his best:

> The foregoing history, apart from the purposes for which it has been given, well illustrates the paradox of form and substance in the development of law. In form, its growth is logical. The official theory is that each new decision follows syllogistically from existing precedents. But just as the clavicle in the cat only tells of the existence of some earlier creature to which a collar-bone was useful, precedents survive in the law long after the use they once served is at an end and the reason for them has been forgotten. The result of following them must often be failure and confusion from the merely logical point of view.
>
> On the other hand, in substance the growth of the law is legislative. And this in a deeper sense than that what the courts declare to have always been the law is in fact new. It is legislative in its grounds. The very considerations which judges most rarely mention, and always

with an apology, are the secret root from which the law draws all the juices of life. I mean, of course, considerations of what is expedient for the community concerned. Every important principle which is developed by litigation is in fact and at bottom the result of more or less definitely understood views of public policy; most generally, to be sure, under our practice and traditions, the unconscious result of instinctive preferences and inarticulate convictions, but none the less traceable to views of public policy in the last analysis. And as the law is administered by able and experienced men, who know too much to sacrifice good sense to a syllogism, it will be found that, when ancient rules maintain themselves in the way that has been and will be shown in this book, new reasons more fitted to the time have been found for them, and that they gradually receive a new content, and at last a new form, from the grounds to which they have been transplanted.

But hitherto this process has been largely unconscious. It is important, on that account, to bring to mind what the actual course of events has been. If it were only to insist on a more conscious recognition of the legislative function of the courts, as just explained, it would be useful, as we shall see more clearly later on.

What has been said will explain the failure of all theories which consider the law only from its formal side, whether they attempt to deduce the *corpus* from *a priori* postulates, or fall into the humbler error of supposing the science of the law to reside in the *elegantia juris,* or logical cohesion of part with part. The truth is, that the law is always approaching, and never reaching, consistency. It is forever adopting new principles from life at one end, and it always retains old ones from history at the other. It will become entirely consistent only when it ceases to grow.[55]

Holmes's statement that the life of the law has not been logic but experience became, in Richard Posner's words, "the most famous sentence he ever wrote."[56] That sentence might have been inspired in part by a work of Rudolph von Jhering that Holmes read while preparing his *Common Law* lectures.[57] Jhering wrote that legal conceptions did not dictate life but, instead, that life shaped them. He declared that law must reflect "not what logic, but what life, intercourse, the sense of right demand."[58] Mathias Reimann attributes to Jhering the idea that "[t]he form of the law . . . often remains unchanged while beneath its surface the substance is adapted to the changing needs of society over time." He notes, "This theory is essentially what Holmes embraces as his fundamental approach to legal evolution in the first lecture of *The Common Law*. In fact, the similarities become more striking the more one analyzes the language used by both Jhering and Holmes."[59]

As Holmes might have acknowledged, his declaration about the life of the law was only half true. Reason and experience interact to generate greater understanding in law, just as they do in other fields. The life of the law has been both logic and experience.[60] As Frederick Maitland observed, "Law is the place where life and logic meet."[61]

The true half of Holmes's half-truth, moreover, did not present the distinctive vision of law that later generations have credited him with articulating. These generations have viewed Holmes's statement (and others like it in *The Common Law*'s best paragraphs) as the battle cry within the legal profession of a broader intellectual revolution—a pragmatic revolution that altered not only law but also philosophy, history, economics, and other fields of inquiry. In an influential essay, Morton White called this revolution "the revolt against formalism" and said that its targets were formalism and deductive reasoning.[62] Andrew Kaufman proclaimed Holmes's statement about the life of the law "the clarion call for the next generation of legal thinkers."[63] Benjamin Cardozo called it "the text to be unfolded. All that is to come will be development and commentary."[64]

Holmes's biographer Liva Baker also maintained that Holmes's vision led to a transformation of American law. She offered this description of the law before Holmes:

> American legal scholarship . . . was ripe for the kind of corrective surgery Holmes was about to perform. The traditions of the natural law—the law of nature transmitted by divine will—as explicated by Blackstone and Kent, its roots running deep into the soil of ancient Greece and Rome, had outlived its usefulness. Its immutable principles comforted. Its abstract and logical nature satisfied. Its simplicity, certainty, and reasonableness continued to be appealing. But its inertia kept it from dealing with the disorder and changefulness and all the other complexities of nineteenth-century life. The traditionalists "discovered" law which was deduced from the unchanging nature of things. . . . That the law's development might have been progressive was not generally recognized.[65]

Some pages later, Baker offered this serenade to Holmes's achievement:

[Holmes] shook the little world of lawyers and judges who had been raised on Blackstone's theory that the law, given by God Himself, was immutable and eternal and judges had only to discover its contents. It took some years for them to come around to the view that the law was flexible, responsive to changing social climates, and amenable to empirical methods of analysis.

But Holmes had . . . broken new intellectual trails, using history to guide him. He had given law a vitality it never before had possessed. He had wrested legal history from the aridity of syllogism and abstraction and placed it in the context of human experience, demonstrating that the corpus of the law was neither ukase from God nor derived from Nature, but, like the little toe and structure of the horse, was a constantly evolving thing, a response to the continually developing social and economic environment.[66]

Baker, White, and innumerable others have mischaracterized the transformation of which Holmes was a part. As noted in chapter 1, this transformation was not a "revolt against formalism" but a revolt against natural law or objective concepts of right and wrong—a revolt whose achievements were mostly negative. For the most part, Holmes, Langdell, and other legal writers of the last third of the nineteenth century did not bring something new to law; they took something away.

Describing mechanical jurisprudence as "the idea that timeless rules are stocked in a conceptual warehouse awaiting discovery," Ronald Dworkin notes that modern lawyers and scholars are right to ridicule its practitioners.[67] Dworkin then suggests a weakness of the claim that Holmes or anyone else led a revolt against this kind of formalism: "[The] difficulty . . . lies in finding practitioners to ridicule. So far [critics] have had little luck in caging and exhibiting mechanical jurisprudents (all specimens captured—even Blackstone and Joseph Beale—have had to be released after careful reading of their texts)."[68]

Lawyers who regard Holmes's declaration as a revolutionary manifesto ought to travel in their minds to the Constitutional Convention of 1787. There they would hear John Dickinson's admonition to his fellow delegates: "Experience must be our only guide. Reason may mislead us."[69] Dickinson's statement was less striking than Holmes's, but his idea was much the same: "The life of the law has not been logic: It has been experience."

Dickinson continued:

> It was not Reason that discovered the singular & admirable mechanism
> of the English Constitution. It was not Reason that discovered or ever
> could have discovered the odd & in the eye of those who are governed
> by reason, the absurd mode of trial by Jury. Accidents probably pro-
> duced these discoveries and experience has given a sanction to them.[70]

The notion that law must adapt to changing circumstances was in fact
familiar long before Dickinson's remarks. More than a century earlier, Sir
Matthew Hale declared that it was the "Nature of Laws" that they are
"accommodated to the Conditions, Exigencies and Conveniences of the
People" as those "Exigencies and Conveniences do insensibly grow upon
the People."[71]

Modern lawyers might also examine the *Federalist Papers* in which
Madison, Hamilton, and Jay argued for ratification of the Constitution.
This work includes James Madison's words:

> Is it not the glory of the people of America, that, whilst they have paid
> a decent regard to the opinions of former times and other nations, they
> have not suffered a blind veneration for antiquity, for custom, or for
> names, to overrule the suggestion of their own good sense, the knowl-
> edge of their own situation, and the lessons of their own experience?[72]

Traveling forward in time, people who imagine that Americans before Holmes believed that they could "deduce law from the unchanging
nature of things" and did not recognize that law's "development might
have been progressive" should examine the highly influential edition of
Blackstone's *Commentaries* that St. George Tucker published with addi-
tions of his own in 1803. In a memorable evolutionary metaphor, Tucker
wrote that a community's law might begin as a seedling oak, advance with
civilization, and put forth "innumerable branches till it covers the earth
with an extensive shade." Every year might be "the parent of new
branches or the destroyer of old ones." Nevertheless,

> a superficial observation of its exterior alone [will not] suffice; the
> roots may be decayed, the trunk hollow, and the monarch of the forest
> ready to fall with its own rottenness and weight at the moment that its
> enormous bulk, extensive branches, and luxuriant foliage would seem
> to promise a millennial duration.[73]

Tucker recognized the need for constant growth, constant pruning, and
occasional uprooting in a forest of evolving law.[74]

If modern lawyers were to examine judicial opinions of the early nineteenth century, they might note this statement of the Pennsylvania Supreme Court in 1813:

> When our ancestors emigrated from England, they took with them such of the English principles as were convenient for the situation in which they were about to place themselves. It required time and experience to ascertain how much of the English law would be suitable to this country. By degrees, as circumstances demanded, we adopted the English usages, or substituted others better suited to our wants, till at length before the time of the Revolution we had formed a system of our own.[75]

From the colonial period onward, American judges announced that they would follow the common law of England only insofar as this law appeared suited to American conditions.[76] These judges could not have recognized more explicitly their duty to adapt law to changing conditions.

Lawyers who believe that judges before Holmes merely found law (or pretended to) must have missed part of law school. They could not have read any opinion by Chief Justice John Marshall. For example, in 1819 in *McCulloch v Maryland*,[77] Marshall recognized that the word *necessary* in the Constitution's necessary and proper clause had many meanings. He wrote:

> Throughout this vast republic, from the St. Croix to the Gulf of Mexico, from the Atlantic to the Pacific, revenue is to be collected and expended, armies are to be marched and supported. The exigencies of the nation may require that the treasure raised in the north should be transported to the south, *that* raised in the east conveyed to the west, or that this order should be reversed. Is that construction of the constitution to be preferred which would render these operations difficult, hazardous, and expensive?[78]

Marshall's language recognized that judges choose and that their choices ought to take account of "the exigencies of the nation." He did not suggest that the appropriate construction of the necessary and proper clause was awaiting discovery by passionless legal technicians. Benjamin Cardozo wrote that Marshall "gave to the constitution of the United States the impress of his own mind; and the form of our constitutional law is what it is, because he moulded it while it was still plastic and malleable in the fire of his own intense conviction."[79] Grant Gilmore declared that Marshall "made law with a sort of joyous frenzy."[80]

Holmes announced that "considerations of what is expedient for the community concerned" are "the secret root from which the law draws all the juices of life." He added that these considerations are rarely mentioned by judges "and always with an apology."[81] Another Supreme Court justice, however, Joseph Story, had sprung the secret a half century earlier. Without an apology, Story had proclaimed, "It is [the] true glory [of the common law] that it is flexible, and constantly expanding with the exigencies of society."[82]

In 1870, at the outset of Holmes's career as a legal scholar, he referred in an offhand way to "the function of judges as law-makers."[83] Holmes did not treat this statement as revolutionary, as requiring any argument or support, or, indeed, as at all controversial.

The inward and inductive turn of American law during the final third of the nineteenth century slowed judicial creativity. This turn generated volumes of wooden analysis and stilted prose. Even at the end of the century, however, explicit judicial innovation in response to changing circumstances did not cease.[84] One's image of Alabama before the turn of the century, for example, may be closer to that of the gulag than to kinder, gentler images of Camelot and the New Deal. In 1887, however, the Alabama Supreme Court reconsidered the scope of the insanity defense:

> We do not hesitate to say that we reopen the discussion of this subject with no little reluctance, having long hesitated to disturb our past decisions on this branch of the law. Nothing could induce us to do so except an imperious sense of duty, which has been excited by a protracted investigation and study, impressing our minds with the conviction that the law of insanity as declared by the courts on many points, and especially the rule of criminal accountability, and the assumed tests of the disease, to the extent which confers legal irresponsibility, have not kept pace with the progress of thought and discovery in the present advanced stages of medical science. Though science has led the way, the courts of England have declined to follow, as shown by their adherence to the rulings in *McNaghten's Case*.[85]

The Alabama court's opinion abandoning *McNaughton* matched almost argument for argument the opinion of the California Supreme Court when it abandoned *McNaughton* almost a century later.[86]

Even the stuffiest of the late-nineteenth-century historicists—that is to say, even Langdell—would have agreed that "the life of the law has not been logic; it has been experience."[87] That was the point of historicism.

Far from taking aim at all the law of his era and all the law that preceded it, Holmes's most famous statement was itself a catchy restatement of Savigny's central thesis. Mathias Reimann comments:

> Savigny's and Holmes's views of the law look strangely similar. In particular, they both viewed law as an ever-growing, never entirely consistent body of rules. They both believed that its true nature is revealed only in its evolution and that we must therefore try to understand its development. Thus we have to trace our present-day rules back through the past to their true source in order to explain their original meaning. This approach was certainly not Holmes's most original idea. It had been the very charter of the historical school and was already half a century old before Holmes ever thought of it. As a matter of fact, it is almost certain that Savigny's ideas were among the sources on which Holmes himself drew.[88]

Holmes wrote in *The Common Law* of "the failure of all theories which consider the law only from its formal side, whether they attempt to deduce the entire *corpus* from *a priori* postulates, or fall into the humbler error of supposing the science of the law to reside in the *elegantia juris,* or the logical cohesion of part with part."[89] For generations, readers of this passage have inferred that someone (perhaps even someone notable) had attempted to deduce the entire corpus of law from *a priori* postulates. Why else would Holmes have disparaged the idea?

Possibly some now-obscure German legal theorist fit Holmes's description of the deductive formalist bogeyman, but I know of no American who did. Certainly Christopher Columbus Langdell did not. As Anthony Sebok has observed, "It is ironic that Langdell was associated with a viewpoint that in an important way was the opposite of what he was trying to argue."[90]

If the word *theologian* is taken to mean something more than "unbending jerk," Holmes's description of Langdell as "our greatest living legal theologian"[91] was misleading.[92] Moreover, Grant Gilmore's assertion that Langdell accepted "the idea of a body of law, fixed for all time and invested with an almost supernatural authority" had no foundation at all.[93] Langdell fit the intellectual pattern of his time and viewed law simply as the product of human custom.[94] As Robert Gordon has observed:

> [Langdellians] agreed that [legal] science should be a positive science based on discoverable, observable facts. . . . In part this commitment

to facts expressed an attitude—a "masculine" readiness to look brute
reality unblinkingly in the face, to throw off the crutches of religion,
moral sentiment, and the stale formulae of conventional professional
wisdom, and to embark upon the strenuous, tough-minded, intellectual path.[95]

Gordon might equally have offered this observation about Holmes.[96]

Richard Posner's declaration that Langdell "focus[ed] on the process
of deduction . . . [while giving] the impression that the premises were
self-evident" was also unfounded.[97] Far from attempting to deduce legal
rules from unexamined premises, Langdell insisted that legal science required the close examination of cases to infer the premises that should
guide future decisions.[98] His method emphasized induction, not deduction.[99] Of course fundamental legal doctrines, once inferred, must be
applied, and the rule application process can be characterized as nomi-
nally deductive.[100] Langdell gave no indication, however, that he viewed
the process of applying legal principles as any more deductive than that
of following a recipe for baked beans. His primary emphasis was on another stage of legal analysis.

It was in fact Langdell's effort to generalize past experience and his
rigidity in adhering to past patterns—his "conceptualism"—that led to
Holmes's criticism. Langdell was innocent of the charge advanced by Gilmore and Posner of attempting to deduce law from *a priori* premises.
Historians can properly convict him only of a lesser crime—"the humbler error of supposing the science of law to reside in the *elegantia juris,*
or the logical cohesion of part with part."[101]

Holmes himself did not charge Langdell with anything more serious. The book review in which Holmes called Langdell a "theologian" did
not mention deducing the entire corpus of law. Instead it declared, "Mr.
Langdell's ideal in the law, the end of all his striving, is the *elegantia juris,*
or *logical* integrity of the system as a system."[102] Exaggerating the differences between Langdell and Holmes, twentieth-century scholars have
misrepresented the positions of both.

Today's lawyers cherish the myth that law once was found but now is
made.[103] Once upon a time, they declare, old fogies led by Mayor Langdell owned the town. Wrapping themselves in black robes, the fogies
persuaded themselves and everybody else that they had mystic powers
and could deduce all of law from the brow of Zeus.[104] One day, however,
a hero rode into town. "Law should serve the real-life needs of ordinary
people," he declared. "Arise from centuries of superstition and consider

at last what law *does.*" People heard the hero's cry and, one by one, joined his crusade. The most devoted of his disciples were the rough-and-ready hands at Realist Ranch. Together they vanquished the fogies, and all lived happily ever after. The hero's name was Holmes.

This story is false or greatly exaggerated in almost every respect. Holmes did resist the rigidity of some of his fellow historicists, and his writings, especially as these works were interpreted by others, helped provide a needed corrective for the wooden legal thought of turn-of-the-century America. Holmes, however, marched arm-in-arm with Langdell, Beale, Carter and other historicists in the central jurisprudential transformation of their era—the revolt against natural law. All of these figures rejected the idea that law could reflect more than "the felt necessities of the time."[105] Moreover, characterizing either the late-nineteenth century historicists or the natural lawyers who preceded them as oblivious to the role of experience in shaping law misrepresents their views entirely. From the beginning, Americans have been determined to make their own law (not to find it or deduce it), and they have recognized the law's need for continual growth and adaptation to meet changing needs.

The pre–Civil War natural lawyers did insist that, in the process of evolution and adaptation, law should adhere to core principles of decency and should seek to advance enduring human goals. In 1835, for example, Francis Hilliard observed that for judges deciding common law issues "general expediency,—public policy,—is often the highest measure of right." At the same time, Hilliard noted that "[i]n law, as in other sciences, there are certain broad and fixed principles, which embody the essence of the system, and remain unchanged amidst the fluctuations of successive ages."[106] The skeptical jurisprudence of the twentieth century has rested on defaming the thought that preceded it.[107]

The Decline of Corrective Justice

Although American lawyers recognized the evolutionary and adaptive nature of law long before Holmes, attitudes toward law, logic, and experience have not remained static from the founding to the present. Apart from the legal profession's loss of faith in core principles of justice, the most significant jurisprudential transformation of the twentieth century was the turn from an essentially retrospective view of the judicial process to a more prospective view. This shift might be described as the decline of corrective justice or as the fading of the idea of courts. Holmes's consequentialism contributed to this change in perspective.

Although American judges always have made law and always have been aware of doing so, they have not always made law with the same focus and for the same purpose as legislatures.[108] In essence, the traditional division of labor between legislatures and courts has been a division between the future and the past. Although the boundary between legislative and judicial tasks was never fixed and always permeable, legislators specialized in governing the future and judges in rectifying past wrongs. The Constitution recognized this allocation of responsibility by forbidding Congress from enacting *ex post facto* laws, bills of attainder, and other retrospective measures while limiting federal courts to the resolution of disputes about past events—"cases of actual controversy."[109]

Judges acted as lawmakers when authoritative sources of law ran out, but they did so largely within this framework. Their primary goal was to render justice to the litigants who came before them. Although they did not turn a blind eye to all forward-looking concerns (for example, promoting commerce by maintaining the predictability of law), they focused mainly on what Aristotle called "corrective justice"—the rectification of past wrongs.[110] Their performance of this task assured each of us that our claims of injustice would be heard, considered, and judged on their merits.

Twentieth-century pragmatism presented a direct challenge to this vision of the judicial role. Although Holmes was not fully a pragmatist,[111] he joined the pragmatists in the belief that all actions—judicial decisions included—should be judged by their consequences alone. This forward-looking perspective afforded no value to corrective justice for its own sake. In that respect, it departed from most of Western thought. A pragmatist could defend a traditional concept of courts only by positing deterrent or other forward-looking goals that this traditional concept might advance.[112]

Referring to Cardozo's *The Nature of the Judicial Process,* Richard Posner explained:

> Legal rules should be viewed in instrumental terms. [In Cardozo's words:] "Few rules in our time are so well established that they may not be called upon any day to justify their existence as means adapted to an end." The instrumental concept of law breaks with Aristotle's influential theory of corrective justice. The function of law as corrective justice is to restore an equilibrium, while in Cardozo's account "not the origin, but the goal, is the main thing. There can be no wis-

dom in the choice of a path unless we know where it will lead. . . .
The rule that functions well produces a title deed to recognition. . . .
The final principle of selection for judges . . . is one of fitness to an
end."[113]

Although a focus on the past might promote a brighter future (primarily
by teaching the public what conduct would lead to sanctions), righting
past wrongs was otherwise valueless.

From a pragmatic perspective, the instrumental goals that a traditional concept of courts might advance were not always decisive, for they
were not the only goals for judges to consider. Pragmatism made *all* potential consequences relevant. In the end, the test of a judicial decision
was how it would affect the entire world for good or ill.

The litigants in a particular case usually are not a major part of the
world, and over the course of the twentieth century, courts (the U.S.
Supreme Court in particular) increasingly came to see litigants as trim-
mings for their rulings. They focused less on corrective justice and more
on concerns like efficiency, deterrence, cost-benefit analysis, the systemic reform of defective institutions, and shaping "the law." As a result,
the sense of individual worth and individual entitlement that has distinguished our culture from some others has diminished, and marking a conceptual line between judicial decisions and legislative enactments has become more difficult.

When pressed to explain why courts should regard governance of
the future as their primary responsibility, pragmatists often have offered
a pragmatic answer: For one reason or another, the *real* legislature has
failed to do the job. On its face, this answer supplies no greater reason
for courts to assume all or part of the legislative role than for Nancy
Schwelb to do it. Laura Kalman observes that long after the Warren
Court era "law professors . . . kept faith in what has been called 'the cult
of the Court,' defined . . . as confidence in the ability of courts to change
society for what judges believe is the better."[114] Kalman's book *The Strange
Career of Legal Liberalism* examines the persistence of a phenomenon she
describes as "trust in the potential of courts to bring about 'those specific
social reforms that affect large groups of people such as blacks, or workers, or women, or partisans of a particular persuasion; in other words,
policy change with nationwide impact.'"[115]

The fading of the idea of courts is a history with many authors. The
Taft Court, the Warren Court, the Burger Court, the Rehnquist Court,
the lower federal courts, some state courts, structural injunctions, the

certiorari power, prospective overruling, class actions, pragmatism, sociological jurisprudence, legal realism, the law and society movement, the law and economics movement, the civil rights movement, widespread police abuses, inhumane prisons and hospitals, mass torts, segregated schools, the assertion of group rights, the political paralysis of state and federal legislatures, the lobbying of law clerks, and a variety of other events, institutions, circumstances, and individuals have contributed to the transformation.

Although Holmes was not the primary author of this change, future-oriented consequentialism like his contributed to the decline of corrective justice. His scholarly writings exhibited little appreciation of the judiciary's essentially retrospective role. *The Common Law*'s introductory chapter declared that "in substance the growth of the law is legislative" and urged "a more conscious recognition of the legislative function of the courts." It spoke repeatedly of "public policy" rather than private justice and maintained that "considerations of what is expedient for the community concerned" are "the secret root from which the law draws all the juices of life."[116] Later, in *The Path of the Law,* Holmes wrote, "I think that judges themselves have failed adequately to recognize their duty of weighing considerations of social advantage."[117] As a champion of judicial restraint, Holmes might not have meant this language as it sounds today and might not have approved the twentieth century's progressive smudging of the line between legislative and judicial lawmaking. Nevertheless, consequentialism like his sowed the seeds.

Assessments of Holmes as an innovative thinker would profit from the disaggregation of distinctive ideas that modern writers have tended to treat as identical. Holmes's consequentialism contributed to the shift from a largely retrospective view of the judicial process to a more prospective view, and Holmes, more than anyone else, led the revolt against natural law. In addition, he resisted the rigid historicism of Dean Langdell. Holmes did not, however, invent the idea that law must take account of changing circumstances, that judges must make law as well as find it, that law should serve everyday human needs, or that "the life of the law has not been logic: It has been experience." Those ideas were the heritage of Americans long before *The Common Law.*

THE REST OF *THE COMMON LAW*

Remembering Maine

The highly regarded writings of the English historicist Sir Henry Maine encouraged historicist scholarship in late-nineteenth-century America. Maine's *Ancient Law: Its Connection with the Early History of Society and Its Relation to Modern Ideas*[118] was published in 1861 and quickly acknowledged as a pathbreaking achievement. Holmes read it as a law student,[119] and it remained the most prominent work of contemporary legal scholarship as Holmes began his own scholarly career.

Maine declared, "[T]he early forms of jural conceptions . . . are to the jurist what the primary crusts of the earth are to the geologist. They contain, potentially, all the forms in which law has subsequently exhibited itself."[120] He claimed that the "unsatisfactory condition in which we find the science of jurisprudence" was attributable to its reliance on "plausible . . . but absolutely unverified" theories rather than "sober research into the primitive history of society and law."[121] After probing ancient sources, Maine announced an arresting historical thesis: "[T]he movement of the progressive societies has . . . been a movement from Status to Contract."[122]

Holmes may have regarded Maine's work as the blueprint for scholarly success. *The Common Law* not only employed the historicist mode of analysis prescribed by Maine, Savigny, and others but also duplicated the organization of Maine's book. As Mark DeWolfe Howe observed, "It is surely something more than a coincidence that for Holmes's lectures on Crimes, Torts, Possession, Contract, and Succession . . . , there were equivalent chapters in Maine's *Ancient Law*."[123] Like Maine, moreover, Holmes announced a sweeping historical thesis, a thesis that he purported to develop in each of his chapters. Law, he said, "by the very necessity of its nature, is continually transmuting . . . moral standards into external or objective ones, from which the actual guilt of the party concerned is wholly eliminated."[124] *The Common Law* offered a narrative, not of movement from status to contract, but of movement from subjective to objective standards of liability.[125] Holmes declared that law had grown "wholly indifferent to the internal phenomena of conscience"[126] and that "the tendency of the law everywhere is to transcend moral and reach external standards."[127] He reiterated again and again his claim that through the adoption of objective standards "public policy sacrifices the individual to the general good"[128]:

The law does undoubtedly treat the individual as a means to an end, and uses him as a tool to increase the general welfare at his own expense.[129]

[J]ustice to the individual is rightly outweighed by the larger interests on the other side of the scale.[130]

[W]hen men live in society, a certain average of conduct, a sacrifice of individual peculiarities going beyond a certain point, is necessary to the general welfare.[131]

The standard of what is called intent is thus really an external standard of conduct under the known circumstances.[132]

[The common law] works out an external standard of what would be fraudulent in the average prudent member of the community, and requires every member at his peril to avoid that.[133]

[A]s the law has grown, even when its standards have continued to model themselves upon those of morality, they have necessarily considered, not the actual condition of the particular defendant, but whether his conduct would have been wrong in the fair average member of the community, whom he is expected to equal at his peril.[134]

Literary Lapses and Scholarly Stumbles

While preparing the articles on which he based *The Common Law,* Holmes wrote of his plans to construct "a new Jurisprudence or New First Book of the law."[135] Edmund Wilson reported that he even "told a friend that he hoped by this book to supersede Blackstone and Kent."[136] Holmes, however, fell short of superseding Blackstone or Kent, or even of coming within hailing distance of Maine.

Calling Holmes's arguments "deeply flawed by sentimental legalistic antiquarianism,"[137] Thomas Grey noted:

The book today reads as a hodgepodge, honeycombed with passages in which ancient cases are treated not as objects of critical historical explanation, but as authoritative precedents, to which Holmes gave ingenious but tendentious lawyerly readings in support of controversial propositions of law he favored.[138]

Robert Gordon commented on the book's "recklessly miscellaneous quality"[139] and Liva Baker on its "dry and turgid" prose.[140] Baker observed that the book offers "only occasional flashes of the stylistic elegance for which Holmes later was recognized. The reader plods through, his or her task only infrequently lightened with an epigram or a felicitous phrase."[141] Grant Gilmore noted, "The lectures have long since become unreadable unless the reader is prepared to put forward an almost superhuman effort of will to keep his attention from flagging and his interest from wandering."[142]

These writers have noted the obstacles that *The Common Law* poses for modern readers. Even at the time of its publication, however, "[t]he book received moderate reviews and had moderate sales."[143] While praising Holmes's originality and his blending of historicist and analytic scholarship, A. V. Dicey[144] objected to Holmes's "uncertainty of aim." Dicey protested that Holmes sometimes "attribute[d] to the sages of the common law a subtlety and acuteness which are really the growth of Mr. Holmes's own mind," and he observed, "[Holmes] hardly distinguishes, in his own mind, between the doctrines of the common law and the dictates of common sense."[145] In the *Nation,* Henry Ware Holland gave *The Common Law* credit for "much that is novel and brilliant" but complained of the book's "tediously discursive and aimless air."[146] Holland noted that the work was "injured by long and philosophical discussion of intent and the like, which if they were worth preserving anywhere, would only be so in a condensed form. . . ."[147] Other reviewers praised *The Common Law*'s insights but described its style as "obscure," "terse," "epigrammatic," "elliptical," and "difficult."[148] No reviewer expressed surprise at Holmes's declaration that the life of the law has been not logic but experience, and none objected that judges must find and never make law.[149]

The Common Law may indeed have had only one highly receptive audience—Dean Langdell and his "formalist" faculty.[150] Within a year of the book's publication, Holmes was appointed to a professorship at the Harvard Law School, one that the school (with the help of Louis D. Brandeis and William F. Weld, Jr.)[151] had created especially to make a place for him. Champions of the claim that Holmes led a "revolt against formalism" might sense some irony in his welcome into the enemy camp.[152] Nevertheless, as G. Edward White observed:

> Principally on the basis of the celebrated passages from Holmes' introductory lecture, especially that contrasting "logic" with "experience" in the "life of the law," *The Common Law* has been seen as a pathbreaking work of legal philosophy, the first example of modernist jurisprudence. . . . But if one considers what Holmes actually engaged in his *Common Law* lectures . . . one finds a methodology strikingly like that

of Langdell. . . . Given the baffling features of Holmes' narrative and the memorable quality of some of his general observations, it is no surprise that readers have focused on the latter and ignored the former.[153]

The Common Law's substance was indeed Langdellian—and worse than its style.[154] The objective theory of liability that Holmes advanced looked primarily to what harms an "average man" would foresee. As the following discussion of Holmes's lectures on crimes and torts will suggest, this theory lacked both descriptive accuracy and normative appeal. The discussion of Holmes's lectures on contracts will reveal, moreover, that he abandoned his general theory when it might have moved the law in a progressive direction. Rather than support legal protection for reasonable reliance on a promise, as the general theory and many judicial precedents indicated he should, Holmes endorsed a formalistic requirement of "bargained for" consideration.

Criminal Law

Holmes claimed to find especially strong support for his thesis in the history of the criminal law. Early criminal prosecutions "were directed only to intentional wrongs,"[155] he said, because "[t]he desire for vengeance . . . takes an internal standard, not an objective or external one, and condemns its victim by that."[156] In modern law, by contrast, "theory and fact agree in frequently punishing those who have been guilty of no moral wrong, and who could not be condemned by any standard that did not avowedly disregard the personal peculiarities of the individuals concerned."[157]

Purporting only to describe the state of the law, Holmes declared that "[p]revention . . . would seem to be the chief and only universal purpose of punishment."[158] He indicated that this external purpose required the abandonment of earlier requirements of *mens rea* or mental culpability:

> Considering this purely external purpose of the law together with the fact that it is ready to sacrifice the individual so far as necessary in order to accomplish that purpose, we can see . . . that the actual degree of personal guilt involved in any particular transgression cannot be the only element, if it is an element at all, in the liability incurred. So far from its being true, as is often assumed, that the condition of a man's heart or conscience ought to be more considered in determining crim-

inal than civil liability, it might almost be said that this is the very opposite of truth. . . .

[W]hen we are dealing with that part of the law which aims more
directly than any other at establishing standards of conduct, we should
expect there more than elsewhere to find that the tests of liability are
external, and independent of the degree of evil in the particular person's motives or intentions. The conclusion follows from the nature of
the standards to which conformity is required.[159]

The argument that a shift from retributive to preventive goals dictates a weakening of *mens rea* requirements is a non sequitur,[160] but
Holmes's position permitted him to respond to "objections to treating
man as a thing" by declaring, "If a man lives in society, he is liable to find
himself so treated."[161] Holmes's enthusiasm for punishing the blameless
also allowed him to invoke his favorite image, the vision of life in society
that often seemed to drive his jurisprudence: "No society has ever admitted that it could not sacrifice individual welfare to its own existence. If
conscripts are necessary for its army, it seizes them, and marches them,
with bayonets in their rear, to death."[162] Punishing blameless people
seemed to Holmes like drafting them and sending them into battle. He
implied that members of the public who accepted the latter brutality
should not quiver about the former.

In a letter to Harold Laski forty-four years after the publication of
The Common Law, Holmes reiterated his willingness to execute someone
for an act that person could not have avoided:

> If I were having a philosophical talk with a man I was going to have
> hanged . . . I should say, I don't doubt that your act was inevitable for
> you, but to make it more avoidable by others we propose to sacrifice
> you for the common good. You may consider yourself a soldier dying
> for your country if you like. But the law must keep its promises.[163]

Holmes's claim that the story of law's development began with requirements of subjective mental culpability confronted an obvious difficulty. Ancient law punished animals and inanimate objects, all of which
lacked any *mens rea* at all. Holmes devoted his first lecture (all of it apart
from his great paragraphs on the development of law) to this ancient
practice. He did not suggest that the killing, forfeiture, banishment, or
destruction of an animal or thing might have served a different purpose
from the punishment of a person. Instead, he argued that primitive law

punished animals and inanimate objects only because it personified them and sought revenge against them.

Nearly all of Holmes's lecture consisted of illustrations of the destruction of things that had caused harm, but because the inventors of these practices had not recorded their motivations, describing the practices failed to advance his argument.[164] As Holmes noted, the Book of Exodus required killing an ox that had gored a person to death, and when someone was killed by a fall from a tree, "the rude Kukis of Southern Asia" required this person's relatives to cut down the tree and scatter it in chips.[165]

Although Holmes offered no evidence to support his thesis, he did reveal how the Yankee from Olympus viewed the common man. Noting that proceedings in admiralty still were brought against vessels and that everyone called vessels "she," he observed: "If [following a ship accident] we should say to an uneducated man to-day, 'She did it and she ought to pay for it,' it may be doubted whether he would see the fallacy, or be ready to explain that the ship was only property. . . ."[166]

Holmes's "mentalist" explanation of the punishment of things seemed implausible, at least in the form necessary to make this explanation compatible with his broader historical assertions. Perhaps ancient law did attribute some vague intentionality to animals and objects,[167] but one doubts that it applied subjective standards in judging these creatures and things. One can imagine, for example, a day on which one of the "rude Kukis of Southeast Asia" protested to his tribal council that, unlike other death-producing trees, a particular tree did not intend the death of the person who fell from it. One may doubt that on this fanciful day the council responded by examining the evidence and ruling on the tree's *mens rea*. Instead, the council might have questioned the sanity of the protesting tribesman (whose protest had revealed that he was, if not mentally ill, at least the very rudest of the Kukis). The council then might have applied a tough, objective, Holmesian standard to the offending tree, treating it as the council treated all other trees that caused death. Only the use of subjective standards would have been consistent with Holmes's claim that law had progressed from subjective to objective standards of liability. Despite Holmes's heroic squirmings, the punishment of animals and things was obviously inconsistent with his thesis.

Early law's treatment of accused criminals was inconsistent with Holmes's thesis too; ancient law typically considered the mental states of people no more than it considered the *mens rea* of trees. Holmes's second lecture examined the punishment of people, and the history he presented in this lecture was backwards.[168] At about the time he wrote, Frederick Maitland, the greatest of English legal historians, was telling the opposite story, noting "the utter incompetence of ancient law to take note of the mental elements of crime."[169] As P. S. Atiyah observed in his Holmes lectures at Harvard, "[T]here are many examples from early English law of a movement from more external to more subjective principles of liability, for example in the law of homicide."[170] Grant Gilmore said of the criminal law lecture and the rest of *The Common Law*, "[T]he historical underpinning was patently absurd."[171]

As Holmes emphasized, the general theory of criminal responsibility that he developed in *The Common Law* was identical to his general theory of civil liability.[172] I will describe the content of this general theory in greater detail and discuss some of its failings in the following discussion of Holmes's torts lectures.

As a justice of the Supreme Judicial Court of Massachusetts, Holmes wrote his objective theory into the state's law of homicide. His opinion in *Commonwealth v Pierce*[173] affirmed the manslaughter conviction of a physician whose stupid but well-intentioned treatment had caused his patient's death. Holmes attempted without success to reconcile his objective standard with an 1809 Massachusetts decision and a seventeenth-century statement of Sir Matthew Hale, both of which had endorsed a subjective standard. He declared that the distinction between murder and manslaughter had nothing to do with the defendant's state of mind; the difference lay only in the degree of danger an objective observer would believe the defendant had created. Malice, the traditional *men rea* of murder, referred to the highest degree of danger; recklessness, the *mens rea* of manslaughter, to a lesser degree.[174] Patrick J. Kelley observed, "Most would agree that *Pierce* was a terrible decision."[175]

Holmes's objectivism still haunts the law of Massachusetts. For example, 113 years after *Pierce*—in 1997—a Massachusetts jury was told that to be guilty of murder a person need neither have intended nor deliberately risked any harm. This jury then returned a conviction of murder in the case of Louise Woodward, a young English au pair charged with murdering the infant in her care. Abruptly backpedaling, the trial judge set aside this generally deplored verdict.[176]

Outside the homeland of Holmes, Holmesian objectivism has not notably influenced the law of crimes. In a ruling that P. S. Atiyah called "notorious" and "catastrophic," the highest court of England—the House of Lords—did briefly embrace Holmes's theory. The Lord Chancellor declared in *Director of Public Prosecutions v Smith*[177] that if a reasonable person would have recognized the likelihood of serious injury or death, "it matters not what the accused in fact contemplated as the probable result or whether he ever contemplated at all." Whatever the accused's own mental state, he was guilty of capital murder.[178] This English decision so troubled the High Court of Australia that it announced unanimously that it would no longer be bound by House of Lords decisions.[179] With the concurrence of the English Law Lords themselves, Parliament soon corrected the House of Lords' decision through legislation.[180] Atiyah reported that even prior to this short-lived misadventure of the House of Lords, "Holmes's view had been abandoned or rejected by all serious criminal lawyers and academics, as well as judges actually engaged in the trial of criminal cases."[181]

Torts

At the beginning of the first of his two lectures on torts, Holmes announced the breadth of his historicist ambitions. He would attempt the ultimate Langdellian breakthrough: "The object of the next two Lectures is to discover whether there is any common ground at the bottom of all liability in tort, and if so, what that ground is. Supposing the attempt to succeed, it will reveal the general principle of civil liability at common law."[182]

As Holmes told his audience, this task was difficult.[183] There were, he said, "two theories of the common-law liability for unintentional harm," and both of these theories had impressive support.[184] One, John Austin's, was that liability "ought only to be based on personal fault." Supporters of this position argued that "negligence means a state of the party's mind."[185] The other theory, however, was "directly opposed." It declared that "under the common law a man *acts* at his peril. . . . [T]he whole and sufficient ground for [liability] is supposed to be that he has voluntarily acted, and that damage has ensued."[186]

Mark DeWolfe Howe said that Holmes devised his general principle of liability to strike a "compromise" between the "two theories . . . competing for dominance,"[187] but Howe mischaracterized the goal of the science in which Holmes was engaged. Holmes's purpose was not to "compromise" the competing theories but instead to "reconcile" the decisions on which the champions of both theories relied to support their claims. Holmes once declared, "The mark of a master is, that facts which before lay scattered in an inorganic mass, when he shoots them through the magnetic current of his thought, leap into an organic order and live and bear fruit."[188] When one ignored the rationales asserted by judges and scholars and examined the raw, bottom-line judicial rulings themselves, one might discern the same principle at work in all of them.[189] This principle, Holmes declared, was neither one of strict liability for every harm produced nor one of fault-based liability. With only minor exceptions, courts held defendants liable in tort whenever an "average" member of the community would have foreseen the harm that the defendant's act produced. This previously unrecognized principle of liability fit nearly all the cases. Holmes explained:

> Foresight is a possible common denominator at the two extremes of malice and negligence. The purpose of the law is to prevent or secure a man indemnity from harm at the hands of his neighbors, . . . excepting, of course, such harm as it permits to be intentionally inflicted. But, as has been shown, he is bound to foresee whatever a prudent and intelligent man would have foreseen, and therefore he is liable for conduct from which a man would have foreseen that harm was liable to follow.[190]

Although Holmes did not mention it, the English Court of Common Pleas had rejected a subjective concept of negligence and endorsed an objective concept in an 1837 decision, *Vaughn v Menlove*.[191] In effect, English law had repudiated Austin's subjective concept of negligence forty-four years before Holmes published *The Common Law*. Indeed, the court had rejected Austin's theory without knowing anything about it, for it was twenty-six years after the decision in *Vaughn v Menlove* that John Austin's widow published a reconstruction of the lectures in which her husband had advanced this concept.[192] As Brian Simpson notes, "There is no reason to suppose that Austin's views on the law of tort . . . ever had the least influence."[193] Although the 1837 decision was known to almost everyone who wrote about torts in the second half of the nineteenth century,[194] Holmes did not acknowledge or cite it. His torts lectures showed how to whip a dead horse, a dead idea, or a straw man. Holmes's objective theory was considerably less creative than he made it seem.[195]

Although there was a deep conflict in the torts decisions of Holmes's era, it was not a conflict between a subjective concept of negligence and strict liability. It was instead a conflict between an *objective* concept of negligence and strict liability. No coherent principle separated the many cases imposing liability only for negligence, objectively defined, from the many imposing strict liability. Holmes might have offered his all-encompassing theory of liability as a means of reconciling these apparently conflicting torts decisions.

Holmes concluded that his general principle—liability for foreseeable harms—was at work in criminal cases too. As he summarized his criminal law lecture, "[I]t was concluded that, subject to exceptions which were explained, the general basis of criminal liability was knowledge, at the time of the action, of facts from which common experience showed that certain harmful results were likely to follow."[196] This principle was in fact more powerful in criminal law than in tort law: "[W]hen we are dealing with that part of the law which aims more directly than any other at establishing standards of conduct, we should expect there more than elsewhere to find that the tests of liability are external, and independent of the degree of evil in the particular person's motives or intentions."[197] Possibly because he sought to lead from strength, Holmes opened *The Common Law*, not with his theory of civil liability, but with his lectures on criminal punishment. Holmes concluded, moreover, that his theory of liability could explain the law of fraud, the law of libel and slander, the law of bailments, the law of trespass, the law of conspiracy, and the law of most other things too.

In an ironic twist of history, Holmes is remembered today, not as the discoverer of the legal equivalent of a unifying theory of macrophysics and microphysics, but as the hero who smashed legal science. His reputation for entering law's temple and overturning the Langdellians' tables was shaped in part by the legal realists of the 1930s. These writers took aim at the "conceptualism" of the preceding generation of scholars.

After proclaiming that "[t]he inherent enemy of realism is conceptualism," Max Radin explained in 1931, "By conceptualism I mean the theory that there are a number of principles which can be stated in a schematic form."[198] Attempting to bring legal cases within stated legal principles was "a piece of harmful and wicked pedantry." This effort appeared attractive only "because it bears the specious garb of certainty."[199] The realists praised the "hunch"[200] and denigrated general principles.[201] Some of them in fact appeared to oppose legal rules altogether.[202]

Noting Holmes's declaration that the life of the law has not been logic, his condemnation of all theories that considered law only from its formal side, and his criticism of Dean Langdell, the realists embraced Holmes as their hero. Karl Llewellyn, who proclaimed and named the realist movement, called Holmes the figure "from whom we all derive."[203] He declared, "Holmes, Holmes almost alone, has cracked open the law of these United States. The time-deep calcine crust is burst forever."[204] Jerome Frank, perhaps the most remembered of the realists after Llewellyn, declared Holmes "the completely adult jurist,"[205] adding that Holmes "almost alone among lawyers, adopted that skeptical attitude upon which modern science has built."[206]

Perhaps because *The Common Law* was close to impenetrable, the realists did not notice who their enemy was. The author of America's most sweeping work of "one size fits all" conceptualism, however, was the figure they most revered, Oliver Wendell Holmes.[207] By discovering and announcing "the general principle of civil [and criminal] liability at common law," Holmes had fulfilled and surpassed Dean Langdell's wildest scholarly fantasies.[208] Fortunately for his reputation among the realists and later generations of lawyers, Holmes had the gift of being obscure and turgid when he needed to be.

When one pieces Holmes's general theory of liability together from his scattered presentation, one discovers seven stages of analysis in both tort and criminal cases:

1. A factfinder[209] must first conclude that the defendant acted. An act, however, is simply a willed muscular contraction.[210] The plaintiff in a torts case or the government in a criminal case may assert any of the defendant's acts as the basis for a claim.
2. The factfinder must determine that the defendant's act was a *sine qua non* of the injury of which the plaintiff or the government has complained.[211]
3. The factfinder must determine what circumstances the defendant knew at the time of his act.[212]
4. The factfinder then must disregard the defendant himself and consider whether an average member of the community who knew what the defendant knew would have foreseen the injury of which the plaintiff or the government complained. If an average member of the community would have perceived a sufficient risk of injury, the defendant must ordinarily be held liable whether or not he was aware of this risk.[213]
5. If, however, the factfinder discovers an extreme impairment of ordinary capacity—infancy or blindness, for example—the defendant may be exempted from liability.[214]
6. The defendant also must be held liable if the factfinder determines that the defendant himself foresaw the plaintiff's or the victim's injury with sufficient clarity. In cases of exceptional foresight, the fact

that an average member of the community might have been unaware of the danger is immaterial.[215]

7. Even if an average member of the community would have foreseen the injury (or the defendant himself foresaw it), the defendant will not be liable if the factfinder determines that he had a recognized legal privilege to inflict the harm.[216]

David Rosenberg appropriately describes Holmes's general theory as one of foresight-based strict liability (strict liability for the foreseeable injuries produced by one's acts). He contrasts this theory with one of cause-based strict liability (liability for *all* of the injuries produced by one's acts) and with negligence (liability only for the injuries produced by one's *unreasonable* acts).[217]

The Common Law's theory of tort liability has been called "the central and most important idea in [Holmes's] jurisprudence,"[218] and scholars have claimed that Holmes greatly influenced American tort law.[219] Holmes's efforts did promote the study of torts as a unified field, and *The Common Law* contributed to the waning of the strong strand of strict liability in English and American law. Holmes did not, however, endorse the cost-benefit analysis that now defines negligence in American law,[220] and his theory also had little in common with the now popular concept of "enterprise liability"—the notion that commercial enterprises should be held strictly accountable for all of the injuries produced by their products to ensure that their prices reflect the full social cost of these products and to spread the economic risk of injury.[221] Rosenberg justly criticizes modern torts scholars for misrepresenting Holmes as a champion of the negligence principle.[222]

Confusion about Holmes's theory of torts, however, is easy to understand. Holmes was confused about it himself. For the most part, he appeared not to recognize the difference that Rosenberg emphasizes between liability for foreseeable harms and liability for unreasonable conduct. He repeatedly indicated that he considered these ideas the same. Holmes seemed strangely oblivious to the fact that the appropriateness of conduct may depend, not only on the gravity and the foreseeability of the risk taken, but also on the justification for taking it.

Holmes wrote, for example, "The question what a prudent man would do under given circumstances is . . . equivalent to the question of what are the teachings of experience as to the dangerous character of this or that conduct under these or those circumstances."[223] Indeed, casting

some doubt on Rosenberg's understanding of the torts chapters, he usually described the issue submitted to juries in torts cases as one of appropriate conduct rather than foreseeability. This issue, he said, was "what
ought to have been done or omitted under the circumstances of the
case"[224] or "whether the defendant had acted as a prudent man would
have done under the circumstances."[225] Holmes wrote that the law does
not hold a person liable unless "he might and ought to have foreseen the
danger, or, in other words, unless a man of ordinary intelligence and fore-
thought would have been to blame for acting as he did."[226] He repeatedly
described his standard of foresight-based liability as identifying conduct
that "would be blameworthy in the average man."[227] Similarly, although
the word *prudence* suggests wisdom and judgment rather than simply
foresight, Holmes described the hypothetical figure at the heart of his
theory as the "average man" and the "prudent man" interchangeably. To
be imprudent is, in ordinary usage, to be negligent. Holmes insisted, "[I]t
would be possible to state all cases of negligence in terms of imputed or
presumed foresight."[228] In short, Holmes usually did not recognize that
judging the propriety of conduct involves more than judging the magnitude of the risk created. He seemed oblivious to the fact that people may
be justified in taking actions that they know risk harm. He apparently
devised his principle of foresight-based liability, not as an alternative to
an objective negligence standard, but as a way of describing it.[229]

Nevertheless, at two points in his torts lectures (as nearly as I can
tell, only two), Holmes did notice briefly that the appropriateness of conduct may depend on its potential benefits as well as its potential costs.[230]
At both of these points, he discussed *Gilbert v Stone*.[231] As Holmes understood this 1647 case, a judge had held the defendant liable although the
defendant had justifiably taken the property of an innocent person in order to save his own life. Holmes reiterated that "in general" the wrongfulness of conduct "will be determined by considering the degree of danger attending the act or conduct under the known circumstances. If there
is danger that harm to another will follow, the act is generally wrong in
the sense of the law."[232] Referring to *Gilbert,* however, Holmes indicated
that "wrong in the sense of the law" might not be wrong in the sense
of the rest of us. He noted that "in some cases the defendant's conduct
may not have been morally wrong, and yet he may have chosen to inflict
the harm, as where he has acted in fear of his life."[233]

Surprisingly, Holmes did not endorse the result in *Gilbert.* In both of
his discussions of the case, he said that courts might reasonably resolve
the issue of liability either way. This issue was "generally unimportant."[234]

"[A]side from such exceptional cases as *Gilbert v. Stone,* the two tests [liability for foreseeable harm and liability for conduct that would be blameworthy in the average member of the community] agree, and the difference need not be considered in what follows."[235] Holmes ended both of his discussions by reiterating the bottom line: "[T]he known tendency of the act under the known circumstances to do harm may be accepted as the general test of conduct."[236]

Holmes thus considered for a moment a case that posed the choice between strict liability for foreseeable harms and liability for inappropriate conduct in unequivocal terms. The issue in *Gilbert v Stone* was which principle governed—that the defendant, although justified in saving his own life, must pay the cost of the foreseeable injuries to others that his conduct inflicted, or that the defendant need not pay because his conduct was justified. With the choice sharply posed, Holmes punted. He declined the opportunity to reiterate his endorsement of foresight-based strict liability, suggesting, perhaps, that he simply did not realize its implications. Although, as David Rosenberg contended, Holmes repeatedly endorsed this standard, he did not notice (or perhaps contrived not to notice) that it differed from an objective negligence standard in anything other than an odd, arcane law school case.[237]

In fact, the choice that Holmes evaded in his discussion of *Gilbert v Stone* runs through much of tort law; it arises whenever a justified activity produces foreseeable harm. For example, before building a suspension bridge, a municipality may be able to predict with near certainty that the construction project will result in injury and death; when a manufacturer appropriately builds a product without a device that would increase its safety while tripling its cost, the manufacturer may realize that selling the product without the device will produce injury and death; when a trucking company places its drivers on the road, it may know with near certainty that some of these drivers will have accidents and produce injury and death. The choice between foresight-based strict liability and liability for negligence seems critical in all of these situations. Holmes, however, declared that the foreseeable-harm standard did not differ enough from a negligence standard to be worth discussing the issue. His unified theory of torts and the criminal law, which invoked the concepts of foresight and appropriate conduct interchangeably, was a muddle.[238]

As a justice of the Supreme Court, Holmes indicated in fact that the common law did not impose foresight-based strict liability; he even appeared to treat the idea as a bit outlandish. In *Southern Pac Co v Berkshire,*[239] a train engineer leaned out of his cab to check the condition of a driving pin that was in danger of overheating. Holmes's opinion assumed that the engineer "was acting in the course of his duty."[240] While leaning from his cab, the engineer was struck and killed by the arm of an extended mail crane about fourteen inches from the cab. Although Holmes's opinion for the majority seemed at times to question the railroad's negligence (which the three dissenting justices called "palpable"),[241] he ultimately did not deny the railroad's fault. Under the Federal Employers' Liability Act, moreover, the case presented no issue of contributory negligence. Holmes and the majority nevertheless rejected the verdict that a jury had returned in favor of the engineer's estate and rejected as well the judgment of two state courts and the views of the three dissenting justices. Although, as the engineer of a freight train that did not carry mail, the decedent had rarely encountered extended mail cranes, the Court held as a matter of law that he had assumed the risk of injury.

In an opinion that veered frequently from the question before the Court, Holmes offered these remarks about liability for the foreseeable injury produced by nonnegligent activity: "When a railroad is built it is practically certain that some deaths will ensue, but the builders are not murderers on that account when the foreseen comes to pass. On the common-law principles of tort the adoption of an improvement in the public interest does not throw the risk of all incidental damage upon those who adopted it. . . ."[242]

Because Holmes's views of tort liability were jumbled and contradictory, his disciples have been able to make of them what they liked. Rosenberg attaches great weight to Holmes's approval of the result in *Rylands v Fletcher*.[243] This case held a mill owner strictly liable for the collapse of his reservoir and the flooding of a nearby mine. Recognizing that the mill owner "could not have found out, the weak point from which the dangerous object [the water] escaped," Holmes sought to bring *Rylands* within his general theory by declaring, "The period of choice was further back, and, although [the mill owner] was not to blame, he was bound at his peril to know that the object was a continual threat to his neighbors, and that is enough to throw the risk of the business on him."[244] Holmes did not explain in *Southern Pac Co v Berkshire* why railroads differed from mills and why a railroad builder was not "bound at his peril to know that the object was a continual threat to his neighbors."

Although Holmes seemed to approve the result in *Rylands,* his primary scholarly goal was to reconcile as many seemingly divergent decisions as possible through his general theory. Holmes therefore disapproved few decisions. Instead, tugging and straining, he presented prior rulings as previously unrecognized illustrations of his general principle of foresight-based liability.

As a judge, Holmes repudiated a theory of responsibility for foreseeable harm when the plaintiff's injury was the result of foreseeable misconduct by someone other than the defendant. For example, in *Elmer v Fessenden*,[245] a doctor falsely told a patient who worked in a buggy-whip factory that the silk used in the factory was contaminated with arsenic. The patient told the doctor's story to co-workers, some of whom quit work. The factory owner then sued the doctor, arguing that repetition of the story and the resulting injury were foreseeable. Holmes's opinion declared the foreseeability of the harm immaterial: "The general rule, that a man is not liable for a third person's actionable and unauthorized repetition of his slander, is settled."[246]

In a later case, Holmes articulated the principle in broader terms: "Wrongful acts of independent third persons, not actually intended by the defendant, are not regarded by the law as natural consequences of his wrong."[247] Holmes offered no normative defense of this limitation of his general principle of foresight-based liability, and as Patrick J. Kelley has shown, prior decisions did not support so broad—and senseless—a restriction.[248] Holmes, however, seemed to regard his restriction of the foreseeability principle as an original and constructive contribution. It was a central theme of several of his Massachusetts opinions,[249] two of his letters to Sir Frederick Pollock,[250] and an 1894 law review article.[251]

Unsurprisingly, Holmes's general theory did not reconcile the strict liability and negligence cases. Despite his contortions, cases imposing strict liability for trespassing upon another's land simply did not reflect the same principle as cases declining to impose strict liability for runaway horses. As Rosenberg observes, "Holmes never explained why the courts should think . . . that trespassing on land was a generally foreseeable risk of choosing to take a walk, while [a] runaway horse . . . was not an expected hazard of saddling-up for a ride."[252]

Moreover, focusing on Holmes's torts lectures, Patrick Kelley noted the same scholarly defect that reviewers have noted from the beginning in *The Common Law* as a whole, a defect that one might call "Langdellianism": The lectures transformed purported historical description into prescription without offering much argument or justification. Holmes's theory was "asserted or suggested, the supporting arguments hinted at obliquely or left out altogether."[253]

A further difficulty with Holmes's theory was that its essential elements remained unspecified—it identified neither the level of risk that would establish *prima facie* liability nor how closely the foreseeable harm must have matched the actual harm. Holmes referred interchangeably to a "possibility of harm,"[254] to whether "harm was liable to follow,"[255] to whether an action "will probably cause some harm,"[256] to a "danger that harm to another will follow,"[257] and to a "manifest danger."[258] Then as now, the resolution of a case through a foreseeability standard is pretty much a resolution *deus ex machina.*[259]

Plausible normative justifications can be offered for both modern negligence doctrine (which imposes liability for objectively wrongful or inefficient conduct) and enterprise liability (which seeks to spread risks and, like the law of negligence, to encourage efficient behavior and sound pricing). Holmes's argument in favor of strict liability for foreseeable harms, however, had no normative appeal at all.

Chief Justice Tindal's 1837 opinion in *Vaughan v Menlove* approved an objective standard of negligence on the ground that a subjective standard would be unworkable: "[W]hether the Defendant had acted honestly and bonâ fide to the best of his own judgment . . . would leave so vague a line as to afford no rule at all, the degree of judgment belonging to each individual being infinitely various."[260] Although Holmes mentioned briefly "the impossibility of nicely measuring a man's powers and limitations," he said that there was "a more satisfactory explanation" for endorsing an objective approach:

> [W]hen men live in a society, a certain average of conduct, a sacrifice
> of individual peculiarities going beyond a certain point, is necessary to
> the general welfare. If, for instance, a man is born hasty and awkward,
> is always having accidents and hurting himself or his neighbors, no
> doubt his congenital defects will be allowed for in the courts of
> Heaven, but his slips are no less troublesome to his neighbors than if
> they sprang from guilty neglect. His neighbors accordingly require
> him, at his proper peril, to come up to their standard, and the courts
> which they establish decline to take his personal equation into ac-
> count.[261]

Holmes's argument proved too much. When a person of average or above-average foresight does not perceive a risk of harm but injures his neighbor nevertheless, "his slips are no less troublesome to his neighbor[ ] than if they sprang from guilty neglect." Pain is pain whatever its cause, and people injured by other people's acts usually want the other people to compensate them. Holmes's pain-is-pain argument for requiring the below-average person to meet the standard of the average man was equally an argument for requiring the average man to meet the standard of the expert. Indeed, in this argument, Holmes offered no reason for stopping short of cause-based strict liability.[262]

Holmes revealed in his criminal law lecture why, although the below-average man must be held to the standard of the average man, the average man could be held to no higher standard: "[A] law which punished conduct which would not be blameworthy in the average member of the community would be too severe for that community to bear."[263] With this declaration, Holmes's power-focused jurisprudence came to the fore, and his general theory's veneer of normative justification vanished.[264]

The dominant power in a democracy can be described as the majority or, less accurately, as the community. It can be personified as the "average man." Although, according to Holmes, the community considered it too severe for the average man to bear responsibility for harms he could not avoid, the average man and the majority had no objection to collecting compensation from the below-average minority for harms this minority could not avoid. A law imposing liability for conduct that was not blameworthy in this hapless minority was not too severe for the community to bear. The community was all for it. Holmes's standard demanded what the average man and the above-average man could provide without difficulty while maximizing their recovery from the less fortunate. As Holmes recognized, "If [the standards to which conformity is required] fall on any one class harder than on another, it is on the weakest."[265]

Holmes wrote, "Unless my act is of a nature to threaten others, unless under the circumstances a prudent man would have foreseen the possibility of harm, it is no more justifiable to make me indemnify my neighbor against the consequences than to make me do the same thing if I had fallen upon him in a fit, or to compel me to insure him against lightning."[266] The test of whether a person could have done better, however, is whether she could have done better, not whether a hypothetical "prudent person" could have done better. Unless a person could have been expected to do better, it seems "no more justifiable to make [her] indemnify [her] neighbor against the consequences than to make [her] do the same thing if [she] had fallen upon him in a fit." Once more, Holmes made no serious effort to justify his use of a "prudent" or "average man" standard rather than, on the one hand, a less-demanding standard taking account of the defendant's own capacities or, on the other, a more-demanding "expert man" standard. The attraction of Holmes's midpoint standard was simply that, compared to either of these alternatives, it maximized the wealth of the dominant power.[267]

Scholars have contended that Holmes minimized the strong element of strict liability in nineteenth-century tort cases because he feared the use of tort law to redistribute wealth.[268] Holmes, however, had no objection to using tort law to redistribute wealth—as long as redistribution proceeded from the weak to the strong. No coherent normative principle supported his general theory of civil and criminal liability; like most of his theories, it rested on the power-centered principle that the "haves" come out ahead.[269]

Contracts

Holmes's three lectures on contracts took the opposite tack from the one his "general principle of civil liability at common law" seemed to require. Taken at face value, Holmes's general principle of foresight-based liability would have made foreseeable detrimental reliance on a promise a sufficient reason for enforcing it. Although the judicial decisions of his era would have provided ample support for protecting the reliance interest, his lectures endorsed an unyielding theory of "bargained for" consideration that excluded reliance as a basis of promissory liability.

Grant Gilmore's book *The Death of Contract*[270] had three scholarly villains. Two of them were familiar hobgoblins, Dean Langdell and Samuel Williston (another prominent Harvard "formalist"). To the amazement of readers, Gilmore's third and principal villain was Oliver Wendell Holmes. At the time Gilmore published *The Death of Contract,* he had been Holmes's official biographer for seven years.[271]

As reviewers demonstrated, Gilmore's book was flawed. He wrote, for example, "[T]he idea that there was such a thing as a general law— or theory—of contract seems never to have occurred to the legal mind until Langdell somehow stumbled across it."[272] The reviewers agreed that this assertion was erroneous; both courts and scholars had recognized general principles of contract law well before Langdell.[273]

As for the theory of contract supposedly launched by Langdell and developed by Holmes and Williston, Gilmore wrote, "Th[is] theory seems to have been dedicated to the proposition that, ideally, no one should be liable to anyone for anything."[274] Even if read in the facetious manner that Gilmore no doubt intended, this remark was unfortunate. The formalist theory attributed to Langdell, Williston, and Holmes sometimes expanded contract liability, as Gilmore himself emphasized.[275] This theory limited excuses for nonperformance and restricted equitable defenses like mistake. It made commercially unsophisticated people more liable in contract, not less.

Gilmore reported that Holmes provided the theoretical basis for narrowing contractual liability by inventing the concept of bargained-for consideration—the notion that no detriment qualifies as consideration unless, in Holmes's words, "the parties have dealt with it on that footing."[276] Noting that the courts commonly treated un-bargained-for reliance as consideration, Gilmore observed, "It seems perfectly clear that Holmes was, quite consciously, proposing revolutionary doctrine and was not in the least interested in stating or restating the common law as it was."[277]

James Gordley reported, however, that six years before the publication of *The Common Law,* Sir Frederick Pollock's treatise on contracts had offered "essentially the same theory" of consideration as Holmes's. Pollock, moreover, had sent Holmes a copy of his work when it was published.[278] As Gordley also observed, the requirement of bargained-for consideration had antecedents prior to Pollock.[279] Although Holmes was not the inventive spinner of doctrine that Gilmore imagined, he might have thrown Gilmore off track by borrowing his concept of consideration from Pollock without attribution.

Despite Gilmore's faulty scholarship,[280] *The Death of Contract* was more right than wrong. Even if Holmes took the concept of bargained-for consideration from Pollock, his most frequent English correspondent, he articulated and endorsed this concept more clearly and forcefully than Langdell or any other American had before him. Rejecting the common view "that any benefit conferred by the promisee on the promisor, or any detriment incurred by the promisee, may be a consideration,"[281] Holmes wrote:

> [I]t is the essence of a consideration, that, by the terms of the agreement, it is given and accepted as the motive or inducement of the promise. Conversely, the promise must be made and accepted as the conventional motive or inducement for furnishing the consideration. The root of the whole matter is the relation of reciprocal conventional inducement, each for the other, between consideration and promise.[282]

This abstraction—unjustified by any normative argument and also unsupported as a matter of description—apparently was designed primarily to rationalize the "formalist" refusal to safeguard reliance. It led courts to conclude that a promise to hold an offer open for a stated time was unenforceable, that there could be no "agreement to agree" or duty to bargain in good faith, that a creditor could recover the full amount of a debt even after agreeing to accept a lesser amount in satisfaction, and (for a time, at least in some places) that a contract to purchase all of an enterprise's requirements of a commodity or service from a particular supplier was no contract at all.[283] The doctrine's insistence on a formal exchange (even if only of a "nominal" consideration like a peppercorn)[284] enhanced the power of the professionally well-advised. Its disallowance of "past" consideration and "moral" consideration disadvantaged the unsophisticated.[285]

Although the requirement of bargained-for consideration was less extravagant than Holmes's "general theory of civil [and criminal] liability," it was, like that general theory, an extreme overgeneralization of the sort that gave the "formalist" era its name. Despite one reviewer's protest that "the firm of Langdell, Holmes, and Williston" was "an unlikely trio of partners,"[286] Gilmore's recognition of the common ground shared by these scholars was appropriate. Although Gilmore may have pushed his point too hard, Langdell, Holmes, and Williston all contributed significantly to the regressive view of contract doctrine that the twentieth-century heroes of the field—Benjamin Cardozo, Arthur Corbin, Lon Fuller, and Friedrich Kessler—criticized and, in the end, vanquished.[287]

Although Holmes's discussion of contracts abandoned without explanation his general principle of responsibility for foreseeable harms, he continued to press his "objectivist" historical thesis. He reiterated, "[A]lthough the law starts from the distinctions and uses the language of morality, it necessarily ends in external standards not dependent on the actual consciousness of the individual."[288] In a handwritten annotation to his personal copy of *The Common Law,* he wrote, "The whole doctrine of contract is formal and external."[289]

Gilmore claimed that the "objective theory of contract" endorsed by Holmes "became the great metaphysical solvent—the critical test for distinguishing between the false and the true."[290] He added that the austerity of this doctrine was not "tempered for the shorn lambs who might shiver in its blast."[291]

Although the objective theory "narrow[ed] the range within which mistake could be successfully pleaded as a defense,"[292] Holmes's bending of the cases to fit his theory made it difficult to tell just how much narrowing he endorsed. For example, in the noted case of *Raffles v Wichelhaus,*[293] a written contract for the sale of cotton declared that the cotton would be sent from Bombay to Liverpool on board the ship *Peerless.* There were, however, two ships with the same name, and they had sailed from Bombay to Liverpool at different times. Although the judges delivered no opinion, they apparently accepted the argument of counsel that there was no "consensus *ad idem*" or meeting of the minds on an essential contractual term.[294] Assuming that the buyer and seller had different ships in mind, the court apparently ruled that no enforceable contract existed.

Holmes concluded that the "true ground of the decision" in *Raffles* was not the ground that had seemed to persuade the judges:

> It is commonly said that such a contract is void, because of mutual mistake as to the subject matter, and because therefore the parties did not consent to the same thing. But this way of putting it seems to me misleading. The law has nothing to do with the actual state of the parties' minds. In contract, as elsewhere, it must go by externals, and judge parties by their conduct. . . . The true ground of the decision was not that each party meant a different thing from the other, as is implied by the explanation which has been mentioned, but that each said a different thing. The plaintiff offered one thing, the defendant expressed his assent to another.[295]

Of course the parties did say the same thing; both of them said "Peerless." If they had meant the same thing, moreover, Holmes and everyone else would have had no difficulty holding them to their contract. The decision in *Raffles v Wichelhaus* did not rest on an objective theory of contract; only the court's requirement of a subjective "meeting of the minds" could have supported its result. As Gilmore observed, however, "The magician who could 'objectify' *Raffles v. Wichelhaus* . . . could . . . objectify anything."[296]

Holmes's lectures on contracts do not warrant declaring *The Common Law* "the best book on law ever written by an American."[297] His lectures on criminal law, torts, and other common law subjects do not justify this description either. Apart from its five great paragraphs, the work was confused, confusing, and turgid. Holmes's attempted masterpiece illustrates as well as any work by Langdell why late-nineteenth-century historicism is treated as a bad dream. Judged as a whole, *The Common Law* was what Saul Touster called it—a "clear failure."[298]

HOLMES AS A COMMON LAW JUDGE

Economists endorse the concept of "revealed preferences." They maintain that people reveal their desires, not through what they say, but through the choices they make.[299] If, as the economists contend, actions speak louder than words, Holmes's rulings in common law cases may reveal more about his judicial philosophy than his general remarks about the life of the law on the first page of *The Common Law.*

Holmes's judicial opinions tend to reinforce the portrait that emerges from the remainder of his book. Despite his reputation as a champion of judicial creativity, Holmes's view of private law issues was mechanistic and his decisions far from progressive. Mark Tushnet read all of the 1,291 opinions Holmes wrote during his twenty years of service on the Supreme Judicial Court of Massachusetts.[300] Tushnet noted the "tension between [Holmes's] judicial opinions, with their forbearance from policy analysis in favor of technicalities, and [Holmes's] more theoretical writings."[301]

Patrick Kelly, the author of another review of Holmes's work on the Supreme Judicial Court, concluded:

> Ultimately, what is so unsatisfactory about Holmes's opinions in these cases is their impoverished vision of law and human beings. . . . [M]orality, custom and human passion are the very things that Holmes leaves out of his pictures. What is ultimately so surprising about Holmes as a judge is his legalistic approach to the law, precisely in the hard cases where a judge has the opportunity to be more than just a legal craftsman.[302]

Although Kelley focused on Holmes's criminal law and torts opinions and Tushnet on his work in many areas, this section describes only a few of Holmes's torts opinions, most of them drawn from Tushnet's and Kelley's studies. Torts is the field of private law in which Holmes is most credited with influencing the life of the law. Both scholars who have viewed him as a progenitor of modern negligence doctrine and David Rosenberg who sees him with greater justification as a champion of foresight-based strict liability have regarded Holmes as a tort law pioneer.[303]

The decisions described in this section were not chosen randomly; they were selected to make a point. The point, however, seems uncontroversial. The tort law of Holmes's era was harsh and unconscionably biased in favor of employers and large-scale business enterprises. Nevertheless, as Holmes's biographer G. Edward White observed, "In general, with the exception of libel cases, [Holmes's] opinions had the effect of confining tort liability rather than extending it."[304] However one interprets the enigmatic lectures of *The Common Law,* Holmes was no tort law pioneer in his judicial decisions.

Two of his most revealing decisions came while he was a justice of the U.S. Supreme Court. One was *Southern Pac Co v Berkshire,*[305] the case described earlier of a railroad engineer killed by an extended mail crane.[306] The other was *United Zinc Co v Britt.*[307] In *Britt,* the parents of two boys sued to recover damages for the boys' deaths. The boys, eight and eleven, had left a campsite and entered land where, several years earlier, the United Zinc Company had operated a plant for manufacturing (among other things) sulfuric acid. When the company tore down its plant, it left a pool of water poisoned by acid and zinc sulfate. According to the dissenting justices, the land was unfenced, and a photograph in the record revealed that the pool had "the appearance of an attractive swimming pool with brick sides and the water coming nearly to the top of the wall. The water [was] described by the witnesses as appearing to be clear and pure, and, on the hot summer day on which the children perished, attractively cool."[308] The adult passers-by who heard the cries of other children and removed the boys from the pool (one of them already dead) suffered acute poisoning themselves. A jury returned a verdict for the children's parents, which a federal appellate court affirmed.

The Supreme Court set aside this verdict. In his opinion for the Court, Holmes declared, "Infants have no greater right to go upon other people's land than adults."[309] Justice Clarke, in a dissenting opinion joined by Justice Day and Chief Justice Taft, objected that the Court had effectively overruled two earlier decisions:

> The courts of our country have sharply divided as to the principles of law applicable to "attractive nuisance" cases, of which this one is typical. At the head of one group, from 1873 until the decision of today, has stood the Supreme Court of the United States, applying what has been designated as the "Humane" doctrine. Quite distinctly the courts of Massachusetts have stood at the head of the other group, applying what has been designated as a "Hard Doctrine"—the "Draconian Doctrine."[310]

In a letter, Holmes called Clarke's dissent "larmoyant" (a French word meaning "suffused with tears"). He said that it contained "more sentiment and rhetoric than reasoning."[311]

The Common Law's torts chapters largely neglected the issues of the day. Holmes described cases of trespass to land, runaway horses, blocking access to light, and keeping fierce animals, but his chapters said virtually nothing about industrial accidents, railroads, the fellow servant rule, medical malpractice, privity, assumption of risk, and contributory negligence. The book's discussion of the responsibility of employers for wrongs committed by employees consisted entirely of an argument that this responsibility was archaic. The doctrine of *respondeat superior* was, Holmes declared, a vestige of the responsibilities of Roman masters for the wrongs of their slaves. He concluded, "If the liability of a master for the torts of his servant had hitherto been recognized by the courts as the decaying remnant of an obsolete institution [slavery], it would not be surprising to find it confined to the cases settled by ancient precedent."[312]

Holmes's appointment to the bench required him to confront the present—in particular, the working conditions of industrialized America and the grisly injuries they produced. The following descriptions of his opinions for the Supreme Judicial Court of Massachusetts reveal less about his theory of torts than about his tough-minded approach to human suffering and his failure to address "considerations of social advantage."

In *Glynn v Central Railroad,*[313] when a worker attempted to couple a railroad car owned by the defendant, his hand was crushed by a defective protruding bolt on the car. Holmes's opinion declared that the defendant owed no duty to the plaintiff because the car had been inspected by another railroad company to which it had been consigned. Holmes recognized that the consignment of the car would not have exempted the defendant from liability if the use of the car that caused the injury had been contemplated by the defendant, but he declared, "[C]ontemplation means a good deal more than simply recognizing a probability."[314]

In *Quinn v New York, New Haven & Hartford Railroad,*[315] a brakeman sitting on top of a railroad car was injured by the overhanging roof of a train station. Holmes's opinion concluded that the brakeman had assumed the risk of injury.

In *Mellor v Merchants Manufacturing Co,*[316] a mill employee complained about defective machinery and was promised that the machinery would be repaired. When it was not, the employee decided to repair it himself. He was injured before beginning his repairs while waiting for the defective machinery to stop. A recent Massachusetts statute had withdrawn the defense of assumption of risk when the risk arose from an employee's contract of service. Holmes's opinion declared the statute inapplicable because the employee's contractual responsibilities did not include repairing machinery.

The plaintiff in *Kelley v Calumet Woolen Co*[317] worked nights in a woolen mill. He was instructed to turn off his spinning equipment whenever he left his post or anything unusual happened. One night, after the lights went out unexpectedly, the plaintiff lost a finger as he attempted to turn off his machine in the dark. Holmes's opinion upheld a verdict for the employer on alternate grounds: first, the plaintiff was contributorily negligent, and second, he had assumed the risk of injury. Holmes wrote, "It is well known that electric lights have been found liable to intermissions in their shining. . . . The order [to turn off the machine] manifestly had no reference to such occasions as the momentary darkening of the electric light."[318]

In *Lamson v American Axe & Tool Co,*[319] Holmes cited an employee's complaints to his employer about the danger posed by an overhead rack of hatchets and the employer's "like it or lump it" response as proof that the employee had assumed the risk of injury from falling hatchets.

Although Holmes's opinion in *Henderson v Boynton*[320] did not reveal the facts of the case, a dissenting opinion supplied them. The defendant, a manufacturer of boot heels, contracted with the master of a house of corrections to use convict labor. The plaintiff, a convict, was ordered to use defective machinery—a heel compressor lacking the mechanical device that permitted ready removal of the compressed heels. The plaintiff also was given an unstable platform on which to stand while prying out the heels by hand. The plaintiff initially refused to use this equipment, but when a supervisor threatened him with solitary confinement, he did as he was told. He was injured when his unsteady platform tipped as he was trying to remove a heel. Justice Lathrop noted in dissent that, as an involuntary laborer, the plaintiff had not willingly assumed the risk of injury. Writing for the court, Justice Holmes concluded as a matter of law that "there was no negligence" on the part of the defendant because the plaintiff knew the platform was unstable and was not required to use it.

Joseph v George C. Whitney Co[321] concerned the scope of a Massachusetts statute declaring employers liable for the negligent acts of their supervisory personnel. Holmes's opinion held that a supervisor had not injured the plaintiff *as a supervisor* when, in responding to another employee's request for instructions, he had inadvertently leaned against a power switch, started an embossing machine, and cut off the plaintiff's hand. In *Joseph,* Holmes evidently sought to limit the doctrine of *respondeat superior* to a narrow scope, just as he had proposed in *The Common Law.*[322]

The plaintiff in *Maloney v United States Rubber Co*[323] was injured when one of several pieces of lumber used to hold felt in place split in two as the felt was pressed into a bale. The shattering piece of wood threw another piece into the plaintiff's face. Holmes's opinion denied liability on the ground that the plaintiff had selected the piece of lumber from a bin maintained for the purpose and might have chosen a less worn piece.

Opinions by Holmes in nonindustrial cases revealed a similarly unsympathetic view of humanity and a similarly mechanistic approach to judging. The plaintiff in *Lorenzo v Wirth*,[324] a recent immigrant from Spain, testified that she had never seen an open coal chute in a sidewalk; she fell into such a chute after walking over a pile of coal. Although two dissenting justices argued that the defendant's negligence was a question for the jury, Holmes's opinion ruled as a matter of law that the defendant was not negligent. It declared, "A heap of coal on a sidewalk in Boston is an indication according to common experience that there very possibly may be a coal hole to receive it."[325]

In *Merrill v Eastern Railroad*,[326] the plaintiff's decedent had been thrown from the steps of an overcrowded train. Holmes's opinion denied recovery on two grounds. First, the decedent knew that the train was overcrowded, and second, he had boarded the train at the engine and was not in a place where passengers were authorized to be.

In *Dietrich v Northampton*,[327] a woman who was four- or five-months pregnant slipped on a defective highway, causing her to miscarry. "[T]here was testimony[, however,] . . . based on observing motion in [the] limbs [of the fetus], that it did live for ten or fifteen minutes."[328] Sir Edward Coke had written that if a person attacked "a woman quick with child," causing her fetus to be born alive and then to die, the batterer would be guilty of murder. No Massachusetts precedent addressed the issue. Holmes concluded that Coke's judgment concerning criminal responsibility did not extend to civil cases. In any event, the miscarried fetus had not quickened; it was not a "person recognized by law" and was incapable of bringing an action.

Mistrustful of juries, Holmes sought without success to transform amorphous standards of tort liability into concrete rules. He wrote, "[T]he sphere in which [a judge] is able to rule without taking [a jury's] opinion at all should be continually growing."[329] The most noted of his failures was *Baltimore and Ohio Railroad v Goodman*.[330]

Nathan Goodman slowed his automobile to five or six miles per hour as he approached a railroad crossing at which his vision was obstructed by a section house. The train that killed him did not slow. Sounding no warning bell or whistle, it proceeded through the intersection at more than sixty miles per hour. The Supreme Court reversed a jury verdict in favor of Goodman's estate on the ground that he was contributorily negligent as a matter of law. Holmes, who never learned to drive, articulated a "stop and look" rule for railroad crossings:

> [I]f a driver cannot be sure otherwise whether a train is dangerously near he must stop and get out of his vehicle. . . . It seems to us that if he relies upon not hearing the train or any signal and takes no further precaution he does so at his own risk. . . . It is true . . . that the question of due care very generally is left to the jury. But we are dealing with a standard of conduct, and when the standard is clear it should be laid down once for all by the Courts.[331]

The Supreme Court abandoned Holmes's "stop and look" rule in an opinion by Justice Cardozo seven years later. Cardozo wrote, "To get out of a vehicle is an uncommon precaution, as everyday experience informs us. Besides being uncommon, it is very likely to be futile and sometimes even dangerous."[332]

Mark Tushnet speculated that Holmes wrote wooden opinions like many of those described above only to placate his judicial brethren.[333] Champions of the Holmes myth appear to be the equals of Ptolemaic astronomers in devising epicycles to maintain their theory. P. J. Atiyah, less inclined than Tushnet to apologize for Holmes, declared, "Throughout Holmes's career as a judge in Massachusetts, he seems to have joined his brethren quite willingly and regularly in denying tort remedies to workers under the Assumption of Risk doctrine."[334]

Whatever the explanation, Holmes's opinions on torts were undistinguished and at least as callous and pedestrian as those of most other jurists of his time. In that respect, these opinions resembled all but five great paragraphs of Holmes's mercifully unread book *The Common Law*.

Chapter Seven

The Descending Trail:
Holmes's *Path of the Law*

In 1897, the *Harvard Law Review* published an article that Sanford Levinson has called "the single most important essay ever written by an American on the law."[1] The article was *The Path of the Law* by Oliver Wendell Holmes, Jr.,[2] and Levinson's appraisal of its significance has been echoed by many others. Morton Horwitz declared, "With 'The Path of the Law' Holmes pushed American legal thought into the twentieth century."[3] Phillip Johnson observed, "This lecture has been so influential in shaping the thinking of American lawyers that it might be described as almost part of the Constitution."[4] Richard Posner proclaimed that *The Path of the Law* may be "the best article-length work on law ever written."[5] Even Saul Touster, who called Holmes's *The Common Law* "a clear failure," described *The Path of the Law* as "Holmes' acknowledged masterpiece in jurisprudence."[6]

Holmes presented this article as an address at the Boston University Law School when he was fifty-five and a justice of the Supreme Judicial Court of Massachusetts. Reiterating ideas that he had sketched in *The Common Law* sixteen years earlier and in other writings extending over more than a quarter century, *The Path of the Law* provided a mature, polished expression of his concept of law.

Four closely related ideas conveyed Holmes's vision. First, his prediction theory of law:

> The prophecies of what the courts will do in fact, and nothing more pretentious, are what I mean by the law.[7]

Second, his "bad man" perspective on law:

If you want to know the law and nothing else, you must look at it as a bad man, who cares only for the material consequences which such knowledge enables him to predict, not as a good one, who finds his reasons for conduct, whether inside the law or outside it, in the vaguer sanctions of conscience.[8]

Third, his opposition to the use of moral terminology in law:

For my own part, I often doubt whether it would not be a gain if every word of moral significance could be banished from the law altogether. . . . We should lose the fossil records of a good deal of history and the majesty got from ethical associations, but by ridding ourselves of an unnecessary confusion we should gain very much in the clearness of our thought.[9]

Fourth, his alternative theory of contract:

Nowhere is the confusion between legal and moral ideas more manifest than in the law of contract. . . . The duty to keep a contract at common law means a prediction that you must pay damages if you do not keep it,—and nothing else.[10]

These statements express in forceful and striking language a concept that I will call "Holmesian positivism."[11]

In examining Holmes's vision of law, this chapter focuses primarily on what Holmes thought law *is.* It examines the analytic side of his legal scholarship. Following this introductory section, the chapter responds to the claim that Holmes's definition of law is incompatible with his concept of law's historical development and that his essay expresses two distinct visions of law. It then reviews some familiar objections to Holmes's definition and asks why this definition spoke of predicting the behavior of courts rather than of other governmental agencies. I argue that Holmes's focus on the judiciary smuggled considerable normativity into his purportedly descriptive definition. A definition that adhered more closely to the "bad man" perspective would not have mentioned courts and would have been more obviously unacceptable.

A section then criticizes Holmes's good-man, bad-man dichotomy. It suggests that this division obscures a reason for law observance that proves decisive much of the time—a sense of reciprocity or mutual obligation that law ought to foster. The following section reviews the confusing and unsatisfactory debate between positivists like Holmes and nonpositivists like Lon Fuller concerning the separation of law and morals. Although law and morality are distinct in some respects, I argue that our thought and language make complete separation of the "is" and the "ought" impossible.

The chapter then notes that efforts to define law are unlikely to succeed without an answer to John Noonan's question, "Why do you want to know?" The usual objective of legal theorists in defining law (even of most positivists although not of Oliver Wendell Holmes) has been to address the question of obligation—to identify directives presumptively entitled to obedience. Taking this theoretical perspective as its starting point, the chapter offers a definition of law that is essentially the opposite of Holmes's: Law consists of those societal settlements that a good person should regard as obligatory. After examining some of the circumstances bearing on the normative issue that this definition emphasizes (and begs), I explain why no theoretical definition of law can be any good.

Following its detour to a different definition of law, the chapter returns to Holmes's essay, examining his proposal to purge moral terminology from the law and his alternative theory of contracts. I contend that Holmes inverted ordinary language for no evident reason, harming rather than enhancing the law's ability to accomplish its ends. The chapter concludes with a reminder of the remarkable influence of Holmes's essay.

WITH FRIENDS LIKE THESE

In addition to its definition of law, *The Path of the Law* reiterates Holmes's views about how law developed and how it should—the same views that Holmes articulated in *The Common Law*. Some writers have claimed that Holmes's picture of law's adaptation to changing circumstances was in tension with his "bad man" concept of law and that *The Path of the Law* offers "conflicting perspectives" on law.[12] A few writers have even maintained that Holmes's essay, which begins with the "bad man" image and then offers his view of law's evolution, follows a "descent–ascent structure."[13] Thomas Grey maintains that the work moves from a "deflationary" to an "elevated" account of law,[14] and Richard Parker asserts that it progresses from cynicism to idealism to romanticism.[15] Oddly, the writers who most revere Holmes appear to be the ones most insistent on "the lack of consistency in his thought."[16]

This chapter will not revisit Holmes's view of law's development, which the last chapter considered at length. The claim that *The Path of the Law* is internally inconsistent and that Holmes's positivism is contradicted by other portions of his essay, however, merits a few comments.

The language that best supports a romantic reading of *The Path of the Law* appears in its very last sentences: "The remoter and more general aspects of the law are those that give it universal interest. It is through them that you . . . connect your subject with the universe and catch an echo of the infinite, a glimpse of its unfathomable process, a hint of the universal law."[17] Two-thirds of the very short (average five-page) commentaries on *The Path of the Law* in the *Harvard Law Review* issue marking the essay's centenary saluted this peroration.[18]

The audience's eyes might have widened, however, as Holmes delivered these words. Had the lecturer suddenly contradicted all that had gone before? Far from offering echoes of the infinite and a hint of the universal law, *The Path of the Law* had insisted that a legal "decision can do no more than embody the preference of a given body in a given time and place."[19]

An attempt to see Holmes's conclusion as more than contradictory or empty rhetoric, however, can be successful. One need only recall Holmes's statements that he did "in a sense worship the inevitable"[20] and that he came "devilish near to believing that might makes right."[21] Holmes not only accepted Darwinian struggle as the order of the universe but also *venerated* power, conflict, violence, death, and survival. Although, as Holmes saw it, a legal decision can do no more than embody the preference of a given body in a given time and place, a sufficiently Olympian observer of the struggles of human beings (and insects) may catch an echo of the infinite, a glimpse of its unfathomable process, a hint of the universal law. As David Luban observes, "[T]he 'hint of the universal law' that Holmes speaks of . . . turns out to be an appreciation of how savage life really is."[22]

Nearly all of the statements that Holmes's admirers treat as proof of his idealism, romanticism, utilitarianism, and moral vision prove compatible on examination with a Nietzschean–Darwinian worldview, yet the attempted reconciliation does not work in the other direction. Holmes's darker statements are rarely subject to rosy interpretations; they are unmistakably what they appear to be. Unless Holmes was the Nietzschean, existentialist, social Darwinist, and Thrasymachian[23] that this book has described, he was indeed incoherent.

One strategy for shielding Holmes (partially) from the kinds of criticisms this book offers is to portray his thought as rich, complex, and contradictory. Another is to declare that he simply did not mean what he said. Robert Gordon wrote, for example, "The 'bad man' turns out to be one of Uncle Alec's practical jokes—a deliberate provocation, a device to shock the audience out of complacency and into an enquiring state of mind."[24] Gordon explained:

> Take the "bad man" and the "prediction theory." This can't possibly be a theory that law has no moral content. "The law is the witness and deposit of our moral life," Holmes says in *The Path,* and elsewhere makes it clear that the law of any age is saturated with "prevalent moral and political theories" as well as "[t]he felt necessities of the time."[25]

Of course one can recognize that moral sentiments shape law (and who could deny it?) and at the same time regard these sentiments as matters of personal taste or as claptrap. Shortly after the passage of *The Path of the Law* that Gordon quotes, Holmes observed that government officials may fail to enact legislation because "the community would rise in rebellion."[26] He wrote, "[T]his gives some plausibility to the proposition that law, if not a part of morality, is limited by it," but he promptly rejected the idea. The limits of public tolerance are "drawn from the habits of a particular people at a particular time," and Holmes in fact "once heard the late Professor Agassiz say that a German population would rise if you added two cents to the price of a glass of beer."[27]

Although Gordon suggests that Holmes must have viewed the "bad man" as a joke and must have valued the moral content of law, on occasion Gordon has appeared to know better. He once wrote that Holmes saw "law and rights [as] only the systems imposed by force by whatever social groups emerged as dominant in the struggle for existence,"[28] and he also wrote of Holmes, "If you are convinced . . . that the growth of law is a Darwinian struggle of powers, interests and unconscious instincts clawing at one another for dominance and survival, the value of being part of the process consists only in being a living link in the food chain, chewing or being chewed."[29]

Thomas Grey maintained that Holmes's declaration, "[I]f my fellow citizens want to go to Hell I will help them," is an "example of Holmes using hyperbole to produce paradox."[30] As one item of proof, Grey noted Holmes's statement in *The Path of the Law* that "[t]he practice of [the law], in spite of popular jests, tends to make good citizens and good men."[31] This statement is a favorite of writers who see Holmes as contradictory but insist that Jeckyll-Holmes prevailed over Hyde-Holmes. Like Gordon, however, Grey has sometimes seemed to know better. He was the author of the insight, noted earlier, that Holmes's speeches on ceremonial occasions never described law "as a force for good . . . whether as the bulwark of liberty, the refuge of the oppressed, the source of order and stability, or the guarantor of prosperity. Their focus is entirely on the intrinsic joys . . . of the lawyer's work."[32] For Holmes, the practice of law made good men only in the sense that it gave them duties and could make them passionate.

Even David Luban, whose perception of Holmes is very close to mine, attempted to resuscitate Holmes at the end of a critical essay on *The Path of the Law*. Luban recited the same declaration Grey did about how the practice of law produces good men, observing that this statement comes "just one paragraph after [Holmes] has introduced the bad man." Luban noted, "The contrast must be intentional. The bad man always treats business as business, and Holmes . . . seems to think that lawyers are different."[33]

But Luban has seemed to know better too. Earlier in the same essay, describing Holmes as a "vitalist," he observed, "[W]hat is noteworthy is that he gives us no hint of what a lawyer's ideal might consist in, beyond having ideals."[34] Luban also wrote:

> [E]specially in his official eulogies . . . for recently deceased Massachusetts lawyers, Holmes adds the unconsoling consolations of stoical devotion to duty, devoid of sentiment and harboring no illusions about higher meaning in lawyer's work. . . . Here is a typical Holmes finale . . . : "We are here—a few men in a room, unhelped, simply stopping for a moment to look the greatest of all facts in the face, to honor the dead, and then like soldiers to go back to the front and fight until we follow our brothers."
>
> By this time Holmes's listeners could surely guess how he would eulogize them. . . . But Holmes was not done: "Both of those whom we commemorate were fighting men and so helped to teach us how to do our fighting—helped us to remember that when war has begun any cause is good, that life is war, and that the part of man in it is to be strong."[35]

Luban observes, "Holmes jerks away even the consoling fiction that lawyers pursue causes they believe right: 'When war has begun any cause is good, [and] life is war.'"[36]

Some scholars' depictions of *The Path of the Law* seem even more idealized. Catharine Pierce Wells declares, "The pragmatic insistence on the primacy of individual perception, the relevance of viewpoint, and the good faith practice of listening as a precondition of knowledge are powerful incentives for respecting—perhaps loving—one's neighbors. For this reason, Holmes's framework is one that may promote a wholesome and moral life."[37] Holmes, who repeatedly declared that "in the last resort a man rightly prefers his own interest to that of his neighbors,"[38] undoubtedly would have balked at Wells's compliment.

David Dolinko's commentary on a version of this chapter published as an article sometimes took the "Holmes couldn't have meant it" tack. Dolinko argued that reading Holmes's work in a "deadly literal" fashion revealed such "obvious" mistakes and "glaring errors" that Holmes probably did not make them.[39] According to Dolinko, responding to what Holmes actually argued in the work his enthusiasts call "the single most important essay ever written by an American on the law" was like shooting fish in a barrel; that task was much too easy. A more charitable hypothesis was that Holmes's predictive theory of law and his advocacy of the "bad man" perspective were "strategies for undermining the misleading picture of law" offered by Dean C. C. Langdell and other late-nineteenth-century thinkers. Dolinko concluded, "Of course [Holmes's] strategies themselves make use of one-sided, exaggerated claims about law that are easy to ridicule."[40] Nevertheless, compared to Dean Langdell, Holmes looked great.

As this book has contended, Langdell and Holmes had much in common, and treating Langdell as a worse villain than Holmes does not alibi Holmes. Moreover, viewing Holmesian jurisprudence as a rhetorical "strategy" or "heuristic device," as Dolinko does, seems to leave this jurisprudence short of greatness and in addition to neglect the extent to which smart people still take it seriously.

The most apt comparison may not be between Langdell and Holmes; refighting their battles may resemble taking sides between the Bolsheviks and Mensheviks. A better comparison might be between Langdell and Holmes on the one hand and Marshall and Lincoln on the other— between American law before and after Darwin. The skepticism of twentieth-century lawyers is so ingrained, however, that few of them have examined this possibility.[41]

Many of Holmes's admirers now grasp at passing phrases, turn a deaf ear to much of his message, treat the central tenets of his jurisprudence as rhetorical gimmicks, and attribute views to him that he would have mocked. I believe that these admirers are wrong to classify Holmes as a utilitarian or pragmatist,[42] but whether they are correct or not, Holmes could have seen law as an exercise of power or of sovereignty without the slightest contradiction. His view of law as power, or as the prediction of judicial decisions from a bad man's perspective, would not have precluded him from arguing that the *content* of law should be shaped by utilitarian objectives. How law functions is one thing, and what it should say is another. The struggle to discover conflict and tension in *The Path of the Law* reveals the determination of some Holmes admirers to minimize the bleak implications of his thought. Unable to deny Holmes's dark side, these admirers treat him as a split personality, then proclaim Jeckyll-Holmes the man behind the mask. The mythical Holmes was always more popular than the man himself.

POSITIVISM AND PREDICTION IN PERSPECTIVE

Holmesian positivism says in essence that the law is what the law does. Sanctions are what count. I may declare, for example, that a teapot is my property. From a Holmesian perspective, I mean that if Professor Helmholz takes the teapot, I can go to court, and the court will order Professor Helmholz to return the teapot to me. Moreover, the court will send the sheriff after Professor Helmholz if he does not comply. Were I unable to secure a judicial order confirming my right to the teapot, I could not sensibly say that the teapot was my property. When I call a teapot my property (and so make a statement of law), I am simply predicting what the courts will do in fact. The introductory paragraph of *The Path of the Law* concluded, "The object of our study . . . is prediction, the prediction of the incidence of public force through the instrumentality of the courts."[43]

Exploring the implications of Holmesian positivism in various contexts reveals its limitations and its artificiality. Viewing a series of issues from the positivist perspective (or trying to) shows that Holmes's definition of law corresponds neither to the ordinary meaning of this word in our language nor to the meaning of law in our lives.

Prediction When the Predictor and the Predicted Are Identical

One defect of Holmes's definition of law has been noted more frequently than any other; from a judge's perspective, predicting legal rulings is mind-boggling. A judge might say to herself, "I would like to decide this case according to law. What is the law?" Justice Holmes might then appear before the judge in a dream and advise her that law is a prediction of what she will do in fact. A judge who began to say to herself, "To decide this case according to law I must predict what I will do," could only hope to wake up.[44]

Although predicting judicial decisions is a small part of the work of judges,[45] it is a substantial part of the work of lawyers engaged in advising clients. Some scholars have doubted, however, that Holmesian positivism appropriately describes law even from a lawyer's vantage point. Henry M. Hart once wrote that he could not understand how the "bad man" view helped lawyers except to make them more effective "counselors of evil."[46] Hart wondered whether the world would be tolerable "if statutes all were drawn, or cases all decided, on the assumption that all lawyers will do this and all clients will want them to."[47]

Do Dissenting Opinions Always Contradict the Law?

When Holmes addressed questions of law in his dissenting opinions, he had little occasion to predict what the courts would do in fact. His fellow justices had done it already. If law is simply a matter of what the courts do in fact, dissenting opinions always have the law wrong.[48]

Other Games

If law is a prediction of what the courts will do in fact, perhaps the rules of baseball are a prediction of what the umpire will do. Like H. L. A. Hart, however, I doubt that they are.[49] I have seen people play baseball without an umpire, and they have followed the rules.

Kangaroo Courts, Nazi Courts, and Massachusetts Courts: Which Courts Count?

Holmes's definition of law purported to be descriptive, but much normativity may lie buried within the word *court*. Power alone does not make a court—as Holmes recognized when he observed that some of a sovereign's commands are enforced by agencies other than courts.[50] Yet Holmes never explained what defines a court or what distinguishes courts from other power-wielding agencies inside and outside government.

I might arm a group of students and, with them, capture Stickney, Illinois. One wonders whether, from a Holmesian perspective, my decrees and judgments would qualify as law until the governor of Illinois mobilized the National Guard and recaptured the town. Some positivists doubtless would carry their concept of law to the point of calling my decrees "the law of Stickney for the moment." Their next step—only slightly less plausible—might be to treat the commands of a bank robber as law.[51]

A bank robber, however, is not a court. I probably am not a court even when cooperative students have captured a village hall and declared me Exalted Justice of the Provisional Revolutionary Tribunal of Stickney. A lynch mob is not a court, and Saddam Hussein is not a court.[52] The word *court* is not self-defining. If this word implies a role, a procedure, a task, a measure of acceptance, or some other indication of legitimacy, Holmes plainly left the work of defining courts (and so of defining law) undone.[53] The uncompleted work, moreover, was apparently a project of normative analysis rather than of power-focused description.[54]

Is Unenforced Law an Oxymoron?

Holmesian positivism denies that unenforced law counts as law. This position may seem plausible in some situations. In others, however, it departs sharply from ordinary understanding.

Consider initially Section 18–6-501 of the Colorado Criminal Code, which provides, "Any sexual intercourse by a married person other than with that person's spouse is adultery, which is prohibited."[55] The statute does not say that adultery is a felony, a misdemeanor, or a petty offense. It imposes no penalty for the act. When a person commits adultery in Colorado, the best prediction of what the courts will do in fact is "nothing." From a positivist perspective, adultery is therefore lawful in Colorado. The law's actions speak louder than its words, and Colorado's purported prohibition of adultery is double-talk.

Similarly, a sign on the highway may proclaim that the speed limit is fifty-five. Every motorist may know, however, that patrol officers do not arrest people for speeding unless they exceed the posted limit by at least five miles per hour. When a motorist drives at fifty-eight miles per hour on the highway, the best prediction of what the courts will do in fact is "nothing." From a Holmesian perspective, the speed limit—the *real* speed limit—is sixty, not fifty-five.[56]

When governmental officials—the state legislature or the state highway patrol—decide unequivocally to refrain from sanctioning any violation of a formal legal prohibition, one may cheer the realism of Holmes's prediction theory. Years before Roscoe Pound suggested a distinction between the "law in the books" and the "law in action,"[57] Holmes emphasized that formal law can differ from the law affecting people's lives.[58] Taking Holmesian positivism seriously becomes difficult, however, when nonenforcement is ad hoc and the product of ignorance, limited economic resources, whim, mercy, kindness, or corruption.

For example, someone who murders a solitary homeless person in an alley at 3:00 A.M. is likely to get away with it. The best prediction of what the courts will do in fact is "nothing." Presumably the killing is un-lawful, yet if Holmes's definition of law were taken literally, it would not be.[59] Perhaps the law in this case is not what a court is likely to do in fact but what a court *would* do if public officials knew all the relevant facts, were honest and principled, and had sufficient resources to capture the killer and prove her guilt. Holmes may have had something like this re-finement of his definition in mind when he said that predictions can be "generalized and reduced to a system" and when he referred to "this body of dogma or systematized prediction which we call the law."[60]

Holmes first articulated his prediction theory twenty-five years be-fore he wrote *The Path of the Law.* Although he declared in his initial itera-tion of the theory that "[t]he only question for the lawyer is, how will the judges act?," he excluded from his calculus "[s]ingular motives, like the blandishments of the emperor's wife." These motives, he said, were "not a ground of prediction" in "the generality of cases."[61] Refining Holmes's concept of law to include only generalized predictions or predictions of appropriate judicial behavior, however, departs from the "bad man" perspective. A bad man does not care why legal pronouncements are un-enforced so long as they are. Corruption and a generalized policy of non-enforcement are all the same to him.[62] David Luban observes:

> There is no hint in *Path* or elsewhere that Holmes understood that risk-benefit analysis by a genuinely bad man 'who cares only for the mate-rial consequences' would consider enforcement probabilities, as well as enforcement outcomes. If Holmes had appreciated this point, I sus-pect he would have seen straightaway that the Bad Man Thesis is pre-posterous. . . .[63]

In defining law, even the simple case of undetected crime may re-quire one to focus on ideals (the ideal of general applicability, for ex-ample) rather than on the deployment of power in fact. In ordinary usage, an official's ignorance of the facts does not alter the law. Bribing a judge might justify a prediction of what the judge's court would do, but an occasional act of bribery does not amend the law. A prosecutor might decline to prosecute a repentant first-offender, but an occasional act of grace does not change the law. Perhaps, despite constitutional provisions to the contrary, a sufficiently generalized revision of law enforcement policy can be seen as amending the law. Even if it can, however, someone who wants to know the law and nothing else must know more than what the courts will do in fact.

How Many Divisions Has the Superior Court?

The divergence of Holmes's definition of law from any ordinary meaning of the term becomes clearer when one asks why Holmesian positivism focuses on predicting the behavior of courts and not the behavior of other governmental agencies. Some observers apparently have viewed Holmes's reference to the courts as incidental. Officialdom frequently uses courts to direct the use of coercive power, but from the bad man's perspective, power alone determines the meaning of the law. Richard Posner, for example, has paraphrased Holmes without speaking of courts:

> The state has coercive power, and people want to know how to keep out of the way of that power. So they go to lawyers for advice. All they want to know is whether the power of the state will come down on them if they engage in a particular course of action. . . . Law is . . . simply a prediction of how state power will be deployed in particular circumstances.[64]

Similarly, Karl Llewellyn declared that "the focus, the center of law, is not merely what the judge does, . . . but what *any* state official does, officially."[65] Holmes's focus on the judiciary, however, was far from incidental; it was a critical part of his positivism.

Before Holmes wrote *The Path of the Law,* he and a like-minded scholar, John Chipman Gray,[66] had published separate papers criticizing what was then the most prominent positivist definition of law. John Austin had defined law as the general command of a sovereign,[67] and Holmes and Gray contended that Austin's definition was too broad.[68] Members of the legal profession did not concern themselves with all of a sovereign's commands. Lawyers considered only those commands that came to the courts for enforcement, and law was a matter of what courts, not other agencies, did. Well before Holmes published *The Path of the Law,* he wrote, "Courts . . . give rise to lawyers, whose only concern is with such rules as the courts enforce. Rules not enforced by them, though equally imperative, are the concern of no profession."[69] Gray objected that if law included every command of the sovereign, it would encompass even "colonel-made and postmaster-made law."[70]

Whatever the situation may have been in Holmes's time, the legal profession today concerns itself with more than the law enforced by courts.[71] No one doubts that administrative law —even "colonel-made and postmaster-made law"—qualifies as law. Thomas Grey has argued, however, that the objection that the Holmesian definition of law is useless to a judge overlooks the definition's original purpose. This definition,

Grey says, was not intended to be of use to a judge. Holmes never meant his predictive positivism to be "a general scientific or conceptual truth about the nature of law."[72] Holmes defined law for practicing lawyers alone.

Grey's argument is intriguing but unpersuasive. If Holmes initially sought to describe law only from the perspective of practicing lawyers, he later forgot that goal. Holmes used positivist, predictive language too often and in too many contexts for anyone to doubt that he viewed this language as expressing "a conceptual truth about the nature of law." When, for example, Justice Holmes wrote for the Supreme Court, "Law is a statement of the circumstances in which the public force will be brought to bear upon men through the courts,"[73] he was not simply de-marking the concern of a specialized profession. Similarly, when Holmes defined "right" as "the hypostasis of a prophesy—the imagination of a substance supporting the fact that the public force will be brought to bear upon those who do things said to contravene it,"[74] he was describing what a right meant to someone who imagined that she had one. Holmes insisted that law was not "sympathetic advice" but "stern monition that the club and the bayonet are at hand ready to drive you to prison or the rope if you go beyond the established lines."[75] He wrote, "All law means that I will kill you if necessary to make you conform to my requirements."[76] These statements are not simply descriptions of what law means to practicing lawyers.

The influence and reputation of *The Path of the Law* certainly rest on the perception that the essay says something about law in general. This work has not attracted high praise merely because Holmes recognized the obvious truth that lawyers, in their professional lives, are concerned with predicting the decisions of judges. Holmes's "bad man" was not in fact a lawyer; he was a consumer of law. Holmes's definition of law was for him.[77]

A passage written by Rudolf von Jhering well before *The Path of the Law* hinted at Holmes's "bad man" imagery. Jhering wrote, "The criminal is not concerned about the purpose of the State or of society. . . . [T]he state says to him: follow your interest, but see to what side the balance inclines when I put punishment in one of the scales."[78] Holmes declared:

> [I]f we take the view of our friend the bad man we shall find that he does not care two straws for . . . axioms or deductions, but that he does want to know what the Massachusetts or English courts are likely to do in fact. I am much of his mind. The prophecies of what the courts

will do in fact, and nothing more pretentious, are what I mean by
the law.[79]

Holmes should have visited with the bad man longer. Contrary to
what this scoundrel told Holmes, he did not care two straws for what the
Massachusetts or English courts would do. He cared what the *sheriff*
would do. The sheriff, not the courts, had the guns, the padlocks, the
battering rams, the handcuffs, the nightsticks, the dogs, the deputies, and
the jails. What the courts did might predict what the sheriff would do,
just as axioms and deductions might predict what the courts would do.
In the end, however, the bad man was concerned about the sheriff. If,
after the courts had spoken, the sheriff would take a bribe and permit the
bad man to flee to Rio, he would laugh at the axioms, the deductions, the
courts of Massachusetts, and the courts of England all together.

A better positivist than Holmes therefore would have defined law
differently: "The prophecies of what the sheriffs will do in fact, and nothing more pretentious, are what I mean by the law." If Holmes had framed
his "power is everything" thesis in this more precise language, however,
no one would have proclaimed *The Path of the Law* the best article-length
work on law ever written.[80] Law plainly is not what the sheriff will do in
fact, for the sheriff may act unlawfully. For example, the sheriff may disregard the orders of a court.

Courts may act unlawfully too. Just as law-abiding sheriffs take their
law from the courts, law-abiding judges take theirs from statute books and
bother authoritative sources (at least when these sources speak clearly).
Once one recognizes that courts can act unlawfully, the Holmesian definition of law collapses. Whatever law may or may not be, it is not a prediction of what the courts will do in fact.

Holmes did not win his quarrel with John Austin. No one maintains
today that law includes only rules enforced by courts and not rules enforced by other agencies. Nevertheless, Holmes's focus on the courts
proved fortuitous. "It is emphatically the province and duty of the judicial
department to say what the law is," Chief Justice John Marshall wrote in
Marbury v Madison.[81] This normative proposition lent color to Holmes's
purportedly hard-edged, descriptive definition. Holmes's concept of law
assumed a norm of American government, and indeed of all civilized governments: Even the bad man looked to the courts to settle his rights. Less
incorrigible than Holmes portrayed him, this shadowy figure submitted
his disputes, not to whoever had the guns, but to decisionmakers characterized by their disinterest and their willingness to hear both sides. The

implicit normativity of Holmes's court-based definition made its defects less evident than they would have been if he had spoken directly of sheriffs, generals, or other public officials with real firepower.[82]

THREE MOTIVES FOR LAW OBSERVANCE: WHY BAD PEOPLE, SAINTS, AND THE REST OF US SOMETIMES OBEY THE LAW

Material Consequences and the Vaguer Sanctions of Conscience
The bad man has crept into the collective unconscious of the legal profession. When I doze off, I may awaken to catch him pushing my pen.

In 1986, for example, the Supreme Court held in *Batson v Kentucky*[83] that prosecutors may not use peremptory challenges to exclude prospective jurors from criminal cases on the basis of race. When I discussed this case with my law school class, my students and I devoted most of an hour to listing the loopholes of *Batson*. The Supreme Court's requirement that a defendant establish a *prima facie* case of discrimination apparently could not be satisfied by showing that a prosecutor had excluded one or two blacks from a jury.[84] In practice, the prosecutor might therefore have one or two "free shots"—enough to eliminate all prospective minority-race jurors in many cases. Moreover, if a defendant succeeded in establishing a *prima facie* case of discrimination, the prosecutor could rebut it by offering racially neutral explanations for her challenges.[85] Such explanations might not be difficult to discover. For example, one prospective juror might have failed to maintain eye contact with the prosecutor,[86] and another might have stared at the prosecutor too long.[87] These ways of evading the apparent holding of *Batson* were only the beginning.[88] By the end of the class, the conclusion seemed plain: any prosecutor worth her salt could drive a truck through the loopholes of the Supreme Court's decision. *Batson* was like the Colorado statute forbidding adultery; it was mostly posturing and pretense. Perhaps the Supreme Court was more interested in ending the appearance of racial discrimination than in changing the reality.

Following the class, a student who worked in a prosecutor's office said to me, "You may be correct, but that decision has changed things a lot downtown." I then recognized that Oliver Wendell Holmes had tricked me again. I had forgotten what law was about. Montesquieu called his classic eighteenth-century study *The Spirit of the Laws*,[89] yet somewhere along the way I had ingested Holmes's *The Spirit of the Loop-*

hole. I had viewed the *Batson* decision from the perspective of a bad man—a prosecutor who wanted to get away with whatever he could. If my student could be believed, many prosecutors were not so incorrigible.[90]

Before *Batson,* the Supreme Court told prosecutors, "As long as you believe that blacks are less likely than other prospective jurors to favor your position in a case, you may challenge them." Many prosecutors did. In *Batson,* however, the Supreme Court declared that challenging blacks for tactical reasons was unconstitutional, and many prosecutors stopped. The difference between the pre-*Batson* regime and the post-*Batson* regime was substantial, yet I had missed it because I had stared too hard at the decision's teeth. The "bad man" prosecutor and the loopholes of cases like *Batson* plainly merit attention, but the "good person" prosecutor merits notice as well. The Holmesian perspective cuts off half the action. It struggles to make law less than it is.[91]

of course

Do Good People Need Law?

Holmes had gone wrong at the first turn, and I had followed him. Contrary to his apparent suggestion, good people do look to law. In assessing the meaning and function of law, they cannot be set aside on the ground that they "find [their] reasons for conduct, whether inside the law or outside it, in the vaguer sanctions of conscience."[92]

Ironically, the belief that human beings possess an innate moral sense is the defining characteristic of the natural lawyer, not of the skeptic or positivist. John Locke maintained that people would recognize core obligations to others even in a state of nature (a state without positive law).[93] For an astonishing moment, Holmes appeared to join him. A true skeptic might better have announced that moral sentiments are not innate; "the vaguer sanctions of conscience" are themselves the product of social institutions like law. Rather than focusing exclusively on sanctions, this skeptic then might have painted a picture of the ways in which law shapes preferences, attitudes, and "the vaguer sanctions of conscience." Indeed, Holmes had outdone Locke. Few, if any, natural lawyers have maintained that good people do not need law. These theorists often have noted explicitly that people who do not need sanctions need guidance.

Neither Socrates nor Aristotle nor Cicero nor Aquinas nor Locke nor Blackstone contended that natural law was all law; the realm of natural law was limited to a few core principles.[94] The distinction between acts that were *mala in se* (or contrary to natural law) and acts that were merely *mala prohibita* (appropriately forbidden although not inherently wrongful) was central to their jurisprudence. Within the realm of things *mala prohibita,* even a saint could not find the reasons for her conduct solely in the sanctions of conscience. Mother Teresa might not have stopped at an intersection if the authorities had posted no stop sign there.

Moreover, reasonably good people may need guidance even in marking the boundaries of things *mala in se.* Although John Locke maintained that people would sense obligations to others in a state of nature, he also contended that self-interest would lead them to underestimate the extent of their responsibilities: "Men being partial to themselves, Passion and Revenge is very apt to carry them too far, and with too much heat, in their own Cases."[95] Only the formation of a civil society could satisfy the need for "a known and indifferent Judge."[96] Similarly, Blackstone maintained that human beings could discover the law of nature by considering what principles would "tend the most effectually to [their] own substantial happiness."[97] Blackstone added, however,

> [I]f our reason were always, as in our first ancestor before his transgression, clear and perfect, unruffled by passions, unclouded by prejudice, unimpaired by disease or intemperance, . . . we should need no other guide than this. But every man now finds the contrary in his own experience; that his reason is corrupt, and his understanding full of ignorance and error.[98]

Perhaps Holmes recognized in a backhanded way that law can work partly through mechanisms other than force. His depiction of the "good man" included a baffling phrase: the good man "finds his reasons for conduct, *whether inside the law or outside it,* in the vaguer sanctions of conscience."[99] Perhaps Holmes's reference to the possibility of acting "inside the law" while still finding the reasons for one's conduct in "the vaguer sanctions of conscience" was meant to acknowledge that, at least in the realm of things *mala prohibita,* no one can rely on conscience alone. People who find their reasons for conduct both "inside the law" and "in the vaguer sanctions of conscience" may be people who would comply with legal requirements even if disobedience would incur no penalty. If, however, this interpretation of Holmes's cryptic phrase is accurate, one wonders why these good people should be disregarded and why "if you want to know the law and nothing else, you must look at it as a bad man." To the extent that law influences people apart from its threat of sanction, you must ask about more than that threat if you want to know the law.

The Excluded Middle: Law Observance and Mutuality

Whether or not Holmes acknowledged in a phrase that law operates partly through noncoercive mechanisms, his "good-man, bad-man" typology missed a central reason for obedience to law. Few people are motivated entirely by concern for others or entirely by a fear of sanctions. These mid-range consumers of law are likely to be affected by both of these motivations and by a third as well—a sense of reciprocity or of mutual obligation. People who are neither totally selfless nor totally selfish may willingly assume a share of the burdens of living in society, but they may balk at assuming a larger than proportional share. The willingness of these consumers to comply with law may depend in part on whether they sense that benefits and burdens are equitably shared.[100]

Somewhere in the psychology of most of us may be an implicit "return-for-giving" or "giving-receiving" ratio. Some people—a few—may give regardless of whether they receive anything in return. These people are called saints. Others may take and never give. These people are called Holmesian bad men. Most consumers of law, however, are neither saints nor bad men. Some may give two, three, or ten times what they receive, yet even these people are likely to cease giving when they sense that the "return-for-giving" ratio has grown too far out of line. Law is one of the social institutions that helps to keep the "return-for-giving" ratio in balance.[101]

Several years ago, Adam moved to a neighborhood in Chicago in which parking regulations were seldom enforced. He frequently found his way and his vision blocked by unlawfully parked, unticketed cars. As Adam grew accustomed to the realities of life in this neighborhood, his own parking behavior changed.

Adam still does not park in traffic lanes, in other people's driveways, beside fire hydrants, or in spaces reserved for the handicapped. When the only available parking space is too close to an intersection to be lawful, however, Adam takes it. Adam was a nicer person and a better citizen when he lived in Colorado. Adam was also happier. When he could improve other people's lives (or, more modestly, facilitate their driving and parking) with confidence that most of them would do the same for him, he felt better about himself and his community.

The lack of parking-law enforcement in Adam's neighborhood has affected his behavior—but Adam is not a Holmesian bad man. Even today, he does not get away with all that he can. Moreover, he would desist from his lawlessness (he really would) if his neighbors would desist from theirs. When Adam must endure the burdens of life among the Holmesians, however, he thinks himself a fool not to capture a portion of the benefits. Neither "the vaguer sanctions of conscience" nor the predicted "material consequences" of parking violations have induced law observance by Adam's neighbors, and Adam is unwilling to do much more than his share. He would prefer a regime of mutual cooperation to one of every person for himself, but he prefers a regime of every person for himself to one of "cooperation for suckers."[102] In Adam's neighborhood in Chicago, the bonds of the social compact have weakened.

Adam does not carry the claim (or rationalization) that "everybody does it" as far as he might. Although he may take the parking space near the crosswalk, he does not take the one marked handicapped even if many of his neighbors would. Were Adam a bad man concerned only for the "material consequences" of disobeying the law, however, the handicapped would have one less space. Sometimes the "vaguer sanctions of conscience" triumph over both Adam's economic calculation of self-interest and his concern that he may be doing more than his share.[103]

And sometimes, to be sure, only threatened material consequences induce Adam to obey the law. Neither concern for others nor a more conditional sense of reciprocity could induce Adam to slow to twenty-five miles per hour while driving on a major highway past a gas station and a general store. Adam nevertheless does slow in Wilson, Wyoming, because he has been told that this "speed trap" finances its government largely through high-priced traffic tickets issued to non-residents.

The vaguer sanctions of conscience may keep Adam from parking in handicapped zones, while threatened material consequences may keep him from speeding in Wilson, Wyoming. With many other issues of law observance, however, Adam's conduct is influenced by the conduct of others. Sanctions matter to Adam less because his own principal reason for law observance is the fear of punishment than because sanctions applied to others reinforce his sense of reciprocity and mutual obligation. Adam, like other *pretty* good people, does need law. A definition of law that leaves out what law means to Adam is woefully incomplete.

THE SEPARATION OF LAW AND MORALS

Holmes announced in *The Path of the Law* that one of his goals was to "dispel a confusion between morality and law."[104] He added, "When I emphasize the difference between law and morals I do so with reference to a single end, that of learning and understanding the law."[105] Legal positivists from John Austin to Holmes (and Holmes's alter ego, John Gray) to Hans Kelsen to H. L. A. Hart have, despite their differences, treated the separation of law and morals as the defining characteristic of positivism.[106] Lon Fuller and other critics of positivism, moreover, have accepted the positivists' formulation of the issue while maintaining that law and morals cannot be separated.[107]

An observer of the debate between positivists and their critics might ask, "What are these people talking about?" Or even, "Is everybody who writes about jurisprudence crazy?" In one clear sense, everyone separates law from morality, and in another clear sense, no one does.

Nonpositivists recognize that law can be unjust—that law and morality are sufficiently distinct to permit the moral criticism of law. Even the declaration of St. Augustine and other natural lawyers that "an unjust law is no law at all"[108] recognizes the distinction. This statement uses the word *law* twice in inconsistent senses. First, when one calls something an unjust law, one does call it a law. This initial usage refers to positive law. Then, when one says that an unjust law is "not law," one means that positive law may not be law in the sense that people should regard it as obligatory.[109] The natural lawyer thus asserts the same separation between positive law and moral law (or morality) that positivists assert when they purport to criticize him. In addition, the critics of positivism recognize that morality may require actions not demanded by law (for example, caring for infirm parents or showing up for a date).

At the same time, the positivists, Holmes included, have recognized that moral sentiments influence the content of law. *The Path of the Law* observed, "The law is the witness and external deposit of our moral life. Its history is the history of the moral development of the race."[110] In one sense, then, law plainly is separate from morals, and in another sense, it plainly is not. Moral sentiments shape law, but law can be immoral.

Someone unable to identify the issue in dispute might become even more baffled upon reading the Hart–Fuller debate, an event considered a notable scholarly watershed when it happened forty years ago. In this debate, H. L. A. Hart, a positivist, conceded the accuracy of most arguments advanced by the positivists' critics. Hart responded, however, that none of the critics' arguments established a "fused identity between law as it is and as it ought to be."[111] Yet Hart did not identify a single critic who had contended that law was always moral—that positive law had fused into just what it ought to be in every jurisdiction from China to Yugoslavia to Iraq.

Insisting on the "inner morality" of even "bad law," Lon Fuller's entry in the debate did not dispel the confusion.[112] Fuller's position was, however, less odd and less dramatic than his insistence on the inseparability of law and morality might have made it seem. Fuller's principal argument was that one often cannot describe positive law—cannot make statements about what the law *is*—without invoking moral norms.[113]

The norms to which Fuller referred concerned both the law's procedural prerequisites and its substantive content. When Fuller spoke of the "inner morality of law," he was referring mainly to procedure. For example, a Nazi accused of war crimes might protest that he had complied with the applicable law of the German state. One familiar response to this sort of defense invokes natural law: A higher law than that of the Third Reich warned the defendant of the wrongfulness of his conduct. Fuller suggested, however, that before turning to natural law, one should consider more closely the meaning and accuracy of the defendant's assertion of compliance with positive law.

Perhaps the defendant's conduct, although contrary to a published German statute, had been ratified after the fact by the Führer himself. The settled rule in Germany was that even secret orders of the Führer could countermand statutory law.[114] If a war crimes tribunal were to ask how the German courts would have viewed the accused war criminal's conduct, the answer would be plain; once the Führer had ratified this conduct, the German courts would have treated it as lawful.

That the Führer had approved the defendant's conduct after the fact, however, would have no bearing on the defendant's argument. The defendant maintained that punishing him for an act that was lawful when he did it would be *unjust,* and the word *law* can be sensibly employed in this sort of moral discourse only if the word has a meaning that makes it relevant to this discourse. In the context of the argument advanced by the accused war criminal, a dictator's secret, *post-hoc* order could not qualify as law. This order might have supplied the rule of decision for the German courts, but even if a war-crimes tribunal were to accept conformity to German law as a defense, it could properly remain indifferent to a rule of decision supplied only by the Führer's *post-hoc* ratification. After-the-fact approval had no bearing on the moral quality of the defendant's act at the time it occurred.[115]

Rather than yield to the rule of decision of the Nazi courts, a war-crimes tribunal could have defined "German law" in a way that served its purpose—to impose only just punishment. Fuller attempted to generalize this insight, maintaining that a system of law requires general, continuing rules announced in advance, consistent with one another, understandable, capable of being obeyed, and adhered to by the agencies charged with administering them.[116] A rule with these procedural characteristics might be immoral, but if it met the requisites of "law," one might speak paradoxically of the "inner morality" of even immoral law.

H. L. A. Hart responded:

> [T]he crucial objection to the designation of these principles of good legal craftsmanship as morality . . . is that it perpetuates a confusion between two notions that it is vital to hold apart: the notions of purposeful activity and morality. Poisoning is no doubt a purposeful activity, and reflections on its purpose may show that it has its internal principles. ("Avoid poisons however lethal if they cause the victim to vomit," or "Avoid poisons however lethal if their shape, color, or size is likely to attract notice.") But to call these principles of the poisoner's art "the morality of poisoning" would simply blur the distinction between the notion of efficiency for a purpose and those final judgments about activities and purposes with which morality in its various forms is concerned.[117]

It was Hart, however, not Fuller, who confounded the distinction between morality and efficiency for a purpose. What one thinks of using an efficacious poison is likely to depend on the merits of the poisoning. One hopes that James Bond will use the most advanced venom while Goldfinger's poison will prove less effective than tap water. Good poisons make good poisonings better and bad poisonings worse. Keeping a law secret, however, always makes the law worse; whether the law is good or bad does not matter. Someone punished for disobeying a law that she had no opportunity to obey is treated *unfairly,* and the injustice does not depend on the secret law's content. The principles comprising Fuller's "inner morality of law" were indeed moral principles, not merely principles of efficiency in implementing a lawgiver's will.

To illustrate the point: Punishing people for driving in the city at forty miles per hour may be a fine idea, but punishing them without first erecting a speed limit sign is unfair. Punishing people for smiling is tyrannical, but the punishment becomes *more* tyrannical when the law against smiling is unpublished. Making *any* law available to the people who must comply with it makes this law better (or less awful) in a way that avoiding ineffective poisons does not make poisoning morally better (or less awful).

Of course keeping a law secret is likely to impede a lawgiver's objective. In that sense, Fuller's moral principles were principles of efficiency too. One could, however, consistently cheer the frustration of a tyrant's objective while decrying her punishment of someone for violating an inaccessible law. That is, one could cheer the inefficiency and boo the immorality. Fuller's "inner morality of law" spoke of law from the consumer perspective. Hart's emphasis on efficiency from the lawgiver's perspective missed the point entirely.

Fuller also noted that statements concerning the content of law typically depend upon moral norms. A nice illustration was provided by James Herget, who asked whether the Constitution empowers Congress to establish an air force.[118] Almost every lawyer would answer this question yes, and the statement that the Constitution empowers Congress to establish an air force is a statement of positive law. The text most directly relevant to this question, however, says only that Congress may "raise and support Armies," "provide and maintain a Navy," and "make Rules for the Government and Regulation of the land and naval forces."[119] If any of the Framers of the Constitution of 1789 anticipated an air force, they knew better than to say so.

Every good law student knows the sort of opinion that a pacifist judge might write to deny Congress the power to establish an air force: "The Constitution provides only for an army and navy, and the function of the judicial branch is to apply the Constitution as it is written, not to keep the Constitution in tune with the times. The Framers of the Constitution specified procedures for amending the document, and the original meaning of the words *land and naval forces* is plain. Even if this court were to take a 'nonoriginalist' perspective, moreover, our decision would be no different. We would hesitate to authorize any action that might make our nation more willing to go to war. We believe that congressional powers that can lead to the killing of innocent people should not be extended beyond their terms."

A good law student also knows that such a judicial opinion would be inappropriate. It would be inappropriate, not because the moral views of its author are plainly unjustified, but because this author would have failed to follow the law. To conclude that this judge disregarded the law, however, one must invoke conventions and understandings that are as much normative as linguistic: "like cases should be treated alike" and "an authoritative text should be interpreted in light of the evident objectives of its framers." These normative-interpretive conventions are strong enough to require judges to supply words not included in the constitutional text. They are strong enough to permit the law student to conclude with confidence, "The Constitution allows Congress to establish an air force. Even a judge who believes that maintaining an air force is immoral must, if true to his oath of office, recognize the air force's constitutionality. I have been to law school and I can make the argument to the contrary, but the argument to the contrary is pettifoggery."

In his commentary on an earlier published version of this chapter, David Dolinko denied that either of the conventions mentioned in the foregoing paragraph qualify as moral principles. He said of the understanding that "an authoritative text should be interpreted in light of the evident objectives of its framers": "*[T]hat* norm surely is not 'moral' at all."[120]

Whether to adhere to the literal meaning of the Constitution or to advance its Framers' larger purposes, however, is a *normative* rather than a purely linguistic question—a question of what *kind* of fidelity a judge owes to the settling power of others. Dolinko recognized that "doing the right thing" includes "acting in conformity to law."[121] That principle— evidently a moral principle—includes judges. A judge who disregarded the objectives of the Framers and offered a narrow reading of the Constitution in order to advance his own pacifist views would merit moral censure, and the principle that "an authoritative text should be interpreted in light of the evident objectives of its framers" is thus a moral *as well as* a linguistic principle.

The fact that Dolinko and I disagree about how to characterize the "evident objectives" principle (and no doubt many others) reveals that separating the "is" from the "ought" (and the "linguistic" from the "moral") is not easy. We lack practice at the task because we usually see no reason to do it. In ordering our experience, we typically speak of all of these things without pausing to notice which is which. We may even combine description and evaluation in a single word: "He gave her a vicious glance." In that sense, Dolinko's and my inability to agree on what qualifies as a moral principle may underscore the practical, everyday compounding of the "is," "ought," "linguistic," and "moral" that makes the positivists' sharp separation of description and evaluation naïve.

Dolinko also regards the principle of treating like cases alike as "not 'moral' at all":

One can view the principle as simply one of the "norms of sound practical reasoning"—a norm of rationality, not specifically moral in nature. Moreover, which respects count as "relevant" will depend on norms independent of the "like cases" principle. If in a given application these supplementary norms are not themselves moral in nature, neither is the "like cases" principle.[122]

Again I disagree. Come with me to visit an isolated tribe, the Wayward, and consider the equality claim of Jotham, eldest son of Uzziah.

From our own social perspective, the Wayward tribe's system of primogeniture (in which a landowner's estate passes automatically on his death to his eldest son) is unjust. Among its defects is its denial of equal treatment to women. Imagine, however, that the Wayward have consistently adhered to their system of primogeniture in every case except one. When Uzziah died, the tribal council awarded his estate, not to Jotham, but to Jotham's younger brother Obed. The council announced no general reform of its system of land tenure in Jotham's case, and it announced no general qualifying principle in the form of, "The father's land shall go to the eldest son except . . . ." The council gave no reason whatever for its action.

Despite the underlying unfairness of the rule of inheritance that Jotham has invoked, I would accept his claim that he has been denied equal treatment and treated unjustly. Just as secret law is unfair regardless of what the law may say, the equality principle is independent of the norms that shape it. It is, moreover, a principle of justice, not just a rule of practical reasoning. People denied equal treatment are treated *unfairly,* even if the unfairness consists simply in failing to adhere to rules applied to everyone else. The skepticism of modern lawyers, however, has led them to disparage even this foundational moral principle.[123]

I would, I recognize, have greater difficulty accepting Jotham's claim of unequal treatment if the tribal council had awarded Uzziah's land, not to Obed, but to Jotham's elder sister Abishom. Equality claims of different sorts often conflict with one another, and choice among them may be unavoidable. Although the principle of equality rarely lends itself to simple, mechanical application, the core intuition that like cases should be treated alike lies at the heart of most conversations about justice and makes them possible.

The normative conventions governing judicial interpretation of the Constitution differ from equally strong conventions governing the interpretation of other laws. Someone who sabotaged the engine of an air force bomber probably would not violate an eighteenth-century penal statute forbidding interference with operations of the "land or naval forces." In the construction of penal statutes, norms of clear warning, of limiting official discretion, and of giving the benefit of the doubt to defendants in matters of law and fact often appear stronger than those of treating like cases alike and of implementing the general purposes of law-givers.[124]

Normative conventions thus can direct answers to questions of positive law even when the words are not there, and they also can direct a judge to disregard the literal meaning of words that are there.[125] Blackstone illustrated both sorts of interpretation with cases that he drew from Pufendorf.[126] A statute forbidding anyone to "lay hands" on a priest forbade injuring a priest with a weapon as well as with one's hands, and a law of Bologna declaring "that whoever drew blood in the streets should be punished" did "not extend to the surgeon who opened the vein of a person that fell down in the street with a fit."[127] Blackstone observed that "the most universal and effectual way of discovering the true meaning of a law . . . is by considering the reason and spirit of it, or the cause which moved the legislator to enact it."[128] He added, "[T]here should be somewhere a power . . . of defining those circumstances which (had they been foreseen) the legislator himself would have expressed."[129] Just as normative conventions may require courts to disregard words that are there and to supply words that are not, they shape and dictate the judicial interpretation of words that bear more than one meaning.

Even more clearly than interpretations of authoritative texts, patterns of decision, common law rules, and customs cannot be discovered empirically but must be constructed normatively. For example, if a buyer were to assert a custom that sellers always pay for delivery, a seller might respond, "No, the custom is different. It is that sellers always pay for delivery except when it will occur in Micanopy, Florida, between 3:00 and 4:00 P.M. on March 28, 2001." Neither the buyer's description of the relevant custom nor the seller's would be inconsistent with prior transactions or decisions. The buyer might respond to the seller's claim, "But the custom you describe would be unprincipled and crazy." This response would carry the dialogue from description to normativity. Every pattern of decisions is subject to multiple descriptions (including the odd sort of description advanced by the Micanopy seller). The choice among these competing descriptions requires normative judgment.[130]

The fact that normative interpretation is unavoidable does not mean that law and morality are coextensive. One can recognize that the Constitution authorizes military forces—even an air force—while criticizing the Constitution for doing so. The process of interpretation, however, remains normative at least in part. The tangle of is and ought cannot be entirely unraveled. The analysis of the interpretative process in which Lon Fuller (and before him Blackstone and Pufendorf) engaged does not exhibit the soft, wishful identification of the "is" and the "ought to be" that positivists have attributed to their critics.[131]

WHY DEFINE LAW?

An armchair sociologist who wished to describe how Americans use the word *law* might conclude, "Law consists of constitutions, statutes, ordinances, administrative regulations, administrative rulings, and judicial decisions. That's about it." This observer might declare, "Those things published by the West Publishing Company of St. Paul, Minnesota, and nothing more pretentious, are what I mean by the law."

This sage's effort to define law from the ground up might stumble over a few cases. Do voluntary sentencing guidelines from which a judge may depart without stating a reason qualify as law? When a prosecutor violates a supervising prosecutor's directive not to enter a plea agreement in a robbery case and then is fired, does the supervisor's directive count as law? If so, does the supervisor's directive to be at work by 9:00 A.M. qualify as law as well?

When challenged to answer these questions, the armchair sociologist might respond: "I know what the relevant rules, customs, and practices are, and I understand their consequences. Why does it matter whether I call them law or not? If forced to resolve the issue, I will say that none of these things are law simply because there is no consensus that they are. In the absence of such a consensus, musing about the issue seems pointless. Every interpretive community may use the word *law* as it likes.[132] I have never heard anyone in America refer to voluntary sentencing guidelines as 'law.' In America, law means constitutions, statutes, ordinances, administrative regulations, administrative rulings, and judicial decisions. That's about it."

John Noonan once wrote that if anyone asks you, "What is law?" your first response should be, "Why do you want to know?"[133] Efforts to define law from the ground up are likely to seem dissatisfying (and insufficiently "theoretical") because the primary reason for seeking a definition of law (at least among legal theorists) is not to explain how this term is used in everyday discourse. The theorists have devoted their ink to the question (lots of it) because, in their view, the answer matters. They believe that the difference between "law" and "not law" has consequences.

In fact, calling a directive "law" privileges it. Someone who has issued a directive and wants it obeyed usually would prefer her audience to treat it as though it were "law." A command that qualifies as law usually has a stronger claim to obedience than a command that does not. Law has a different *moral* status than "not law."

Most law-defining theorists have asked explicitly or implicitly, "What commands should one recognize as law and therefore obey (or treat as presumptively worthy of obedience)?" If, however, the principal reason for defining law is to identify an institution whose directives are entitled to obedience most of the time, the positivists seem to have confounded law and morals more than the natural lawyers. Without always recognizing it, these positivists have struggled to get their ought from an is.[134]

The positivists' task is not inherently impossible. In philosophers' language, moral judgments "supervene" upon factual judgments. In other words, moral judgments are always judgments *about* facts. Two factual situations cannot differ from each other only in terms of some moral quality; they must always differ in ways that one might, in principle, describe in nonevaluative terms. Whenever something differs from something else in a moral quality, it must differ in one or more other characteristics as well.

Imagine, then, a moral quality called "entitled to obedience," and imagine that this moral quality supervenes on one and only one set of facts (or that all situations upon which it supervenes share a common characteristic). A person might define "law" by describing this set of facts (or this characteristic) in nonevaluative language. Such a definition would identify an "is" and an "ought" at the same time. The definition would describe in nonevaluative terms all factual circumstances upon which the moral quality, "entitled to obedience," supervenes. It would call these factual circumstances "law." In theory, a positivist definition of law could therefore address the normative question of obligation.

Now, however, consider a different world, one that the next section of this chapter will contend is our own. In this world, any of a very large number of circumstances tends to obligate, and any of a very large number of circumstances tends to excuse obedience (or even to demand disobedience). Imagine, further, that these circumstances can be combined in nearly infinite varieties. Suppose, for example, that the pronouncements of a democratic government have a stronger claim to obedience than the pronouncements of a monarch, that rules that apply to everyone have a stronger claim to obedience than rules that apply to an individual or to a small group, that rules that are usually enforced have a stronger claim to obedience than rules that are rarely enforced, that published rules have a stronger claim to obedience than unpublished rules, and on and on. In this tangled world, no *manageable* definition of law could specify the directives upon which the moral quality, "entitled to obedience," supervenes.

No one in fact has offered a definition of law that purports to resolve comprehensively the question of obligation. Some positivists, however, have undertaken a less ambitious task—specifying a set of circumstances that *presumptively* entitle governmental pronouncements to obedience. At least initially, this task seems too easy. When many circumstances tend to obligate, one can pack as many or as few of them as one likes into a "presumptive" definition. For example:

> By law, I mean all pronouncements that are intended by the public officials who promulgate them to promote the welfare of society as a whole.

> By law, I mean all authorized pronouncements of reasonably democratic governments.

> By law, I mean societal rules that have been announced in advance, that are general in form, and that are enforced largely through procedures affording hearings before impartial tribunals.

> By law, I mean all governmental rules that have been authorized by written or unwritten constitutions recognized by most members of a society as authoritative.

Anyone can list a set of mildly motivating circumstances and call herself a theorist. When one is seeking a presumption and not an answer, being a theorist should be a snap. That so many people have botched the job therefore seems surprising.

Although John Austin, Hans Kelsen, and H. L. A. Hart implicitly or explicitly addressed the question of obligation,[135] some recent positivist writers have given up the normative ghost and have advanced what Philip Soper calls "a remarkably counterintuitive claim"[136] —that there is no *prima facie* obligation to obey the law.[137] Moreover, unlike most other positivist writers, Holmes's goal probably was not to address the question of obligation. His implicit message was tougher—that the question of obligation was not worth asking. Law was simply an exercise of power so that one could not sensibly ask what commands should be obeyed. Sanctions and only sanctions made law.[138] To speak of a moral duty to obey was pretense—one more effort of human beings to envision themselves personal friends of God.[139]

Just as Holmes's goal was not to address the question of obligation, his goal probably was not to describe how the word *law* is used in everyday discourse. However, a list of only two reasons—the normative and the sociological—for seeking an answer to the question "What is law?" does not exhaust the possibilities. If one really were a bad man, for example, or if one were a lawyer advising clients, Holmes's answer would become plausible. Perhaps Steve Allen's character "the Question Man" or Johnny Carson's "Carnack the Magnificent" could identify the question to which Holmes's definition was the answer.[140]

WHAT IS LAW?

An appropriate definition of law for the purposes most often pursued by legal theorists might be the opposite of Holmes's: Law consists of those societal settlements that a good person should regard as obligatory.[141] This definition begs rather than answers the question of obligation, but the question it begs may be the right one—one that lies at the root of most theoretical efforts to define law.[112] The following discussion of obligation will carry this chapter some distance from *The Path of the Law,* but criticism of Holmes's concept of law probably should be accompanied by an indication of what law does mean to good people. Some preliminary notes on the suggested definition:

1. The word *settlement* seems preferable to words like *command* and *directive.* This word is broad enough to encompass several types of law whose distinctiveness was emphasized by H. L. A. Hart—commands of the sort found in criminal codes; rules facilitating private ordering through wills, marriages, contracts and the like; and rules governing dispute resolution and the creation and alteration of law. For example, a state constitution might declare that the legislative power shall be vested in a General Assembly. This declaration, although undoubtedly a law, would not directly command anyone to do something or to refrain from doing something. Viewing this declaration as a "settlement" seems easier than viewing it as a "command."[143]

2. For the most part, Americans view only governmental pronouncements as law. The phrase *societal settlements* is somewhat broader. This phrase leaves open the possibility that custom may qualify as law in some societies (and perhaps even in today's international community). Under the proposed definition, however, only customs regarded as obligatory qualify as law; other widely observed customs, such as the rules of etiquette, do not. Treating directives that are neither "societal" nor "govern-

mental" as law would seem odd (parental commands, for example, or the rules and regulations of a private university). Nevertheless, when the goal is to address the question of obligation, the conventional limitation of the concept of law to governmental or societal settlements may not be very helpful.

3. When the definition speaks of settlements that a "good person" should regard as authoritative, it declares that the appropriate perspective for determining what qualifies as law is that of a person who takes seriously her moral responsibilities to others. It emphasizes that the appropriate vantage point is not that of Holmes's bad man. Everyone, however, should be a good person; that statement is close to a truism. The definition therefore could be broadened from "good people" to "everyone" without changing its meaning.[144]

4. To some extent, the words *societal settlement* may incorporate the customary requirement that law be "general." Very specific governmental commands (for example, a government officer's directive to a subordinate to file a letter) are not usually seen as law. Although these specific orders may be given by officers who represent society, it would seem strange to describe them as "societal settlements" or as law. Some specific directives, however, may be seen as law: "I sentence you to ten years" or "Judgment for the plaintiff." Unlike an official's order to file a paper, these products of formal deliberative processes may be seen as embodying more than the conclusions of the people who voice them. Metaphorically (or mystically), they may be seen as "societal settlements" and as "law." A defendant who refuses to obey a court's judgment then may be regarded as violating the "law" embodied in the court's command. The suggested definition does not resolve the question of how general law must be. Although the generality of a settlement is one of many circumstances that affect whether the settlement will be recognized as law, I am unsure that limiting the concept of law at the outset to general settlements advances rather than conceals the normative inquiry.[145]

Legal scholars generally have addressed the question of obligation in two stages. They have asked what rules qualify as law and then what circumstances justify the disobedience of law. For the most part, moreover, the scholars who have addressed the first phase of the inquiry (law recognition) have neglected the second (determining when disobedience is appropriate). Although these scholars have noted that civil disobedience sometimes may be justified, they have left the question of when this disobedience may be justified to others.[146] Similarly, those who have written about civil disobedience have neglected the law-recognition process. They apparently have viewed law recognition as a task presenting issues distinct from the normative issues they seek to address.[147]

It seems appropriate, at least initially, to collapse the two related stages and to ask directly what purported social settlements a good person should respect—in other words, which purported social settlements qualify as law.[148] The attempt to answer this question directly will reveal that it does not yield to a definition, a formula, or a rule of recognition. Moreover, the conventional bifurcation of the issue into "law identification" and "obedience to law" helps only slightly.[149] The respect owed settlements that purport to be binding varies with countless circumstances.

For one thing, the respect owed a directive that on its face governs all members of a society may vary with one's social role. In a debate with Stephen A. Douglas, Abraham Lincoln declared that if he were elected to the Senate he would vote to enact a fugitive slave law. "[A]lthough it is distasteful to me," Lincoln said, "I have sworn to support the Constitution."[150] At the time of Lincoln's statement, the most relevant provision of the Constitution was Article IV, Section 2, Clause 3, which provided that a slave who fled to a free state "shall be delivered up on Claim of the Party to whom [the escaped slave's] Service or Labour may be due." Had the delegates to the Constitutional Convention not agreed to this clause, there would have been no Constitution.

Article IV, Section 2, Clause 3 did not expressly require Congress to enact a fugitive slave law, but interpreting the clause as self-executing would have rendered it a dead letter. Lincoln emphasized this point when he explained his own interpretation of the clause: "[T]here is a constitutional right which needs legislation to enforce it. . . . [Having sworn to support the Constitution,] I cannot conceive that I do support it if I withheld from that right any necessary legislation to make it practical."[151] Because a normative-interpretive convention required members of Congress to supply words not there,[152] Abraham Lincoln announced his willingness to support a fugitive slave law—a law that he considered repugnant.

Surely no slave, however, owed any respect to the fugitive slave clause,[153] and someone who was neither a slave nor a member of Congress might have occupied a position different from both Lincoln's and the slave's. This person would have had options not open to a person in bondage. Most notably, if white, adult, and male,[154] he could have sought amendment of the fugitive slave clause through the political process.[155]

Nevertheless, unlike Lincoln (if successful in his campaign to become a senator), this person would not have sworn to respect the settlement embodied in Article IV, Section 2, Clause 3.

Especially with the benefit of hindsight, one might conclude that no member of American society should have respected the fugitive slave clause.[156] Returning an escaped slave to her master was so great an evil that Lincoln might better have refused to swear to support the Constitution, thereby disqualifying himself from serving in Congress. Or, even better, Lincoln might have sworn to support the Constitution and then not done so.[157] Nevertheless, different roles in society plainly give rise to different obligations to treat purported settlements as binding.[158]

Two more commonly recognized determinants of the respect owed purported social settlements are the legitimacy or illegitimacy of the authority that has promulgated these settlements[159] and the justice or injustice of the settlements themselves. Even the interplay between these two core considerations may suggest that the question of obligation is complex and that respect for law requires painful choices.

On the one hand, even the declarations of an essentially legitimate government may not merit obedience. The Constitution of the United States was ratified through what was (at the time) an extraordinarily democratic process.[160] The ratification occurred after public debate of the highest quality, and ratification of the Constitution established the most democratic nation-state on earth. Nevertheless, most of us now admire the dissenters who had the wisdom and courage not to respect the Constitution's fugitive slave clause as "law."[161]

On the other hand, even the declarations of a tyrant may have a claim—a moral claim—to obedience. If, for example, only Joseph Stalin has posted stop signs, set speed limits, and declared whether to drive on the right- or the left-hand side of the road, a driver's regard, not for Stalin, but for the safety of her fellow citizens ought to prompt obedience. (Concerted disobedience of traffic regulations designed to promote political change might be appropriate, however.) Between the kinder, gentler pronouncements of tyrants and the inhuman pronouncements of legitimate governments lie a variety of purported societal settlements that sometimes give good people difficult choices.

Indeed, within a single government, some legitimate lawgiving authorities may have more authority and greater settling power than others. In *Cooper v Aaron,*[162] the Supreme Court observed that "Article VI of the Constitution makes the Constitution the 'supreme Law of the Land.'" Noting Chief Justice Marshall's statement in *Marbury v Madison*[163] that "[i]t is emphatically the province and duty of the judicial department to say what the law is," the Court declared, "It follows that the interpretation of the Fourteenth Amendment enunciated by this Court . . . is the supreme law of the land. . . ."[164]

The Court thus equated its interpretation of the Constitution with the text of the Constitution itself.[165] In an extreme case, however, an opinion of the Court might contradict the constitutional text, and in this situation, a citizen (and, even more clearly, a president sworn to protect and defend the Constitution) ought to honor the text rather than the Court's opinion.[166] Both Thomas Jefferson and Andrew Jackson went further. As president, Jefferson pardoned people whom the federal courts had convicted of violating the Sedition Act, which he considered unconstitutional. In a letter to Abigail Adams in 1804, Jefferson explained, "[N]othing in the Constitution has given [the judiciary] a right to decide for the Executive, more than to the Executive to decide for them. Both magistracies are equally independent in the sphere of action assigned to them."[167]

In 1832 Andrew Jackson used similar language to explain his veto of a bill to recharter the Bank of the United States (a decade and more after the Supreme Court had upheld the Bank's constitutionality): "The Congress, the Executive, and the Court must each for itself be guided by its own opinion of the Constitution. Each public officer who takes an oath to support the Constitution swears that he will support it as he understands it, and not as it is understood by others."[168] The apparent claim of Jefferson and Jackson was that chief executives (at least)[169] should resolve constitutional issues without regard to opinions of the Supreme Court. Like the Supreme Court's assertion of judicial authority in *Cooper v Aaron,* this assertion of executive authority was excessive.

In a rare departure from ordinary practice, each of the nine justices of the Supreme Court signed the Court's opinion in *Cooper v Aaron.*[170] The Court's claim of ultimate interpretive authority in this case had strong provocation—Little Rock's "massive resistance" to the school desegregation decreed by *Brown v Board of Education.*[171] The hateful crowds, the National Guard troops deployed by a governor to block a schoolhouse door, the federal troops required to permit nine black students to enter Central High—all suggest the fearful consequences of not according general settling power to Supreme Court interpretations of the Constitution.[172] Presidents and the rest of us sometimes must defer to the Court's rulings even when we take a different view of the Constitution, even when we have not been parties to lawsuits before the Court, and even when we have not ourselves been afforded opportunities to be heard. The Supreme Court may have gone overboard in *Cooper v Aaron,* but Jefferson and Jackson were equally far from the deck on the ship's other side.[173]

Decisions of the Supreme Court, however, often may have less settling power than legislative enactments. Every scholar who has examined the issue apparently agrees that *Brown v Board* yielded little school desegregation; progress toward desegregation began only when Congress embraced this goal in the Civil Rights Act of 1964,[174] As an empirical matter, doubters and dissenters proved more willing to accept a settlement produced in a political forum than to yield to one reached by a court. The Civil Rights Act of 1964 was shaped by representatives of all parts of the nation under the skillful leadership of a new president following the assassination of John F. Kennedy. Perhaps there were reasons—moral reasons—why this watershed event had greater settling power than the Supreme Court's decision in *Brown.*[175]

To view Supreme Court decisions generically and to compare them with legislation or with the text of the Constitution, however, often may sweep too broadly. Abraham Lincoln argued that the Supreme Court's ruling in *Dred Scott v Sanford*[176] bound the parties to that case and, in addition, that third parties should respect the Court's conclusion that Dred Scott remained a slave despite his presence on free soil.[177] Lincoln, however, refused to yield to the Court's broader holdings—first, that Congress's prohibition of slavery in federal territories deprived slaveowners of their property without due process of law and, second, that no person of African descent could ever be a citizen of the United States.[178] Although Lincoln declared in his debates with Stephen A. Douglas that his respect for the Constitution would lead him to support a fugitive slave law, he said that he would vote to prohibit slavery in the territories despite *Dred Scott.*[179]

Lincoln noted that only defiance of the Supreme Court's decision could enable the Court to overrule it, and he added:

> [D]ecisions apparently contrary to that decision, or that good lawyers thought were contrary to that decision, have been made by that very court before. It is the first of its kind; it is an astonisher in legal history. It is a new wonder of the world. It is based upon falsehood in the main as to the facts.[180]

All of the circumstances that Lincoln mentioned bore on what settling power the *Dred Scott* decision should have. Chief Justice Earl Warren recognized that a decision's settling power depends on case-specific circumstances when he discouraged concurring and dissenting opinions in *Brown v Board* and when, in circulating the first draft of his opinion to members of the Court, he noted that the draft had been "prepared on the theory that the opinion[ ] should be short, readable by the lay public, non-rhetorical, unemotional and, above all, non-accusatory."[181]

The appropriateness of a person's disregard of a purported settlement depends not only on the character of the settlement but also on the form and extent of this person's defiance. Again, however, the issue of obedience does not yield to a formula. Martin Luther King's *Letter from Birmingham City Jail* declared, "One who breaks an unjust law must do it *openly, lovingly* . . . and with a willingness to accept the penalty."[182] Others have echoed King's insistence that open, nonviolent disobedience coupled with an acceptance of the prescribed punishment is the only legitimate form of noncompliance with civil authority.[183] Some have added that although disobedience of an unjust rule itself can be appropriate, disobedience of another rule cannot.[184] On this view, the violation of a criminal trespass statute to protest a war of aggression would be improper if the protester had no quarrel with the criminal trespass statute itself.

Harriet Tubman, however, a former slave who returned nineteen times to slave territory to lead over three hundred others to freedom,[185] did not defy rules openly and with a willingness to accept the penalty. If she had, she could not have rescued very many slaves. Tubman surely has a place among the saints.[186]

At a war conference on July 20, 1944, Colonel Heinz Brandt moved aside the briefcase of Colonel Klaus von Stauffenberg so that Brandt could better see a map. A few minutes later, a bomb in Stauffenberg's briefcase exploded, killing Brandt and three others but causing only minor injuries to its primary intended target, Adolf Hitler.[187] The motives that prompted Stauffenberg to try to kill Hitler were more complex than those that prompted Harriet Tubman to free slaves, and Stauffenberg's actions were far more violent. My guess, however, is that Klaus von Stauffenberg is among the saints too. Even prohibitions of homicide are not quite categorical imperatives.[188]

As this chapter has indicated, the extent to which prohibitions are enforced and the extent to which they are observed by others bear on their claims to obedience. Settlements that both on paper and in operation distribute social burdens equitably have stronger claims to obedience than settlements that do not. Moreover, civil authority cannot properly demand obedience to secret rules or compliance with contradictory commands. The requisites of law emphasized by Lon Fuller—publication, comprehensibility, consistency, prospectivity, and the like—also influence the recognition of binding settlements.

This discussion has not exhausted all of the circumstances that influence the identification of law. That task would be impossible. The discussion has indicated, however, why no definition of law can be any good. "Law" is a matter of more-or-less rather than yes-or-no.[189] Law identification depends on assessments of social roles, the legitimacy of the authority that has promulgated a rule, the justice or injustice of the rule itself, the form and extent of one's noncompliance, the degree to which the rule has been enforced or obeyed, the observation of procedures that make compliance possible, and countless other circumstances.

Ronald Dworkin once asked how a constitution could have "any power at all to create . . . rights." This constitution might have been approved long ago and might have lacked unanimous support then. Dworkin said that the

> answer must take some form such as this. The constitution sets out a general political scheme that is sufficiently just to be taken as settled for reasons of fairness. Citizens take the benefit of living in a society whose institutions are arranged and governed in accordance with that scheme, and they must take the burdens as well, at least until a new scheme is put into force. . . .[190]

Dworkin's answer emphasizes that only a reasonably just constitution obligates. In addition, this answer suggests that whether a constitution truly qualifies as a constitution and as law depends as much or more upon its content and the extent of its acceptance as upon its historical pedigree. Dworkin, moreover, appropriately identifies the principal source of obligation as a sense of reciprocity (accepting burdens along with benefits). Yet Dworkin does not discuss the extent of a person's obligation when a generally fair and accepted constitution—a constitution whose benefits she welcomes and that she would not renounce in favor of a state of nature—contains a fugitive slave clause.

David Luban offers a useful checklist that refines Dworkin's concept of legal obligation.[191] Luban argues that cooperative schemes[192] create obligations when

(1) they create benefits;

(2) the benefits are general: They accrue to the whole community;

(3) widespread participation in the scheme is necessary for it to succeed;

(4) the scheme actually elicits widespread participation; and

(5) the scheme is a reasonable and important one.[193]

Luban's list probably comes as close as any categorical checklist can to identifying those societal settlements that a good person should regard as obligatory. Like Dworkin's theory, however, it is incomplete. For one thing, "cooperative schemes" do not always come neatly packaged. If someone in the antebellum period concluded that the U.S. Constitution as a whole satisfied the checklist criteria, should she have felt an obligation to honor the fugitive slave clause? Or was this clause a *distinct* "cooperative scheme" that badly failed the "general benefits" and "reasonability" requirements?[194]

Moreover, Luban's checklist does not seem to leave room for obligation to vary with social role. Whether one is a senator, a judge, a person who has discovered a fugitive slave in her hayloft, or a free black ineligible to hold office does not appear to affect one's answers to the checklist questions. Similarly, Luban's categorical approach does not treat obligation as a matter of degree. The list, for example, does not indicate that one might treat the fugitive slave clause as "half-law"—with enough settling power, say, to make it improper to injure a public official in order to rescue a fugitive slave[195] but without enough settling power to lead one to return a slave or to refrain from concealing the slave by lying to the official.

Bifurcating the question of obedience into two stages does seem helpful. One might employ Dworkin's concept of legal obligation or Luban's to identify bodies of doctrine (the laws of the state of Florida or the customs of the sea) that appear to be presumptively entitled to obedience. Or, more simply, one might use the word *law* as it is employed in everyday discourse (law "from the ground up"). A person who disobeys Dworkin-law, Luban-law, or law as it is understood by people who do not theorize about it should bear the burden of justifying her disobedience. The word *law* in this two-stage inquiry merely allocates the burden of justifying noncompliance and need not be defined very precisely. One should recognize, moreover, that the presumption in favor of obedience may not always be strong.[196]

In his first inaugural address, just after taking the oath of office from the author of the *Dred Scott* opinion, Abraham Lincoln promised faithful enforcement of the fugitive slave law. Then he reiterated his unwillingness to respect the holdings of *Dred Scott*. He articulated a position somewhere between that of President Jackson's bank veto message and the position of the Supreme Court in *Cooper v Aaron:*

> [I do not] deny that [constitutional decisions of the Supreme Court] must be binding in any case upon the parties to a suit as to the object of that suit, while they are also entitled to very high respect and consideration . . . by all other departments of Government. And while it is obviously possible that such decision may be erroneous in any given case, still the evil effect [of] following it . . . can better be borne than could the evils of a different practice. At the same time, the candid citizen must confess that if the policy of the Government upon vital questions affecting the whole people is to be irrevocably fixed by decisions of the Supreme Court, . . . the people will have ceased to be their own rulers, having to that extent practically resigned their Government into the hands of that eminent tribunal.[197]

What Lincoln said about the Supreme Court might be said of every other law-giving or law-settling authority, and what he said about the people might be said of every person. Respect for the settling power of others is indispensable if a person is to live in society, yet she should not defer so completely that she ceases to be her own ruler. To remain fully human, she must retain the power to choose and must accept responsibility for her actions.[198]

Lincoln concluded that respect for the settling power of the Constitution demanded support of a fugitive slave law, yet respect for the settling power of the Supreme Court did not require acquiescence in the *Dred Scott* decision. Lincoln confronted challenging issues of responsibility and citizenship with sensitivity and judgment.[199] It might have been easier for him to think of law just as an exercise of power, as a dogmatic datum, as a prediction of what the courts will do in fact.

Lincoln had learned his law from Blackstone, however, and law meant more to him than the prediction of judicial decisions. At the age of twenty-nine, in one of his earliest public addresses, Lincoln urged "reverence for the laws" as "the political religion of the nation":

> As the patriots of seventy-six did to support the Declaration of Independence, so to the support of the Constitution and Laws, let every American pledge his life, his property, and his sacred honor;—let every man remember that to violate the law, is to trample on the blood

of his father, and to tear the character of his own, and his children's liberty. Let reverence for the laws, be breathed by every American mother, to the lisping babe, that prattles on her lap—let it be taught in schools, in seminaries, and in colleges; let it be written in Primers, spelling books, and in Almanacs;—let it be preached from the pulpit, proclaimed in legislative halls, and enforced in courts of justice.[200]

One cannot revere predictions of what the courts will do in fact; patriots have never pledged their lives, their property, or their sacred honor to the prediction of judicial decisions; and no mothers have told their babies to predict and honor whatever the courts will do. Lincoln's view of law observance became more sophisticated with the passage of time and with the challenge of *Dred Scott*. His rhetoric became less flowery. Even in subdued form, however, Lincoln's rhetoric about reverence for law would evoke raised eyebrows today. We owe our raised eyebrows partly to thinkers like Holmes.

Holmesian positivism falsifies Lincoln's experience. Holmes could not see the complexity, the difficulty, and the richness of the choices that confronted Lincoln, Andrew Jackson, Harriet Tubman, Klaus Stauffenberg, Martin Luther King, the crowds outside Central High in Little Rock, and the young people who defied them. What Lincoln said of Douglas might better have been said of Holmes: "[H]e is blowing out the moral lights around us."[201]

In fact, the same respect for the settling power of government that led Stephen A. Douglas to support *Dred Scott* also led him, following his defeat by Lincoln in the presidential election of 1860, to give his support to the Union. When Lincoln spoke in his inaugural address of the authority of law and of its limits, Douglas stood close to him to underline his endorsement of Lincoln's efforts to maintain the nation intact. A brisk wind was blowing, and Douglas held Lincoln's stovepipe hat.[202] That evening, "in a hall decorated with shields and flags and brilliantly lighted with gas, Douglas escorted Mrs. Lincoln to the inaugural ball, and at midnight he danced the quadrille with her."[203]

Following the attack on Fort Sumter, Lincoln asked Douglas to the White House and showed him a draft of the proclamation he intended to issue the next day. Douglas had one suggestion: Rather than call for seventy-five thousand volunteers, "I would make it 200,000."[204] Months earlier, Douglas had told the Senate, "No man will go further than I to maintain the just authority of the Government, to preserve the Union, to put down rebellion, to suppress insurrection, and to enforce the laws."[205] Following Fort Sumter, in an address to the Illinois General Assembly, Douglas declared that party creeds and platforms must be set aside. "The first duty of an American citizen is obedience to the constitution and laws of the county. . . . Give me a country first, that my children may live in peace."[206] One critic asked, "What means this evident weakness of Mr. Douglas for Mr. Lincoln?," and another suggested that Douglas had "gone over to the Republicans."[207]

Douglas's action contributed notably to the unity of the North. When he died at the age of forty-eight with the Civil War barely underway, his final words were, "Tell my children to obey the laws and uphold the Constitution."[208] Douglas probably did not mean, "Tell my children to uphold the best predictions of what the courts will do in fact." A closer paraphrase might be, "Tell my children to uphold the settlements that all of us must honor if we mean to live with one another in peace."

MORAL TERMINOLOGY AND THE
ALTERNATIVE THEORY OF CONTRACTS

In *The Path of the Law,* Holmes listed five words to illustrate the sort of moral terminology he proposed to banish from law—rights, duties, malice, intent, and negligence.[209] Of these, the word *duty* appeared to be the principal object of his scorn.[210]

Holmes indicated the force of his objection to this word in his presentation of the alternative theory of contracts:

> Nowhere is the confusion between legal and moral ideas more manifest than in the law of contract. Among other things, here again the so called primary rights and duties are invested with a mystic significance beyond what can be assigned and explained. The duty to keep a contract at common law means a prediction that you must pay damages if you do not keep it,—and nothing else. If you commit a tort, you are liable to pay a compensatory sum. If you commit a contract, you are liable to pay a compensatory sum unless the promised event comes to pass, and that is all the difference. But such a mode of looking at the matter stinks in the nostrils of those who think it advantageous to get as much ethics into the law as they can.[211]

Holmes proposed to "wash [the notion of duty] with cynical acid and expel everything except the object of our study, the operations of the law."[212] With the success of his positivist project, lawyers have come to view "breach of duty" as a conclusory term meaning "any conduct to which the law attaches burdensome consequences."

This view, however, turns the word *duty* upside down. When the state of Florida takes Ernest's house to build a highway, it does not violate a legal duty. When Clare burns Ernest's house to the ground while negligently performing stunts in an airplane a few feet above Ernest's roof, Clare does violate a legal duty. In each case, however, the law imposes essentially the same material consequences upon the taker or destroyer of Ernest's house. When the state takes Ernest's house to build a highway, it must pay him what a jury thinks his house is worth. When Clare destroys Ernest's house by crashing an airplane into its roof, Clare, too, must pay Ernest what a jury thinks his house is worth.

When an act is not considered wrongful so long as one pays, we do not speak of a duty to refrain from the act. When an act is considered wrongful even if one pays, we do speak of duty not to perform the act. To people who use the English language in orthodox ways, the word *duty* tells people what the law expects of them, not what consequences it attaches to their conduct.[213]

Society does not view Clare's destruction of Ernest's house in the same way that it views the Florida Highway Department's destruction of Ernest's house, and it expresses this judgment by applying the words *breach of duty* to Clare's conduct and not to the Highway Department's. The words tell Clare (and everyone else) that Clare has done something we wish she had not done. The phrase expresses our judgment that the "alternative theory of eminent domain" makes sense but the "alternative theory of low-altitude stunt flying" does not.[214]

Holmes insisted that the law should tell people only what it would do to them and not what it expected of them. He did not explain why. A mood of unsentimental, clear-eyed realism somehow required that the law not speak of its ends but only of its means. The case of Ernest's house was, I confess, not my illustration. It was Holmes's:

Leaving the criminal law on one side, what is the difference between . . . statutes authorizing a taking by eminent domain and the liability for what we call a wrongful conversion of property where restoration is out of the question? In both cases the party taking another man's property has to pay its fair value as assessed by a jury, and no more. What significance is there in calling one taking right and another wrong from the point of view of the law?[215]

Holmes added immediately after this passage:

It does not matter, so far as the given consequence, the compulsory payment is concerned, whether the act to which it is attached is described in terms of praise or in terms of blame, or whether the law purports to prohibit or allow it. If it matters at all, still speaking from the bad man's view, it must be because in one case and not in the other some further disadvantages, or at least some further consequences, are attached to it by the act of the law.[216]

To a Holmesian bad man, law is a system of prices, and only material prices matter. The law's price may include damages, an injunction, a contempt citation, a fine, a prison term, or even death by hanging. Nevertheless, a man tough enough to pay the price always has the option of noncompliance with the law's directives.

Holmes, however, balked at this evident implication of his positivism. He qualified his claim that there was no greater reason to apply words like *breach of duty* to wrongful conversions of property[217] than to takings by eminent domain with this preface: "Leaving the criminal law on one side." Holmes, the author of the alternative theory of contracts (and the alternative theory of torts)[218] did not advance an alternative theory of criminal punishment. More strikingly, Holmes rescinded his banishment of moral terminology—and welcomed back even the murky term *duty*—in some tort and contract cases:

> [T]here are some cases in which a logical justification can be found for speaking of civil liabilities as imposing duties in an intelligible sense. These are the relatively few in which equity will grant an injunction, and will enforce it by putting the defendant in prison or otherwise punishing him unless he complies with the order of the court. But I hardly think it advisable to shape general theory from the exception. . . .[219]

Holmes again advanced a baffling position without explaining it. Why he failed to assert the "alternative theory of everything" remains a mystery. As the law's price increased and changed in kind (from awards of damages to injunctions, contempt citations, and jail sentences), Holmes apparently abandoned descriptive positivism and reverted to traditional moral terminology. That he failed to recognize the implications of his positivism seems unlikely, yet Holmesian moralism seems almost as unlikely as Holmesian stupidity.

Perhaps, in a momentary lapse, a flicker of normativity did infect

Holmes. When the law *really* sought compliance with its commands—when courts imposed severe, afflictive sanctions to enforce these commands—the language of duty seemed, even to Holmes, more appropriate than the language of pricing.

Holmes's midstream leap to the moralist horse, however, raised more questions than it answered. Holmes apparently agreed that the law meant what it said when it used the word *duty* in criminal cases and in injunctive actions. Why, then, did the law not mean what it said when, in an action for damages, it called Clare's careless stunt flying a breach of her duty to Ernest? When the law's response to a tort (or to a breach of contract) is an award of damages, does this response truly indicate indifference between committing the tort (or breaking the contract) and satisfying the award? Would use of the word *duty* be justified in an action for *punitive* damages? *Should* Claire have an option free from any hint of moral censure to risk burning down Ernest's house as long as she is willing to pay the price?

Some history may help to explain Holmes's apparent incoherence. Twenty-five years before publishing *The Path of the Law*, he wrote:

> The notion of duty involves something more than a tax on a certain course of conduct. A protective tariff on iron does not create a duty not to bring it into the country. The word imports the existence of an absolute wish on the part of the power imposing it to bring about a certain course of conduct, and to prevent the contrary. A legal duty cannot be said to exist if the law intends to allow the person supposed to be subject to it an option at a certain price. . . . The imposition of a penalty is therefore only evidence tending to show that an absolute command was intended (a rule of construction). . . .
>
> Liability to pay the fair price or value of an enjoyment . . . is not a penalty; and this is the extent of the ordinary liability to a civil action at common law. In a case of this sort, where there are no collateral consequences attached . . . , it is hard to say that there is a duty in strictness. . . .[220]

This first statement of Holmes's alternative theory described it from the perspective of "the law" or the lawgiver. Holmes declared that when "the power imposing" a law wishes "to bring about a certain course of conduct," it creates a duty. When this power wishes to allow alternatives, however, its sanctions should be viewed as a tax. The nature and magnitude of the sanctions imposed are relevant, but only as evidence of the lawgiver's intention. Holmes's initial presentation of his alternative theory was unsatisfactory only in failing to offer any support for the idea that some common-law lawgiver had truly intended to afford tortfeasors a free option to kill, injure, and destroy property as long as they were prepared to pay the price.

In *The Path of the Law,* Holmes presented his alternative theory from a very different perspective—that of a consumer of law. He spoke of what your duty to keep a contract means to you—"a prediction that you must pay damages if you do not keep it."[221] He noted that he was "still speaking from the bad man's point of view."[222] As with Holmes's prediction theory,[223] what apparently began as a qualified thesis emerged as a grander conceptual truth about the nature of law.

In speaking of law as the prediction of judicial decisions, Holmes moved over time from the viewpoint of a lawyer advising clients to that of a bad man or consumer of law; in describing his alternative theory, Holmes again changed perspectives—this time, from that of a lawgiver to that of a consumer of law. The switch was so much quicker than the eye that even the magician seemed not to notice it.

Holmes, who initially distinguished the imposition of a legal duty from the imposition of a tax on conduct, spoke in *The Path of the Law* of abandoning the concept of duty altogether. Talk of exceptional cases in which one might speak of "duties in an intelligible sense" persisted, but this talk had become unintelligible. From the bad man's perspective, all of law is a tax on conduct. The bad man cares no more for "duty" than he does for axioms and deductions. In damage actions, injunctive actions, and criminal proceedings alike, his concern is simply what the courts will do to him. In Holmes's words, "A man who cares nothing for an ethical rule which is believed and practiced by his neighbors is likely nevertheless to care a good deal to avoid being made to pay money, and will want to keep out of jail if he can."[224] This person's perspective requires an alternative theory of everything, but Holmes failed to keep his perspectives straight.

The Path of the Law has molded American legal consciousness for more than a century, and lawyers now carry gallons of cynical acid to pour over words like *duty, obligation, rights,* and *justice.* Holmes's alternative theory of contracts, however, remains what it was at the beginning—a hopeless jumble of ill-considered prescriptive and descriptive ideas.

Although Holmes did not assert an alternative theory of everything, many of his heirs in the law and economics movement have. These disciples have taken Holmes's declaration in *The Common Law* that "general principles of criminal and civil liability are the same"[225] a bit further than

Holmes did himself. To these economically minded scholars, the criminal law (and all of law) is nothing but a system of pricing.

For example, Richard Posner has suggested that, were it not for the fact that some criminals are insolvent, criminal law could be abandoned altogether. The law of torts determines the optimal price for harmful conduct, and if all criminals could pay the full social costs of their behavior, the deterrence of antisocial behavior could be left to tort law.[226] Imprisonment in Posner's view is necessary only for criminals who have caused more social harm than they can pay for. Moreover, before sentencing someone to imprisonment (a sanction that takes money out of the public treasury), courts always should exhaust the offender's financial resources through a fine (a sanction that puts money into the public treasury). Only offenders without money or other financial resources should go to jail.[227]

One apparent implication of Posner's view—an implication that he seems to have overlooked—is that imprisonment should be authorized for ordinary tort and contract defendants who lack funds. Until these defendants (like the people we now call criminals) face a risk of imprisonment, they will lack appropriate incentives for efficient or socially desirable behavior. Posner's approach does not explain why many harmful acts that give rise to civil liability have not been made crimes.[228]

Law and economics scholars speak of optimal deterrence. They voice their concern that excessive punishment would deter "efficient crimes." Readers of their analyses might wonder whether we do not punish murder more severely because we worry that we might not get enough of it.[229] By extending Holmes's alternative theory of contract and tort throughout the legal universe, law and economics scholars have made Holmes's theory more coherent—and also more chilling and absurd.[230]

Although, in the area of contracts, Holmes apparently offered his alternative theory as a matter of description, the appropriateness of this theory depends upon a normative judgment. One plausible ethical view is that when a person can break a contract, pay damages to the nondefaulting party, and still profit from the breach, she ought to break the contract. In this situation, the defaulting party is better off; the nondefaulting party is apparently no worse off; and the breach increases aggregate social utility. Law and economics scholars refer to contractual default in this situation as "efficient breach."[231] When society's judgment is that the defaulting party ought to default, we surely should not call the default a breach of duty. We might better speak of a duty to *break* one's promises.[232]

There is, however, a competing ethical view. Broken promises are among the harmful things that human beings do to other human beings, and damages often cannot remedy the injuries that broken promises inflict.[233] If our social judgment is that contractual default remains objectionable even when the defaulting party pays damages, the alternative theory of contract is inappropriate. We might better speak of duty.[234]

Frederick Pollock thought the moralistic position closer to the ordinary person's understanding of ordinary contracts. Pollock noted that when a person contracts with a tailor for the delivery of a coat, he does not envision himself as making a bet with the tailor. Similarly, the purchaser does not see himself as purchasing an insurance policy. The purchaser wants a coat.[235]

A defaulting tailor might report that the day before he was scheduled to deliver a coat, a billionaire named Trump noticed the coat and offered to pay him five thousand dollars to deliver it to Trump rather than to the person who had ordered it. The tailor then might return the purchaser's money with interest and might add something to cover the cost of purchasing a coat elsewhere. Economically minded scholars might praise the tailor for a wealth-maximizing breach, but Frederick Pollock and the purchaser might judge the tailor's act wrongful.[236]

Amidst the jumbled jurisprudence of the realist Karl Llewellyn, a coherent sentence sometimes appeared. Here is one:

> [The right to recover damages for breach of contract] could rather more accurately be phrased somewhat as follows: if the other party does not perform as agreed, you can sue, and *if* you have a fair lawyer, and nothing goes wrong with your witnesses or the jury, *and* you give up four or five days of time and some ten to thirty percent of the proceeds, and wait two to twenty months, you will *probably* get a judgment for a sum considerably less than what the performance would have been worth—which, if the other party is solvent and has not secreted his assets, you can in further due course collect with six percent interest for delay.[237]

Llewellyn offered this sentence shortly after deriding Roscoe Pound as "a man partially caught in the traditional precept-thinking of an age that is passing."[238] As Llewellyn characterized the views of Pound, "It is a heresy when . . . Holmes speaks of a man having liberty under the law to perform his contract or to pay damages, at his option."[239]

Llewellyn's observation suggests, however, why (even from an economic perspective) the payment of damages often is not a satisfactory alternative to the performance of a contract, and why realism argues against rather than in favor of the alternative theory of contract. If Holmes's theory makes sense, it does so only for the defaulting party who does not force resort to process, who does not squabble, who resolves doubts about what he owes in favor of the nondefaulting party, and who promptly sends the nondefaulting party a check for this amount. The normative version of Holmes's alternative theory—the version now apparently endorsed by law and economics scholars—depends on a formalist fiction, the "juridically assumed" adequacy of legal and other remedies for breach of contract. Only this fiction enables scholars to treat as "efficient" many breaches of contract that plainly are not. When efficiency is the goal, encouraging performance (or rescission by mutual consent) is probably preferable in the overwhelming majority of cases to encouraging resort to costly dispute resolution procedures.[240]

For plausible reasons, however, the common law has been reluctant to tie contracting parties too tightly to their promises.[241] Treating damages as normatively equivalent to performance may be appropriate for some kinds of contracts and not for others. For purposes of this chapter, these issues need not be resolved. The important point is simply that whether one endorses Frederick Pollock's view of ordinary contracts or the economists' relentless ethic of wealth maximization, the law should say what it means. When the law does not seek to encourage the performance of contracts, it should speak in terms of unfreighted alternatives. When, however, it prefers performance, it should use words like *duty*. Contrary to the claim of Oliver Wendell Holmes, descriptive honesty does not demand the abandonment of traditional moralistic language.

Words in fact are cheap; and if words of censure can discourage harmful or inefficient conduct even slightly, they are worth the price. When language describing the law's normative judgments succeeds in shaping consciousness and influencing conduct, this language is likely to be far more cost effective than damage awards or other sanctions. There can be only one explanation for the failure of Holmes and of modern law and economics scholars to embrace moral terminology as a masterpiece of efficiency: Such a mode of looking at the matter "stinks in the nostrils" of those who think it advantageous to get as much morality out of the law as they can.[242]

—

Holmes once wrote of "the secret isolated joy of the thinker, who knows that, a hundred years after he is dead and forgotten, men who never heard of him will be moving to the measure of his thought,——the subtle rapture of a postponed power . . . which to his prophetic vision is more real than that which commands an army."[243] Holmes surely was writing about Holmes, and more than one hundred years after *The Path of the Law,* descriptions of this article as an "acknowledged masterpiece in jurisprudence," "the single most important essay ever written by an American on the law," and perhaps "the best article-length work on law ever written" confirm Holmes's prophetic vision of his intellectual power.[244]

At the conclusion of a tour of Holmes's dark, elegant, engaging, and destructive essay, however, the praise seems flawed. Morton Horwitz's judgment appears more appropriate: "With 'The Path of the Law' Holmes pushed American legal thought into the twentieth century."[245] The only thing flawed about this pronouncement is that Horwitz apparently meant it as a compliment to Holmes, to the century, and to American law.

Chapter Eight

The Beatification of
Oliver Wendell Holmes

THE SOURCES OF HOLMES'S REPUTATION

To an obvious question—how and why a man brutalized by war became the great oracle of American law—there are obvious answers. Oliver Wendell Holmes was brilliant. He wrote captivating prose. He had extraordinary charm. He took his work seriously and drove himself hard. Some of his writings offered a needed corrective for the mechanistic legal thought of turn-of-the-century America. Moreover, history has judged Holmes right and most of his Court wrong on the two most important constitutional issues of his time—the protection to be afforded freedom of expression and the permissibility of social welfare legislation. This book does not deny his greatness.

Although these explanations of Justice Holmes's reputation are both accurate and adequate, they are not quite complete. The fictionalized Holmes of Catherine Drinker Bowen's *Yankee from Olympus* said of the massive Hopkinson portrait that dominates part of the reading room of the Harvard Law School Library, "That isn't me, but it's a darn good thing for people to think that it is."[1] In explaining Holmes's reputation, one should note not just his intellect but also his height (six-foot-three)[2], his eyes,[3] his bearing, and his mustache.

One should note as well the lack of plausible liberal heroes on the bench of the U.S. Supreme Court during the first three decades of the twentieth century. As ill-suited as Holmes was for the role, he may have been as close to a liberal hero as frustrated progressives could find.[4] One must note, too, that Holmes's misanthropic letters reached print (contrary to his wishes)[5] only after his reputation was secure. Finally, one should note the public relations efforts on Holmes's behalf (deliberate mythmaking in Grant Gilmore's opinion)[6] by Felix Frankfurter and other young admirers of Holmes.

G. Edward White concluded, "Holmes' 'greatness' was . . . the conscious product of a systematic campaign of publicity, a campaign in which Holmes participated. Holmes was fortunate to have as one of his principal boosters a person who was eminently suited to launch such a campaign and highly motivated to do so [Frankfurter]."[7] White declared, "The 'discovery' of Holmes in the last two decades of his tenure on the Court testifies to the fortuitous process by which judicial reputations are created."[8]

Frankfurter was born the same year that Holmes became a justice of the Massachusetts Supreme Judicial Court. When they met in 1912, Frankfurter was thirty and Holmes seventy-one. White reports that, after their first meeting, Frankfurter

> began . . . to write Holmes flattering letters. One . . . said that "from the first time I came in contact with you, as a freshman in the Law School, through your *Common Law*, you had . . . 'the gift of imparting ferment.'" "That this bounty," Frankfurter continued, "should be enriched by the passion and persuasiveness of the living fire is a good fortune that makes my indebtedness everlastingly alive."
>
> This letter set the tone for Frankfurter's early correspondence with Holmes. . . . One familiar with Frankfurter's career can easily recognize both the excessively flattering tone and the stilted language, common in his correspondence with persons he regarded as mentors or patrons. And one familiar with Holmes' career could anticipate the pleasure he would take in the receipt of such flattery, notwithstanding the awkward way in which it was phrased.[9]

Reviewing the Holmes-Frankfurter correspondence, Sanford Levinson observes that "genuine dialogue" is "almost entirely absent from this collection" and that "[i]f anyone ever collected the letters of, say, the president of the Frank Sinatra fan club to [Sinatra], I suspect they would have much the same tone of Frankfurter's missives to Holmes."[10]

Four years after meeting Holmes, Frankfurter organized a symposium in the *Harvard Law Review* to commemorate Holmes's seventy-fifth birthday.[11] In the symposium, he said that Holmes's contribution to the law in his commerce clause and due process opinions was "the outstanding characteristic of constitutional history in the last decade" and that "[t]o discuss Mr. Justice Holmes' opinions is to string pearls."[12] In 1922,

Frankfurter published a second flattering article[13] and also persuaded the editors of the *New Republic* to commemorate the twentieth anniversary of Holmes's appointment to the Supreme Court with a congratulatory editorial.[14] In 1926, Frankfurter solicited contributions to an issue of the *New Republic* to celebrate Holmes's eighty-fifth birthday. His own contribution to the issue spoke of the "tender, wise and beautiful being who is Mr. Justice Holmes," adding that Holmes "vivifies life for all who come within his range."[15] In 1931, with Holmes still a member of the Supreme Court, Frankfurter edited and contributed to a volume celebrating Holmes's ninetieth birthday. The volume included praise from Learned Hand, Benjamin Cardozo, Morris Cohen, John Dewey, John Wigmore, and Walter Lippmann.[16] Following Holmes's death, Frankfurter continued to celebrate Holmes's contributions to law and life.[17]

Harold Laski was twenty-two and Holmes seventy-five when the two men met in 1916.[18] Liva Baker observes that following this meeting, Laski wrote Holmes that the occasion had been

> the realisation of one of my dreams—and if I could write a fairy-story of the happiness men hope for I should try to analyse the vigorous refreshment you gave to all I hold most dear. I do not say "thank you"— not merely because it is inadequate but because from one's master one learns that it is simply duty to receive. You teach our generation how to live.[19]

Baker observes, "Laski set in this first note to Holmes . . . the tone that dominates Laski's side of the correspondence, a flattering and reverential one, every letter a genuflection."[20]

Four years after meeting Holmes, Laski edited and published the first collection of Holmes's nonjudicial writings.[21] Although Holmes wrote in the preface to this work that he was "unable to do more than run my eye over" the manuscript, Sheldon Novick reports that "he actually read the proofs carefully, and submitted corrections."[22] Laski also published *Mr. Justice Holmes—for His 89th Birthday*[23] and *The Political Philosophy of Mr. Justice Holmes.*[24]

Liva Baker observed that Frankfurter and Laski turned Holmes

> into a judicial ancestor of the New Deal and dedicated civil libertarian, neither of which he was. But their outspoken veneration inspired others, and Morris Cohen, . . . Max Lerner, and Francis Biddle . . . soon joined the cult of Holmes's admirers. Writing in the professional journals, they focused on the liberalism they had found in Holmes's juris-

prudence, a liberalism they also happened to embrace. In the popular press—*Atlantic Monthly, New Republic, Harper's*—they disseminated the wit and wisdom of the man.[25]

Over the course of his years as a Supreme Court justice, Holmes hired thirty high-ranking graduates of the Harvard Law School as his "law secretaries."[26] These clerks worked in an office adjacent to Holmes's at his house on I Street.[27] They paid his household bills, kept his checkbook,[28] summarized briefs and records, and carried out his instructions to "embellish this [opinion] with citations from my favorite author [Holmes of course]."[29]

Holmes gave his secretaries little official work. He encouraged them to read books, attend plays and lectures, golf, and socialize. One clerk noted that his "most regular duty was to take [Holmes] to walk from five to six, after his return from the Court."[30] Another spent four days on the job before receiving a work assignment. In the interim, he heard Holmes's economic views, visited with Mrs. Holmes, dined with Justice and Mrs. Holmes at the Willard, observed a Supreme Court argument, golfed, and received a tour of Holmes's personal library.[31] In conversations with his secretaries, Holmes recounted tales, true and false, of his war experience and sought, in the words of I. Scott Messinger, "to create a mythical image of himself."[32]

When Felix Frankfurter began to select Holmes's clerks following the death of John Chipman Gray, he assured Holmes, "I think you need have no fear that our candidates will possessive [*sic*] any obtrusive Christian virtues."[33] Holmes instructed Frankfurter not to nominate a married man "as it means a major interest outside his work." He explained, "It is true that the work is not very much but if baby has the megrims, papa won't have the freedom of mind and spirit that I like to find."[34] Ten years later, Frankfurter apparently had forgotten his duty, and Holmes reminded him: "I would not have taken [W. Barton] Leach had I known earlier that he was married. . . . I want a free man, and one who may be a contribution to society."[35] Holmes's former secretaries ultimately published at least thirty-one books, articles, and book reviews praising him.[36]

HOLMES'S MESSAGE AND HIS TIMES

Indisputable brilliance, an eloquent style, great wit and charm, a famous father, heroic service in wartime, a stunning mustache, longevity, historic vindication on some great issues of his time, and the service of admiring public relations agents all contributed to Holmes's reputation. Still the explanation does not seem complete. At least in academic circles, the esteem in which Holmes is held does not appear to rest on myth and misunderstanding but rather on the message he delivered.

This book has argued that Morton White mischaracterized America's intellectual revolution at the end of the nineteenth century. Contrary to the argument of White's *The Revolt against Formalism,* [37] the principal target of this revolution was not formalism or deductive reasoning; it was moral realism or natural law. Oliver Wendell Holmes was at the forefront of this revolution, and his contribution towers above the rest.

Holmes was not alone, however, and over the course of the twentieth century, moral skepticism like his came to dominate nearly every field of knowledge. The revolution that Holmes helped lead would have happened without him. Holmes led this revolution, however, partly because the disillusionment induced by his war experience fit neatly with the social Darwinism that he discovered "in the air" [38] and then embraced.

With the smell of war in his nostrils, Holmes concluded that every cause—the abolition of human slavery included—was a personal taste of no notable significance. The postwar Holmes ranked the prewar Holmes with the Trotskyites, the pacifists, and the Christian Scientists. He evidently thought himself a fool to have believed in a cause beyond himself. Experiencing the death of comrades, the flow of senseless orders, the sight of lifeless bodies piled deep in the trenches, the rush of blood from his mouth, a bullet in the neck, a bullet in the chest, and a bullet in the ankle, Holmes concluded that right could never be more than the will of the strongest—"what a given crowd will fight for."

The postwar Holmes adopted as his motto the Darwinian truism, "Winners win" or "survival of the fittest" (with "the fittest" defined as "those who survive"). He reiterated this truism in countless ways: The prophecies of what the courts will do in fact, and nothing more pretentious, are what I mean by the law; the foundation of jurisdiction is physical power; truth is the power of a thought to gain its acceptance in the marketplace; if you want to know the law and nothing else, you must view it as a bad man; when a government may prohibit, it may prohibit with the privilege of avoiding the prohibition in a certain way; there can be no such thing as a right created by law against the sovereign by which the right is created; the duty to keep a contract means only a prediction that you must pay damages if you do not keep it; legislation is a means by which a body puts burdens disagreeable to itself on the shoulder of somebody else; the natural outcome of a dominant opinion must prevail even if it will take us to hell; and no test of excellence can be found except correspondence to the actual equilibrium of force in the community. Although many later lawyers did not take moral skepticism as far as Holmes did, the message he brought from the Civil War killing ground found a receptive audience.

Chapter Nine

Ending the Slide from Socrates and Climbing Back

The current ethical skepticism of American law schools (in both its utilitarian and law-as-power varieties) mirrors the skepticism of the academy as a whole. Some twentieth-century pragmatists, extending their incredulity further than Holmes, have abandoned the idea that human beings can perceive external reality—not only right, wrong, and God (issues on which Holmes took a skeptical stance) but also gravity, suffering, and even chairs (issues on which Holmes was a realist).

These pragmatists maintain that the only test of truth is what works,[1] and a century of pragmatic experimentation has given that question a clear answer: Pragmatism and moral skepticism don't. They are much more conducive to despair than to flourishing. They fail their own test of truth. We have walked Holmes's path and have lost our way.

SKEPTICISM AND SOCIETY

I do not know the extent to which intellectual movements shape society or if they do so at all. Nevertheless, "the nation's mood is sullen."[2] The vices of atomism, alienation, ambivalence, self-centeredness, and vacuity of commitment appear characteristic of our culture.[3] Americans have become indolent, cynical, and bitter[4]—envious of those above, reproachful toward those below, and mistrustful of those around them.[5] In 1960, 58 percent of Americans agreed that "most people can be trusted"; in 1994, only 35 percent did.[6] A sense that the people around us are looking out for themselves and that we will be suckers unless we become a little bit like them seems pervasive.[7] A distinguished national study group concludes, "[O]ur democracy is growing weaker because we are using up, but not replenishing, the civic and moral resources that make our democracy possible."[8] Our malaise is remarkable partly because many indicators of the material conditions of our lives—employment rate, inflation rate, longevity, educational level, water and air quality, occupational safety, and others—have improved in recent decades.[9]

Current American politics are the politics of resentment—resentment of government especially,[10] but also of the rich, of the poor on welfare, of white-collar criminals, of street criminals, of drug dealers, of financial institutions, of taxes, of unions, of extravagantly paid executives, of the media, of health care providers, of insurance companies, of tobacco companies, of drunk drivers, of child abusers, of date rapists, of pornographers, of prying journalists, of partisan prosecutors, of political action committees, of terrorists, of telemarketers, of militant feminists, of lawyers, of landlords, of auto repair shops, of public utilities, of teenage mothers, of absconding fathers, of corporations, of polluters, of environmentalists, of paperwork, of bureaucracy, of computers, of computer technicians, of people who have benefited from affirmative action (minorities and women especially), of people who have benefited from traditional favoritism (whites and men especially), of prisoners with access to weight-lifting equipment, of entrepreneurs who have prospered while their customers have remained poor, of homosexuals, of homophobes, of evangelists, of Muslims, of new-agers, of illegal aliens, and of legal aliens. Of course our resentments are justified (yours and mine, that is), but resentments move in a circle.[11]

Our selfish consumerism has turned us into the world's principal debtor nation. We buy much more than we produce or earn,[12] and the largest part of what we consume is electronic junk. Eighty percent of the leisure time of Americans is devoted to passive consumption (essentially solitary consumption), and most of this passive consumption consists of watching television.[13] Our art has become blunt, ugly, angry and dissociative.[14] Our popular culture is violent and bitter.[15]

The number of inmates in state and federal prisons increased from 196,000 in 1972 to 1,159,000 in 1997—a nearly sixfold increased in twenty-five years.[16] A similar explosion in local jail populations brought the total number of Americans behind bars to 1,726,000.[17] Nearly one out of three black men in their twenties is currently under some form of penal supervision—prison, jail, probation, or parole.[18] Between 1975 and 1998, the proportion of U.S. income received by the poorest 20 percent of the population declined 22 percent while that received by the wealthiest 5 percent increased 35 percent.[19] Homelessness is evident on the streets of every city. As Albert Borgmann observes, the nation's troubled mood is evident "not only in . . . broadly measurable phenomena but also in diffuse and anecdotal ways, in numberless incidents of careless service, shoddy work, wasted time, scattered trash, and mindless consumption."[20]

To say so is reminiscent of doomsayers since Plato, but the signs of social disintegration are especially manifest among the young. Almost every measure confirms that America's youth are in trouble.[21] Although the rate of teen pregnancies has declined 17 percent since 1990, nearly one of ten women between the ages of fifteen and nineteen became pregnant in 1996, the last year studied.[22] This rate was twice that of England and Canada and ten times that of the Netherlands and Japan.[23] Approximately one-third of all children born in the United States and three-quarters of black children are born out of wedlock.[24] Most fathers of these children assume no responsibility for their care or support.[25] To the limited extent that anyone can measure this closeted phenomenon, child abuse has increased.[26]

Despite a recent decline, the juvenile homicide rate in 1997 was twice what it had been in 1985.[27] Within three years—in 1997, 1998, and 1999—teenagers and one preteenager in Mississippi, Arkansas, Kentucky, Pennsylvania, Oregon, Colorado, and Georgia brought firearms to school and began to fire at random, killing twenty-six students and three teachers and wounding sixty-nine others in the seven incidents.[28] The number of deaths caused by random school shootings in the years prior to 1997 was zero. Thirty percent of all high school seniors report that, at some point within the past two weeks, they have drunk five or more alcoholic drinks in a row.[29] Between 1982 and 1996, the number of children in foster care grew by 93 percent.[30] Since 1970, the percentage of teens and children who are overweight has increased approximately 150 percent.[31] One high school student in five reports that she has seriously contemplated suicide within the past year, and the number of suicides among young people has tripled since the 1950s.[32]

One cannot blame teen pregnancies on Oliver Wendell Holmes. The intellectual revolution that Holmes helped to spark has affected nearly every field of knowledge, and this revolution surely would have happened without him. How much this revolution has influenced today's culture and practice is anyone's guess. One can speak only of affinities, symbols, parables, and paradigms. Nevertheless, when Perry Farrell, the lead singer of Porno for Pyros, shouts the central lyric of twentieth-century American jurisprudence, "Ain't no wrong, ain't no right, only pleasure and pain,"[33] another storm cloud may appear on the horizon. Perhaps, amidst signs of cultural discouragement and decay, one should expect to hear this lyric from orange-headed, leather-clad rock stars as well as Richard Rorty and Richard Posner.

A NEW EPISTEMOLOGY AND AN OLD PATH

As American culture and pragmatism foundered, post–World War II writers supplied a better test of truth.[34] This new epistemology goes by many names—coherency, reflective equilibrium, holism, and inference to the best explanation.[35] As Michael Moore describes the core idea, "Any belief, moral or factual, is justified only by showing that it coheres well with everything else one believes. . . . [O]ne matches one's own particular judgments with one's more general principles without presupposing that one group must necessarily have to yield where judgments and principles contradict each other."[36] Nelson Goodman explains, "[R]ules and particular inferences alike are justified by being brought into agreement with each other. A rule is amended if it yields an inference we are unwilling to accept; an inference is rejected if it violates a rule we are unwilling to amend."[37] Howard Margolis offers a distinct but related proposition: "[W]e recognize patterns in making sense of the world; we . . . use patterns to guide activity in the world."[38]

We have become increasingly aware that human reasoning does not resemble the operations of a hand-held calculator as much as it does the workings of a computer ranging over a large set of everchanging data to determine a "best fit" line. In trying to make sense of our experience, we use all the tools at our command—including tacit knowledge,[39] emotional knowledge,[40] empirical generalization, normative generalization, and the testing of normative and empirical hypotheses against new experience. Both consciously and unconsciously, we generalize, test generalization against experience, and generalize again. We collapse analogy, induction, and deduction into a single continuous process. We seek patterns in complex, holistic, and provisional ways, continuously updating our understanding of those patterns as we observe the world more closely. We don't just make these patterns up.

Pragmatism, by treating the utility of perceptions and patterns in shaping the future as the only test of their truth, has undervalued their importance in making sense of the present and the past. Where pragmatism invites people to "construct" reality and await possible payoffs,[41] the new epistemology emphasizes the need to make sense of our experience.

Working to make the world more comprehensible does lead to payoffs, but we require no reward beyond coherency itself. In focusing entirely on consequentialist payoffs, pragmatism puts second things first.

An earlier chapter of this book presented an analysis of the problem of obligation that illustrates how people reason about values and how the new epistemology works. Like the man who was astonished to discover that he had been speaking prose all his life, you may be surprised that you have used this epistemology for as long as you can remember and probably longer.

The earlier chapter offered this sort of interplay between the general and the specific: Should I accept Martin Luther King's belief that all legitimate disobedience of public authority must be open? This view attracts me when I consider King's marches and sit-ins, but it is not a belief that fits well (or at all) when I consider Harriet Tubman's journeys along the underground railway. Can I at least join King in the belief that legitimate disobedience must be nonviolent? Probably not; what do I believe about Klaus Stauffenberg's attempt to assassinate Adolf Hitler? Should I conclude, then, that the directives of murderous tyrants like Hitler are not entitled to obedience? Well, what about Hitler's traffic regulations? Must legitimate "law" always be prospective? Must it always be general? Must it always be published?

In testing provisional hypotheses—both ethical and empirical—one seeks to attain the highest level of generality that one can consistent with one's specific beliefs, and one may abandon specific beliefs that do not "fit" otherwise very powerful generalizations. When the attempt to generalize fails, however (as mine did in trying to resolve issues of law recognition and obligation), one reluctantly accepts an inability to discover clear patterns and learns to tolerate disorder. As Albert Einstein explained, "Everything should be made as simple as possible, but not more so."[42]

One then may discover that the inability to articulate clear patterns does not mean that one has made no progress at all toward their discovery. Patterns, like law, are a matter of more-or-less—sometimes blurry and sometimes sharp. The attempt to fit beliefs into patterns may have yielded an inarticulate "best fit" line. When one then confronts a new question of obedience (Should I resist the draft? How guilty should I feel about smoking marijuana? Would anything really be wrong with cheating on my taxes when everyone else seems to be doing it?), one's answer may be informed by inarticulate but reasonably coherent views concerning law observance in general, views that may have been formed in part by thinking about Martin Luther King, Harriet Tubman, Abraham Lincoln, John Wilkes Booth, Klaus Stauffenberg, Operation Rescue, Little Rock's massive resistance to school desegregation, and a false 1998 deposition by President Bill Clinton concerning his personal conduct. Whether one is a Holmesian "bad man," a stern authoritarian, or a person who often parks illegally but never takes a space marked handicapped, one's position on a "law-authoritarianism" scale may be shaped by a series of experiences and beliefs that, consciously or unconsciously, one has managed to fit into a pattern.

This epistemological model suggests a conclusion inconsistent with Holmes's declaration that our tastes and values are "finalities."[43] To suppose that one's position on such things as the "law-authoritarianism" scale is dogmatic or simply a matter of taste is probably wrong. You may not be able to explain why you are no more authoritarian than you are, and I may not be able to give you "an argument" about why you should become more or less authoritarian. But you are in fact seeking the soundest position you can locate on the "law-authoritarianism" scale, not just any position. Like a theoretical physicist developing a unified theory of the universe or a child learning the English language, you are seeking the simplest, most heuristic ordering of the largest amount of experience that you can. My talk can give you (vicariously) new experiences and new attempted generalizations. Our discussion can contribute to the search for coherency in which both of us are engaged.

Of course you and I have been engaged in this process for a long time, and my words are unlikely to change your life very much. A dozen new data points on a graph that already includes one hundred thousand such points cannot greatly alter the best-fit line. My words, however, may change your position on the "law-authoritarianism" scale just a little. They may bring you a bit closer to the knowledge that you seek. Your words can do the same for me.

How people regard the process of knowing (epistemology) bears on what kinds of things they think exist (ontology). Older images of human reasoning set up morals for a kill. They suggested that "logic" always could be pushed to a "premise" and that reaching this premise ended the game. At this endpoint, it was everyone for herself.

As Holmes expressed this viewpoint:

> Deep-seated preferences cannot be argued about—you can not argue
> a man into liking a glass of beer—and therefore, when differences are
> sufficiently far reaching, we try to kill the other man rather than let

him have his way. But that is perfectly consistent with admitting that, so far as it appears, his grounds are just as good as ours.[44]

From this still prevalent perspective, values are the product of "can't helps." In the end, a person can do no more than assert her own personal, existential belief—a belief that may not move any other rational person and that she is likely to assert either apologetically and without conviction or with indefensible conviction. Unreasoning plunges over Niagara Falls seem unavoidable for everyone engaged in normative discourse.

The new epistemology emphasizes that premises do not come from nowhere. They are usually the product of efforts to generalize our experience of the world. We may do this job of inference well or poorly—perceiving patterns sharply or dimly, misperceiving them, or missing them altogether. We move from induction to deduction to induction to deduction in continuous, hopefully progressive spirals.[45]

Gilbert Harman puts it this way: "If we suppose that beliefs are to be justified by deducing them from more basic beliefs, we will suppose that there are beliefs so basic that they cannot be justified at all."[46] Traditional images of human reasoning portray the most important of our beliefs as the least justified. Harman underlines the new epistemology's response: "These skeptical views are undermined . . . once it is seen that the relevant kind of justification is not a matter of derivation from basic principles but is rather a matter of showing that a view fits in well with other things we believe."[47]

Holmes wrote, "[O]ne's general attitude toward the universe . . . is determined largely by early associations and temperament. . . . Men to a great extent believe what they want to—although I see in that no basis for a philosophy that tells us what we should want to want."[48] The new epistemology stresses what this statement overlooks. Like a person's position on the "law-authoritarianism" spectrum, her position on the more general spectrum that ranges from global doubt to unquestioning credulity is not simply a matter of taste, personality, and early associations. Like other values and empirical beliefs, her position on this "skepticism" spectrum is likely to be the product of active consideration throughout her lifetime, and although there may not be precisely correct answers to where along that spectrum she belongs, there are plainly wrong ones.

Holmes's own position on the "skepticism" spectrum apparently changed dramatically with his experience in the Civil War. Unlike a disillusioning personal experience of the sort he endured, this book is not apt to alter your position very much. It may, however, prompt some reconsideration of where Holmesian skepticism is likely to lead. This reconsideration may move you toward a stance that I consider sounder than Holmes's—a stance of moderate credulity.

By moderate credulity, I mean the provisional acceptance of what seems to be real until better understanding becomes available—proceeding by the light that is given without worrying too much about how dim the light may be. Like Holmes before the Civil War and unlike Holmes after, you probably consider your beliefs about the abolition of slavery more than a purely personal preference. Perhaps your sense is mistaken, and you might be unable to satisfy a doubter that any significant difference exists between your moral objection to slavery and your fondness for apples. As Bernard Williams has observed, however, "[I]t is a mistake . . . to think that there is some objective presumption in favor of the nonethical life, that ethical skepticism is the natural state. . . ."[49] The burden of justification should rest as much or more on people who claim that things are not as they seem as on people who trust appearances.[50]

Firing a demand for hogchoker proof at every belief may leave one without beliefs, and one may turn to "uneconomic" bursts of will or energy in an effort to overcome a sense of emptiness and despair. The new epistemology, however, exposes the brooding and the leaps of the Holmesians as petulant and destructive. This epistemology leaves room for "sez who?'s" but not for refusals to believe in the absence of hogchoker responses. The name of the game at the outset of the twenty-first century is neither hogchoker proof nor blind "can't helps." It is reflective equilibrium, coherency, and inference to the best explanation. The failure of clear Euclidean proof justifies neither despair nor blind assertions of personal will. There is a world between.

For Holmes to retreat to sneers and "can't helps" because he lacked a clear vision of the universe was a cop-out. Arresting though his iconoclastic views of moral issues often were, these views were more adolescent than profound.[51] The oracle of American law, bearing the scars and applauding the lessons of Ball's Bluff, Antietam, and Chancellorsville, led twentieth-century law down the wrong path. Few of his followers, however, had as much excuse for believing the old soldier's message as he did.

Notes

Chapter One

1. Holmes to Lady Pollock, Sept 6, 1902, in 1 *The Holmes–Pollock Letters: The Correspondence of Mr. Justice Holmes and Sir Frederick Pollock, 1874–1932* at 105 (Mark DeWolfe Howe ed) (Harvard Univ Press, 2d ed 1961).

2. See Albert W. Alschuler, *Failed Pragmatism: Reflections on the Burger Court,* 100 Harv L Rev 1436 (1987).

3. Thomas C. Grey, *Hear the Other Side: Wallace Stevens and Pragmatist Legal Theory,* 63 So Cal L Rev 1569 (1990).

4. Cornel West, *The American Evasion of Philosophy: A Genealogy of Pragmatism* 5 (Univ of Wisconsin Press, 1989).

5. See, for example, *Foreword: Symposium on the Renaissance of Pragmatism in American Legal Thought,* 63 So Cal L Rev i, vii–viii (1990) ("Pragmatism does not seek a final, objective conception of truth or meaning. Rather, it finds truth in the consensus of a community, in lived experience. . . .").

6. Richard Rorty, *Contingency, Irony and Solidarity* 41 (Cambridge Univ Press, 1989). See also Richard Rorty, *The Banality of Pragmatism and the Poetry of Justice,* 63 S Cal L Rev 1811, 1813 (1990) (observing that the banality of pragmatism is illustrated by the ease with which such diverse scholars as Roberto Unger, Ronald Dworkin, and Richard Posner are accommodated under this rubric); Thomas C. Grey, *Holmes and Legal Pragmatism,* 41 Stan L Rev 787, 814 (1989) ("Pragmatist theory of law is, like much pragmatist theory, essentially banal.").

7. Yogi Berra, *The Yogi Book* 102 (Wortman, 1998).

8. The standard list includes Holmes as well as Chauncey Wright, Nicholas St. John Green, William James, Charles Sanders Peirce, and John Dewey. See, for example, Philip P. Wiener, *Evolution and the Founders of Pragmatism* (Univ of Pennsylvania Press, 1972). Holmes, however, both rejected and mocked pragmatism. See chapter 2 at 18–19.

9. Thomas Grey describes Holmes as "an instrumentalist without an adequate system of ends." Grey, *Holmes and Legal Pragmatism,* 41 Stan L Rev at 850. He might have extended this criticism to pragmatists generally.

10. Pragmatists often recognize the need for general philosophical objectives while treating philosophy as a matter of fitness to one's environment and leaving the concept of fitness unspecified. See 1 *Collected Papers of Charles Sanders Peirce* 591 (Charles Hartshorne and Paul Weiss eds) (Harvard Univ Press 1934) ("Every man has certain ideals of the general description of conduct that befits a rational animal in his particular station in life, what most accords with his total nature and relations.")

11. See Roscoe Pound, *Juristic Problems of National Progress,* 22 Am J Soc 721, 724 (1917) (declaring that the appropriate function of both law and society is simply the "satisfaction of a maximum of wants with a minimum of sacrifice of other wants"); Hans Kelsen, *The Pure Theory of Law,* 50 L Q Rev 474, 482 (1934) ("From the standpoint of rational knowledge, there are only interests and conflicts of interests. . . . Justice is an irrational ideal.").

12. See, for example, Cass R. Sunstein, *Legal Interference with Private Preferences,* 53 U Chi L Rev 1129 (1986).

13. See Richard A. Posner, *The Economics of Justice* 48–87 (Harvard Univ Press, 1983) (a revised version of Richard A. Posner, *Utilitarianism, Economics, and Legal Theory,* 8 J Legal Stud 103 (1979)).

14. Id at 82 (emphasis in the original). Later, in the course of denouncing *all* moral theories articulated by academics, Posner conceded that his own effort was "doomed." See Richard A. Posner, *1997 Oliver Wendell Holmes Lectures: The Problematics of Moral and Legal Theory,* 111 Harv L Rev 1637, 1670 and n62 (1998). On similarly skeptical grounds, the most prominent of the critical legal studies scholars, Duncan Kennedy, renounced the theoretical contribution for which he was most noted. See Duncan Kennedy, *The Structure of Blackstone's Commentaries,* 28 Buff L Rev 205, 211–12 (1979) (announcing "the fundamental contradiction"); Duncan Kennedy and Peter Gabel, *Roll Over Beethoven,* 36 Stan L Rev 1, 14 (1984) (renouncing "the fundamental contradiction").

15. Arthur Allen Leff, *Unspeakable Ethics, Unnatural Law,* 1979 Duke L J 1229, 1244.

16. Robert H. Bork, *Neutral Principles and Some First Amendment Problems,* 47 Ind L J 1, 10 (1971).

17. See Aristotle, *The Nicomachean Ethics* bk I, ch 7, at 75–76 (J. A. K. Thompson transl) (Penguin, 1983) (declaring that "sentient life" is "shared by horses and cattle and animals of all kinds," while "a practical life of the rational part" is the distinctive function of man).

   Thomas Aquinas wrote, "At first sight it seems obvious that animals choose. Bees, spiders and dogs behave in marvelously clever ways. . . ." Aquinas maintained, however, that "when animals behave cleverly it is because they are following out superlatively designed processes by natural instinct. . . . [T]hey are not themselves reasoning or choosing, as we see from the fact that all members of the same species behave in the same way." Thomas Aquinas, 2 *Summa Theologiae: A Concise Translation* 188–89 (Timothy McDermott ed) (Eyre and Spottiswoode, 1989). Roger Baldwin's antislavery argument before the Supreme Court in *United States v Libellants of the Schooner Amistad,* 40 US 518 (1841), maintained that references to property in a treaty encompassed animals but not human slaves. Animals, Baldwin said, were universally regarded as appropriate subjects of ownership because they were "irrational." 40 US at 558.

18. See Mary Midgley, *Beast and Man: The Roots of Human Nature* 160 (Cornell Univ Press, 1978).

19. James M. Gustafson, 1 *Ethics from a Theocentric Perspective* 286 (Univ of Chicago Press, 1981).

20. See id at 284–87.

21. Ludwig Wittgenstein, *Philosophical Investigations* 134e (G. E. M. Anscome transl) (Macmillan, 3d ed 1958).

22. Arthur Leff's classic article, *Unspeakable Ethics, Unnatural Law* (cited in note 15), reveals the critical role of the "sez who?" in skeptical thought.

23. Jeremy Bentham, *Anarchical Fallacies,* in 2 *Works of Jeremy Bentham* 105 (John Browning ed) (Russell & Russell, 1962).

24. Justice Holmes used the phrase "brooding omnipresence in the sky" to deflate traditional concepts of the common law. *Southern Pac Co v Jensen,* 244 US 205, 222 (1917) (Holmes dissenting). The phrase has provided a nice device for ridiculing the idea of natural justice as well.

25. A standard "boundary" problem of utilitarianism is whether to include animals in the group whose happiness one seeks to maximize. Jeremy Bentham counted hippopotamuses "in," but he added that we should nevertheless eat whatever animals we want. See Jeremy Bentham, *The Principles of Morals and Legislation* 282b (J. H. Burns and H. L. A. Hart eds) (Methuen, 1970).

26. Richard A. Posner, *The Jurisprudence of Skepticism,* 86 Mich L Rev 827, 829 (1988).

27. Holmes to Harold Laski, July 23, 1925, in 1 *The Holmes–Laski Letters: The Correspondence of Mr. Justice Holmes and Harold J. Laski, 1916–1935* at 761, 762 (Mark DeWolfe Howe ed) (Harvard Univ Press, 1953).

28. Holmes, *Natural Law,* 32 Harv L Rev 40, 42 (1918), reprinted in 3 *The Collected Works of Justice Holmes: Complete Public Writings and Selected Judicial Opinions of Oliver Wendell Holmes* 445, 447 (Sheldon M. Novick ed) (Univ of Chicago Press, 1995) (hereinafter cited as *Collected Works*).

29. See, for example, Richard A. Posner *The Problems of Jurisprudence* 354–55 (Harvard Univ Press, 1990).

30. Oliver Wendell Holmes, Jr., *The Gas Stokers' Strike,* 7 Am L Rev 582 (1873), reprinted in 1 *Collected Works* at 323, 325.

31. See, for example, Frank H. Easterbrook, *Foreword: The Court and the Economic System,* 98 Harv L Rev 4, 42 (1984); Frank H. Easterbrook, *Statutes' Domains,* 50 U Chi L Rev 533, 543 (1983). For criticism of this position, see Mark L. Movesian,

Are Statutes Really "Legislative Bargains"? The Failure of the Contract Analogy in Statutory Interpretation, 76 NC L Rev 1145 (1998).

32. See James M. Buchanan and Gordon Tullock, *The Calculus of Consent: Logical Foundations of Constitutional Democracy* (Univ of Michigan Press, 1962) (describing politics as a process of exchange between rent-seeking interest groups and rent-yielding governmental officials).

33. Jonathan R. Macey and Geoffrey P. Miller, *Origin of the Blue Sky Laws,* 70 Texas L Rev 347 (1991).

34. Mark A. Cohen, *Explaining Judicial Behavior or What's "Unconstitutional" about the Sentencing Commission?* 7 J of Law, Econ, and Organization 183 (1991).

35. Fred C. McChesney, *Government Prohibitions on Volunteer Fire Fighting in Nineteenth-Century America: A Property Rights Perspective,* 15 J Legal Stud 69 (1989).

36. Morris P. Fiorina, *Congress: Keystone of the Washington Establishment* 46–47 (Yale Univ Press, 1977).

   In recognition of his role in establishing public choice as a distinct field of economic inquiry, James M. Buchanan received the Nobel Prize in economics in 1986. See *U.S. Economist Wins Nobel Prize,* Chicago Tribune, Oct 17, 1986, at § 1, p 1.

37. Sometimes taken with a tequila chaser. See, for example, Peter Gabel and Duncan Kennedy, *Roll Over Beethoven,* 36 Stan L Rev 1 (1984).

38. Of course this catchphrase cannot entirely capture a movement that has generated hundreds of books and articles. Nevertheless, it will do for starters. See John Henry Schlegel, *Notes toward an Intimate, Opinionated, and Affectionate History of the Conference on Critical Legal Studies,* 36 Stan L Rev 391, 410–11 (1984) ("If the liberal conceit continues to unravel, and all concerned become aware that the postulated dichotomy between the public sphere of politics and the private sphere of law is fraudulent—that, in a phrase, LAW IS POLITICS, pure and simple—then the movement and its visible organ, the Conference [on Critical Legal Studies], may be of some significance in the world"); Frederick R. Kellogg, *Legal Scholarship in the Temple of Doom: Pragmatism's Response to Critical Legal Studies,* 65 Tul L Rev 15, 17 (1990) ("[T]he main premise of CLS [is] that there is no practical dividing line between law and politics."); David Kairys, *Law and Politics,* 52 Geo Wash L Rev 243, 247 (1984); Owen M. Fiss, *The Death of the Law?,* 72 Corn L Rev 1, 2 (1986).

39. Politics is "the science or art of political government." *The American Heritage Dictionary of the English Language* 1015 (Houghton Mifflin, 1981).

40. See Duncan Kennedy, *The Role of Law in Economic Thought: Essays on the Fetishism of Commodities,* 34 Am U L Rev 939, 969 (1985) (referring to "the mind-fucks of capitalism"); Duncan Kennedy, *On Gramsci and Ideology* 4 (Sept 1979) (mimeographed), quoted in Louis B. Schwartz, *With Gun and Camera through Darkest CLS-Land,* 36 Stan L Rev 413, 453 n199 (1984) (liberalism portrayed as "a gigantic mind fuck"); Duncan Kennedy, *First Year Law Teaching as Political Action,* 1 L and Soc Probs 47, 49 (1980) (referring to "encrustations of the shit-hierarchy"); Catharine A. MacKinnon, *Toward a Feminist Theory of the State* 149–50 (Harvard

Univ Press, 1989) ("The mind fuck of all of this makes liberalism's complicitous collapse into 'I chose it' feel like a strategy for sanity."). See also K. C. Worden, Note, *Overshooting the Target: A Feminist Deconstruction of Legal Education,* 34 Am U L Rev 1141, 1152 (1985) (student note describing "the reified, ideological shit blocked up inside me" and declaring, "This Article may be but another enema").

41. The term *radical feminist* is a term of art. It describes feminists whose central goal is neither to afford women the same opportunities currently enjoyed by men (the principal object of liberal feminists) nor to provide greater recognition of and reward for women's customary roles and distinctive qualities (the principal object of cultural feminists) but simply to afford women more power. Catharine MacKinnon is the most prominent radical feminist among today's law school academics.

42. Kimberle Crenshaw, *A Black Feminist Critique of Antidiscrimination Law and Politics,* in *The Politics of Law: A Progressive Critique* 195, 201 (David Kairys ed) (Pantheon, rev ed 1990).

43. Ann Scales, *The Emergence of Feminist Jurisprudence: An Essay,* 95 Yale L J 1373, 1385 (1986).

44. Id at 1390.

45. Catharine A. MacKinnon, *Feminism Unmodified: Discourses on Life and Law* 43–44 (Harvard Univ Press, 1987).

46. *Plato's The Republic* 19 (Benjamin Jowett transl) (Collier, rev ed 1901). In his dialogue with Socrates, Thrasymachus said other things that seem inconsistent with this declaration, and people have disputed whether this initial statement truly captures his views. See Julia Annas, *An Introduction to Plato's Republic* 34–58 (Clarendon, 1981). My sense, however, is that Thrasymachus's contradictions are the product of Plato's portrayal of his inept defense of the contention that might makes right and that one may appropriately take his initial statement at face value.

Thrasymachus was not alone. Plato complained that many philosophers had misled the youth of Athens by teaching "that the principles of justice have no existence at all in nature, but that mankind are always disputing about them and altering them; and that the alterations which are made . . . have no basis in nature, but are of authority for the moment and at the time at which they are made . . . ." Plato, *Laws,* in 4 *The Dialogues of Plato* 458 (Benjamin Jowett transl) (Clarendon, 4th ed 1953).

47. *Plato's The Republic* at 43.

48. Id at 44–45.

49. Cicero, *De Re Publica* 211 (Clinton Walker Keyes transl) (Putnam, Loeb Classical Library, 1928).

50. Thomas Hobbes, *Leviathan* 32 (Blackwell, 1957). Hobbes would be described by an American legal realist as "the grandfather of realistic jurisprudence." Felix S. Cohen, *Transcendental Nonsense and the Functional Approach,* 35 Colum L Rev 809, 836 (1935).

51. See Sheldon M. Novick, *Editor's Introduction,* in 1 *Collected Works* at 181.

52. Oliver Wendell Holmes, Jr., *Codes, and the Arrangement of the Law,* 5 Am L Rev 1 (1870), reprinted in 1 *Collected Works* at 212.

53. See Thomas C. Grey, *Langdell's Orthodoxy,* 45 U Pitt L Rev 1 (1983).

54. Some writers who began publishing before 1865 continued to publish for decades thereafter, and their views rarely underwent a radical transformation. Primarily because two scholarly generations overlapped, expressions of natural law sentiment coexisted with more skeptical depictions of law throughout the final third of the nineteenth century.

55. Thomas M. Cooley, who began publishing before the final third of the century, may be an exception to the generalization in text. Cooley declared in his edition of Blackstone's *Commentaries* that "the law of God" established "immutable principles of right and justice." Thomas M. Cooley, *Suggestions Concerning the Study of the Law,* in William Blackstone, *Commentaries on the Laws of England* at v, x (Thomas M. Cooley ed) (Callaghan, 3d rev ed 1884). Nevertheless, Stephen Siegel's judgment concerning Cooley's work seems justified: "Cooley would have . . . denied that he was a natural-law jurist." See Stephen A. Siegel, *Historism in Late Nineteenth-Century Constitutional Thought,* 1990 Wis L Rev 1431, 1515. See also Alan Jones, *Thomas M. Cooley and "Laissez-Faire Constitutionalism": A Reconsideration,* 53 J Am Hist 751, 763 (1967) ("[Cooley] cannot be classified as a defender of a doctrine of natural rights. As he explicitly noted . . . , rights were historically created by the law in a process of continuing change.").

56. This characterization began with the realist Karl Lewellyn's description of the "Grand Style" in *The Common Law Tradition: Deciding Appeals* 36–45, 62–72 (Little, Brown, 1960). Grant Gilmore declared, "The pre-Civil War period was our Golden Age. . . . After the Civil War all the gold, by a sort of reverse alchemy, was transmuted into lead." Grant Gilmore, *The Ages of American Law* 12 (Yale Univ Press, 1977). Gilmore titled his chapter on the antebellum period "The Age of Discovery." Id at 19–40. Morton Horwitz spoke of a "paradigm shift" from an "instrumental" to a "formalist" or "Classical" mode of reasoning following the Civil War. See Morton J. Horwitz, *The Transformation of American Law, 1789–1860* at 253–66 (Harvard Univ Press, 1977).

57. See Morton White's influential essay, *The Revolt against Formalism in American Social Thought of the Twentieth Century,* 8 J Hist of Ideas 131 (1947) (also published as chapter 2 of White's *Social Thought in America* (Viking, 1949)). This essay is criticized in chapter 6 at 93–100.

58. Sheldon M. Novick, *Honorable Justice: The Life of Oliver Wendell Holmes* (Little, Brown, 1989).

59. Liva Baker, *The Justice from Beacon Hill: The Life and Times of Oliver Wendell Holmes* (HarperCollins, 1991); G. Edward White, *Justice Oliver Wendell Holmes: Law and the Inner Self* (Oxford Univ Press, 1993).

60. Gary J. Aichele, *Oliver Wendell Holmes, Jr.: Soldier, Scholar, Judge* (Twayne, 1989).

61. See, for example, *The Legacy of Oliver Wendell Holmes, Jr.* (Robert W. Gordon ed) (Stanford Univ Press, 1992) (containing essays by Robert W. Gordon, J. W. Bur-

row, Morton J. Horwitz, Mathias W. Reimann, Stephen Diamond, Robert A. Ferguson, Peter Gibian, and David Hollinger); *Symposium:* The Path of the Law *After One Hundred Years,* 110 Harv L Rev 989 (1997) (containing essays by William W. Fisher III, Robert W. Gordon, Tracey E. Higgins, Martha Minow, Sheldon M. Novick, Richard D. Parker, Richard A. Posner, David Rosenberg, and G. Edward White); *Symposium:* The Path of the Law *100 Years Later: Holmes' Influence on Modern Jurisprudence,* 63 Brook L Rev 1 (containing essays by Anthony J. Sebok, Richard A. Posner, Thomas C. Grey, Catharine Pierce Wells, G. Edward White, Gary Minda, Neil Duxbury, David Dyzenhaus, William Twining, and John C. P. Goldberg); *Symposium,* The Path of the Law *Today,* 78 BU L Rev 78 (1998) (containing essays by Lewis Kornhauser, Frederick Schauer, Robin L. West, Ruth Gavison, Clayton P. Gillette, Robert Cooter, Sanford Levinson, Jack Balkin, Gerald Leonard, Jack Beerman, and Richard McAdams); *"The Path of the Law" and Its Influence: The Legacy of Oliver Wendell Holmes, Jr.* (Steven J. Burton ed) (Cambridge Univ Press, 2000); David Rosenberg, *The Hidden Holmes: His Theory of Torts in History* (Harvard Univ Press, 1995); Sheldon M. Novick, *Editor's Introduction,* in 1 *Collected Works* at 1; Sheldon M. Novick, *Justice Holmes's Philosophy,* 70 Wash U L Q 703 (1992); Sheldon M. Novick, *Justice Holmes and the Art of Biography,* 33 Wm & Mary L Rev 1219 (1992); Richard A. Posner, *Introduction* to *The Essential Holmes: Selections from the Letters, Speeches, Judicial Opinions and Other Writings of Oliver Wendell Holmes, Jr.* ix (Richard A. Posner ed) (Univ of Chicago Press, 1992); Morton J. Horwitz, *The Transformation of American Law, 1870–1960* (Oxford Univ Press, 1992); David J. Seipp, *Holmes's Path,* 77 B U L Rev 515 (1997); Robert Brauneis, *"The Foundation of Our 'Regulatory Takings' Jurisprudence": The Myth and Meaning of Justice Holmes's Opinion in* Pennsylvania Coal Co. v. Mahon, 106 Yale L J 619 (1996); William Michael Treanor, *Jam for Justice Holmes: Reassessing the Significance of* Mahon, 86 Geo L J 813 (1998); Richard A. Epstein, Pennsylvania Coal v. Mahon: *The Erratic Takings Jurisprudence of Justice Holmes,* 86 Geo L J 875 (1998); Robert Brauneis, *Treanor's* Mahon, 86 Geo L J 907 (1998); William Michael Treanor, *Understanding* Mahon *in Historical Context,* 86 Geo L J 933 (1998); William P. LaPiana, *Victorian from Beacon Hill: Oliver Wendell Holmes's Early Legal Scholarship,* 90 Colum L Rev 809 (1990); Louis Menand, *Bet-tabilitarianism,* New Republic, Nov 11, 1996, at 47; Mathias Reimann, *Why Holmes?,* 88 Mich L Rev 1908 (1990); Thomas C. Grey, *Holmes and Legal Pragmatism,* 41 Stan L Rev 787 (1989); Thomas C. Grey, *Molecular Motions: The Holmesian Judge in Theory and Practice,* 37 Wm & Mary L Rev 19 (1995); Catherine Wells Hantzis, *Legal Innovation within the Wider Intellectual Tradition: The Pragmatism of Oliver Wendell Holmes, Jr.,* 82 Nw U L Rev 541 (1988); Anne C. Dailey, *Holmes and the Romantic Mind,* 48 Duke L J 429 (1998); David Dolinko, *Alschuler's Path,* 49 Fla L Rev 421 (1997); James Gordley, *When Paths Diverge: A Response to Albert Alschuler on Oliver Wendell Holmes,* 49 Fla L Rev 441 (1997); Winston P. Nagin, *Not Just a Descending Trail: Traversing Holmes' Many Paths of the Law,* 49 Fla L Rev 463 (1997).

For more critical views of Holmes, see David Luban, *Justice Holmes and the Metaphysics of Judicial Restraint,* 44 Duke L J 449 (1994); David Luban, *The Bad Man and the Good Lawyer: A Centennial Essay on Holmes's* Path of the Law, 72 NYU L

Rev 1547 (1997); Louise Weinberg, *Holmes' Failure,* 96 Mich L Rev 691 (1997) (criticizing Holmes for his focus on private rather than public law and also for his focus on common law rather than equity); Patrick J. Kelley, *Was Holmes a Pragmatist? Reflections on a New Twist to an Old Argument,* 14 S Ill L J 427 (1990); Patrick J. Kelley, *Holmes on the Supreme Judicial Court: The Theorist as Judge,* in *The History of the Law in Massachusetts: The Supreme Judicial Court 1692–1992* at 275 (Russell K. Osgoode ed) (Supreme Judicial Court Historical Socy, 1992).

For a noncommittal view, see Robert M. Mennel and Christine L. Compson, *Introduction* to *Holmes and Frankfurter: Their Correspondence, 1912–1934* xi (Robert M. Mennel and Christine L. Compson eds) (Univ Press of New England, 1996).

62. See Mortimer J. Adler, *Legal Certainty,* 31 Colum L Rev 91 (1931) (book review).

63. See H. L. Mencken, *The Great Holmes Mystery,* 26 Am Mercury 123 (May 1932) (book review) (describing Holmes as moved less by "a positive love of liberty than [by] an amiable and half contemptuous feeling that those who longed for it ought to get a horse-doctor's dose of it, and so suffer a really first-rate belly-ache").

64. See Yosal Rogat, *Mr. Justice Holmes: A Dissenting Opinion* (part 1), 15 Stan L Rev 3 (1962); Yosal Rogat, *Mr. Justice Holmes: A Dissenting Opinion* (part 2), 15 Stan L Rev 254 (1963); Yosal Rogat, *The Judge as Spectator,* 31 U Chi L Rev 213 (1964). See also Yosal Rogat and James M. O'Fallon, *Mr. Justice Holmes: A Dissenting Opinion—The Speech Cases,* 36 Stan L Rev 1349 (1984) (O'Fallon's completion of work that Rogat left unfinished at the time of his death).

65. See Saul Touster, *In Search of Holmes from Within,* 18 Vand L Rev 437 (1965); see also Saul Touster, *Holmes a Hundred Years Ago: The Common Law and Legal Theory,* 10 Hofstra L Rev 673 (1982).

66. See Edmund Wilson, *Patriotic Gore: Studies in the Literature of the American Civil War* 743–96 (Oxford Univ Press, 1962).

67. The works of these scholars are cited and described in chapter 2 at 15 and in notes 21 and 22 on page 204.

68. See Mark DeWolfe Howe, *Justice Oliver Wendell Holmes: The Proving Years* 46 n41 (Harvard Univ Press, 1963) (quoting a letter from Holmes to James Bryce, Sept 17, 1919).

69. Richard A. Posner, *Foreword: Holmes,* 63 Brook L Rev 7, 14 (1997). Posner, who combines a Holmesian worldview with personal warmth, grace, and generosity, proves the truth of this proposition himself. See my remarks about him in the acknowledgments.

70. Oliver Wendell Holmes, *Natural Law,* 32 Harv L Rev 40 (1918), reprinted in 1 *Collected Works* at 445, 446.

71. Holmes to Harold Laski, July 23, 1925, in 1 *Holmes–Laski Letters* at 762.

72. Holmes, *The Gas Stokers' Strike,* 7 Am L Rev at 587, reprinted in 1 *Collected Works* at 325.

73. Oliver Wendell Holmes, *The Path of the Law,* 10 Harv L Rev 457, 459 (1897), reprinted in 3 *Collected Works* at 392.

Chapter Two

1. Benjamin N. Cardozo, *Mr. Justice Holmes,* 44 Harv L Rev 682, 691 (1931).

2. Id at 684.

3. Felix Frankfurter, *Mr. Justice Holmes and the Constitution,* in *Mr. Justice Holmes* 46, 54 (Felix Frankfurter ed) (Coward-McCann, 1931).

4. Felix Frankfurter, *Mr. Justice Holmes,* 48 Harv L Rev 1279, 1280 (1935).

5. Charles Wyzanski, *The Democracy of Justice Oliver Wendell Holmes,* 7 Vand L Rev 311, 323 (1954).

6. Henry Steele Commager, *The American Mind* 382 (Yale Univ Press, 1950).

7. Thomas C. Grey, *Holmes and Legal Pragmatism,* 41 Stan L Rev 787 (1989).

8. Karl N. Llewellyn, *Holmes,* 35 Colum L Rev 485, 490 (1935).

9. Morton J. Horwitz, *The Place of Justice Holmes in American Legal Thought,* in *The Legacy of Oliver Wendell Holmes, Jr.* 31 (Robert W. Gordon ed) (Stanford Univ Press, 1992).

10. Richard A. Posner, *Introduction* to *The Essential Holmes: Selections from the Letters, Speeches, Judicial Opinions and Other Writings of Oliver Wendell Holmes, Jr.* ix (Richard A. Posner ed) (Univ of Chicago Press, 1992).

11. Harry Kalven and Hans Zeisel, *Law, Science and Humanism,* in *The Humanist Frame* 329, 331 (Julian Huxley ed) (Harper, 1961).

    Alexander Bickel declared, "It has been remarked that no other man of comparable intellect and spirit has been a judge . . . among English-speaking peoples." Alexander Bickel, *The Unpublished Opinions of Mr. Justice Brandeis* 241 (Harvard Univ Press, 1957).

    Learned Hand wrote of Holmes:

    > They say the soul of Rabelais roams the earth gathering spirits for the Abbey of Theleme, those who are gay, nimble, courteous, feat, witty, amorous, simple, courtly, kind, pleasing, happy, genial, wise, humble, tolerant, joyous. Now the initiated tell us that among these there is none he has more certainly chosen than the captain of Antietam. . . .

    Learned Hand, *Book Review,* 36 Pol Sci Q 528, 530 (1921) (reviewing Oliver Wendell Holmes, *Collected Legal Papers* [Harcourt, Brace and Howe, 1920]).

12. G. Edward White, *Justice Oliver Wendell Holmes: Law and the Inner Self* 486 (Oxford Univ Press, 1993).

13. Richard A. Posner, *Cardozo: A Study in Reputation* 76 at table I (Univ of Chicago Press, 1990).

14. See Thomas G. Grey, *Molecular Motions: The Holmesian Judge in Theory and Practice,* 37 Wm & Mary L Rev 19 (1995) (referring to the confirmation hearings for Ruth Bader Ginsburg and Stephen G. Breyer).

15. The novel by Catherine Drinker Bowen is *Yankee from Olympus* (Atlantic/Little Brown, 1944). The play by Emmet Lavery and the motion picture bear the title *The Magnificent Yankee.*

16. See Saul Touster, *Holmes a Hundred Years Ago: The Common Law and Legal Theory,* 10 Hofstra L Rev 673 (1982).

17. Mathias Reimann, *Why Holmes?,* 88 Mich L Rev 1908, 1912 (1990).

18. William James to Henry Bowdich James, May 22, 1869, in Ralph Barton Perry, 1 *The Thought and Character of William James* 295, 297 (Little, Brown, 1935).

19. Mortimer J. Adler, *Book Review,* 31 Colum L Rev 91, 107 (1931).

20. H. L. Mencken, *Mr. Justice Holmes,* 26 The American Mercury 123, 124 (May 1932).

21. See, for example, Francis E. Lucey, *Jurisprudence and the Future Social Order,* 16 Soc Sci 211 (1941); Francis E. Lucey, *Natural Law and American Legal Realism,* 30 Geo L J 439 (1942); Francis E. Lucey, *Holmes—Liberal—Humanitarian—Believer in Democracy?,* 39 Geo L J 523 (1951); Paul L. Gregg, *The Pragmatism of Mr. Justice Holmes,* 31 Geo L J 262 (1943); John C. Ford, *The Fundamentals of Holmes' Juristic Philosophy,* 11 Fordham L Rev 255 (1942). These writers understood Holmes better than the lawyers and scholars who viewed him as a liberal hero. Some of them, however, did not enhance their credibility when they denounced Holmes's agnosticism and linked him with Hitler.

22. Ben W. Palmer, *Hobbes, Holmes and Hitler,* 31 ABA J 569 (1945). Harold R. McKinnon called Holmes's philosophy "a symbol of . . . intellectual wretchedness" but added "that there was a real inconsistency in Holmes' thought and . . . in his work as a judge he actually repudiated some of the nihilism of his legal theory." Harold R. McKinnon, *The Secret of Mr. Justice Holmes,* 36 ABA J 261, 345, 343 (1950).

23. Lucey, *Holmes—Liberal—Humanitarian—Believer in Democracy?,* 39 Geo L J at 524.

24. Reimann, *Why Holmes?,* 88 Mich L Rev at 1918, 1923.

25. Daniel Boorstin, *The Elusiveness of Mr. Justice Holmes,* 14 New Eng Q 478 (1941).

26. Touster, *Holmes a Hundred Years Ago,* 10 Hofstra L Rev at 679.

27. White, *Justice Oliver Wendell Holmes* at 4.

28. Francis Biddle, *Mr. Justice Holmes* 95 (Scribner's, 1942).

29. Sheldon M. Novick, *Honorable Justice: The Life of Oliver Wendell Holmes* vii (Little, Brown, 1989).

30. Id at xvii. Novick presumably did not mean the word *fascist* to be taken literally; nothing in Holmes's letters suggests support for the economic program of Benito Mussolini. Perhaps, while trying to avoid use of the more inflammatory word *Nazi,* Novick meant something like "Nazi junior-grade."

31. Richard A. Posner, *Introduction* to *The Essential Holmes* at ix, xxviii n31.

32. Id at xviii.

33. See id at xxviii–xxix.

34. Richard A. Posner, *Foreword: Holmes,* 63 Brook L Rev 7, 17 (1997). See also Posner, *Introduction* to *The Essential Holmes* at xxviii (describing Holmes as "remarkably unprejudiced for his time").

35. See Edmund Wilson, *Patriotic Gore: Studies in the Literature of the American Civil War* 783 (Oxford Univ Press, 1962).

36. See id at 784–85; David A. Hollinger, *The "Tough-Minded" Justice Holmes, Jewish Intellectuals, and the Making of an American Icon,* in *The Legacy of Oliver Wendell Holmes, Jr.* at 216.

37. See I. Scott Messinger, *The Judge as Mentor: Oliver Wendell Holmes, Jr., and His Law Clerks,* 11 Yale J of Law and the Humanities 119, 140 (1999). The one exception was a white, male, *married,* high-ranking graduate of the Harvard Law School. Holmes hired this clerk, W. Barton Leach, without realizing his marital status— and protested when he discovered it. See chapter 8 at 184.

38. Holmes to Sir Frederick Pollock, Apr 5, 1919, in 2 *The Holmes–Pollock Letters: The Correspondence of Mr. Justice Holmes and Sir Frederick Pollock, 1874–1932* at 8 (Mark DeWolfe Howe ed) (Harvard Univ Press, 1941).

39. See Sheldon M. Novick, *Justice Holmes's Philosophy,* 70 Wash U L Q 703, 730 (1992).

40. Holmes to Harold Laski, Mar 7, 1928, in 2 *The Holmes–Laski Letters: The Correspondence of Mr. Justice Holmes and Harold J. Laski, 1916–1935* at 1034, 1035 (Mark DeWolfe Howe ed) (Harvard Univ Press, 1953).

41. 261 US 525 (1923).

42. 261 US at 569–70.

43. 223 US 59 (1917).

44. 223 US at 63.

45. Holmes to Laski, Sept 27, 1921, in 1 *Holmes–Laski Letters* at 372 (also remarking, "I can't . . . think the play *Othello* other than disagreeable.").

46. Holmes to Laski, Nov 5, 1926, in 2 id at 893.

47. See White, *Justice Oliver Wendell Holmes* at 335 (describing Holmes as "particularly unsympathetic to ideas of racial equality"); Robert W. Gordon, *Law as a Vocation: Holmes on the Lawyer's Path,* in *"The Path of the Law" and Its Influence: The Legacy of Oliver Wendell Holmes, Jr.* (Steven J. Burton ed) (Cambridge Univ Press, forthcoming) ("[Holmes] voted more regularly even than his conservative colleagues to deny petitions of blacks claiming violations of their civil rights. . . .").

48. See Ben W. Palmer, *The Totalitarianism of Mr. Justice Holmes: Another Chapter in the Controversy,* 37 ABA J 809 (1951).

49. See G. Edward White, *The Rise and Fall of Justice Holmes,* 39 U Chi L Rev 51, 74 (1971).

50. For an extended argument that Holmes was a utilitarian, see H. L. Pohlman, *Justice Oliver Wendell Holmes and Utilitarian Jurisprudence* (Harvard Univ Press, 1984). For a demonstration that he plainly was not, see David Luban, *Justice Holmes and the Metaphysics of Judicial Restraint,* 44 Duke L J 449, 517–23 (1994).

51. See, for example, Frederick R. Kellogg, *Introduction* to *The Formative Essays of Justice Holmes: The Making of an American Legal Philosophy* (Frederick R. Kellogg ed) (Greenwood Press, 1984); Thomas C. Grey, *Holmes and Legal Pragmatism,* 41 Stan

L Rev 787 (1989); Catharine Wells Hantzis, *Legal Innovation within the Wider Intellectual Tradition: The Pragmatism of Oliver Wendell Holmes, Jr.,* 82 Nw U L Rev 541 (1988); Note, *Holmes, Peirce and Legal Pragmatism,* 84 Yale L J 1123 (1975). For a historical answer to the claim that Holmes was a pragmatist, see Patrick J. Kelley, *Was Holmes a Pragmatist? Reflections on a New Twist to an Old Argument,* 14 S Ill U L J 427 (1990) (maintaining that Holmes's views about the growth of the law reflected the positivism of Auguste Comte and John Stuart Mill rather than the pragmatism of Charles Sanders Peirce and William James).

52. Oliver Wendell Holmes, Jr., *The Gas Stokers' Strike,* 7 Am L Rev 582 (1873), reprinted in 1 *The Collected Works of Justice Holmes: Complete Public Writings and Selected Judicial Opinions of Oliver Wendell Holmes* 325 (Sheldon M. Novick ed) (Univ of Chicago Press, 1995) (hereinafter cited as *Collected Works*).

53. Id.

54. Novick, *Honorable Justice* at 432 n23.

55. Sheldon M. Novick, *Editor's Introduction* to 1 *Collected Works* at 1, 42.

56. Richard A. Posner, *Book Review,* 53 Geo Wash L Rev 870, 872 (1985).

57. Immanuel Kant, *Groundwork of the Metaphysics of Morals* 75 (2d ed 1786), in *The Moral Law: Kant's Groundwork of the Metaphysics of Morals* 95 (H. J. Paton transl) (Hutchinson, 1948).

58. Oliver Wendell Holmes, *Ideals and Doubts,* 10 Ill L Rev 1 (1915), reprinted in 3 *Collected Works* at 442, 443.

59. See Holmes to Pollock, June 17, 1908, in 1 *Holmes–Pollock Letters* at 138, 139; Holmes to Lewis Einstein, June 17, 1908, in *The Holmes–Einstein Letters: Correspondence of Mr. Justice Holmes and Lewis Einstein 1903–1935* at 34, 35 (James B. Peabody ed) (St. Martin's, 1964); Holmes to Pollock, July 6, 1908, in 1 *Holmes–Pollock Letters* at 140. As this chapter will reveal, utilitarianism, Kantianism, and pragmatism are merely three entries on a nearly endless list of beliefs at which Holmes scoffed.

60. Holmes to Pollock, July 6, 1908, in 1 *Holmes–Pollock Letters* at 140.

61. Holmes to Pollock, June 17, 1908, in 1 id at 139. See also Holmes to Einstein, Sept 27, 1909, in *Holmes–Einstein Letters* at 51, 52 (James "believes in miracles if you will turn down the lights").

62. Holmes to Laski, Mar 29, 1917, in 1 *Holmes–Laski Letters* at 69, 70. See also Holmes to Pollock, Sept 1, 1910, in 1 *Holmes–Pollock Letters* at 166, 167 (Holmes's comment following the death of William James that he had "little sympathy" for James's pragmatism).

By contrast, at age eighty-five Holmes called *Experience and Nature* by the pragmatist John Dewey "truly a great book." He added, however, that he "could not have summed up a chapter or a page" and that "after [Dewey,] Henderson on *The Federal Trade Commission* is an easy task." Holmes insisted that the reason for his praise was not that Dewey "quotes me in [the book] as one of our great American philosophers." Instead, "with all [the book's] defects of expression, [Dewey] seems to me to hold more of existence in his hand and more honestly to see behind all the current philosophers than any book I can think of on such themes." Holmes to Laski, Dec 15, 1926, in 2 *Holmes–Laski Letters* at 904–05. See also Holmes to John Wu, Jan 30, 1928, in *Justice Holmes to Doctor Wu: An Intimate Correspondence, 1921–1932* (Central Book, undated).

63. See David Luban, *What's Pragmatic about Legal Pragmatism?*, 18 Cardozo L Rev 43 (1996).

64. See Luban, *Justice Holmes and the Metaphysics of Judicial Restraint,* 44 Duke L J at 488.

65. In addition, as Anne Dailey observes, Holmes viewed much of human psychology as innate and did not regard "man's emotional life primarily as an adaptive response to his environment." Unlike the pragmatists of his era, who, in Dailey's words, wrote optimistically about "the unfolding of human adaptation," Holmes's view of humanity was pessimistic. See Anne C. Dailey, *Holmes and the Romantic Mind,* 48 Duke L J 429, 483 (1998).

66. Responding to Thomas Grey's argument that Holmes was a pragmatist, Patrick J. Kelley observes that Grey's analysis disregards both Holmes's work as a whole and the accomplishments that Holmes regarded as primary. In Kelley's words, Grey's argument focuses on "bits and pieces" and "off-hand comments." See Kelley, *Was Holmes a Pragmatist?*, 14 S Ill U L J at 466–67.

67. Oliver Wendell Holmes, *Law in Science and Science in Law,* 12 Harv L Rev 443, 452 (1899), reprinted in 3 *Collected Works* at 406, 412.

68. David Luban offers some of the relevant evidence in *The Bad Man and the Good Lawyer: A Centennial Essay on Holmes's* Path of the Law, 72 NYU L Rev 1547, 1553–54 (1997). I present other evidence throughout this book.

69. See Jean-Paul Sartre, *Existentialism* 15 (Bernard Frechtman transl) (Philosophical Library, 1947) (presenting Sartre's basic statement of the existentialist position, "Existence preceeds essence," which means, apparently, that "essence" is something that people just make up).

70. One scholar who has used this label is Morton Horwitz. See Morton J. Horwitz, *The Transformation of American Law, 1870–1960: The Crisis of Legal Orthodoxy* 177 (Oxford Univ Press, 1992). See also Posner, *Introduction* to *The Essential Holmes* at xix–xx (including existentialism among eighteen "ism's" that one can find in Holmes's thought "together with the explicit rejection of most" of them).

71. J. W. Burrow, *Holmes in His Intellectual Milieu,* in *The Legacy of Oliver Wendell Holmes, Jr.* at 17, 29. See Posner, *Introduction* to *The Essential Holmes* at xxviii (calling Holmes "the American Nietzsche"); Richard A. Posner, *The Problems of Jurisprudence* 239–41 (Harvard Univ Press, 1990) (describing some parallels and differences between the two men); Luban, *Justice Holmes and the Metaphysics of Judicial Restraint* (an elegant and thorough comparison).

72. Id at 466.

73. The last two items of the series are taken from id at 465 n41. For documentation of the preceding items, see Walter Kaufmann, *Nietzsche: Philosopher, Psychologist, Antichrist* (Princeton Univ Press, 1974); Carl E. Pletch, *A Psychoanalytic Study of*

Friedrich Nietzsche (unpublished doctoral dissertation, Univ of Chicago, 1977); Darren Olofson, *A Comparative Study of Oliver Wendell Holmes, Jr. and Friedrich Nietzsche* (unpublished senior paper, Univ of Chicago, 1993).

74. Oliver Wendell Holmes, *Ideals and Doubts,* 10 Ill L Rev at 3, reprinted in 3 *Collected Works* at 442, 443. See also Holmes to Baroness Moncheur, Dec 30, 1915, quoted in Novick, *Honorable Justice* at 319.

75. Luban, *Justice Holmes and the Metaphysics of Judicial Restraint,* 44 Duke L J at 487–88.

76. See id at 484–88.

77. Id at 464. Holmes himself observed, "There is much [in Nietzsche] that I long have believed, after or independently of him—much that I don't care for. He . . . must see man as a little god to be happy . . . —I prefer more serenity." Holmes to Morris R. Cohen, Aug 28, 1924, in Felix S. Cohen, *The Holmes–Cohen Correspondence,* 9 J Hist Ideas 3, 41 (1948).

78. Later chapters will reveal more fully why Holmes merits the Darwinist label.

79. The views of the philosopher Thrasymachus are described in chapter 1 at 8.

80. For material permitting informed speculation about the nature of Holmes's relationship with Castletown, see Novick, *Honorable Justice* at 207–19 (setting forth some of Holmes's letters to Castletown). Holmes biographer G. Edward White, a Virginian and a gentleman, declares that Holmes's early letters to Castletown "do not sound like those of one who has been physically intimate with his correspondent." White regards the tone of a later letter, however, as "that of one who has become intimate with his correspondent, at least emotionally if not physically." White, *Justice Oliver Wendell Holmes* at 239, 241.

    Biographer Sheldon Novick draws a stronger inference:

    > Holmes had a good deal of sexual energy, and the intensity and speed with which he worked . . . was at least partly intended to keep his weekends and summers free for trips to New York and London, for the love affairs and the courtly flirtations that energized his work. Although one can never know what happened behind closed doors, its seems likely that . . . he had affairs. Holmes' love letters to Lady Castletown, for instance, do not reveal the secrets of the bedroom, but they do not leave any doubt about the fundamental nature of the relationship.

    Sheldon M. Novick, *Editor's Introduction* to 1 *Collected Works* at 35.

81. Holmes to Clare Fitzpatrick, Lady Castletown, April 10, 1897, quoted in Novick, *Honorable Justice* at 216.

82. Id.

83. See Oliver Wendell Holmes, *The Soldier's Faith: An Address Delivered on Memorial Day at a Meeting Called by the Graduating Class of Harvard University,* May 30, 1895, reprinted in 3 *Collected Works* at 487. Holmes's remarks on this subject are quoted in chapter 4 at 48.

84. Id at 488.

85. Oliver Wendell Holmes, Jr., *Speech to the Twentieth Regiment, Massachusetts Volunteers,* Dec 10, 1892, in 3 *Collected Works* at 512, 513.

86. Oliver Wendell Holmes, Jr., *Remarks at a Tavern Club Dinner for Paul Bourget,* Dec 4, 1893, in 3 *Collected Works* at 513, 514.

87. Oliver Wendell Holmes, *Speech at a Dinner Given to Chief Justice Holmes by the Bar Association of Boston on March 7, 1900,* in 3 *Collected Works* at 498, 499. Holmes made the point again: "The joy of life is to put one's power in some natural and useful or harmless way. There is no other." Id. Holmes used nearly identical language at the fiftieth reunion of his Harvard College class. See Oliver Wendell Holmes, *The Class of '61: At the Fiftieth Anniversary of Graduation,* June 28, 1911, in 3 *Collected Works* at 504, 505.

    In a speech given in 1902 shortly after his nomination to be a justice of the Supreme Court, Holmes wrote: "[T]he fiercest joy is in the doing. Those who run hardest . . . find, I am sure, that they know most of the joy of life when at top speed. . . . That is the universal romance of man—to face obstacles and to measure his force by the number that he overcomes. . . . [T]he fight is joy." Oliver Wendell Holmes, *Address at a Dinner of the Chicago Bar Association,* Oct 21, 1902, in 3 *Collected Works* at 532, 532–33.

88. Holmes, *Speech at a Dinner Given to Chief Justice Holmes,* reprinted in 3 *Collected Works* at 499.

89. Id at 500.

90. Id.

91. White, *Justice Oliver Wendell Holmes* at 482.

92. Holmes to Ellen Curtis, Jan 7, 1901, quoted in Novick, *Justice Holmes's Philosophy,* 70 Wash U L Q at 734–35.

93. Grey, *Holmes and Legal Pragmatism,* 41 Stan L Rev at 851.

94. Oliver Wendell Holmes, *The Profession of the Law,* in 3 *Collected Works* at 471, 472. Holmes's remarks on this occasion did not claim that the legal profession provided greater opportunities for self-realization than other work: "Every calling is great when greatly pursued." Id at 26. On another occasion, however, Holmes indicated that the legal profession was distinctive: "And what a profession it is! . . . [W]hat other gives such scope to realize the spontaneous energy of one's soul? In what other does one plunge so deep in the stream of life—to share its passions, its battles, its despair, its triumphs—both as witness and actor." *Justice Holmes on the Bench and at the Bar,* 31 Alb L J 419, 420 (1885).

95. Quoted in Novick, *Honorable Justice* at 374. Compare the remarks of Justice William Brennan on his ninetieth birthday: "If I have drawn one lesson in 90 years, it is this: To strike a blow for freedom allows a man to walk a little taller and raise his head a little higher. While he can he must." William J. Brennan, *What the Constitution Requires,* NY Times, Apr 28, 1996, § 4 at 13.

96. Holmes, *On Receiving the Degree of Doctor of Laws, Yale University Commencement,* June 30, 1886, in 3 *Collected Works* at 473.

97. Holmes, *Address of Chief Justice Holmes at the Dedication of the Northwestern University Law School Building, Chicago,* Oct 20, 1902, in 3 *Collected Works* at 529.

98. Id.

99. Holmes, *Remarks at a Tavern Club Dinner for Rudolph C. Lehmann,* Nov 24, 1896, in 3 *Collected Works* at 516–17.

100. Holmes to Morris R. Cohen, Feb 5, 1919, in *The Holmes–Cohen Correspondence,* 9 J Hist Ideas at 15.

101. Holmes, *The Soldier's Faith,* reprinted in 3 *Collected Works* at 486. Chapter 4 describes this address and its influence at 47–48.

102. Id at 489.

103. Jerome K. Jerome, *Three Men on the Bummel* in *Three Men In a Boat* 181, 333 (Dutton, 1966 [1900]).

104. Holmes to Laski, July 1, 1927, in 2 *Holmes–Laski Letters* at 958. See also Holmes to Einstein, Feb 8, 1931, in *Holmes–Einstein Letters* at 321 ("Solitaire seems always an epitome of life. One says to oneself why do I care whether I win the game or not, and then one answers, why do you care to live, or like beer . . . or why do you work?").

> G. Edward White observes:

> The images through which Holmes described [intellectual] ambition reflect physical robustness. . . . They also convey a sense of danger and disappointment, of great striving after rewards that might prove elusive. Life was like an ice floe, or like a quest for a golden chalice—the adventurer could exhaust himself or the cup might prove bitter. . . . The metaphors sought to capture the vast, and at the same time the quixotic, nature of the enterprise.

> G. Edward White, *Holmes's "Life Plan": Confronting Ambition, Passion, and Powerlessness,* 65 NYU L Rev 1409, 1432 (1990) (footnote omitted).

105. Leo Strauss, *Natural Right and History* 47–48 (Univ of Chicago Press, 1953).

106. Wilson, *Patriotic Gore* at 789.

107. Perry, 2 *The Thought and Character of William James* at 250–51 (quoting a letter from William James to Frances R. Morse).

108. Oliver Wendell Holmes, *The Path of the Law,* 10 Harv L Rev 457, 467 (1897), reprinted in 3 *Collected Works* at 391, 398.

109. Holmes to Lewis Einstein, Aug 19, 1909, quoted in Posner, *Introduction* to *The Essential Holmes* at xxv–xxvi. Note the use of "kerosene" as a verb. Holmes's prolific letters confirm his mastery of style and make plausible his biographer's claim that he never wrote more than one draft of anything. See Novick, *Honorable Justice* at 374.

110. Holmes to Pollock, Aug 30, 1929, in 2 *Holmes–Pollock Letters* at 251, 252. See also Holmes to Laski, Jan 11, 1929, in 2 *Holmes–Laski Letters* at 1112, 1125. ("I regard [man] as I do the other species . . . having for his main business to live and propagate, and for his main interest food and sex. A few get a little further along and get pleasure in it, but are fools if they are proud.").

111. McKinnon, *The Secret of Mr. Justice Holmes,* 36 ABA J at 264 (quoting a letter from Holmes to Frederick Pollock).

112. Holmes to Pollock, Feb 1, 1920, in 2 *Holmes–Pollock Letters* at 36. Holmes added, "I should be glad . . . if it could be arranged that the death should precede life by

provisions for a selected race, but we shall not live to see that." Id. See also Holmes to Laski, Jan 14, 1920, in 1 *Holmes–Laski Letters* at 232 ("I repeat my old aphorism that everything is founded on the death of men—society, which only changes the modes of killing—romance, to which . . . generations of dead, on the memorial tablets of a great war, are necessary.").

113. Holmes to John Gray, Sept 3, 1905, quoted in Novick, *Honorable Justice* at 283. Compare Friedrich Nietzsche, *Thus Spoke Zarathustra,* in *The Portable Nietzsche* 115, 129–30 (Walter Kaufmann transl) (Viking, 1954) ("One still works, for work is a form of entertainment.").

114. Letter from Holmes to Lady Pollock, Sept 6, 1902, in 1 *Holmes–Pollock Letters* at 105.

115. Holmes, *Address of Chief Justice Holmes at the Dedication of the Northwestern University Law School Building,* in 3 *Collected Works* at 530.

116. Arthur E. Sutherland, *Book Review,* 32 Cornell L Q 617 (1947).

117. See chapter 3 at 38.

118. William Blackstone, 1 *Commentaries* * 127. See Albert W. Alschuler, *Rediscovering Blackstone,* 145 U Pa L Rev 1, 34–36 (1996) (noting the similar views of other political theorists from the medieval period through the Enlightenment).

119. Holmes to Laski, July 23, 1925, in 1 *Holmes–Laski Letters* at 761, 762.

120. Holmes to Laski, June 14, 1922, in 1 id at 431.

121. Holmes to Felix Frankfurter, Mar 27, 1917, in *Holmes and Frankfurter: Their Correspondence, 1912–1934* at 69, 70 (Robert M. Mennel and Christine L. Compston eds) (Univ Press of New England, 1996).

122. Holmes to Laski, Aug 6, 1917, in 1 *Holmes–Laski Letters* at 96. As Holmes put the matter on another occasion, "The notion that with socialized property we should have women free and a piano for everybody seems to me an empty humbug." Oliver Wendell Holmes, *Ideals and Doubts,* 10 Ill L Rev at 4, reprinted in 3 *Collected Works* at 442, 443.

123. Oliver Wendell Holmes, Jr., Introduction to *Rational Basis of Legal Institutions,* in 3 *Collected Works* at 399, 400.

124. Holmes to Laski, June 1, 1922, in 1 *Holmes–Laski Letters* 429, 430.

125. Holmes to Einstein, Dec 19, 1910, in *Holmes–Einstein Letters* at 57, 59.

126. Holmes to Einstein, May 21, 1914, in id at 92, 93.

127. Holmes to Pollock, July 6, 1908, in 1 *Holmes–Pollock Letters* at 140, 140.

128. Holmes to Pollock, April 26, 1912, in id at 191, 191–92.

129. Holmes to Alice Stopford Green, Feb 7, 1909, quoted in Novick, *Justice Holmes's Philosophy,* 70 Wash U L Q at 721.

130. Luke 2: 29–32 (King James).

131. Holmes to J. C. H. Wu, July 1, 1929, in *Justice Oliver Wendell Holmes: His Book Notices and Uncollected Letters and Papers* 201, 202 (Harry C. Shriver ed) (Central Book, 1936).

132. Holmes to Laski, Aug 1, 1925, in 1 *Holmes–Laski Letters* at 768, 769.

133. Holmes to Laski, May 12, 1927, in 2 id at 941, 942.

134. Holmes to Laski, June 1, 1927, in id at 948.

135. Holmes to Laski, Sept 15, 1916, in 1 id at 20, 21.

136. Oliver Wendell Holmes, *Natural Law,* 32 Harv L Rev 40 (1918), reprinted in 3 *Collected Works* at 445–46.

137. Id, reprinted in 3 *Collected Works* at 447. On reading Holmes's remarks about natural law in the *Harvard Law Review,* Frederick Pollock wrote him:

   > [I]f you mean to imply that no one can accept natural law (= natural justice = reason as understood in the Common Law) without maintaining it as a body of rules known to be absolutely true, I do not agree. . . .
   >   If you deny that any principles of conduct at all are common to and admitted by all men who try to behave reasonably—well, I don't see how you can have any ethics or any ethical background for law.

   Pollock to Holmes, Dec 20, 1918, in 1 *Holmes–Pollock Letters* at 274, 274–75. Holmes replied, "I didn't expect you to agree with me altogether. As to Ethics I have called them a body of imperfect social generalizations expressed in terms of emotion." Holmes to Pollock, Jan 24, 1919, in 2 id at 3.

138. Holmes to Laski, Sept 7, 1916, in 1 *Holmes–Laski Letters* at 16.

139. Holmes to Laski, April 13, 1929, in 2 id at 1146.

140. United States v Schwimmer, 279 US 644, 654 (1929) (Holmes dissenting).

141. Holmes to Laski, April 13, 1929, in 2 *Holmes–Laski Letters* at 1146.

142. Holmes to J. H. Wigmore, Nov 1915, quoted in Novick, *Honorable Justice* at 469 n11.

143. Holmes to Laski, Dec 3, 1917, in 1 *Holmes–Laski Letters* 115, 116. See also Holmes to Laski, Aug 5, 1926, in 2 id 862 ("Pleasures are ultimates and in cases of difference between oneself and another there is nothing to do except in unimportant matters to think ill of him and in important ones to kill him.").

144. Holmes to Sir Frederick and Lady Pollock, Sept 20, 1928, in 2 *Holmes–Pollock Letters* 230.

145. Holmes, *Ideals and Doubts,* 10 Ill L Rev at 3, reprinted in 3 *Collected Works* at 443.

146. Holmes to Clare Fitzpatrick, Lady Castletown, Aug 19, 1897, quoted in Novick, *Justice Holmes's Philosophy,* 70 Wash U L Q at 729.

147. Holmes to Einstein, Aug 6, 1917, in *Holmes–Einstein Letters* 144, 145. Note that this statement followed the one cited in the preceding footnote by twenty years.

148. Holmes, *The Soldier's Faith,* reprinted at 3 *Collected Works* at 487.

149. Oliver Wendell Holmes, *Law and the Court,* Feb 15, 1913, in 3 *Collected Works* at 505, 507.

150. Oliver Wendell Holmes, *Law and Social Reform,* in *The Mind and Faith of Justice Holmes* 399, 401 (Max Lerner ed) (Little, Brown, 1943).

151. Holmes to Frankfurter, Sept 3, 1921, in *Holmes and Frankfurter: Their Correspondence* at 124, 125. Holmes added, "I don't know enough to say that I want it but

I think it the condition of intelligent socialism." Id. Holmes apparently believed that a regime of *laissez-faire* capitalism might eliminate unfit infants without governmental executions but that a successful socialist regime required them.

152. Id at 126. See also Holmes to Pollock, Feb 26, 1922, in 2 *Holmes–Pollock Letters* at 89, 90 ("I always say that society is founded on the death of men—if you don't kill the weakest one way you kill them another.").

153. Holmes to J. C. H. Wu, July 21, 1925, in *Justice Oliver Wendell Holmes: His Book Notices, Uncollected Letters and Papers* at 181.

154. Lucey, *Jurisprudence and the Future Social Order,* 16 Soc Sci at 214–15.

155. Posner, *Introduction* to *The Essential Holmes* at xxix.

156. Novick, *Justice Holmes's Philosophy,* 70 Wash U L Q at 732.

157. The organizers of the First and Second International Congresses of Eugenics kept the topic of birth control entirely off the agenda. *Eugenics Then and Now* 52 (Carl Jay Bajema ed) (Dowden, Hutchinson & Ross 1976). Recalling her disagreements with other participants in the Sixth International Malthusian and Birth Control Conference, Margaret Sanger declared, "[E]ugenics without birth control seemed to me a house built upon sands." Id at 51.

158. Edgar Schuster, *Eugenics* 254 (Warwick and York, 1912).

159. *Buck v Bell,* 274 US 200 (1927). This opinion is discussed in chapter 5 at 65–67.

160. Ian Dowbiggin, *Keeping America Sane: Psychiatry and Eugenics in the United States and Canada, 1880–1940* at 78 (Cornell Univ Press, 1997).

161. Id.

162. S. J. Holmes, *The Eugenic Predicament* 148 (Harcourt, Brace, 1933). In 1912, Edgar Schuster advocated measures "for the care and control of the feeble-minded." He did not endorse sterilization but did declare that "[t]his control should be of a sufficiently effective and permanent kind to preclude the possibility of such persons propagating their kind." Schuster then added, "The passing of such a measure is the only directly Eugenic legislation which can at present be advocated." Schuster, *Eugenics* at 250–51.

163. See Daniel Kevles, *In the Name of Eugenics: Genetics and the Uses of Human Heredity* 21, 63, 94 (Knopf, 1985). Francis Galton, the cousin of Charles Darwin who gave the eugenics movement its name, once met Laski, one of Holmes's acolytes and correspondents. Galton described Laski as "simply a *beautiful* youth of the Jewish type." Id at 86.

164. Apart from Holmes himself, I know of only one American who seemed to voice approval of execution as a tool of eugenic policy during Holmes's lifetime, and that writer's approval was unclear. Madison Grant wrote in 1919, "Mistaken regard for what are believed to be divine laws and a sentimental belief in the sanctity of human life tend to prevent both the elimination of defective infants and the sterilization of such adults as are themselves of no value to the community." Madison Grant, *The Passing of the Great Race: Or, the Racial Basis of European History* 49 (Scribner's, 1919). Grant's work as a whole suggests, however, that he meant to

"eliminat[e] defective infants" only through such measures as forbidding inter-racial marriage and withdrawing charitable aid to the poor. Following Holmes's death, Grant did praise Adolf Hitler's views on racial purity and sent copies of his work to Hitler's scientific advisers. At that time, other Americans also voiced their approval of Hitler's eugenic policies, and a few endorsed execution of the "feebleminded." See William H. Tucker, *The Science and Politics of Racial Research* 124–25, 243, 318 n298 (Univ of Illinois Press, 1994).

165. See White, *Justice Oliver Wendell Holmes* at 320, 408.

166. Oliver Wendell Holmes, *The Class of '61; At the Fiftieth Anniversary of Graduation,* June 28, 1911, in 3 *Collected Works* at 504, 505.

167. Id. Holmes's admirers tend to emphasize transcendental statements like these. They also may note that his letters were full of chatter about books read, walks taken, and drives in Rock Creek Park "through all manner of tender greens with the white of the dogwood blossoms flashing. . . ." Holmes to "Marchioness" (Lewis Einstein's daughter), May 6, 1925, in *Holmes–Einstein Letters* at 238, 239.

168. Holmes, *The Soldier's Faith,* reprinted in 3 *Collected Works* at 489.

169. See text at 23–24.

170. See, for example, Richard D. Parker, *The Mind of Darkness,* 110 Harv L Rev 1033, 1033 (1997). But see Dailey, *Holmes and the Romantic Mind,* 48 Duke L J at 483 & n268 (calling Holmes a romantic while recognizing that he "consistently empha-sized the individual's selfish and aggressive instincts").

171. The following conclusion of a speech indicates how Holmes's existentialism blended with his view of the cosmos:

> The law of the grub and the hen is the law also for man. We all have cosmic destinies of which we cannot divine the end, if the unknown has ends. Our business is to commit ourselves to life, to accept at once our functions and our ignorance and to offer our heart to fate.

Oliver Wendell Holmes, *Remarks at a Dinner of the Alpha Delta Phi Club,* Sept 27, 1912, in 3 *Collected Works* at 539, 541.

Chapter Three

1. Sheldon M. Novick, *Honorable Justice: The Life of Oliver Wendell Holmes* (Little, Brown, 1989).

2. For a description of Holmes's relationship with these admirers, see David A. Hol-linger, *The "Tough-Minded" Justice Holmes, Jewish Intellectuals, and the Making of an American Icon,* in *The Legacy of Oliver Wendell Holmes, Jr.* 216, 227 (Robert W. Gor-don ed) (Stanford Univ Press, 1992).

3. See Novick, *Honorable Justice* at xvi–xvii.

4. Grant Gilmore, *The Ages of American Law* 48–49 (Yale Univ Press, 1977).

5. Sheldon M. Novick, *Editor's Introduction* to 1 *The Collected Works of Justice Holmes: Complete Public Writings and Selected Judicial Opinions of Oliver Wendell Holmes* 1, 6

(Sheldon M. Novick ed) (Univ of Chicago Press, 1995) (hereinafter cited as *Collected Works*).

6. See Novick, *Honorable Justice* at xvii.

7. Novick, *Editor's Introduction* to *Collected Works* at 6.

8. Catherine Drinker Bowen, *Yankee from Olympus* (Atlantic/Little, Brown, 1944). On Bowen's inability to secure access to the Holmes papers, see Novick, *Editor's Introduction* to *Collected Works* at 5.

9. Unlike the other authorized biographers, Frankfurter was not disillusioned with Holmes, but his appointment as a justice of the Supreme Court precluded his completion of the biography. Frankfurter's admiration for Holmes and his role in promoting Holmes's reputation are described in chapter 8 at 182–83.

10. Robert M. Mennel and Christine L. Compston, *Introduction* to *Holmes and Frankfurter: Their Correspondence, 1912–1934* at xi, xxix–xli (Robert M. Mennel and Christine L. Compston eds) (Univ Press of New England, 1996).

11. Sheldon M. Novick, *Justice Holmes and the Art of Biography,* 33 Wm & Mary L Rev 1219, 1219–20 (1992).

12. G. Edward White, *Justice Oliver Wendell Holmes: Law and the Inner Self* 410–11 (Oxford Univ Press, 1993).

13. Id at 467.

14. See Novick, *Honorable Justice* at 129–31, 428 n20.

15. See Liva Baker, *The Justice from Beacon Hill: The Life and Times of Oliver Wendell Holmes* 218–19 (HarperCollins, 1991).

16. Oliver Wendell Holmes, Sr., *The Poet at the Breakfast Table* 69 (James R. Osgood, 1872).

17. Id at 279.

18. Id at 166.

19. Oliver Wendell Holmes, *The Profession of the Law,* reprinted in 3 *Collected Works* at 471, 472–73.

20. Letter from Oliver Wendell Holmes to Lady Burghclere, Sept 17, 1898, quoted in White, *Justice Oliver Wendell Holmes* at 102.

21. Id.

22. Novick, *Honorable Justice* at 33.

23. White, *Justice Oliver Wendell Holmes* at 105.

24. The second volume carried the story of Holmes's life to his appointment to the Supreme Judicial Court of Massachusetts in 1882. See Mark DeWolfe Howe, *Justice Oliver Wendell Holmes: The Shaping Years, 1841–1870* (Harvard Univ Press, 1957); Mark DeWolfe Howe, *Justice Oliver Wendell Holmes: The Proving Years, 1870–1882* (Harvard Univ Press, 1963).

25. Howe, *Justice Oliver Wendell Holmes: The Proving Years* at 8; see White, *Justice Oliver Wendell Holmes* at 102, 103.

26. Baker, *The Justice from Beacon Hill* at 196.

27. Holmes to Ellen Curtis, Mar 21, 1903, quoted in White, *Justice Oliver Wendell Holmes* at 311.

28. Holmes to Patrick Sheehan, Dec 15, 1912, in *The Holmes–Sheehan Correspondence: Letters of Justice Oliver Wendell Holmes, Jr. and Canon Patrick Augustine Sheehan* 56 (David M. Burton ed) (Kennikat Press, 1976).

29. Novick, *Honorable Justice* at 120.

30. Id at 145.

31. Id at 155; Baker, *The Justice from Beacon Hill* at 260–61.

32. Baker, *The Justice from Beacon Hill* at 261.

33. Id at 221, 224.

34. Novick, *Honorable Justice* at 336.

35. Id at 137, 143, 220, 225–26, 233; White, *Justice Oliver Wendell Holmes* at 102.

36. Holmes to Lady Ethel Scott, Jan 6, 1912, quoted in Howe, *Justice Oliver Wendell Holmes: The Proving Years* at 103.

37. Holmes to Lewis Einstein, June 1929, in *The Holmes–Einstein Letters: The Correspondence of Mr. Justice Holmes and Lewis Einstein* 59 (James Bishop Peabody ed) (St. Martin's, 1964).

38. White, *Justice Oliver Wendell Holmes* at 105.

39. Novick, *Honorable Justice* at 201.

40. Id at 285–86, 317, 337–38.

41. Holmes to Lord and Lady Pollock, May 24, 1929, in 2 *The Holmes–Pollock Letters: The Correspondence of Mr. Justice Holmes and Sir Frederick Pollock 1874–1932* at 243 (Mark DeWolfe Howe ed) (Harvard Univ Press, 1941).

42. White, *Justice Oliver Wendell Holmes* at 460.

43. Holmes to Lewis Einstein, Aug 31, 1928, in *Holmes–Einstein Letters* at 269.

44. Id.

45. Letter from Hand to Mark DeWolfe Howe, April 29, 1959, quoted in Howe, *Justice Oliver Wendell Holmes: The Proving Years* at 8 n17.

46. See, for example, Novick, *Honorable Justice* at 14.

47. James answered "no, he was not bothered that way."

48. Howe, *Justice Oliver Wendell Holmes: The Shaping Years* at 11–12.

49. Howe, *Justice Oliver Wendell Holmes: The Proving Years* at 255.

50. Holmes to James, Dec 15, 1867, in Ralph Barton Perry, 1 *The Thought and Character of William James* 506 (Little, Brown, 1935).

51. James to Holmes, Jan 3, 1868, in id at 508. James earlier had written notes to "Sweet Wendell" and had signed the notes "Thine Till Death." Novick, *Honorable Justice* at 95, 422 n4. After addressing James as "Bill, my beloved," Holmes's declared, "In spite of my many friends I am almost alone in my thoughts and inner feelings. And whether I ever see you much or not, I think I can never fail to derive a secret comfort and companionship from the thought of you. I believe I shall always respect and love you whether we see much or little of each other."

Sheldon Novick infers on the basis of extremely thin evidence that Holmes had a sexual liaison with William James's brother Henry. See Sheldon M. Novick, *Henry James: The Young Master* 109–110 (Random House, 1996). Whatever the relationship between Holmes and Henry James may have been, the romantic tone of some of Holmes's exchanges with William James seems merely playful. Although no available evidence can entirely prove the negative, William James later declared that "homosexuality affects us with horror." Michael Kenney, *The Big Literary Debate: Did They or Didn't They? Bio Claims Holmes, Henry James Tryst,* Boston Globe, Dec 19, 1996, at E1. Moreover, the correspondence between the two men includes offhand references to their interest in women. See, for example, Holmes to James, Apr 19, 1868, in Perry, 1 *The Thought and Character of William James* at 510 (referring to the "not infrequent times when . . . a girl of some trivial sort can fill the hour for me"). The relationship between Holmes and William James may in fact have been complicated by their romantic interest in the same women, including the woman whom Holmes later married. See Novick, *Honorable Justice* at 103 (describing James's courtship of Fanny Dixwell).

Throughout his life, Holmes "treated flirtation as both a treasured opportunity for self-revelation and a parlor exercise," and he regarded "intimacy itself . . . as something of a game." White, *Justice Oliver Wendell Holmes* at 31. Following Holmes's appointment to the Supreme Court, he wrote to various women correspondents:

> I have not looked upon a woman save in the way of kindness. I see no probability of new ventures.
>
> [I have decided] to close out that department [romantic flirtations] and be a kindly cynic . . . and . . . a survivor.
>
> It remains true that I see no one intimately. One is in such a high light that eternal discretion is necessary.
>
> I somehow found myself talking to a very pretty girl . . . & she told me I might play in her backyard if I didn't play with other girls. . . . But I fear the tragedy ends there, as I don't have time to play in backyards. . . . I am hoping to read some philosophy or law in the breathing spells—that does me more good than playing in backyards.

White, *Justice Oliver Wendell Holmes* at 308–10 (quoting letters from Holmes to Ellen Curtis, Dec 21, 1902; Holmes to Anna Codman, Feb 15, 1903; Holmes to Ellen Curtis, April 1, 1903; and Holmes to Nina Gray, Feb 8, 1904). The best inference on the basis of the available evidence is that Oliver Wendell Holmes was heterosexual and exclusively so. See Kenney, *The Big Literary Debate* at E1 (noting Louis Menand's description of Holmes as a "rabid heterosexual").

52. James to Holmes, May 15, 1868, in Perry, 1 *The Thought and Character of William James* at 514.

53. William James to Henry James, Oct 2, 1869, in id at 307.

54. William James to Henry James, July 5, 1876, in id at 371.

55. In 1888, James attributed Holmes's decision to vote for Benjamin Harrison to his desire "to show the shady side of himself." William James to Alice James, Oct 14, 1888, in id at 408.

56. Holmes to Sir Frederick Pollock, Sept 1, 1910, in 1 *Holmes–Pollock Letters* at 166, 167. My account of the Holmes–James relationship is drawn partly from Novick, *Honorable Justice* and from Thomas C. Grey, *Holmes and Legal Pragmatism,* 41 Stan L Rev 787, 865–68 (1989).

57. Mary James to Henry James, Jr., Feb 28, 1873, quoted in White, *Justice Oliver Wendell Holmes* at 89–90. Earlier, Mary James wrote that Minnie Temple, who once had been attracted to Holmes, had become "quite disenchanted, and evidently looks at Holmes with very different eyes from what she did; that is she sees him as others do, talks of his thinness and pinchedness, as well as of his beautiful eyes, and seems to see his egotism." Mary James to Alice James, Jan 1867, quoted in White, *Justice Oliver Wendell Holmes* at 92. See id at 14 ("[C]ontemporaries of Holmes . . . , especially during his late twenties and thirties, remarked on his self-preoccupation and singlemindedness."); id at 478 ("[Holmes's] early self-preoccupation [was] periodically rendered by contemporaries as selfishness.").

58. Baker, *The Justice from Beacon Hill* at 210.

59. Novick, *Honorable Justice* at 164.

60. Id at 166.

61. Howe, *Justice Oliver Wendell Holmes: The Proving Years* at 263–64.

62. Id at 264 n19. The Weld Professor at the Harvard Law School is now Charles R. Nesson. Another William F. Weld, a graduate of the Harvard Law School, was governor of Massachusetts from 1991 until 1997. Captain Joseph Weld, a seventeenth-century ancestor of William F. Weld, Jr. and reputedly the richest person in the Massachusetts Bay Colony, was among the first donors to Harvard College. See *Other Merchants and Sea Captains of Old Boston: Being More Information about the Merchants and Sea Captains of Old Boston Who Played Such an Important Part in Building Up the Commerce of New England Together with Some Quaint and Curious Stories of the Sea* 60–62 (Walton Advertising and Printing Co., 1919) (material supplied by Governor William F. Weld). Our democracy is not entirely without its dynasties.

63. Holmes to Harvard president Charles William Eliot, Nov 1, 1881, in Howe, *Justice Oliver Wendell Holmes: The Proving Years* at 260, 261.

64. Novick, *Honorable Justice* at 169.

65. Howe, *Justice Oliver Wendell Holmes: The Proving Years* at 267.

66. Id at 267.

67. Id at 267–68.

68. Id at 270–71.

69. Francis Biddle, *Justice Holmes, Natural Law, and the Supreme Court* 7 (Macmillan, 1961).

70. See Baker, *The Justice from Beacon Hill* at 7–8, 642; Gary J. Aichele, *Oliver Wendell Holmes, Jr.: Soldier, Scholar, Judge* 93 (Twayne, 1989) ("No record remains to indicate any interest in politics, civic, or charitable activities."); id at 106 ("[T]here is no record that Holmes ever represented the oppressed or downtrodden of Bos-

ton."); Howe, *Justice Oliver Wendell Holmes: The Proving Years* at 110 ("If any of the partners [of Holmes's firm] had a social conscience his practice did not reveal it.").

71. Edmund Wilson, *Patriotic Gore: Studies in the Literature of the American Civil War* 796 (Oxford Univ Press, 1962).

72. I. Scott Messinger, *The Judge as Mentor: Oliver Wendell Holmes, Jr., and His Law Clerks,* 11 Yale J of Law and the Humanities 119, 133 n57 (1999) (quoting the unpublished diary of the law clerk, Chauncey Belknap).

73. Baker, *The Justice from Beacon Hill* at 642. On the Supreme Court's recommendation, Congress approved the use of Holmes's legacy to fund two "non-productive enterprises"—the publication of a collection of his writing and the establishment of a park in his honor. Fifteen years later, with neither project underway, Congress enacted legislation establishing The Permanent Committee of the Oliver Wendell Holmes Devise. This committee approved the funding of three projects—a history of the Supreme Court, a series of Oliver Wendell Holmes Lectures at American law schools, and a memorial volume of Holmes's writings. See Novick, *The History of This Edition,* in 1 *Collected Works* at 3, 4–5. The collection of Holmes's writings was published only in 1995. See *Collected Works*. Despite substantial recent progress, the Holmes Devise history of the Supreme Court has not been completed sixty-five years after Holmes's death. Most of the prominent scholars who initially agreed to write volumes in the series failed to do so. See *The Oliver Wendell Holmes Devise History of the Supreme Court,* Virginia Journal 33, 34–35 (fall 1999). Despite the fizzles that followed it, I personally do not believe that Holmes's money was cursed.

74. Novick, *Honorable Justice* at 186.

75. White, *Justice Oliver Wendell Holmes* at 228 (quoting Holmes to Owen Wister, Apr 14, 1889). While Holmes was a justice of the Supreme Court, he and Mrs. Holmes provided an apartment in their house on I Street for an orphaned cousin of Holmes, Dorothy Upham. Novick, *Honorable Justice* at 264. Moreover, Justice Holmes answered almost all of his own mail. As John Wu learned when he began his correspondence with Holmes, a student could write to him, refer to a paper that the student had published, and receive a handwritten reply. See letters from Oliver Wendell Holmes to J. C. H. Wu (Apr 19, 1921 and Apr 20, 1921), in *Justice Oliver Wendell Holmes: His Book Notices and Uncollected Letters and Papers* 151–52 (Harry C. Shriver ed) (Central Book, 1936) (offering words of advice concerning a law review article written by Wu). At age 22, John Wu was not in fact a student, but Holmes apparently believed that he was. Upon recognizing his error, the justice wrote a second, longer reply to the letter Wu had sent him.

76. Novick, *Honorable Justice* at 180.

77. *Webster's American Biographies* 193 (Charles Van Doren ed) (G. & C. Merriam, 1984).

78. Baker, *Justice from Beacon Hill* at 293.

79. Id.

80. One sees in Holmes's correspondence occasional hints of excitement at brutal thoughts. Whether or not Clare Castletown and Oliver Wendell Holmes were lovers, Castletown unmistakably evoked strong sexual feelings in Holmes. A letter from Holmes to Castletown in 1897 contained the following passage:

   > [U]ntil you substitute artificial selection for natural by putting to death the inadequate, or get the whole world to limit procreation to the visible means of support, I do not believe you will see socialism successful. Existing society is founded on the death of men. While I write in this abstract way I am thinking of you until you seem almost present—and I can hardly go on.

   Holmes to Clare Fitzpatrick, Lady Castletown, Aug 19, 1897, quoted in Sheldon M. Novick, *Justice Holmes's Philosophy*, 70 Wash U L Q 703, 729 (1992). Sheldon Novick observes that "[s]imilarly brutal passages within very affectionate letters were not unusual for Holmes." Id.

81. Richard H. Rovere, *The American Establishment and Other Reports, Opinions, and Speculations* 149 (Harcourt Brace-World, 1962).

82. See White, *Justice Oliver Wendell Holmes* at 489.

83. Novick doubts that Holmes in fact met Adams, though Holmes's father did take him to the late president's funeral when Holmes was almost seven. Holmes, however, grew up "in the presence of the local literary peerage" including such figures as James Russell Lowell, Henry Wadsworth Longfellow, Ralph Waldo Emerson, William H. Prescott, John Greenleaf Whittier, Nathaniel Hawthorne, and Herman Melville. See Baker, *The Justice from Beacon Hill* at 15.

84. Novick, *Honorable Justice* at 422 n37. But see Howe, *Justice Oliver Wendell Holmes: The Shaping Years* at 168–69 & 304 n76 (describing Felix Frankfurter's recounting of Holmes's story as "the most reliable version" of events, describing Harold Laski's version as "imaginative," and reciting evidence that makes both versions seem highly improbable).

85. Novick, *Honorable Justice* at 376.

86. See Posner, *Introduction* to *The Essential Holmes: Selections from the Letters, Speeches, Judicial Opinions, and Other Writings of Oliver Wendell Holmes, Jr.* xiv (Richard A. Posner ed) (Univ of Chicago Press, 1992).

87. See 1 & 2 *Holmes–Pollock Letters*.

88. Wilson, *Patriotic Gore* at 788.

89. G. Edward White, *Holmes as Correspondent*, 43 Vand L Rev 1707, 1761 (1990).

90. I owe this thought and most of this paragraph to John C. P. Goldberg.

Chapter Four

1. As a child, Holmes was described as "docile" and "amiable." Mark DeWolfe Howe, *Justice Oliver Wendell Holmes: The Shaping Years, 1841–1870* at 5 (Harvard Univ Press, 1957) (quoting a letter from one of Holmes's schoolmasters, T. Russell Sullivan, to another, Epes Sargent Dixwell [the father of Fanny Dixwell, whom Holmes married twenty-one years later], Sept 29, 1851). In college, however,

Holmes was disciplined several times for minor misconduct. This misconduct once took the form of "repeated and gross indecorum in the recitation of Professor Bowen." Liva Baker, *The Justice from Beacon Hill: The Life and Times of Oliver Wendell Holmes* 80, 81–82 (HarperCollins, 1991). The pieties of Francis Bowen, the Alford Professor of Natural Religion, were apparently too much for Holmes, but as the following paragraphs in the text reveal, Holmes did not scoff at all religious belief.

2. Oliver Wendell Holmes, Jr., *Books,* 4 Harv Mag 408 (1858), reprinted in 1 *The Collected Works of Justice Holmes: Complete Public Writings and Selected Judicial Opinions of Oliver Wendell Holmes* 139 (Sheldon M. Novick ed) (Univ of Chicago Press, 1995) (hereinafter cited as *Collected Works*). See G. Edward White, *Justice Oliver Wendell Holmes: Law and the Inner Self* 38–39 (Oxford Univ Press, 1993) ("It may be surprising for those who have come to associate Holmes with the philosophical perspectives of skepticism, empiricism, or even resignation, to come to grips with the fact that in his initial effort at critical writing he was assuming the role of an Emersonian camp follower.").

3. *Plato,* 2 Univ Quart 205, 213 (Oct 1860), reprinted in 1 *Collected Works* at 145. Despite this criticism, Holmes wrote of Plato and his teacher Socrates, "I should wish my last words to be those of the reverence and love with which this great man and his master always fill me."

4. Howe, *Justice Oliver Wendell Holmes: The Shaping Years* at 54.

5. Id at 56.

6. *Plato,* 2 Univ Quart at 210, reprinted in 1 *Collected Works* at 148.

7. Id at 209, 212, reprinted in 1 *Collected Works* at 148, 149.

8. *Notes on Albert Durer,* 7 Harv Mag 41 (Oct 1860), reprinted in 1 *Collected Works* at 153, 157.

9. Howe, *Justice Oliver Wendell Holmes: The Shaping Years* at 46–47.

10. Id at 48. The more conservative group to which Holmes referred limited its membership to students who "heartily assent[ed] to the fundamental truths of the Christian religion" and who provided evidence of "a saving change of heart." Id at 46.

11. Holmes to Arthur Garfield Hays, April 20, 1928, quoted in Howe, *Justice Oliver Wendell Holmes: The Shaping Years* at 49. Recall Holmes's statement, quoted in chapter 2 at 17: "[W]hen I was a sophomore, I didn't like the nigger minstrels because they seemed to belittle the race. . . . [Now] I fear you would shudder . . . at the low level of some of my social beliefs."

12. See Sheldon M. Novick, *Honorable Justice: The Life of Oliver Wendell Holmes* 15 (Little, Brown, 1989).

13. Baker, *The Justice from Beacon Hill* at 58.

14. Howe, *Justice Oliver Wendell Holmes: The Shaping Years* at 67.

15. Baker, *The Justice from Beacon Hill* at 57.

16. Howe, *Justice Oliver Wendell Holmes: The Shaping Years* at 65–67.

17. See id at 69–76.

18. Id at 71.

19. Id at 75. For discussion of the role of Hallowell in Holmes's war experience, see text at 44–46.

20. See Novick, *Honorable Justice* at 48–51.

21. See undated diary entry, in *Touched with Fire: Civil War Letters and Diary of Oliver Wendell Holmes, Jr., 1861–1864* at 24 (Mark DeWolfe Howe ed) (Harvard Univ Press, 1946).

22. Holmes to his mother, Oct 23, 1861, in id at 13, 18. In the Battle of Ball's Bluff, more than half the Union troops were killed, wounded, or captured. The commander of the Union forces was among the dead, and the commander of Holmes's regiment was among the captured. White, *Justice Oliver Wendell Holmes* at 52.

23. This at least was the story told by Holmes Sr. Novick offers evidence that his trip to the war zone had been planned for journalistic purposes before he learned of his son's injuries. Novick, *Honorable Justice* at 419 n27.

24. See Howe, *Justice Oliver Wendell Holmes: The Shaping Years* at 131–32; Baker, *The Justice from Beacon Hill* at 8.

25. Novick, *Honorable Justice* at 78.

26. Undated diary entry, in *Touched with Fire* at 25.

27. Holmes to his parents, June 2, 1862, in id at 47, 50–51.

28. Holmes to his mother, Dec 12, 1862, in id at 74, 78. Holmes wrote this letter while "miserably sick with the dysentery" and hospitalized behind the lines. He wrote that he and a companion had climbed a hill from which they watched the Battle of Fredericksburg. For the first time, Holmes's regiment was engaged in heavy fighting without him. "We couldn't see the men but we saw the battle," Holmes wrote. Saul Touster suggested that this letter offered a metaphor of Holmes's postwar view of humanity. Following the war, he would be able to see the battle but not the men. See Saul Touster, *In Search of Holmes from Within,* 18 Vand L Rev 437, 459 (1965).

29. Diary entry for May 8, 1864, in *Touched with Fire* at 108, 109.

30. Holmes to his mother, May 11, 1864, in id at 114.

31. Diary entry for May 13, 1864, in id at 117.

32. Holmes to his parents, May 16, 1864, in id at 121–22.

33. Id at 122.

34. Diary entry for May 18, 1864, in id at 125, 126.

35. Holmes to his sister Amelia, Nov 16, 1862, in id at 70, 73.

36. See White, *Justice Oliver Wendell Holmes* at 27, 31.

37. See Baker, *The Justice from Beacon Hill* at 108.

38. See *Touched with Fire* at 27, 18, 42, 60.

39. Id at 45.

40. Id at 65–66.

41. See Howe, *Justice Oliver Wendell Holmes: The Shaping Years* at 153 (quoting a letter of Governor John A. Andrew).

42. Hallowell to Holmes, Feb 7, 1863, in id at 152.

43. See Mark DeWolfe Howe, *Preface* to *Touched with Fire* at viii–ix.

44. Howe, *Justice Oliver Wendell Holmes: The Shaping Years* at 152 (suggesting that Governor Andrew would not have rejected Holmes's application).

45. W. E. B. Du Bois, *Black Reconstruction in America* 104 (A. Saifer, 1935) ("Nothing else made Negro citizenship conceivable, but the record of the Negro as a fighter."). For the estimate of the number of black soldiers killed, see Jack D. Foner, *Blacks and the Military in American History* 32 (1974).

46. Herbert Spencer, *Social Statics* (John Chapman, 1851). Compare *Lochner v New York,* 198 US 45, 75 (1905) (Holmes dissenting) ("The Fourteenth Amendment does not enact Mr. Herbert Spencer's *Social Statics*.").

47. Decades later, Holmes would write of Abbott:

    In action he was sublime. . . . [At Fredericksburg, h]is first platoon had vanished . . . in an instant, ten men falling dead by his side. He had quietly turned back to where the other half of his company was waiting, had given the order, "Second platoon, forward!" and was again moving on, in obedience to superior command, to certain and useless death, when the order he was obeying was countermanded. . . . [F]or us, who not only admired, but loved, his death seemed to end a portion of our life also.

    Oliver Wendell Holmes, *Memorial Day,* in 3 *Collected Works* at 462, 465. Although Holmes's account declared, "His few surviving companions will never forget the awful spectacle of his advance along with his company . . . ," Holmes had not been present. See White, *Justice Oliver Wendell Holmes* at 77–78.

48. Howe, *Justice Oliver Wendell Holmes: The Shaping Years* at 159.

49. Novick, *Honorable Justice* at 80.

50. Holmes to his mother, June 7, 1864, in *Touched with Fire* at 141, 143. According to Sheldon Novick, "Both [of Holmes's] parents urged him to reenlist until the war's end, although that seemed to him to mean almost certain death." Sheldon M. Novick, *Justice Holmes's Philosophy,* 70 Wash U L Q 703, 709 (1992). Liva Baker notes, "Holmes's letters from his parents have not survived, but it seems apparent from his defiant answers during this time that he was being criticized for his decision to resign." Baker, *The Justice from Beacon Hill* at 149.

51. Holmes to Laski, Sept 18, 1918, in 1 *The Holmes–Laski Letters: The Correspondence of Mr. Justice Holmes and Harold J. Laski, 1916–1935* at 163, 164 (Mark DeWolfe Howe ed) (Harvard Univ Press, 1953).

52. Holmes to Laski, June 1, 1927, in 2 id at 948. Immediately before this sentence, Holmes wrote, "I . . . would fight for some things—but instead of saying that they ought to be I merely say they are part of the kind of world that I like, or should like."

53. Holmes to Laski, July 10, 1930, in 2 id at 1265.

54. Holmes to Laski, Oct 24, 1930, in 2 id at 1291.

55. Touster, *In Search of Holmes from Within,* 18 Vand L Rev at 449.

56. Holmes to his parents, May 30, 1864, in *Touched with Fire* at 135.

57. As noted in chapter 3 in text at 33–34, Holmes Sr. described his son several years after the war as a "strange unearthly being" with eyes "turned away from all human things"—"further away from life than any student whose head is bent downward over his books."

58. Holmes's appointment to the Supreme Judicial Court of Massachusetts in 1882 led to invitations to speak at memorial occasions, and these occasions provided opportunities for reflection on his military experience. See Holmes, *Memorial Day,* in 3 *Collected Works* at 462 (the first of Holmes's commemorative speeches).

59. G. Edward White observes that Holmes "glorif[ied] war and its codes" and that he "emerged . . . with considerable survivor guilt." White, *Justice Oliver Wendell Holmes* at 477.

60. Holmes, *Memorial Day,* in 3 *Collected Works* at 467.

61. Holmes to Lewis Einstein, Mar 27, 1912, in *The Holmes–Einstein Letters: Correspondence of Mr. Justice Holmes and Lewis Einstein* 66, 67 (James Bishop Peabody ed) (St. Martin's, 1964).

62. Oliver Wendell Holmes, Jr., *Edward Avery and Erastus Worthington,* in 3 *Collected Works* at 521, 522.

63. Holmes to Laski, Dec 31, 1916, in 1 *Holmes–Laski Letters* 49.

64. See Novick, *Honorable Justice* at 234–35.

65. John A. Garraty, *Holmes's Appointment to the U.S. Supreme Court,* 22 New Eng Q, 291, 296 (1949) (quoting Lodge's letter). As G. Edward White observes, not only were Roosevelt, Lodge, and Holmes all Harvard men, they were all members of the socially elite Porcellian Club. White, *Justice Oliver Wendell Holmes* at 299.

66. See White, *Justice Oliver Wendell Holmes* at 299–303; Baker, *The Justice from Beacon Hill* at 348–51.

67. Holmes traveled to Sagamore Hill on July 24, 1902, and conferred with the president the next morning. He wrote on his reading list, "July 25. Presdt offered me Judgeship." Baker, *The Justice from Beacon Hill* at 349. Holmes nevertheless told the reporters who informed him of his nomination on August 11, "Personally I know nothing of the matter beyond what you tell me, my first intimation that I had been, or was going to be, chosen coming from the press." Id at 351.

68. Oliver Wendell Holmes, *The Soldier's Faith: An Address Delivered on Memorial Day at a Meeting Called by the Graduating Class of Harvard University,* May 30, 1895, in 3 *Collected Works* at 486, 489.

69. Id at 490. Holmes had spoken in an earlier speech of "that something more which led men . . . to toss life and hope like a flower at the feet of their country and their cause." Quoted in Baker, *The Justice from Beacon Hill* at 286.

70. Oliver Wendell Holmes, *The Fraternity at Arms: Remarks at a Meeting of the 20th Regimental Association,* Dec 11, 1897, in 3 *Collected Works* at 519, 519.

71. Holmes, *The Soldier's Faith,* in 3 *Collected Works* at 486–87. Compare Jean Bethke Elshtain, *Women and War* 173 (Basic Books, 1987) ("The only dead the Spartans 'named'—their names were inscribed on tombstones—were men who had died in war and women who had succumbed in childbirth.").

72. Holmes, *The Soldier's Faith,* in 3 *Collected Works* at 487.

73. Roosevelt to Lodge, June 5, 1895, in 1 *Selections from the Correspondence of Theodore Roosevelt and Henry Cabot Lodge* 146 (Henry Cabot Lodge and Charles F. Redmond eds) (Scribner's, 1925). Not everyone admired *The Soldier's Faith* as much as Roosevelt did. Wendell Phillips Garrison, Holmes's college classmate and editor of the *Nation,* described Holmes's remarks as "sentimental Jingoism." Baker, *The Justice from Beacon Hill* at 309 (quoting 61 Nation 440–41 (1895)). Holmes wrote, "Fancy my speech of last Memorial Day being treated as a jingo document! . . . Garrison . . . a most watery person but one who is, was, and ever will be flat, walked into me with a blunt knife. . . ." Holmes to Pollock, Dec 27, 1895, in 1 *The Holmes–Pollock Letters: The Correspondence of Mr. Justice Holmes and Sir Frederick Pollock, 1874–1932* at 66, 67 (Mark DeWolfe Howe ed) (Harvard Univ Press, 1941).

74. Oliver Wendell Holmes, *Address to the Banquet of the Middlesex Bar Association,* Dec 3, 1902, in 3 *Collected Works* at 535, 537.

75. Baker, *The Justice from Beacon Hill* at 356.

76. 193 US 197 (1904).

77. Adams to Elizabeth Cameron, Mar 20, 1904, quoted in White, *Justice Oliver Wendell Holmes* at 307.

78. *Lincoln v United States,* 197 US 419 (1905) (Holmes), *aff'd on reargument,* 202 US 484 (1906) (Fuller).

79. See Novick, *Honorable Justice* at 278–79.

80. Roosevelt to Lodge, Sept 4, 1906, quoted in Garraty, *Holmes's Appointment to the U. S. Supreme Court,* 22 New Eng Q at 301.

81. Holmes to Pollock, Feb 9, 1921, in 2 *Holmes–Pollock Letters* at 64. Edmund Wilson noted that Holmes took an invariably patronizing attitude toward the presidents under whom he served, Edmund Wilson, *Patriotic Gore: Studies in the Literature of the American Civil War* 785 (Oxford Univ Press, 1962), and Holmes adopted a similar attitude toward other notable figures. See, for example, Mark DeWolfe Howe, *Justice Oliver Wendell Holmes: The Shaping Years, 1841–1870* at 228, 248–49 nb (Harvard Univ Press, 1957) (reporting Holmes's critical or highly qualified views of John Stuart Mill, Henry Maine, James Fitzjames Stephen, Leslie Stephen, Albert V. Dicey, John Morley, and James Bryce).

82. (J. C. Winston, 1859).

83. (John Chapman, 1851). See note 46.

84. Because Spencer and Thomas Malthus (a similarly dismal thinker) wrote before Darwin and because Malthus influenced Darwin, Phillip Johnson suggests that it would be better to call Darwin's theory of natural selection "biological Spencerism" than to call Spencer's *laissez-faire* social principles "social Darwinism." Phillip E. Johnson, *Objections Sustained: Subversive Essays on Evolution, Law & Culture* 35 (InterVarsity Press, 1998).

85. See James E. Herget, *American Jurisprudence, 1870–1970* at 26 (Rice Univ Press, 1990). Evolutionary sentiment in the second half of the nineteenth century led to two distinct social movements, social Darwinism and reform Darwinism. Social Darwinists saw life as an enduring struggle among people for limited resources. Reform Darwinists believed that social science and social planning could expand resources and provide for the welfare of all. Both groups saw human evolution as rapid and as burdened by ideas and institutions that had outlived their usefulness. See Herbert Hovenkamp, *Evolutionary Models in Jurisprudence,* 64 Tex L Rev 645, 660–62 (1985).

86. See Richard Hofstadter, *Social Darwinism in American Thought* 26 (Univ of Pennsylvania Press, 1945).

87. Holmes to Morris Cohen, Feb 5, 1919, quoted in Novick, *Honorable Justice* at 412 n11.

88. Howe, *Justice Oliver Wendell Holmes: The Shaping Years* 156. Holmes did not read Darwin until 1907. Id.

89. Holmes to Lady Pollock, July 2, 1895, in 1 *Holmes–Pollock Letters* at 57, 58.

90. Baker, *The Justice from Beacon Hill* at 159.

91. Wilson, *Patriotic Gore* at 758.

92. Id at 759.

93. Novick, *Honorable Justice* at 80. Chapter 3 describes in text at 38–39 Holmes's unusual interest in John Jay Chapman following Chapman's self-mutilation and the loss of his hand.

94. Baker, *The Justice from Beacon Hill* at 523.

95. Id at 480–81. On his first trip to Europe, Holmes was delighted to see "one of those who tumbled down the Matterhorn"—a mountaineer who survived a fall in which four other mountaineers plunged over a 4,000-foot precipice and died. Id at 183.

96. Holmes to Laski, Dec 3, 1917, in 1 *Holmes–Laski Letters* at 115, 116.

97. See Holmes to Ellen Curtis, Jan 7, 1901, quoted in Sheldon M. Novick, *Justice Holmes's Philosophy,* 70 Wash U L Q at 734–35.

98. Touster, *In Search of Holmes from Within,* 18 Vand L Rev at 437.

99. Wilson, *Patriotic Gore* at 775.

100. Robert W. Gordon, *Introduction: Holmes's Shadow,* in *The Legacy of Oliver Wendell Holmes, Jr.* 1 (Robert W. Gordon ed) (Stanford Univ Press, 1992).

    Mark DeWolfe Howe, a cautious scholar and a former Holmes law clerk, concluded that "[w]ar did not make any fundamental change in Holmes's character."

Howe, *Justice Oliver Wendell Holmes: The Shaping Years* at 102. Howe seems nearly alone in this judgment, and even he observed that, unlike the Civil War *in fact,* "the war in retrospect" might have been "dominantly formative of [Holmes's] philosophy." Mark DeWolfe Howe, *Preface,* in *Touched with Fire* at vii.

101. Attributed to a graduation address, Michigan Military Academy, June 19, 1879. See *Familiar Quotations* 492 (John Bartlett ed) (Little, Brown, 16th ed 1992).

102. In accordance with Holmes's wishes, his gravestone in Arlington National Cemetery reads:

OLIVER WENDELL HOLMES
Captain and Brevet Colonel
20th Massachusetts Volunteer Infantry, Civil War
Justice Supreme Court of the United States
March 1841–March 1935

Chapter Five

1. See Richard A. Posner, *Foreword: Holmes,* 63 Brook L Rev 7, 17 (1997) (claiming that Holmes is the victim of a "temporal parochialism" that holds "people who lived in different times . . . accountable for having failed to anticipate the sensitivities of today."). Of course no one objects to giving people who lived in earlier eras credit for *anticipating* the sensitivities of today—as we do when we praise Holmes's dissenting opinions on freedom of speech and the constitutionality of social welfare legislation.

2. See *Lafayette Ins Co v French,* 59 US (18 How) 404, 407 (1855) (although a state can prevent out-of-state corporations from doing business within its territory, conditions on doing business must be "reasonable" and "not repugnant to the constitution or laws of the United States"); *Ducat v Chicago,* 77 US (10 Wall) 410, 415 (1870); *Insurance Co v Morse,* 87 US (20 Wall) 445, 457–59 (1874) ("A man may not barter away his life or his freedom, or his substantial rights."); *Barron v Burnside,* 121 US 186, 200 (1887) ("As the Iowa statute makes the right to a permit dependent upon the surrender by the foreign corporation of a privilege guaranteed to it by the Constitution and law of the United States, the statute requiring the permit must be held to be void."); *Southern Pac Co v Denton,* 146 US 202, 207 (1892); *Martin v Baltimore & O RR,* 151 US 673, 684 (1894); *Barrow SS Co v Kane,* 170 US 100, 111 (1898).

3. *Western Union Tel Co v Kansas,* 216 US 1, 54 (1910) (Holmes dissenting). Holmes also dissented from the Court's invocation of the doctrine of unconstitutional conditions in *Pullman Co v Kansas,* 216 US 56 (1910), and *Frost & Frost Trucking Co v Railroad Comm'n,* 271 US 583, 594 (1926). In the latter case, the Supreme Court said, "If the state may compel the surrender of one constitutional right as a condition of its favor, it may, in like manner, compel a surrender of all. It is inconceivable that the guarantees embedded in the Constitution of the United States may thus be manipulated out of existence." Holmes replied, "'[T]he power to exclude

altogether generally includes the lesser power to condition.'" Id at 602 (Holmes dissenting, quoting *Packard v Banton,* 264 US 140, 145 (1924)).

4. *Western Union Tel Co v Kansas,* 216 US at 53 (Holmes dissenting). See also *Western Union Tel Co v Foster,* 247 US 105 (1918) (Holmes) (describing a state's power to grant privileges as "absolutely arbitrary"); *Pullman Co v Adams,* 189 US 420, 422 (1903); *Pennsylvania Fire Ins Co v Gold Issue Mining Co,* 243 US 93, 96 (1917).

5. *McAuliffe v New Bedford,* 155 Mass 216, 220, 29 NE 517, 517 (1892).

6. 155 Mass at 220, 29 NE at 518.

7. *Commonwealth v Davis,* 162 Mass 510, 39 NE 113 (1895), *aff'd,* 167 US 43 (1897).

8. 162 Mass at 511, 39 NE at 113.

9. Kenneth Culp Davis, 3 *Administrative Law* § 25.01 at 437 (1958).

10. *Heard v Sturgis,* 146 Mass 545, 548, 16 NE 437, 441 (1888).

11. *The Western Maid,* 257 US 419, 432 (1922).

12. *Raymond v Chicago Union Traction Co,* 207 US 20, 41 (1907) (Holmes dissenting) (the action of the state "was to be found in its Constitution" and "no fault could be found . . . until the authorized interpreter of that constitution, the [state] Supreme Court, had said that it sanctioned the alleged wrong"). The Supreme Court itself had endorsed Holmes's position in *Barney v City of New York,* 193 US 430 (1904). *Raymond* was apparently inconsistent with *Barney,* but the majority purported to distinguish rather than to overrule the earlier case.

13. *McDonald v Mabee,* 243 US 90, 91 (1917). See also *Michigan Trust Co v Ferry,* 228 US 346, 353, 356 (1913) (Holmes); *Fall v Eastin,* 215 US 1, 15 (1909) (Holmes concurring).

14. See Albert Ehrenzweig, *The Transient Rule of Personal Jurisdiction: The "Power" Myth and Forum Conveniens,* 65 Yale L J 289 (1956).

15. *Blackstone v Miller,* 188 US 189, 205 (1903) ("[I]t is plain that the transfer does depend upon the law of New York . . . because of the practical fact of its power over the person of the debtor.").

16. See Stephen Diamond, *Citizenship, Civilization, and Coercion: Justice Holmes on the Tax Power,* in *The Legacy of Oliver Wendell Holmes, Jr.* 115 (Robert W. Gordon ed) (Stanford Univ Press, 1992).

17. 163 US 537 (1896).

18. *Berea College v Kentucky,* 211 US 45 (1908).

19. *Chiles v Chesapeake & O Ry,* 218 US 71 (1910).

20. Holmes to Sir Frederick Pollock, Apr 5, 1919, in 2 *The Holmes–Pollock Letters: The Correspondence of Mr. Justice Holmes and Sir Frederick Pollock 1874–1932* at 7, 8 (Mark DeWolfe Howe ed) (Harvard Univ Press, 1941).

21. 235 US 151 (1914).

22. 235 US at 161–62.

23. Merlo Pusey, 1 *Charles Evans Hughes* 291 (Macmillan, 1951).

24. 123 Fed 671 (MD Ala 1903).

25. 219 US 219 (1911).

26. 219 US at 243.

27. 219 US at 246–47 (Holmes, joined by Lurton, dissenting). Of course Alabama did not similarly punish a defaulting employer.

28. *United States v Reynolds,* 235 US 133, 150 (1914) (Holmes concurring).

29. Id.

30. 189 US 475 (1903).

31. See Yosal Rogat, *Mr. Justice Holmes: A Dissenting Opinion* (Part 2), 15 Stan L Rev 254, 262 n237 (1963) (quoting Edward S. Corwin, *The Constitution of the United States: Analysis and Interpretation* 1163 (U.S. Govt Printing Office 1952)). Rogat's article reviews in detail Holmes's decisions in cases involving issues of racial equality. See id at 254–75. For criticism of the ruling in *Giles,* see Louise Weinberg, *Holmes' Failure,* 96 Mich L Rev 691, 710–11 (1997) (contrasting Holmes's statement that it would be "impossible" to order the registration of eligible voters because "[t]he traditional limits of proceedings in equity have not embraced a remedy for political wrongs," with *Marbury v Madison,* 5 US (1 Cranch) 137 (1803) (Marshall, CJ) (approving an equitable remedy for the political wrong of withholding a commission of office from a person entitled to that office)).

32. 273 US 13 (1927).

33. Robert W. Gordon, *Law as a Vocation: Holmes on the Lawyer's Path,* in *"The Path of the Law" and Its Influence: The Legacy of Oliver Wendell Holmes, Jr.* (Steven J. Burton ed) (Cambridge Univ Press, forthcoming).

34. *Lorden v Coffey,* 178 Mass 489, 60 NE 124 (1901) (holding that an improper apportionment between landowners and the general public rendered an assessment for street improvements unconstitutional). Holmes also wrote one opinion holding a Vermont statute unconstitutional. *Woodward v Central Vermont Ry,* 180 Mass 599, 62 NE 1051 (1902).

     Mark Tushnet and G. Edward White both report that Holmes wrote only one opinion declaring Massachusetts legislation unconstitutional, but the two scholars cite different opinions. See Mark Tushnet, *The Logic of Experience: Oliver Wendell Holmes on the Supreme Judicial Court,* 63 Va L Rev 975, 1025 n239 (1977) (citing *Lorden v Coffey* above); G. Edward White, *The Integrity of Holmes' Jurisprudence,* 10 Hofstra L Rev 633, 655 (1982) (mistakenly citing *Opinion of the Justices,* 155 Mass 598, 607, 30 NE 1142, 1146 (1892), in which Holmes, disagreeing with most of his colleagues, would have permitted the Massachusetts legislature to authorize municipalities to sell coal and wood as fuel).

     Sheldon Novick describes *Miller v Horton,* 152 Mass 540, 26 NE 100 (1891), as an opinion by Holmes declaring a Massachusetts statute invalid. Sheldon M. Novick, *Editor's Introduction,* in 1 *The Collected Works of Justice Holmes: Complete Public Writings and Selected Judicial Opinions of Oliver Wendell Holmes* at 1, 64–65 (Sheldon M. Novick ed) (Univ of Chicago Press, 1995) (hereinafter cited as *Collected Works*). In *Miller,* however, Holmes merely construed a statute that permitted the destruction of diseased horses. He read this statute literally, saying that although it permitted the destruction of diseased horses, it did not permit the destruction of horses that officials had mistakenly *declared* diseased. This narrow construction avoided the constitutional issue that would have been presented if the statute had authorized the destruction of horses without affording judicial review of the determination that the horses were diseased.

35. Holmes to his sister Amelia, Nov 16, 1862, in *Touched with Fire: Civil War Letters and Diary of Oliver Wendell Holmes, Jr.* at 70, 71 (Mark DeWolfe Howe ed) (Harvard Univ Press, 1947).

36. Oliver Wendell Holmes, Jr., *The Gas-Stoker's Strike,* 7 Am L Rev 582, 583–84 (1873), reprinted in 1 *Collected Works* at 323.

37. Holmes to Felix Frankfurter, Mar 24, 1914, in *Holmes and Frankfurter: Their Correspondence, 1912–1934* at 19 (Robert M. Mennel and Christine L. Compston eds) (Univ Press of New England, 1996).

38. Oliver Wendell Holmes, *Ideals and Doubts,* 10 Ill L Rev 1, 2 (1915), reprinted in 3 *Collected Works* at 442, 443.

39. Oliver Wendell Holmes, *Montesquieu,* in 3 *Collected Works* at 425, 429.

40. Holmes to Frankfurter, Mar 24, 1914, in *Holmes and Frankfurter: Their Correspondence* at 19.

41. Holmes to Canon Patrick Sheehan, Nov 23, 1912, in *The Holmes–Sheehan Correspondence: The Letters of Justice Oliver Wendell Holmes and Canon Patrick Sheehan* 52, 52–53 (Kennikat Press, 1976).

42. Holmes to Pollock, Apr 23, 1910, in *Holmes–Pollock Letters* at 163.

43. Oliver Wendell Holmes, *Address at a Banquet of the Middlesex Bar Association,* Dec 3, 1902, in 3 *Collected Works* at 535, 536.

44. See *Plato's The Republic* 19 (Benjamin Jowett transl) (Collier, rev ed 1901).

45. Plato, *Gorgias* 53 (Donald Zeyl transl) (Hackett, 1987).

46. *Plato's The Republic* at 20.

47. Id at 24–27.

48. See Donald Kagan, *Pericles of Athens and the Birth of Democracy* 2 (Free Press, 1991) (describing democracy as "one of the rarest, most delicate and fragile flowers in the jungle of human experience").

49. Bernard Williams, *Ethics and the Limits of Philosophy* 30 (Harvard Univ Press, 1985).

50. A dissenting justice might claim that his position reflected the will of the dominant power if he meant to predict that a revolution or other political event would prevent implementation of the majority's decision. It is doubtful, however, that Holmes meant his statements concerning dominant forces to be read as predictions that judges would not get away with declaring legislation unconstitutional.

51. This remark—probably the most quoted one-liner in the history of American sports—is persistently attributed to Lombardi. Lombardi, however, claimed that the writers who reported his remark were mistaken. He had said only, "Winning

is not everything—but making the effort to win is." See 1 *Vince Lombardi on Football* 16 (George L. Flynn ed) (Wallynn, 1973).

52. I suspect that no one—not Thrasymachus nor even Holmes—truly believed that might makes right. My guess is that people who talk this way believe, "There isn't any right." Judging would seem an inauspicious career choice for someone who believes "there isn't any right."

53. Holmes apparently saw the legislative power as superior not only to the judicial power but also to the executive power. In *Myers v United States,* 227 US 52 (1926), the Supreme Court held unconstitutional legislation that purported to restrict the president's ability to remove a member of the executive branch from office. Emphasizing that Congress had created the executive office and could abolish it at will, Holmes dissented. Id at 177.

54. Thomas Grey has written, "Holmes showed no trace of public-choice style skepticism; he evidently did not doubt that democratic legislation was the best index of the actual balance of preference in the community." Thomas C. Grey, *Molecular Motions: The Holmesian Judge in Theory and Practice,* 37 Wm & Mary L Rev 19, 39 n68 (1995). Holmes's talk of force, his acclaim of "survival of the fittest" in the political process, and his description of legislation as "simply shifting the place where the strain or rub comes" make it doubtful that he regarded legislative action simply as a device for aggregating preferences. Contrary to Grey's perception, Holmes did recognize rent seeking in the political process; he simply did not care. Unprincipled political struggle provided the nearest Darwinian metaphor, and that was enough for him.

55. See chapter 2 at 17–18.

56. Holmes's dissent in *Lochner v New York,* 198 US 45, 74 (1905), spoke of "the natural outcome of a dominant *opinion*" (emphasis added). See text at 62–63. This phrasing seemed broad enough to satisfy both Darwinists and utilitarians; a dominant opinion could be simply the wishes or desires of the greatest number. Success, however, is certainly not the "natural outcome" of a political opinion whose "dominance" is measured only by the number of its adherents.

57. David Luban, *Justice Holmes and the Metaphysics of Judicial Restraint,* 44 Duke L J 449, 510 (1994).

58. Between 1899 and 1937, the Supreme Court held 197 state or federal regulations invalid under the due process clause. An even larger number of regulations survived scrutiny. See Laurence H. Tribe, *American Constitutional Law* 567 n2 (West, 2d ed 1988).

59. See Robert W. Gordon, *Introduction: Holmes's Shadow,* in *The Legacy of Oliver Wendell Holmes, Jr.* at 1, 3 (noting the number of Holmes's dissents in regulatory cases); Sheldon M. Novick, *Editor's Introduction* to 1 *Collected Works* at 1, 14 (noting the total number of Holmes's opinions).

    Holmes did not always dissent. Most notably, Holmes wrote the majority opinion in *Pennsylvania Coal Co v Mahon,* 260 US 393 (1922), holding unconstitutional a statute that forbade coal mining when the mining operation would cause subsidence in surface land not owned by the mining company. Holmes's brief opinion relied, not on the due process clause, but on the constitutional requirement of just compensation when private property is taken for public use. The key sentence of his opinion declared, "The general rule at least is that while property may be regulated to a certain extent, if the regulation goes too far it will be recognized as a taking." 260 US at 415. As Richard Epstein comments, "[T]he 'too far' test is wholly silent on whether the relevant test is dollar or percentage loss." Moreover, focusing on what a property owner has *left* after a governmental action bears no relationship to the goals of the takings clause. Richard A. Epstein, Penn sylvania Coal v. Mahon; *The Errotis Takings Jurisprudence of Justice Holmes,* 86 Geo L J 875, 893, 899 (1998). Epstein concludes that Holmes's opinion in *Mahon* "has condemned takings law to eternal incoherence." Id at 900. Nevertheless, this opinion has been the subject of extended analysis by judges and scholars seeking its true meaning. For recent examples, see Robert Brauneis, "*The Foundation of Our 'Regulatory Takings' Jurisprudence*": *The Myth and Meaning of Justice Holmes's Opinion in* Pennsylvania Coal Co. v. Mahon, 106 Yale L J 619 (1996); William Michael Treanor, *Jam for Justice Holmes: Reassessing the Significance of* Mahon, 86 Geo L J 813 (1998); Robert Brauneis, *Treanor's* Mahon, 86 Geo L J 907 (1998); William Michael Treanor, *Understanding* Mahon *in Historical Context,* 86 Geo L J 933 (1998).

60. 198 US 45 (1905).

61. Sheldon M. Novick calls the *Lochner* dissent Holmes's most famous in *Honorable Justice: The Life of Oliver Wendell Holmes* 463 n27 (Little, Brown, 1989).

62. *Lochner,* 198 US at 74, 76 (Holmes dissenting).

63. J. F. Wall, *Social Darwinism and Constitutional Law with Special Reference to* Lochner v. New York, 33 Annals Sci 465, 475–76 (1976). Wall also observes, "Nowhere in the lengthy briefs submitted by counsel . . . to either the New York Court of Appeals or the United States Supreme Court is there any reference which could be construed as having its source within Spencer's *Social Statics,* or any evidence that the attorneys were arguing for survival of the fittest." Id at 471.

64. Morton J. Horwitz, *The Jurisprudence of* Brown *and the Dilemmas of Liberalism,* in *Have We Overcome: Race Relations since* Brown 173, 174 (Michael Namorato ed) (Univ of Mississippi Press, 1978).

65. See Richard A. Epstein, *Takings: Private Property and the Power of Eminent Domain* 108–09, 128, 280–81 (Harvard Univ Press, 1985).

66. For a defense of Holmes's view of the due process clause, see Albert W. Alschuler, *Preventive Pretrial Detention and the Failure of Interest-Balancing Approaches to Due Process,* 85 Mich L Rev 510 (1987).

67. Holmes to Frankfurter, Dec 23, 1921, in *Holmes and Frankfurter: Their Correspondence* at 132, 133.

68. Holmes to Lewis Einstein, Oct 28, 1912, in *The Holmes–Einstein Letters: Correspondence of Mr. Justice Holmes and Lewis Einstein* 73, 74 (James Bishop Peabody ed) (St. Martin's, 1964).

69. Holmes to Pollock, Apr 23, 1910, in 1 *Holmes–Pollock Letters* at 163.

Holmes wrote Felix Frankfurter that he wished God would write in letters of fire on the sky:

> The Crowd has all there is
> The Crowd pays for everything.

Holmes to Frankfurter, Aug 10, 1916, quoted in Sheldon M. Novick, *Justice Holmes's Philosophy,* 70 Wash U L Q 703, 726 (1992). Novick remarked that letters of fire might not have been enough for Frankfurter, whose writings later depicted Holmes as sympathetic to efforts to redistribute wealth.

Apparently because Holmes thought some wealthy women too egalitarian, he wrote, "I used to tell my wife or she used to tell me, it was a joint opinion, that the manner of the Beacon Street women toward their servants and employees did more than the women were worth to upset the existing order. . . . I think that the crowd now has substantially all there is. . . ." Holmes to Harold Laski, May 24, 1919, in 1 *The Holmes–Laski Letters: The Correspondence of Mr. Justice Holmes and Harold J. Laski* 207 (Mark DeWolfe Howe ed) (Harvard Univ Press, 1953). See also Holmes to Frankfurter, Nov 30, 1919, in *Holmes and Frankfurter: Their Correspondence* at 76, 77 ("People damned Rockefeller when he embodied the inevitables. They didn't say, damn order of the universe or the Great Panjandrum yet it was the order of the universe they disliked.").

70. Holmes to Charles Evans Hughes, quoted in Pusey, 1 *Charles Evans Hughes* at 287.

71. Holmes to Laski, Mar 4, 1920, in 1 *Holmes–Laski Letters* at 248, 249.

72. H. L. Mencken, *Mr. Justice Holmes,* 26 American Mercury 123 (May 1932). Another writer remarked that Holmes's "indulgence of the legislature . . . rested at least as much on contempt as tolerance." Martin Hickman, *Mr. Justice Holmes: A Reappraisal,* 5 W Pol Q 66, 83 (1952).

73. Recall Holmes's declaration that he "loathed the thick-fingered clowns we call the people," see Holmes to his sister Amelia, Nov 16, 1862, in *Touched with Fire* at 70, and his statement that he "doubt[ed] that a shudder would go through the spheres if the whole ant heap were kerosened." See Holmes to Lewis Einstein, Aug 19, 1909, in *Holmes–Einstein Letters* at 49, 50.

74. 219 US 219 (1911). *Bailey* is discussed in text at 57.

75. 217 US 349 (1910).

76. 217 US at 364.

77. Technically, the Philippines statute violated a provision of that country's Bill of Rights whose language duplicated that of the Eighth Amendment. The applicability of the Constitution to American territories was still unresolved, and the Court did not consider whether the restrictions of the Eighth Amendment applied directly.

78. 217 US at 373.

79. 217 US at 382 (White, joined by Holmes, dissenting).

80. 262 US 390 (1923).

81. 262 US at 412 (Holmes dissenting). Holmes did agree with the majority that an Ohio statute prohibiting only the teaching of German was unconstitutional. 262 US at 413.

82. Yosal Rogat, *Mr. Justice Holmes: A Dissenting Opinion,* 15 Stan L Rev 3, 10–44 (1962). See also White, *Justice Oliver Wendell Holmes: Law and the Inner Self* 343–48 (Oxford Univ Press, 1993).

83. 232 US 138 (1914).

84. 232 US at 145.

85. Rogat, *Mr. Justice Holmes,* 15 Stan L Rev at 42 13 & n191. Holmes's first opinion for the Supreme Court upheld a statute prohibiting the sale of stock on margin. It declared, "[W]e cannot say that there might not be conditions of public delirium" in which such a prohibition would be sensible. *Otis v Parker,* 187 US 606, 609 (1902).

86. 274 US 200 (1927).

87. 274 US at 206.

88. 274 US at 205, 207.

89. Novick, *Honorable Justice* at 478 n65.

90. See Robert J. Cynkar, *Buck v. Bell: "Felt Necessities" v. Fundamental Values?,* 81 Colum L Rev 1418, 1458 (1981).

91. See Paul Lombardo, *Three Generations, No Imbeciles: New Light on* Buck v Bell, 60 NYU L Rev 30, 61 (1985).

92. Cynkar, Buck v. Bell, 81 Colum L Rev at 1439.

93. Mary Dudziak, *Oliver Wendell Holmes as a Eugenic Reformer,* 71 Iowa L Rev 833, 863 n206 (1986).

94. See Cynkar, Buck v. Bell, 81 Colum L Rev at 1437–40, 1457.

95. Novick, *Honorable Justice* at 478 n65.

96. See Cynkar, Buck v. Bell, 81 Colum L Rev at 1454–55.

97. See Lombardo, *Three Generations, No Imbeciles,* 60 NYU L Rev at 53.

98. Id at 60 & n185, 35 n24.

99. 274 US at 207.

100. Saul Touster, *Holmes a Hundred Years Ago: The Common Law and Legal Theory,* 10 Hofstra L Rev 673, 678 (1982).

101. 274 US at 208.

102. Holmes to Laski, May 12, 1927, in 2 *Holmes–Laski Letters* at 942.

103. Holmes to Einstein, May 19, 1927, in *Holmes–Einstein Letters* at 267. For further discussion of *Buck v Bell,* see S. J. Gould, *The Mismeasure of Man* 335–37 (Norton 1981); Robert L. Burgdorf and Marcia Pearce Burgdorf, *The Wicked Witch Is Almost Dead:* Buck v. Bell *and the Sterilization of Handicapped Persons,* 50 Temple L Q 995 (1977).

104. Theodore Roosevelt to Henry Cabot Lodge, July 10, 1902, quoted in White, *Justice Oliver Wendell Holmes* at 300.

105. 176 Mass 492, 505, 57 NE 1011, 1016 (1900) (Holmes dissenting).

106. 167 Mass 92, 95, 44 NE 1077, 1079 (1896) (Holmes dissenting).

107. 167 Mass at 107, 44 NE at 1081 (Holmes dissenting). See also Oliver Wendell Holmes, Jr., *The Gas Stokers' Strike,* 7 Am L Rev 582 (1873).

108. 167 Mass at 108, 44 NE at 1081.

109. 167 Mass at 106, 44 NE at 1081.

110. Holmes to Pollock, Feb [*sic:* probably Sept] 23, 1902, in 1 *Holmes–Pollock Letters* at 106.

111. 276 US 518, 533 (1928) (Holmes dissenting).

112. 41 US (16 Pet) 1 (1842).

113. 304 US 64 (1938).

114. See *Kuhn v Fairmont Coal Co,* 215 US 349, 370–72 (1910) (Holmes dissenting); *Southern Pac Co v Jensen,* 244 US 205, 222 (1917) (Holmes dissenting).

115. The reference is to John Austin, who defined law as the command of a sovereign. The two chapters that follow this one will note and consider some aspects of Austin's jurisprudence.

116. Compare Oliver Wendell Holmes, *The Path of the Law,* 10 Harv L Rev 457, 465 (1897), reprinted in 3 *Collected Works* at 391, 396 ("[J]udicial dissent often is blamed, as if it meant simply that one side or the other were not doing their sums right. . . ."). For an argument that it was Holmes who had not done his sums right and that his Austinian focus on sovereignty had no bearing on the issues in *Swift* and *Erie,* see Jack Goldsmith and Steven Walt, Erie *and the Irrelevance of Legal Positivism,* 84 Va L Rev 673 (1998).

117. White, *Justice Oliver Wendell Holmes,* at 379.

118. See *Swift,* 41 US (16 Pet) at 19.

119. See Geoffrey C. Hazard, Colin C. Tate, and William A. Fletcher, *Pleading and Procedure: State and Federal: Cases and Materials* 483–87 (Foundation, 7th ed 1994).

120. 249 US 47 (1919).

121. 249 US at 52.

122. 250 US 616 (1919).

123. 250 US at 630–31 (Holmes dissenting).

124. *McAuliffe* and *Davis,* cited and discussed at 54 and 228 nn5 & 7. This chapter has noted Holmes's dissent in *Meyer v Nebraska,* 262 US 390 (1923), a ruling establishing the constitutional right to teach foreign languages in private grade schools. *Meyer* was argued and decided under the due process clause rather than the First Amendment, but one doubts that invoking the First Amendment would have persuaded Holmes to join the majority. The year before *Meyer,* Holmes joined an opinion holding the guarantee of free speech inapplicable to the states, *Prudential Ins Co v Cheek,* 259 US 530, 538 (1922), and in *Meyer* itself, he maintained that a state could properly restrict the teaching of foreign languages as a means of promoting a common tongue.

125. *Burt v Advertiser Newspaper Co,* 154 Mass 238 (1891).

126. *Cowley v Pulsifer,* 137 Mass 392 (1884). Holmes recalled twenty-eight years later that *"The Nation* [had] pitched into" his opinion. Holmes to Pollock, Dec 15, 1912, in 1 *Holmes–Pollock Letters* at 204. See 39 Nation 7 (July 3, 1884); David S. Bogen, *The Free Speech Metamorphosis of Mr. Justice Holmes,* 11 Hofstra L Rev 97, 122–23 (1982).

127. 205 US 454 (1907).

128. The First Amendment, which provides that "Congress shall make no law . . . abridging the freedom of speech, or of the press," refers only to the federal government and only to the legislative branch of this government. The defendant had argued, however, that the Fourteenth Amendment, which declares that no state shall deprive a person of life, liberty, or property without due process of law, protects the freedoms of speech and of the press against abridgment by the states. The Supreme Court rejected this argument in 1922 in an opinion that Holmes joined. *Prudential Ins Co v Cheek,* 259 US 530, 538 (1922) ("the Constitution . . . imposes on the States no obligation to confer upon those within their jurisdiction . . . the right of free speech"). Three years later, Holmes declared in dissent in *Gitlow v New York,* 268 US 652, 673 (1925), that the "general principle of free speech . . . must be taken to be included in the Fourteenth Amendment in view of the scope that has been given to the word 'liberty' as there used." Somewhat more tentatively, the majority in *Gitlow* assumed for purposes of decision that the freedom of speech was "incorporated" within the Fourteenth Amendment's due process clause. Later cases have treated *Gitlow* as resolving the issue.

129. 205 US at 462 (emphasis in the original).

130. Id.

131. Id. In 1922, in a letter to Zechariah Chafee, Holmes recanted this position, saying, "I surely was ignorant." Holmes to Chafee, June 12, 1922, quoted in Bogen, *The Free Speech Metamorphosis of Mr. Justice Holmes,* 11 Hofstra L Rev at 100. Blackstone had contended that the freedom of speech in England was limited to an immunity from prior restraint. William Blackstone, 4 *Commentaries* * 151–53.

 Among the circumstances of which Holmes appeared to be ignorant was the fact that Blackstone's view had been contested in the United States from the beginning. A number of courts, including the Supreme Judicial Court of Massachusetts, had endorsed this view, but many noted American lawyers including Thomas Jefferson, James Madison, Alexander Hamilton, James Kent, St. George Tucker, John Adams, William Cushing, and Thomas Cooley had denounced Blackstone's position. Some of these critics had insisted that a primary purpose of the free speech provisions of state and federal constitutions was to repudiate the Blackstonian view. See Bogen, *The Free Speech Metamorphosis of Mr. Justice Holmes,* 11 Hofstra L Rev at 108 n50, 109 n60, 110 n65, 116–18. Whether the freedom of speech included more than freedom from prior censorship was an especially salient issue in the early American Republic. This issue divided the Federalists who supported the Sedition Act from the Republicans and the other Federalists who regarded the act as unconstitutional. Holmes's and the Supreme

Court's casual and unexplained endorsement of Blackstone's position was therefore astonishing, especially since the question had not been briefed or argued.

Criticism of the Blackstonian position persisted in the years following Holmes's
opinion. See, for example, Roscoe Pound, *Equitable Relief against Defamation and
Injuries to Personality,* 29 Harv L Rev 640 (1916); Zechariah Chafee, *Freedom of
Speech,* New Republic, Nov 16, 1918, at 66, 67 ("This definition of liberty of the
press originated with Blackstone, and ought to be knocked on the head once and
for all."). By the time *Debs v United States,* 249 US 211 (1919) (Holmes), came
before the Supreme Court, the government mentioned the Blackstonian position
but disclaimed reliance upon it. See Bogen, *The Free Speech Metamorphosis of Mr.
Justice Holmes,* 11 Hofstra L Rev at 148–49.

132. 205 US at 465 (Harlan dissenting).

133. 236 US 273 (1915).

134. Holmes to Frankfurter, March 27, 1917, in *Holmes and Frankfurter: Their Correspondence* at 69, 70.

135. 249 US 47 (1919).

136. 249 US 204 (1919).

137. 249 US 211 (1919).

138. As David M. Rabban has observed, however, the Court did confront significant
First Amendment issues earlier in a number of cases. See David M. Rabban, *The
First Amendment in Its Forgotten Years,* 90 Yale L J 514 (1981). See also David P.
Currie, *The Constitution in the Supreme Court: The Second Century* 115 (Univ of Chi-
cago Press, 1990).

139. 244 F 535 (SDNY), *rev'd,* 246 F 24 (2d Cir 1917).

140. 244 F at 540.

141. Id.

142. Id.

143. Debs v United States, 249 US 211, 214 (1919).

144. Id.

145. 249 US at 214–15. See White, *Justice Oliver Wendell Holmes* at 420 ("*Debs* . . .
established the principle that one could be convicted for opposing war generally."). Holmes once observed, "In practice the sacred right of free speech means
that I will let you say anything that does not shock *me.*" Holmes to Kentaro Ka-
neko, June 16, 1925, quoted in Liva Baker, *The Justice from Beacon Hill: The Life and
Times of Oliver Wendell Holmes* 589 (HarperCollins, 1991).

146. 249 US 47, 52 (1919). *Schenck* was probably the strongest of the three cases for
the government. The defendants had sent a circular to men who had been called
and accepted for military service. The circular argued that the draft violated the
Thirteenth Amendment and said, "Do not submit to intimidation." *Frohwerk* was
closer to *Debs.* The defendant had been sentenced to ten years' imprisonment for
publishing newspaper articles arguing that the United States had taken the wrong

side in World War I and that Americans who violated draft laws, although "technically wrong," were "more sinned against than sinning."

147. Vincent Blasi, *Learned Hand and the Self-Government Theory of the First Amendment:
Masses Publishing Co. v. Patten*, 61 U Colo L Rev 1, 17 (1990); see White, *Justice
Oliver Wendell Holmes* at 420 (*"Debs* . . . was not a 'clear and present danger' case
unless Holmes was treating that formula as merely codifying the 'tendency' element of criminal attempt law."). Robert Cover wrote that the clear and present
danger test was "born . . . as an apology for repression." Robert Cover, *The Left,
The Right and the First Amendment: 1918–1928*, 40 Md L Rev 349, 372 (1981).

148. 249 US at 216. Both the jury instruction and Holmes's opinion mentioned the
statutory requirement that Debs *intend* to obstruct recruiting. In assessing the
original meaning of "clear and present danger," however, the relevant portion of
the trial court's instruction is not its description of the necessary mental state but
its discussion of how proximate the threatened harm must have been. Zechariah
Chafee observed that the instruction "gave the jury such a wide scope that Debs
was probably convicted for an exposition of socialism, merely because the jury
thought his speech had some tendency to bring about resistance to the draft."
Zechariah Chafee, *Free Speech in the United States* 84 (Harvard Univ Press, 1941).

149. As Blasi notes:

> In none of the cases did the prosecution produce evidence that any material conse-
> quences followed from the writings or speeches of the defendants. Nor does it
> seem surprising, given the nature of the speeches and writings and the circum-
> stances of their dissemination, that they had no apparent immediate effect. Writ-
> ings and speeches of the sort involved in the three cases could be expected to have
> material consequences only by creating a general sense of disaffection with the war
> effort that might in time lead some persons to resist the war or the draft. In this
> scenario, the consequences would be speculative, delayed, and not readily traceable
> to the incremental impact of any particular statement.

Blasi, *Learned Hand and the Self-Government Theory of the First Amendment*, 61 U Colo
L Rev at 17.

150. Rabban, *The First Amendment in Its Forgotten Years*, 90 Yale L J at 582–84.

151. 249 US at 51.

152. 249 US at 52.

153. Id.

154. Holmes to Hand, June 24, 1918, quoted in White, *Justice Oliver Wendell Holmes*
at 425.

155. Holmes to Pollock, Apr 27, 1919, in 2 *Holmes–Pollock Letters* at 10, 11 (cited in
note). See also Holmes to Pollock, June 17, 1919, in id at 15; Holmes to Laski,
Mar 16, 1919, in 1 *Holmes–Laski Letters* at 189, 190.

156. Nick Salvatore, *Eugene V. Debs: Citizen and Socialist* 328 (Univ of Illinois Press,
1982).

157. On Debs's release from prison on Christmas Day, 1921, the warden of the Atlanta
Penitentiary, "in violation of every prison regulation, . . . opened each cell block

to allow the more than 2300 inmates to throng to the front of the jail building." The inmates' roar brought tears to Debs's eyes, and he turned and stretched out his arms to the prisoners. Id at 317–28.

158. Id at 328.

159. See 2 *Holmes–Laski Letters* at 971 & n3, 974 & n1.

160. Touster, *Holmes a Hundred Years Ago,* 10 Hofstra L Rev at 675 (quoting Harold Laski, *Mr. Justice Holmes for His Eighty-Ninth Birthday,* in *Mr. Justice Holmes* 138, 162 (Felix Frankfurter ed) (Coward-McCam, 1931), and letters from Holmes to Laski, Aug 24, 1927 and Aug 18, 1927, in 2 *Holmes–Laski Letters* at 974, 971.)

161. Baker, *The Justice from Beacon Hill* at 610–11 (quoting Holmes's letters). One wonders whether the dedication of political activists to what Holmes would have regarded as foolish and hopeless causes might have seemed "enchanting" to him, as when a man "nearly kills himself for an end which derives its worth simply from his having affirmed it." See Holmes to Clare Fitzpatrick, Lady Castletown, Apr 10, 1897, quoted in Novick, *Honorable Justice* at 216. The radicals of Holmes's era were fully as passionate as the explorers and other physical adventurers whom Holmes romanticized, and these radicals boldly risked long terms of imprisonment for speaking, publishing articles, and distributing leaflets. Nevertheless, Holmes's admiration for anarchists and syndicalists was evidently limited. Radical politics were not "uneconomic" enough to match boat races, solitaire, violent duels, and suicide.

162. 250 US 616 (1919).

163. 250 US at 623.

164. 250 US at 618–19.

165. 250 US at 630–31 (Holmes dissenting).

166. Max Lerner, *The Mind and Faith of Justice Holmes* 306 (Little, Brown, 1943).

167. Sheldon M. Novick, *The Unrevised Holmes and Freedom of Expression,* 1992 S Ct Rev 303, 305. Novick hinted that Samuel Konefsky and Yosal Rogat marched in the revisionist army as well. His roll call also might have included Robert Cover. See Cover, *The Left, the Right and the First Amendment,* 40 Md L Rev at 372. Since Novick wrote, moreover, both Vincent Blasi and G. Edward White have enlisted. See Blasi, *Learned Hand and the Self-Government Theory of the First Amendment,* 61 U Colo L Rev at 16–27; White, *Justice Oliver Wendell Holmes* at 427 ("*Abrams . . .* represented a major change in Holmes' attitude toward free speech. . . ."); G. Edward White, *Justice Holmes and the Modernization of Free Speech Jurisprudence: The Human Dimension,* 80 Calif L Rev 391, 427 (1992). David Bogen contends that, although Holmes abandoned his early view of the freedom of speech, the conversion occurred prior to *Schenck* rather than between *Schenck* and *Abrams.* See Bogen, *The Free Speech Metamorphosis of Mr. Justice Holmes,* 11 Hofstra L Rev 97 (1982).

168. *Abrams v United States,* 250 US 616, 621 (1919).

169. 250 US at 627 (Holmes dissenting).

170. See, for example, Oliver Wendell Holmes, *The Common Law* 38 (Dover, 1991

(1881)) ("[Law], by the very necessity of its nature, is continually transmuting . . . moral standards into external or objective ones, from which the actual guilt of the party concerned is wholly eliminated."). Chapter 6 examines Holmes's historical thesis and his preference for objective standards in greater detail. It also considers the claim of Morton Horwitz that Holmes abandoned his objectivism prior to the *Abrams* decision.

171. See text at 81, chapter 6 at 110.

172. 250 US at 626–27.

173. In light of the clear statutory basis for Holmes's approval of a subjective standard, Sheldon Novick's claim that Holmes saw the First Amendment as comparable to a common law privilege that could be defeated by proof of an improper motive seems immaterial. See Novick, *The Unrevised Holmes and Freedom of Expression,* 1992 S Ct Rev at 305.

174. 248 US 593 (1918).

175. In addition, although Holmes's dissent was extraordinarily vague in its discussion of the defendants' constitutional rights, the First Amendment's assurance of the right to petition for the redress of grievances should have immunized the defendants' conduct.

176. See Novick, *The Unrevised Holmes and Freedom of Expression,* 1992 S Ct Rev at 328–35 (the author's discussion of *Baltzer*) and at 388–90 (setting forth Holmes's unpublished dissent in an appendix).

177. Gerald Gunther, *Learned Hand and the Origins of Modern First Amendment Doctrine: Some Fragments of History,* 27 Stan L Rev 719, 720 (1975).

178. 250 US at 627 (emphasis added).

179. 250 US at 628 (emphasis added).

180. 250 US at 630 (emphasis added).

181. 250 US at 630–31 (emphasis added).

182. See *Schaeffer v United States,* 251 US 466, 482 (1920) (Brandeis joined by Holmes dissenting); *Pierce v United States,* 252 US 239, 253 (1920) (Brandeis joined by Holmes dissenting); *Gitlow v New York,* 268 US 652, 672 (1925) (Holmes joined by Brandeis dissenting); *Whitney v California,* 274 US 357, 376–77 (1927) (Brandeis joined by Holmes—formally a concurring opinion but in effect a dissent).

183. See White, *Justice Oliver Wendell Holmes* at 412 ("[W]hen Holmes altered his position toward speech issues, beginning with his 1919 dissent in *Abrams v. United States,* that alteration was to an important extent a response to suggestions implicitly and explicitly made to Holmes by others."); id at 450 ("The evidence suggests that Holmes' shift resulted primarily from his personal experiences and relationships.").

184. 32 Harv L Rev 932 (1919).

185. Id at 967.

186. Rabban, *The First Amendment in Its Forgotten Years,* 90 Yale L J at 590. G. Edward White refers to Chafee's statement as "astonishing." White, *Justice Holmes and the Modernization of Free Speech Jurisprudence,* 80 Calif L Rev at 429.

187. See Holmes to Laski, Dec 17, 1920, in 1 *Holmes–Laski Letters* at 297.

188. Holmes to Pollock, June 21, 1920, in 2 *Holmes–Pollock Letters* at 45.

189. See Rabban, *The First Amendment in Its Forgotten Years,* 90 Yale L J at 594 n449.

190. See White, *Justice Holmes and the Modernization of Free Speech Jurisprudence,* 80 Calif L Rev at 425.

191. Holmes to Clare Castletown, June 20, 1916, quoted in Novick, *Honorable Justice* at 316.

192. In 1882, Brandeis facilitated Holmes's appointment to the Harvard Law School faculty. See chapter 3 at 37.

193. William Howard Taft to Henry L. Stimson, May 18, 1928, quoted in Baker, *The Justice from Beacon Hill* at 560.

194. Taft had offered similar observations about Brandeis's influence since 1923 when Holmes was eighty-two. See Taft to Helen Taft Manning, June 1, 1923, quoted in White, *Justice Oliver Wendell Holmes* at 319 ("I think perhaps [Holmes's] age makes him a little more subordinate or yielding to Brandeis, who is his constant companion, than he would have been in his prime."); Taft to Robert A. Taft, March 7, 1926, quoted in id at 321 (attributing Holmes's failures as a constitutional lawyer partly to the "influence which Brandeis has had on him").

   In 1921, the same year that Taft joined the Supreme Court, Holmes conceded that Brandeis sometimes influenced him. He wrote that a phrase in one of Nina Gray's letters—"If only you stay thoroughly Anglo-Saxon"—"tickled" him:

   > I take the innuendo to be that I am under the influence of the Heb's. I am comfortably confident that I am under no influence except that of thoughts and insights. Sometimes my brother B. seems to me to see deeper than some of the others—and we often agree. There is a case now on in which his printed argument convinced me contrary to my first impressions—I do not remember any other case in which the agreement was not independent. In two or three cases he has perhaps turned the scale on the question whether I should write—but in each of those I was and am more than glad that I did. . . . On the Cuba question I had written repeatedly before I ever knew or cared what he thought—and on free speech my best ebullition was independent though the Gov't prevented my opinion appearing by confessing error. . . . I don't suppose that I shall change your prepossession by what I say, but I am confident that you need not be uneasy on the score.

   Holmes to Nina Gray, Mar 5, 1921, quoted in White, *Justice Oliver Wendell Holmes* at 319. See also id at 322 ("In Holmes' correspondence with Harold Laski . . . there are numerous references to Brandeis' being a catalytic factor in Holmes' decision to issue a dissenting opinion."); id at 410 (Holmes "did not achieve the intimacy with any of his [judicial] colleagues, except Brandeis, that he did with, for example, Nina Gray, Frankfurter, Pollack [*sic*], or Laski, friends he saw only occasionally.").

195. See, for example, *Bailey v Alabama,* 219 US 219 (1911) (discussed in text at 57); *Weems v United States,* 217 US 349 (1910) (discussed in text at 64); *Kepner v United States,* 195 US 100 (1904) (discussed in text at 81–82).

196. *Frank v Mangum,* 237 US 309, 345 (1915) (Holmes dissenting) (supporting habeas corpus relief for a prisoner convicted at a mob-dominated trial).

197. White, *Justice Oliver Wendell Holmes* at 348, 353.

198. Holmes did continue to dissent from majority decisions sustaining substantive due process claims. He did so even in *Meyer v Nebraska,* 262 US 390 (1923) (discussed in text at 64 and in note 124), which one could regard as closer to a modern personal rights case than to other substantive due process decisions.

199. See the decisions on freedom of expression cited in notes 162, 182, and 201 and *Olmstead v United States,* 277 US 438, 470 (1928) (Holmes dissenting). Although Holmes often has been called the Great Dissenter, see, for example, Jan Vetter, *The Evolution of Holmes, Holmes and Evolution,* 72 Calif L Rev 343, 361 (1984); William J. Brennan, *In Defense of Dissents,* 37 Hastings L J 427, 429 (1985), he in fact dissented less often than most other members of his Court. See Ruth Bader Ginsburg, *Remarks on Writing Separately,* 65 Wash L Rev 133, 142 (1990). The shift in the direction of Holmes's dissents was substantial, but this shift did not mark a major change in the direction of all of his votes and opinions considered together. For example, Holmes's majority opinion in *Buck v Bell* (an opinion joined by Justice Brandeis) came when Holmes was eighty-six—in the same year that Holmes joined Brandeis's concurrence in *Whitney v California,* 274 US 357 (1927), and one year before Holmes and Brandeis dissented in *Olmstead v United States,* 277 US 438 (1928).

200. Novick, *The Unrevised Holmes and Freedom of Expression,* 1992 S Ct Rev at 305.

201. Novick, *Honorable Justice* at 353. See *Milwaukee Social Democratic Pub Co v Burleson,* 255 US 407, 437 (1921) (Holmes dissenting); *Leach v Carlile,* 258 US 138, 140 (1922) (Holmes and Brandeis dissenting).

202. See Baker, *The Justice from Beacon Hill* at 488–89, 519–20. On the nature of the relationship between Holmes and these admirers, see note 204 and chapter 8 at 182–84; David A. Hollinger, *The "Tough-Minded" Justice Holmes, Jewish Intellectuals, and the Making of an American Icon,* in *The Legacy of Oliver Wendell Holmes, Jr.* at 216.

203. See Novick, *The Unrevised Holmes and Freedom of Expression,* 1992 S Ct Rev at 357. Laski wrote Chafee that he had twice read Chafee's article criticizing Holmes's opinion in *Debs,* and "I'll go to the stake on every word." Referring to the tea party at which he had arranged for Chafee and Holmes to meet, Laski added, "We must fight on it." See White, *Justice Holmes and the Modernization of Free Speech Jurisprudence,* 80 Calif L Rev at 429. Compare Erwin N. Griswold, *Foreword* to 1 *Collected Works* at xiii, xv ("Mark Howe found some statements in the letters written by Laski which, to put it politely, were not so.").

204. In his later years, the childless Holmes may have been anxious to maintain the admiration of his bright, youthful followers. He wrote to Felix Frankfurter of his "rather fearful hope that I may never fall from the place you have given me" and of his "expectation that always while I live . . . I shall have great cause to be proud

of having counted for something in your life." Holmes to Frankfurter, Mar 9, 1915, quoted in G. Edward White, *Holmes's "Life Plan": Confronting Ambition, Passion, and Powerlessness,* 65 NYU L Rev 1409, 1472 (1990). A later letter declared, "You have brought a great deal of comfort and companionship to the natural loneliness of old age and I ask nothing better than that it may continue while I last." Holmes to Frankfurter, Sept 25, 1919, quoted in id at 1473.

205. For a stronger statement that Holmes's admirers prompted his dissent in *Abrams,* see White, *Justice Holmes and the Modernization of Free Speech Jurisprudence,* 80 Calif L Rev at 419–33. See also White, *Justice Oliver Wendell Holmes* at 450 ("[I]t is apparent that Holmes's exchange of views with younger intellectuals influenced him to abandon the analogy between the free speech cases and criminal-attempt cases and to reconfigure free speech as a broader principle.").

206. See White, *Justice Holmes and the Modernization of Free Speech Jurisprudence,* 80 Calif L Rev at 441.

207. Oliver Wendell Holmes, *Law in Science and Science in Law,* 12 Harv L Rev 443, 449 (1899), reprinted in 3 *Collected Works* at 406, 411.

208. Oliver Wendell Holmes, *Holdsworth's English Law,* 25 Law Q Rev 412 (1909), reprinted in 3 *Collected Works* at 434, 435. See also Oliver Wendell Holmes, *Law and the Court,* Feb 15, 1913, in 3 *Collected Works* at 505, 506–07 ("law embodies beliefs that have triumphed in the battle of ideas").

209. In *Gitlow v New York,* 268 US 652 (1925), the Supreme Court sustained a conviction for violating the New York Criminal Anarchy Act, which proscribed advocating the violent overthrow of the government. The majority held that, in judging the validity of the statute, the clear and present danger standard was inapplicable. Unlike the Federal Espionage Act, which had outlawed the obstruction of recruitment efforts by any means, the New York statute identified and outlawed certain speech. The majority said that the clear and present danger standard had "no application . . . where the legislative body itself has previously determined the danger of substantive evil arising from utterances of a specified character." 268 US at 671.

The majority's argument may have troubled Justice Holmes. In an earlier case in which Justice Brandeis, in dissent, had used the clear and present danger standard to test the validity of legislation, Holmes had joined neither Brandeis's opinion nor the majority's but had concurred without opinion in the majority's result. *Gilbert v Minnesota,* 254 US 325, 334 (1921). Nevertheless, in *Gitlow,* Holmes dissented. He indicated that, on the facts of the case, the defendant's speech was constitutionally protected; "there was no present danger of an attempt to overthrow the government by force." 268 US at 673 (Holmes dissenting). Holmes's opinion, however, did not consider how much weight, if any, the Court should afford a legislative determination that speech was unprotected. He did not contend that the New York Criminal Anarchy Act was itself unconstitutional.

Holmes later joined an opinion by Justice Brandeis that did address the issue he had elided in *Gilbert* and *Gitlow.* Concurring in *Whitney v California,* 274 US 352 (1927), Brandeis wrote, "Where a statute is valid only in case certain conditions exist, the enactment of the statute cannot alone establish the facts which are essential to its validity. . . . The legislative declaration . . . creates merely a rebuttable presumption that these conditions have been satisfied." 274 US at 374, 379.

210. White, *Justice Oliver Wendell Holmes* at 413.

211. See Sheldon M. Novick, *Justice Holmes and the Art of Biography,* 33 Wm & Mary L Rev 1219, 1243 (1992) ("Holmes had a characteristic Malthusian argument on behalf of [his] theory of the First Amendment, but I should say that what carries across the generations is not his hard-minded, faintly crackpot, evolutionism. . . .").

212. Ideas, unlike men, need not consume limited resources to survive.

213. As noted in chapter 2 at 18, Holmes's skepticism concerning values did not extend to facts, and he criticized pragmatism for its refusal to acknowledge any mind-independent reality.

214. Holmes to Alice Stopford Green, Oct 1, 1901, quoted in Novick, *Justice Holmes's Philosophy,* 70 Wash U L Q at 718.

215. Holmes to John Gray, Sept 3, 1905, quoted in Novick, *Honorable Justice* at 283.

216. Holmes to Laski, Jan 11, 1929, in 2 *Holmes–Laski Letters* at 1124.

217. Holmes to Laski, April 6, 1920, in 1 id at 258, 259.

218. Oliver Wendell Holmes, *Natural Law,* 32 Harv L Rev 40 (1918), reprinted in 3 *Collected Works* at 445, 446.

219. *The American Heritage Dictionary of the English Language* 1378 (William Morris ed) (Houghton Mifflin, 1969).

220. Holmes, *Natural Law,* 32 Harv L Rev at 41, reprinted in 3 *Collected Works* at 446.

221. *Book Review,* 91 Colum L Rev 1221, 1236 (1991).

222. Richard A. Posner, *The Problems of Jurisprudence* 221 (Harvard Univ Press, 1990).

223. Luban, *Justice Holmes and the Metaphysics of Judicial Restraint,* 44 Duke L J at 503.

224. See, for example, Andrea Dworkin, *Pornography: Men Possessing Women* 17 (Perigree Books, 1981) (arguing that the marketplace of ideas subordinates women because "[m]ale supremacy is fused into the language, so that every sentence both heralds and affirms it. Thought, experienced primarily as language, is permeated by the linguistic and perceptual values developed expressly to subordinate women."); Richard Delgado, *More Than Speech Was at Stake,* ABA J, Dec 1993, at 32 ("Recent scholarship has shown that free speech may be a reasonably good corrective for small errors. . . . But it is a poor way of correcting systemic social ills, like racism or sexism. . . ."). See also David A. Strauss, *Persuasion and Autonomy,* 91 Colum L Rev 334, 349 (1991) ("[T]here is no theory that explains why competition in the realm of ideas will systematically produce good or truthful or otherwise desirable outcomes.").

To be a society's best available test of truth, however, survival in a marketplace of ideas need not be a very *good* test of truth. The market need be only a better test of truth than a board of censors, a state legislature, a jury, or some other official arbiter. In economic terms, arguments for regulation are always incomplete unless they address the likelihood of regulatory failure as well as the likelihood of market failure. *Accord, American Booksellers v Hudnut,* 771 F2d 323, 330–31 (7th Cir 1985) (Easterbrook) ("A power to limit speech on the ground that truth has not yet prevailed and is not likely to prevail implies the power to declare truth. . . . If the government may declare the truth, why wait for the failure of speech?").

225. Holmes to Laski, Oct 26, 1919, in 1 *Holmes–Laski Letters* at 217. See also Holmes to Pollock, Oct 26, 1919, in 2 *Holmes–Pollock Letters* 27, 29 ("[I]n the abstract, I have no very enthusiastic belief [in freedom of speech], though I hope I would die for it.").

226. *Nash v United States,* 229 US 373, 377 (1913) (adding that at common law "a man might have to answer with his life for consequences . . . he neither intended nor foresaw").

227. See, for example, *Commonwealth v Pierce,* 138 Mass 165, 178 (1884) (discussed in chapter 6 at 110).

228. *Brown v United States,* 256 US 335 (1921). Joseph Henry Beale, who would become one of the scholars most ridiculed by the legal realists, see chapter 6 at 87, was the principal academic defender of the common law rule. Beale denounced the "hip-pocket ethics" and "brutality" of courts in the South and West that had abandoned the duty to retreat. Joseph H. Beale, *Retreat from a Murderous Assault,* 16 Harv L Rev 567, 577, 580 (1903) (concluding "that one man should live rather than . . . another man should stand his ground in a private conflict"); Joseph H. Beale, *Homicide in Self-Defense,* 3 Colum L Rev 526 (1903). See generally Richard Maxwell Brown, *No Duty to Retreat: Violence and Values in American History* (Oxford Univ Press, 1991).

229. See text at 64.

230. *Kepner v United States,* 195 US 100, 134 (1904) (Holmes dissenting).

231. 212 US 78 (1909).

232. 218 US 245, 252–53 (1910).

233. 265 US 57 (1924).

234. 284 US 390 (1932).

235. *Frank v Mangum,* 237 US 309, 345 (1915) (Holmes dissenting).

236. See id (decrying "lynch law" and "a mob intent on death" in the case of Leo Frank, who later was lynched); *Moore v Dempsey,* 261 US 86 (1923).

237. *People v DeFore,* 150 NE 585, 587–88 (NY 1926).

238. *Olmstead v United States,* 277 US 438, 470 (1928) (Holmes dissenting). In recent years, the Supreme Court has rejected Holmes's surprisingly moralistic justification for the exclusionary rule and has placed the rule on an instrumental basis. Then it has declared the rule's instrumental justification—its utility in discouraging police misconduct—inapplicable in many situations. See, for example, *United States v Janis,* 428 US 433 (1976); *Stone v Powell,* 426 US 465 (1976); *Immigration*

and *Naturalization Service v Lopez-Mendosa,* 468 US 1032 (1984); *United States v Leon,* 468 US 897 (1984).

239. *Silverthorne Lumber Co v United States,* 251 US 385 (1920). Justice Frankfurter used the phrase "fruit of the poisonous tree" in *Nardone v United States,* 308 US 338 (1939). Again the Supreme Court later lost sympathy for Holmes's position. In *United States v Calandra,* 414 US 338 (1974), it distinguished Holmes's *Silverthorne* opinion on thin and technical grounds.

240. 277 US 438, 469 (1928) (Holmes dissenting).

241. The Supreme Court overruled *Olmstead* and held that the term *search* includes the interception of private conversations in *Katz v United States,* 389 US 347 (1967), and *Berger v New York,* 388 US 41 (1967).

242. Baker, *The Justice from Beacon Hill* at 614.

243. Id at 616.

244. See H. L. Mencken, *Mr. Justice Holmes,* 26 American Mercury 123, 124 (May 1932). One sees little sign of a mellower Holmes, however, in his correspondence. In general, Holmes's long life seems remarkable for its lack of growth or development following the changes in his personality and outlook wrought by the Civil War.

Chapter Six

1. See Sheldon M. Novick, *Editor's Introduction* to *The Common Law,* in 3 *The Collected Works of Justice Holmes: Complete Public Writings and Selected Judicial Opinions of Oliver Wendell Holmes* 109 (Sheldon M. Novick ed) (Univ of Chicago Press, 1995) (hereinafter cited as *Collected Works*). Holmes kept the champagne cork, which was found in the front drawer of his desk following his death fifty-four years later.

2. See Holmes to James Bryce, Aug 17, 1879, quoted in Mark DeWolfe Howe, *Justice Oliver Wendell Holmes: The Proving Years, 1870–1882* at 280 (Harvard Univ Press, 1963) ("I hate business and dislike practice, apart from arguing cases.")

3. Envisioning Holmes's eleven chapters as lectures is difficult. They are of varying length, with the longest (the first lecture on torts) about three times longer than the shortest (on contract elements). Holmes noted in his preface, "The lectures as actually delivered were a good deal simplified." Oliver Wendell Holmes, *The Common Law* xxiii (Dover, 1991). One member of the audience reported that Holmes gave them without referring to his manuscript. See G. Edward White, *Justice Oliver Wendell Holmes: Law and the Inner Self* 293 (Oxford Univ Press, 1993). However simplified the lectures might have been, all but a small portion would have been too specialized, too obscure, and too technical for a general audience. John Lowell, Jr., a textile manufacturer, had endowed the Lowell Institute in 1836 to present public lectures demonstrating "the truth of those moral and religious precepts, by which alone . . . men can be secure of happiness in this world and that to come." Id at 148. Holmes's father had delivered the Lowell Lectures in 1853. See Edward Weeks, *The Lowells and Their Institute* 65 (Little, Brown, 1966).

4. Holmes, *The Common Law* at 1.

5. Id at 35–36.

6. Posner said it twice. See Richard A. Posner, *Cardozo: A Study in Reputation* 20 (Univ of Chicago Press, 1990); Richard A. Posner, *Introduction* to *The Essential Holmes: Selections from the Letters, Speeches, Judicial Opinions, and Other Writings of Oliver Wendell Holmes, Jr.* x (Richard A. Posner ed) (Univ of Chicago Press, 1992).

7. White, *Justice Oliver Wendell Holmes* at 3.

8. Andrew L. Kaufman, *Cardozo* 201 (Harvard Univ Press, 1998).

9. P. S. Atiyah, *The Legacy of Holmes through English Eyes,* 63 B U L Rev 341, 376 (1983).

10. Saul Touster, *Holmes a Hundred Years Ago: The Common Law and Legal Theory,* 10 Hofstra L Rev 673, 685 (1982).

11. Sheldon M. Novick, *Editor's Introduction* to 1 *Collected Works* at 1, 10.

12. Id at 118.

13. Id at 86.

14. Id at 120.

15. For an extended discussion of Langdell's jurisprudence, see William P. LaPiana, *Logic and Experience: The Origin of Modern American Legal Education* (Oxford Univ Press, 1994).

16. John Austin, 1 *Lectures on Jurisprudence* 178 (Robert Campbell ed) (Murray, 5th ed 1885).

17. For an outstanding history and description of the work of Savigny and other German "legal scientists," see Mathias Reimann, *Nineteenth Century German Legal Science,* 31 B C L Rev 842 (1990). For an equally outstanding description of the reception of Savigny's historicism in America, see Stephen A. Siegel, *Historism in Late Nineteenth-Century Constitutional Thought,* 1990 Wis L Rev 1431. Savigny's historicism, which dominated the scholarship of post–Civil War American writers, also influenced the work of some American writers who began publishing earlier. These earlier writers included John Norton Pomeroy, Francis Lieber, and Joel Bishop, all of whom blended historicism with natural law. See id at 1452 (noting that historicism mediated the transition from the theism and natural law that preceded it to the agnosticism and positivism of our era).

18. Oliver Wendell Holmes, Jr., *Book Review,* 6 Am L Rev 134 (1871), reprinted in 1 *Collected Works* at 266.

19. *American Banana Co v United Fruit Co,* 213 US 347, 356 (1909) (Holmes).

20. See Patrick J. Kelley, *Was Holmes a Pragmatist? Reflections on a New Twist to an Old Argument,* 14 S Ill L J 427, 451 n111 (1990) (noting that Holmes saw "both *morals* and *law* [as] reducible to scientific laws of antecedence and consequence").

21. Mathias W. Reimann, *Holmes's* Common Law *and German Legal Science,* in *The Legacy of Oliver Wendell Holmes, Jr.* 72, 79 (Robert W. Gordon ed) (Stanford Univ Press, 1992). See James C. Carter, *Law: Its Origin, Growth and Function: Being a Course of Lectures Prepared for Delivery before the Law School of Harvard University* 268

(Putnam's, 1907) (attributing the weakness of earlier jurisprudence to the fact that "[t]he law of Evolution so dominating in its influence upon recent thought, had not been stated"—and to unawareness that "society, like every other phenomenon in nature, was a condition resulting from the operation of causes reaching back into periods infinitely remote").

22. Charles Malcom Platt, *The Character and Scope of Analytical Jurisprudence,* 24 Am L Rev 603, 613 (1890).

23. Siegel uses the word *historism* to refer to a particular form of historicism. For my purposes, the more inclusive and familiar term seems more appropriate.

24. Siegel, *Historism in Late Nineteenth-Century Constitutional Thought* at 1435–36.

25. Although scholars today seem united in regarding the late-nineteenth-century historicists as formalists, they are not at all united about what the word *formalism* means. As Brian Simpson has remarked poetically, "[T]he name 'formalism' . . . seems to me . . . in general use, to be little more than a . . . term of abuse." A. W. B. Simpson, *Legal Iconoclasts and Legal Ideals,* 58 Cinn L Rev 819, 835 (1990). The rhyme is admittedly the product of my ellipses; Simpson and I should be listed as co-poets.

26. See, for example, Robert Samuel Summers, *Instrumentalism and American Legal Theory* 26–27 (Cornell Univ Press, 1982) (offering Langdell and Beale as the author's principal exemplars of formalism).

27. See Laura Kalman, *Legal Realism at Yale, 1927–1960* at 26 (Univ of North Carolina Press, 1986); Jerome Frank, *Law and the Modern Mind* 53–61 (Brentano, 1930).

28. Joseph H. Beale, *The Development of Jurisprudence During the Past Century,* 18 Harv L Rev 271, 283 (1905).

29. Id.

30. Oliver Wendell Holmes, Jr., *The Arrangement of the Law—Privity,* 7 Am L Rev 46, 46 (1872), reprinted in 1 *Collected Works* at 303.

31. See id at 48, reprinted in 1 *Collected Works* at 305; Oliver Wendell Holmes, Jr., *The Theory of Torts,* 7 Am L Rev 652, 663 (1873), reprinted in 1 *Collected Works* at 326, 334.

32. Oliver Wendell Holmes, Jr., *Codes, and the Arrangement of the Law,* 5 Am L Rev 1 (1870), reprinted in 1 *Collected Works* at 212, 213.

33. Holmes, *The Common Law* at 219.

34. Id.

35. Langdell to T. D. Woolsey, Feb 6, 1871, quoted in LaPiana, *Logic and Experience* at 77.

36. Id.

37. James E. Herget, *Organic Natural Law: The Legal Philosophy of George Hugh Smith,* 41 Cath U L Rev 383, 412–13 (1992).

38. Oliver Wendell Holmes, Jr., *Book Review,* 1 Am L Rev 554 (1867), reprinted in 1 *Collected Works* at 188.

39. Holmes to John C. H. Wu, July 1, 1929, in *The Mind and Faith of Justice Holmes* 435 (Max Lerner ed) (Little, Brown, 1943).

40. C. C. Langdell, *Cases on Contracts* vi–vii (Little, Brown, 1871).

41. Oliver Wendell Holmes, *The Path of the Law,* 10 Harv L Rev 457, 457–58 (1897), reprinted in 3 *Collected Works* at 391.

42. C. C. Langdell, *A Summary of the Law of Contracts* 20–21 (Little, Brown, 2d ed 1880) (presenting Langdell's infamous analysis of "the mailbox rule").

43. Holmes himself seemed to criticize Langdell for straying from the pack. The labels that Holmes applied to Langdell (they are quoted in text at note 52) apparently were meant to ridicule the dean and to indicate his extremism.

44. Samuel Williston, *Life and Law* 200 (Little, Brown, 1940).

45. See, for example, Mathias Reimann, *The Historical School against Codification: Savigny, Carter and the Defeat of the New York Civil Code,* 37 Am J Comp L 95 (1989); Stephen A. Siegel, *Joel Bishop's Orthodoxy,* 13 Law & Hist Rev 215, 251 (1995).

46. James C. Carter, *The Proposed Codification of Our Common Law* 86 (Evening Post Job Printing Office, 1884).

47. Warren J. Samuels, *Joseph Henry Beale's Lectures on Jurisprudence, 1909,* 29 U Miami L Rev 260, 305 (1975) (consisting of Robert L. Hale's class notes on lectures by Beale together with an introduction by Samuels). See also Holmes, *Codes, and the Arrangement of the Law* at 2, reprinted in 1 *Collected Works* at 213 (arguing against codification on the ground that "[n]ew cases will arise which will elude the most carefully constructed formula"); Oliver Wendell Holmes, Jr., *Book Review,* 5 Am L Rev 114 (1870), reprinted in 1 *Collected Works* at 223 (arguing against codification on the ground that it would "put an end to the function of judges as lawmakers").

48. Holmes, *The Common Law* at 2.

49. Oliver Wendell Holmes, *Law in Science and Science in Law,* 12 Harv L Rev 443, 443–44 (1899), reprinted in 3 *Collected Works* at 406.

50. Holmes, *The Path of the Law* at 469, reprinted in 3 *Collected Works* at 399. Lord Mansfield had offered a similar observation more than one hundred years earlier: "The law would be a strange science . . . if after so large an increase of commerce, arts and circumstances accruing, we must go to the time of Richard I to find a case, and see what is the law." *Jones v Randall,* 98 Eng Rep 706, 707 (KB 1774).

51. This stance seems consistent with Holmes's general skepticism. Holmes did not venerate the wisdom of the past any more than he venerated anything else except war and struggle. The ardor for historicism voiced by Carter, Beale, and other writers would have moved him no more than most other enthusiasms.

52. *Book Review,* 14 Am L Rev 233, 234 (1880), reprinted in 3 *Collected Works* at 102, 103.

53. Id.

54. Holmes, *The Common Law* at 1–2.

55. Id at 35–36.

56. See Richard A. Posner, *Introduction* to *The Essential Holmes* at ix, xx.

57. According to James Herget, Holmes read Jhering's *Von Geist des römischen Rechts* in both the original German and a French translation. Letter from James E. Herget to author, Aug 11, 1998; see Reimann, *Holmes's* Common Law *and German Legal Science* at 103; Mark DeWolfe Howe, *Justice Oliver Wendell Holmes: The Proving Years* at 151 (Harvard Univ Press, 1963).

58. Jhering wrote, "Das Leben is nicht der Begriffe, sondern die Begriffe sind des Lebens wegen da. Nicht was die Logik, sondern was das Leben, der Verkehr, das Rechtsgefuehl postuliert, hat zu geschehen, moege es logisch deduzierbar oder unmoeglish sein." Rudolph von Jhering, 3 *Von Geist des römischen Rechts* 321 (Scietia Verlag Aalen, 1968).

   James Herget offers the following literal translation: "Life is not the conceptions, but the conceptions are there from life. Not what logic, but what life, intercourse, the sense of right demand is what must happen, whether it is logically deducible or impossible." Herget observes that, without citing Jhering, Holmes supplied a more artful translation on the first page of *The Common Law*. Letter from Herget to author.

59. Reimann, *Holmes's* Common Law *and German Legal Science* at 103. Jhering's work also may have helped inspire Holmes's "bad man" metaphor. See chapter 7 at 144.

60. Note Holmes's recognition of a role for logic in the sentences immediately preceding his famed declaration: "To accomplish the task, other tools are needed besides logic. It is something to show that the consistency of a system requires a particular result, but it is not all."

61. Quoted in William Holdsworth, *Some Aspects of Blackstone and His Commentaries,* 4 Cambridge L J 261, 266 (1932).

62. Morton White, *The Revolt against Formalism in American Social Thought of the Twentieth Century,* 8 J Hist of Ideas 131 (1947) (also published as chapter 2 of White's *Social Thought in America* (Viking, 1949)). See Howe, *Justice Oliver Wendell Holmes: The Proving Years* at 155 (describing Holmes's statement as "the repudiation of a traditional understanding of the judicial process").

63. Kaufman, *Cardozo* at 201.

64. Benjamin Cardozo, *Mr. Justice Holmes,* 44 Harv L Rev 682, 683 (1931).

65. Liva Baker, *The Justice from Beacon Hill: The Life and Times of Oliver Wendell Holmes* 249 (HarperCollins, 1991).

66. Id at 257–58.

67. Ronald Dworkin, *Taking Rights Seriously* 15 (Harvard Univ Press, 1977).

68. Id at 15–16.

69. Max Farrand, 2 *Records of the Federal Convention of 1787* at 278 (Yale Univ Press, 1911).

70. Id. See also *Barwell v Brooks,* 99 Eng Rep 702, 703 (KB 1784) ("As the usages of society alter, the law must adapt itself to the various situations of mankind.").

71. Matthew Hale, *History of the Common Law of England* 39 (Charles Gray ed) (Univ of Chicago Press, 1971). This statement introduced an extended discussion of the development of the English common law, see id at 39–46, and Hale's discussion included the comment that judicial decisions are not the law but merely evidence of the law. Id at 45; see William Blackstone, 1 *Commentaries* * 69 (similarly declaring that judicial decisions are merely evidence of the law); *Swift v Tyson,* 41 US (16 Pet) 1, 18–19 (1842) (Story) (same); LaPiana, *The Logic of Experience* at 36–37 (reciting similar statements by many American authorities).

The familiar declaration of seventeenth-, eighteenth-, and nineteenth-century writers that judicial decisions are merely evidence of the law has been cited as showing that judges once envisioned their role to be that of discovering and articulating timeless principles of justice. See, for example, LaPiana, *The Logic of Experience* at 34 ("Belief in a law of principles which transcends human attempts to discover and elucidate those principles explains the oft-repeated statement that cases are the mere evidence of law and not law itself."). Hale's discussion (including the statement quoted in text) reveals, however, that he plainly did *not* endorse the "oracular" view that law is timeless and merely awaiting discovery. As far as I can tell, neither did any of the authorities who repeated his comment. The statement that judicial decisions are merely evidence of the law referred, not to natural law, but to positive law. As Hale and other writers emphasized, the common law was customary law. It changed over time and was influenced by many sources, including judicial decisions. As Hale put it, judicial decisions had been a frequent source of "alterations" in the law. Hale, *History of the Common Law of England* at 39–40. At the same time, a judge could be mistaken about customary law, just as he could about the meaning of a statute. Accordingly, a judicial decision was no more than evidence of what the common law (the customary law) provided. See id at 45 (declaring that a judicial decision, although authoritative, was less authoritative than a statute).

72. *The Federalist No. 14* at 72 (James Madison) (Michael Lloyd Chadwick ed) (Global Affairs, 1987).

73. St. George Tucker, *Introduction* to 1 *Blackstone's Commentaries: With Notes of Reference, to the Constitution and Laws, of the Federal Government of the United States; and of the Commonwealth of Virginia* xv (St. George Tucker ed) (Birch & Small, 1803).

74. For a fuller description of Tucker's work, see Albert W. Alschuler, *Rediscovering Blackstone,* 145 U Pa L Rev 1, 11–14 (1996).

75. *Guardians of the Poor v Greene,* 5 Binney 554 (Pa 1813).

76. See *Van Ness v Pacard,* 27 US (2 Pet) 137, 144 (1829) ("The common law of England is not taken in all respects to be that of America. Our ancestors brought with them its general principles, and claimed it as their birthright; but they brought with them and adopted only that portion which was applicable to their situation."); Letter from John Marshall to St. George Tucker, Nov 27, 1800,

reprinted in Stewart Jay, *Origins of Federal Common Law* (Part 2), 133 U Pa L Rev 1231, app A at 1326 (1985) ("My own opinion is that our ancestors brought with them the laws of England both statute & common law as existing at the settlement of each colony, so far as they were applicable to our situation.").

In *Campbell v Hall,* Lofft 655, 678, 98 All ER 848 (KB 1774), Lord Chief Justice Mansfield construed the general language of a directive to a colonial governor and wrote: "[T]he laws of England are to prevail, and, as near as may be consistent with local circumstances, are to be enjoyed as the general privilege of British subjects, there as here." The principle that judges should apply the common law only when this law was suited to local circumstances ultimately was accepted throughout the British Commonwealth.

77. 17 US (4 Wheat) 316 (1819).

78. 17 US at 408.

79. Benjamin N. Cardozo, *The Nature of the Judicial Process* 169–70 (Yale, 1921).

80. Grant Gilmore, *Legal Realism: Its Cause and Cure,* 70 Yale L J 1037, 1045 (1961).

81. Holmes, *The Common Law* at 35.

82. Joseph Story, *Value and Importance of Legal Studies* (1829), in *The Miscellaneous Writings of Joseph Story* 503, 526 (William Story ed) (Little, Brown, 1852, reprint 1972).

Grant Gilmore wrote of Story, "[He] was an easy-going pragmatist who looked on rules of law not as mystical absolutes but as tentative approximations subject to change as the conditions which called them forth themselves changed." Grant Gilmore, *Book Review,* 39 U Chi L Rev 244, 244–45 (1971).

83. See Oliver Wendell Holmes, Jr., *Book Review,* 5 Am L Rev 114 (1870), reprinted in 1 *Collected Works* at 223 ("Perhaps the question on which the desirableness of a code depends is whether it is desirable to put an end to the function of judges as law-makers. We confess we doubt it.").

84. The Supreme Court declared in 1884, "[F]lexibility and capacity for growth and adaptation is the peculiar boast and excellence of the common law." *Hurtado v California,* 110 US 516, 530 (1884).

85. *Parsons v State,* 81 Ala 577, 582, 2 So 854, 857 (1887).

86. See *People v Drew,* 583 P2d 1318, 22 Cal 3d 333 (1978).

87. See Siegel, *Historism in Late Nineteenth-Century Constitutional Thought* at 1547.

88. Reimann, *Holmes's Common Law and German Legal Science* at 97–98. Reimann observes that Holmes's knowledge of Savigny might have come through his reading of the work of John Norton Pomeroy. He adds that he "almost suspects" that Holmes plagiarized Pomeroy's phrases in his declarations that the common law "has grown from barbarism to civilization," that it "is forever adopting new principles from life at the one end and . . . always retains old ones from history at the other, which have not yet been absorbed or sloughed off," that it will never become entirely consistent, and that it reflects "the felt necessities of the time, the prevalent moral and political theories, intuitions of public policy." Id at 258 n110.

Unlike Reimann, I do not "almost suspect" Holmes of plagiarism, but Reimann correctly notes the similarity between Pomeroy's historicism and that of Holmes. Pomeroy wrote, for example, "The common law . . . is not now, and never was, and never will be a complete system . . . ; it is rather a power continually reproducing itself, taking up fresh material, and converting it into new regulations, new maxims, new applications. . . ." John Norton Pomeroy, *Introduction to Municipal Law* 19 (Appleton, 1864). Pomeroy, a prolific writer, a superb scholar, and a pathbreaking educator, added, "As civilization is a product of religion, philosophy, letters, arts, trade, commerce, government, and above all, the ethnic life of a people, so do these elements enter into and shape their law." Id at 168.

89. Holmes, *The Common Law* at 36.

90. Anthony J. Sebok, *Misunderstanding Positivism,* 93 Mich L Rev 2054, 2086 (1995).

91. See text at 90.

92. Certainly the word *God* does not appear in Langdell's writings just as it does not appear in the writings of Joseph H. Beale, James B. Ames, Francis B. Sayre, Austin W. Scott, Samuel Williston, or any other "formalist" member of the late-nineteenth-or early-twentieth-century Harvard Law School faculty.

  Joel Bishop, a popular nineteenth-century treatise writer who did speak often of God, lived near the Harvard campus and was sometimes called "the foremost law writer of the age." Although many honored Bishop, the Harvard faculty did not give him "the slightest recognition." See Siegel, *Joel Bishop's Orthodoxy* at 215–16. Siegel offers a possible explanation: "The Harvard school was post-Darwinian, attributing legal development to a morally ambiguous evolutionary process. Bishop was pre-Darwinian. . . ." Id at 258.

93. See Grant Gilmore, *The Ages of American Law* 64 (Yale Univ Press, 1977). Gilmore wrote that the product of American courts in the post–Civil War era could be described as "Langdellianism in action." Id at 61–62. He said that this product

> seems to start from the assumption that law is a closed, logical system. Judges do not make law; they merely declare the law which, in some Platonic sense, already exists. The judicial function has nothing to do with the adaptation of rules of law to changing conditions; it is restricted to the discovery of what the true rules of law are and indeed always have been. Past error can be exposed and in that way minor corrections can be made, but the truth, once arrived at, is immutable and eternal.

  (Id at 62).

94. Recall Langdell's statement (quoted in text at 89), "Each of these doctrines has arrived at its present state by slow degrees; in other words, it is a growth extending in many cases through centuries."

95. Robert W. Gordon, *Legal Education and Practice: The Case for (and against) Harvard,* 93 Mich L Rev 1231, 1240 (1995). See Siegel, *Joel Bishop's Orthodoxy* at 253 ("Langdell and his followers . . . were among the first Western jurists to adopt a wholly secular approach to law."); C. C. Langdell, *Classification of Rights and Wrongs* (Part 2), 13 Harv L Rev 659, 673 (1900) (declaring it "impossible that there should be any other actual rights than such as are created by the State"); LaPianna, *Logic and Experience* at 122–23; Stephen M. Feldman, *From Premodern to*

Modern American Jurisprudence: The Onset of Positivism, 50 Vand L Rev 1387, 1426 (1997) ("Langdellians repudiated . . . natural law notions. . . . Instead, generally consistent with a positivist outlook and a historicist . . . sensibility, Langdellians understood legal principles as developing or evolving over time.").

96. William LaPiana observes:

> Much of what we associate with Holmes as his unique contribution to legal thought, especially his "bad man" theory of law and his refusal to equate law with morality, are elaborations of a rich stream of legal thought in which he was a participant. . . .
>
> [T]he new legal scientists sought to study law as it was without considering what it should be. Their goal was to develop a jurisprudence that would properly classify and arrange the principles of the law. . . .
>
> Holmes blended historical and analytical jurisprudence, concluding that the former confirmed the latter. His final position was shared by the law teachers who were transforming the Harvard Law School. . . . Holmes himself is in some ways an intellectual comrade of Christopher Columbus Langdell.

William P. LaPiana, *Victorian from Beacon Hill: Oliver Wendell Holmes's Early Legal Scholarship,* 90 Colum L Rev 809, 810–11 (1990). See also id at 817 ("[C]ontrary to what many have assumed, Holmes and Langdell were more intellectual allies than enemies.").

97. See Richard A. Posner, *Legal Formalism, Legal Realism, and the Interpretation of Statutes and the Constitution,* 37 Case W Res L Rev 179, 182 (1986). Posner used this language to describe "the nineteenth-century formalists" rather than Langdell alone, but he later defined "Langdellism" as "the fallacy in legal reasoning of smuggling the conclusion into the premise." Id at 184. He declared, "The problem was not that Langdell was a bad formalist, in the sense of making errors of logic, but that he was uncritical about his premises." Id at 183. Posner also has written, "Both Langdellian legal theory and economic theory are deductive systems, but Langdell wanted to stop with deduction—with comparing the facts of a case to a rule derived from a priori concepts." Richard A. Posner, *Overcoming Law* 19 (Harvard Univ Press, 1995).

98. Langdell simply did not choose premises the same way that Posner does.

99. Joseph Beale made clear that his own "formalism" was not deductive. He wrote that "juristic" reasoning (one of two forms of reasoning that he considered essential to the development of law)

> is not necessarily a logical process. . . . [U]sually it does not proceed in accordance with formal logic. It will depend on a judgment or intuition more subtle than any articulate major premise. It does, however, necessarily, proceed on some ideal conception of legal truth, whether that conception be one of the older stages of law or the conception of liberty, equality, and fraternity of law in its most modern dress. How far does the proposed rule conform . . . with social or economical needs or with current morality?

Joseph H. Beale, *Juristic Law and Judicial Law,* 37 W Va L Q 237, 248 (1931). Compare C. C. Langdell, *Report* in *Annual Reports of the President and Treasurer of Harvard College, 1876–1877* at 96–97, quoted in LaPianna, *Logic and Experience* at

122–23 ("Law has not the demonstrative certainty of mathematics . . . nor does it acknowledge truth as its ultimate test and standard, like natural science. . . .").

100. Richard Posner observes, "A legal rule has the form of the major premise of a syllogism. For example: no contract is enforceable without consideration; the contract in suit has no consideration; therefore the contract is unenforceable." Richard A. Posner, *The Problems of Jurisprudence* 42 (Harvard Univ Press, 1990).

101. See Holmes, *The Common Law* at 36.

102. 14 Am L Rev 233, 234 (1880), reprinted in 3 *Collected Works* at 102, 103.

103. A. W. B. Simpson once wrote, "[W]e all know that since the time of Bentham it has been the accepted orthodoxy that judges do make law. . . ." A. W. B. Simpson, *Innovation in Nineteenth Century Contract Law,* 91 L Q Rev 247, 247 (1975). People in fact realized well prior to Bentham that judges made law. See generally Alschuler, *Rediscovering Blackstone.* Simpson was too optimistic, however, in using the words *we all know.* See, for example, John Monahan and Laurens Walker, *Social Science in Law* 1 (Foundation, 3d ed 1994) (declaring that until the turn of the twentieth century American law was "dominated by the belief that a single, correct legal solution could be reached in every case by the application of rules of logic to a set of natural and self-evident principles"); G. Edward White, *The Canonization of Holmes and Brandeis: Epistemology and Judicial Reputation,* 70 NYU L Rev 576, 580 (1995) (referring to a pre-twentieth-century "jurisprudential orthodoxy that legal principles were not created by the judges who applied them but existed in some disembodied, timeless state, external to their interpreters"); Thomas C. Grey, *Molecular Motions: The Holmesian Judge in Theory and Practice,* 37 Wm & Mary L Rev 19, 21 (1995) ("The legal formalist believes that . . . [j]udges can and must find existing law that will decide cases in a determinate way. . . . [J]udicial opinions about policy and fairness have no proper place in the decisional process if the Rule of Law is to be respected. This has been the orthodox jurisprudence of the bench and bar, at least until recent times.").

104. See Paul D. Carrington, *The Missionary Diocese of Chicago,* 44 J Legal Ed 467, 468–73 (1994) ("Langdell's faith . . . was a form of mystification, a technique of government employed by most if not all tribal chieftains. . . . Unlike his primitive predecessors, he found law not in the stars or in the entrails of sheep, but at least partly in his navel."); Kaufman, *Cardozo* at 200 ("In the late nineteenth and early twentieth centuries, debate focused on whether judges 'found' or 'made' law."); George C. Thomas III, *Law's Social Consequences,* 51 Rutgers L Rev 845, 846 (1999) (crediting the legal realists with "replac[ing] the myth of common law formalism with a frank acknowledgment that judges were part of the equation of making law—that judges helped make the law of a particular case, rather than finding the law in a transcendent reality and then applying it mecanically").

105. See Holmes, *The Common Law* at 1. See also Feldman, *From Premodern to Modern American Jurisprudence* at 1446 ("As modernists—the realists, the Langdellians, and the Holmesians—all rejected the antebellum . . . commitment to natural law principles. . . .").

106. Francis Hilliard, *The Elements of Law* v–vi (Hilliard, Gray, 1835, reprint 1972).

107. Before deriding all American legal thought prior to the publication of *The Common Law,* critics ought to have a better-than-comic-book understanding of what this thought was. See Alschuler, *Rediscovering Blackstone* at 18.

108. Although judges are also more insulated from interest group pressures than legislators, the discussion in text does not focus on this difference. This discussion centers on the differing goals and products of the legislative and judicial processes rather than the differing inputs and procedures.

109. See US Const, art I, § 3, cl 3 (prohibiting *ex post facto* laws and bills of attainder); US Const, amend V (due process clause); US Const, art III, § 2 (case or controversy requirement).

110. See Aristotle, *The Nicomachean Ethics* bk V, ch 4, at 111, 114–17 (David Ross transl) (Oxford Univ Press, 1980).

111. See chapter 2 at 18–19.

112. See, for example, Richard A. Posner, *The Concept of Corrective Justice in Recent Theories of Tort Law,* 10 J Legal Stud 187 (1981).

113. Richard A. Posner, *Overcoming Law* 391 (Harvard Univ Press, 1995) (quoting Benjamin N. Cardozo, *The Nature of the Judicial Process* 98, 102–03 (Yale Univ Press, 1921)).

114. Laura Kalman, *The Strange Career of Legal Liberalism* 4 (Yale Univ Press, 1996).

115. Id at 2 (emphasis in the original) (quoting Gerald Rosenberg, *The Hollow Hope: Can Courts Bring About Social Change?* 4 (Univ of Chicago Press, 1991)).

116. Holmes, *The Common Law* at 35–36.

117. Holmes, *The Path of the Law* at 466–67, reprinted in 3 *Collected Works* at 398.

118. Sir Henry Sumner Maine, *Ancient Law: Its Connection with the Early History of Society and Its Relation to Modern Ideas* 3 (Sir Frederick Pollock ed) (Murray, 1906 (1861)).

119. Howe, *Justice Oliver Wendell Holmes: The Proving Years* at 149.

120. Maine, *Ancient Law* at 2–3.

121. Id at 3.

122. Id at 165.

123. Howe, *Justice Oliver Wendell Holmes: The Proving Years* at 149 n31. See also Touster, *Holmes a Hundred Years Ago* at 684; White, *Justice Oliver Wendell Holmes* at 194 ("Holmes adopted the same organizational structure of Maine's *Ancient Law*"); Neil Duxbury, *The Birth of Legal Realism and the Myth of Justice Holmes,* 20 Anglo-Am L Rev 81, 88 (1991); Edmund Wilson, *Patriotic Gore: Studies in the Literature of the American Civil War* 765 (Oxford Univ Press, 1962); J. W. Burrow, *Holmes in His Intellectual Milieu,* in *The Legacy of Oliver Wendell Holmes, Jr.* at 17, 25–28. Holmes not only borrowed much of Maine's structure; he also replayed some of the themes that Maine had sounded. See Reimann, *Holmes's* Common Law *and German Legal Science* at 72, 252 n65 ("The idea that legal forms have survived as mere shells while their substance has changed . . . —one of the central themes in *The Common Law*—had already been developed by Maine in his discussion of legal

fictions."). Nevertheless, references to Maine were conspicuously absent from Holmes's text. Touster, *Holmes a Hundred Years Ago* at 686. Holmes wrote of Maine, "I do not think he will leave much mark on the actual structure of jurisprudence, although he helped many others to do so." Holmes to Sir Frederick Pollock, Mar 4, 1888, in 1 *The Holmes–Pollock Letters: The Correspondence of Mr. Justice Holmes and Sir Frederick Pollock, 1874–1932* at 31 (Mark DeWolfe Howe ed) (Harvard Univ Press, 1941). G. Edward White observed that in *The Common Law* Holmes "sought to distinguish himself, principally through erroneous citations or the absence of citation, from contemporaries whose insights he had adopted or extended, notably Maine, Pollock, and Pomeroy." White, *Justice Oliver Wendell Holmes* at 193.

124. Holmes, *The Common Law* at 38.

125. See Thomas C. Grey, *Holmes and Legal Pragmatism,* 41 Stan L Rev 787, 841–42 (1989) (Holmes "obviously thinks [his 'objective theory'] is comparable to Maine's hypotheses of the law's tendency to move from status to contract, or from communal to individual ownership.").

126. Holmes, *The Common Law* at 110.

127. Id at 135.

128. Id at 41.

129. Id at 46–47.

130. Id at 48.

131. Id at 108.

132. Id at 134.

133. Id at 137.

134. Id at 162. Patrick Kelley notes a strong parallel between Holmes's claim that the history of law is one of movement from subjective to objective standards and Auguste Comte's theory that human thought on any subject progresses through three stages or styles—a theological mode, a metaphysical mode, and a positivist mode. Kelley argues that Holmes's view of the development of law was influenced more by the positivism of Comte and John Stuart Mill than by the pragmatism of C. S. Pierce, William James, and John Dewey. See generally Kelley, *Was Holmes a Pragmatist?,* 114 S Ill L J 427 (1990).

135. Holmes to A. G. Sedgwick, July 12, 1879, quoted in Robert W. Gordon, *Holmes's Common Law as Social and Legal Science,* 10 Hofstra L Rev 719 (1982).

136. Wilson, *Patriotic Gore* at 756.

137. Grey, *Holmes and Legal Pragmatism* at 813.

138. Id.

139. Gordon, *Holmes's* Common Law *as Social and Legal Science* at 719.

140. Baker, *The Justice from Beacon Hill* at 254.

141. Id. Baker did call *The Common Law* "a distinguished and original contribution to legal scholarship," id at 254, but this judgment rested on her unfair caricature of the law before Holmes. See text at 93–94.

142. Gilmore, *The Ages of American Law* at 52. Even David Rosenberg, a fervent Holmes admirer, observes:

> [C]ontrary to what most readers expect, Holmes's writings are not easily accessible. They are characterized by peaks of sparkling insight punctuating long passages of dense, abstruse detail; by crucial ideas expressed in delphic aphorisms; by arguments directed to bygone issues, knowledge of which is taken for granted; by use of terms with multiple meanings; and by simultaneous development of multiple lines of thought with only context to guide the reader.

David Rosenberg, *The Hidden Holmes: His Theory of Torts in History* 164 (Harvard Univ Press, 1995). But see White, *Justice Oliver Wendell Holmes* at 112 (referring to *The Common Law*'s "distinctive perspective and arresting style").

143. Novick, *Editor's Introduction* to *The Common Law,* in 3 *Collected Works* at 109.

144. Vinerian Professor of Law at Oxford and later the author of the influential *Introduction to the Study of the Law of the Constitution* (Macmillan, 1885).

145. *Book Review, Spectator,* June 3, 1882, at 745 (literary supplement). This review is reprinted in Touster, *Holmes a Hundred Years Ago* at 712–17 and is discussed in id at 686, 696 & n93, 702–03.

146. 32 *Nation* 464, 465 (1881). Mark De Wolfe Howe identified Holland as the author of this review in *Justice Oliver Wendell Holmes: The Proving Years* at 249.

147. 32 *Nation* at 465. Arthur Sedgwick, the editor of the *Nation,* formerly had been a law clerk with Holmes at the firm of Chandler, Shattuck and Thayer and also had been co-editor with Holmes of the *American Law Review.* Holmes had written to Sedgwick that he would welcome mention of his work in the *Nation,* referring specifically to an article he later incorporated in *The Common Law.* Baker, *The Justice from Beacon Hill* at 251.

148. See White, *Justice Oliver Wendell Holmes* at 182 (citing [Roger Foster], *Holmes on the Common Law,* 23 Albany L J 380 (1881); [John Warren], *Holmes's Common Law,* 15 Am L Rev 331 (1881); and 25 J of Jurisprudence 646 (1881)).

People who know Holmes's frequently masterful style may find it difficult to realize how ponderous and dense his book is until they try to read it. Although this book contains five paragraphs of Holmes at his best, it contains hundreds of paragraphs of Holmes at his worst. Moreover, perhaps because Holmes had a deadline, the quality of his writing deteriorated throughout the volume. Holmes's prose was, to be sure, no more dreary than that of Langdell, Beale, and other writers of his era, but anyone who suspects that only our distance in time accounts for the flatness and obscurity of Holmes's language ought to consider the clear, engaging prose of a classic fully twice as old as *The Common Law,* Blackstone's *Commentaries.* Or that reader might examine the still-crisp prose of Holmes's English contemporaries Pollock, Stephen, and Maitland—or the writings of outstanding American legal and political authors prior to Holmes such as Madison, Marshall, Tucker, Pomeroy, and Lincoln. Classics are timeless, and Holmes's five great paragraphs *are.* The bulk of his book isn't.

149. See Rosenberg, *The Hidden Holmes* at 45–46 (describing the book reviews, citing several nineteenth-century tort cases in which judges explicitly made policy, and

commenting, "Holmes may well have overestimated the extent to which judges were shy to acknowledge their policy-making role."). Despite Rosenberg's recognition of Holmes's error on this point, he continually portrayed Holmes as struggling heroically against an *a priori*-ism that was everywhere around him. Citing only a secondary source, he declared, "Emulating Euclidean geometry, formalist legal science presented law as a syllogistic scheme operating from fixed postulates and deductively derived rights to produce mathematically determinate decisions." Id at 17. Citing nothing, he characterized nineteenth-century legal science as proclaiming, "Formulated in the image of the syllogistic ideal, law . . . would become not only entirely consistent and determinate but, more importantly, untroubled by choices among competing policies and social interests." Id at 3. Rosenberg, who accuses Mark DeWolfe Howe, G. Edward White, Lawrence Friedman, Richard Posner, Guido Calabresi, Morton Horwitz, Robert Gordon, and Grant Gilmore of "scholarly defects of the most elementary kind" including uncritical reliance on secondary sources, see id at 8–9, 164, lives in a glass house himself.

150. Mark DeWolfe Howe observed that when Holmes gave his lectures "[i]t is not unlikely that Langdell, Thayer, Ames, and Gray—the entire Faculty of the Harvard Law school—were in the audience." Howe, *Justice Oliver Wendell Holmes: The Proving Years* at 157. See also White, *Justice Oliver Wendell Holmes* at 151.

   Of course Holmes's own high opinion of *The Common Law* was unshaken by the book's reception. See Holmes to Harold Laski, Feb 1, 1919, in 1 *The Holmes–Laski Letters: The Correspondence of Mr. Justice Holmes and Harold J. Laski, 1916–1935* at 182–84 (Mark deWolfe Howe ed) (Harvard Univ Press, 1953) ("so far as I know my attempt stands almost alone").

151. See chapter 3 at 37.

152. Or they might suppose that Langdell and his colleagues were unusually broad-minded formalists.

153. White, *Justice Oliver Wendell Holmes* at 170–71.

154. See Feldman, *From Premodern to Modern American Jurisprudence* at 1442–43 ("[I]n many ways, the early Holmes was strongly aligned with his Langdellian contemporaries. . . . *The Common Law* was deeply reductionistic—attempting to condense the entire common law into one principle—and for that reason, it was highly abstract, formal, and conceptual. In short, in many ways it strongly resembled a work of Langdellian jurisprudence."); LaPiana, *Logic and Experience* at 169 (Langdell and Holmes "were deeply situated in the intellectual life of their age, and their ideas about law were far more alike than different."); A. W. Brian Simpson, *Book Review,* 95 Mich L Rev 2027, 2035 (1997) ("There is not a single example in *The Common Law* where Holmes explained the legal evolution in tort law in terms of factors external to the law except for a few vague, empirically unfounded remarks that represent Holmes at both his persuasive rhetorical best and his intellectual worst.").

155. Holmes, *The Common Law* at 39.

156. Id at 40.

157. Id at 44–45.

158. Id at 46.

159. Id at 49–50.

160. The goal of preventing harm may not be furthered by punishing people who lack the capacity to prevent it. Moreover, the endorsement of preventive goals does not imply that these goals should be pursued without regard to human and economic costs. The error of Holmes's argument seemed evident once he revealed that his own objective standard neither imposed strict liability for producing "external" harm nor always demanded the highest care of which a member of the community was capable. As Holmes's endorsement of a non-strict-liability standard implicitly recognized, difficult lines remain to be drawn even after one renounces the imposition of deserved punishment as an objective of the criminal law. In the absence of greater empirical knowledge than Holmes had (or we have), one might favor traditional *mens rea* requirements as the most cost-effective means of satisfying preventive goals. See Glanville Williams, *Criminal Law: The General Part* 123 (Sweet & Maxwell, 2d ed 1961) ("[T]he deterrent theory . . . finds itself in some difficulty when applied to negligence.").

161. Holmes, *The Common Law* at 44.

162. Id at 43.

163. Holmes to Harold Laski, Dec 17, 1925, in 1 *Holmes–Laski Letters* 806 (adding that Holmes felt "neither doubt nor scruple" about this position).

164. Holmes did show that the forfeiture of animals and things usually was not a way of imposing strict criminal liability on the owners of these animals and things.

165. Holmes, *The Common Law* at 7, 19.

166. Id at 28–29.

167. There is, however, little reason to believe that it did. One can easily imagine other reasons for destroying an animal or object that has produced harm—a desire not to leave this instrumentality as a visible reminder of the injury, a belief that demons had infested the creature or object (which differs from the view that the object itself intended harm), or the need for a ceremonial act to erase the past and symbolize the closure of a painful incident. See Paul Schiff Berman, *An Anthropological Approach to Modern Forfeiture Law: The Symbolic Function of Legal Actions against Objects,* 11 Yale J L & Human 1 (1999). In addition, ancient kings realized what the generals of today's war on drugs know too—that the forfeiture of "accursed things" can be a nice source of revenue. See Eric Blumenson and Eva Nilsen, *Policing for Profit: The Drug War's Hidden Economic Agenda,* 65 U Chi L Rev 35 (1998).

168. See Touster, *Holmes a Hundred Years Ago* at 686–87 & n72.

169. Frederick Maitland, *The Early History of Malice Aforethought,* in 1 *Collected Papers of Frederick William Maitland* 304, 327 (H. A. L. Fisher ed) (Cambridge Univ Press, 1911) (Hein 1981).

170. Atiyah, *The Legacy of Holmes through English Eyes* at 344. Atiyah added, "And certainly the modern history of criminal law over the past century or more shows a strong movement in the same direction." Id.

171. Gilmore, *The Ages of American Law* at 52. See also Grey, *Holmes and Legal Pragmatism* at 842 ("As a historical thesis, Holmes' theory is wholly unconvincing.").

    Gilmore declared that casting Holmes's "essentially philosophical statement about the nature of law" in "the misleading disguise of pseudo-history" was absurd even apart from the fact that Holmes on occasion "deliberately distorted" his history. Gilmore's speculation about Holmes's reasons for using history to make his arguments, including his suggestion that Holmes's historical method might have been "an elaborate joke," revealed Gilmore's unawareness of the dominance of historicist methodology in late-nineteenth-century legal scholarship. Gilmore's mischaracterization of Langdell's work reflected the same ignorance. See text at 98 and 253 n93.

172. See Holmes, *The Common Law* at 44 ("[T]he general principles of criminal and civil liability are the same.").

173. 138 Mass 165, 178 (1884). See also *Commonwealth v Chance*, 174 Mass 245, 252, 54 NE 51, 554 (1899); *Commonwealth v Kennedy*, 170 Mass 18, 20, 48 NE 770 (1897) ("[T]he aim of the law is not to punish sins, but is to prevent certain external results. . . .").

174. *Pierce*, 138 Mass at 178. In general, Holmes viewed words like *malice, intent, recklessness, negligence,* and *mischance* as denoting "tiers" of objectively determined danger rather than subjective mental states. See, for example, Oliver Wendell Holmes, *Privilege, Malice and Intent*, 8 Harv L Rev 1 (1894), reprinted in 3 *Collected Works* at 371, 371–72 ("If the manifest probability of harm is very great, and the harm follows, we say that it is done maliciously or intentionally; if not so great, but still considerable, we say that the harm is done negligently; if there is no apparent danger, we call it mischance."); *White v Duggan*, 140 Mass 18, 20 (1885) ("[T]he difference between intent and negligence, in a legal sense, is ordinarily nothing but the difference in the probability, under the circumstances known to the actor and according to common experience, that a certain consequence, or class of consequences, will follow from a certain act. . . ."); Holmes, *The Common Law* at 59–60.

175. Patrick J. Kelley, *Holmes on the Supreme Judicial Court: The Theorist as Judge*, in *The History of the Law in Massachusetts: The Supreme Judicial Court 1692–1992* at 275, 284 (Russell K. Osgoode ed) (Supreme Judicial Court Historical Socy, 1992).

176. The trial judge had denied the jury the option of convicting the defendant of manslaughter, and the state's Holmes-warped jury instruction declared that she would be guilty of murder if, "in the circumstances known to [her], a reasonably prudent person would have known that, according to common experience, there was a plain and strong likelihood that death would follow the contemplated act." *Commonwealth v Woodward*, 427 Mass 659, 670 n14, 694 NE2d 1277, 1286 n14 (1998). The Supreme Judicial Court later explained that the only difference between murder and involuntary manslaughter in Massachusetts lay "in the degree

of risk of physical harm that a reasonable person would recognize was created by particular conduct, based on what the defendant knew." A murder conviction required proof of "a plain and strong likelihood of death," while a manslaughter conviction required only proof of "a high degree of likelihood that substantial harm will result to another." *Woodward,* 427 Mass at 670, 694 NE2d at 1286. The murder conviction of the apparently no-worse-than-negligent Woodward sparked public outcry, and the trial judge, denying that this outcry influenced him at all, replaced the murder verdict with the involuntary manslaughter verdict he had precluded the jury from returning. The judge promptly imposed a sentence that released Woodward from custody. The Supreme Judicial Court affirmed his ruling, and so ended another Massachusetts close encounter with Holmesian objectivism.

177. [1961] AC 290.

178. Id at 327.

179. *Parker v The Queen,* [1962–63] 111 CLR 610, 632 (Austl). The Privy Council acquiesced in Australia's secession, and the sun then set on the British Empire even in law. See Atiyah, *The Legacy of Holmes through English Eyes* at 348.

180. Criminal Justice Act, 1967, ch 80, § 8.

181. Atiyah, *The Legacy of Holmes through English Eyes* at 347.

182. Holmes, *The Common Law* at 77. Holmes's view of tort law had changed in the ten years since his first publication on the subject, a book review in which he noted the grab-bag nature of the field and declared, "We are inclined to think that Torts is not a proper subject for a law book." Oliver Wendell Holmes, Jr., *Book Notice,* 5 Am L Rev 340, 341 (1871) (reviewing C. G. Addison, *The Law of Torts* (abridged) (Little, Brown, 1870)).

183. Holmes, *The Common Law* at 77 ("Such a general view is very hard to find.").

184. Id at 81.

185. Id at 82.

186. Id.

187. Howe, *Justice Oliver Wendell Holmes: The Proving Years* at 187–89.

188. Oliver Wendell Holmes, Jr., *The Use of Law Schools,* Nov 5, 1886, in 3 *Collected Works* at 474.

189. One of the statements most responsible for Langdell's lasting reputation as a fogie was: "[L]aw is a science, and . . . all the available materials of that science are contained in printed books." C. C. Langdell, *Teaching Law as a Science,* 11 Am L Rev 123 (1887). Langdell also declared that the law library is to legal academics "all that the museum of natural history is to the zoologists, all that the biological garden is to the botanists." *Record of the Commemoration, November Fifth to Eighth 1886, on the Two Hundred and Fiftieth Anniversary of the Founding of Harvard College* 87 (John Wilson & Son, 1887). Note Sir Henry Maine's earlier use of a similar analogy in remarks quoted in text at 104.

190. Holmes, *The Common Law* at 146–47. See Simpson, *Book Review* at 2035 ("Holmes,

as it seems to me, wrote of tort law . . . in one of his alternative modes, Holmes-the-unreconstructed-legal-scientist, desperate, somehow or other, to cobble together a theory that presented the entire law of tort as an internally consistent whole, based upon a single, timeless principle of liability, awaiting 'discovery' through a doctrinal analysis of the reported cases, an analysis that assumes the law must be internally consistent.").

191. 132 Eng Rep 490, 493–94 (CP 1837).

192. Sarah Austin, a noted editor and translator, pieced her departed husband's views together from notes on lectures that he had delivered in 1843 or earlier. She published her reconstruction in 1863. See John Austin, 1 *Lectures on Jurisprudence of the Philosophy of Positive Law* 34, 422, 438–43 (Robert Campbell ed) (John Murray, 3d ed 1869); Simpson, *Book Review* at 2032. Brian Simpson notes that, by the time Holmes wrote, "Austin's views about negligence had long been overtaken by events." Id.

193. Simpson, *Book Review* at 2028.

194. See, for example, C. G. Addison, *Wrongs and Their Remedies, Being a Treatise on the Law of Torts* 131, 132, 135 (V. and R. Stevens and Sons, 1860); Thomas M. Cooley, *A Treatise on the Law of Torts* 591 (Callaghan, 1879); Francis Hilliard, *The Law of Torts or Private Wrongs* 120 (Little, Brown, 3d ed 1866); Thomas W. Saunders, *A Treatise on the Law Applicable to Negligence* 5, 7 (Robert Clarke, 1872); Francis Wharton, *A Treatise on the Law of Negligence* 786, 866, 867 (Kay and Brother, 1874); Seymour D. Thompson, 1 *The Law of Negligence in Relations Not Resting in Contract* 121, 148, 150, 171, 489 (F. H. Thomas, 1880).

195. Chief Justice Tindal's objective standard in *Vaughn v Menlove* differed from that of Holmes. Tindal's standard imposed liability for failing to exercise "caution such as a man of ordinary prudence would observe" while Holmes's imposed liability for harms that a prudent person would have *foreseen.* As this chapter will indicate, Holmes was oblivious to the difference between these two formulations.

196. Holmes, *The Common Law* at 130–31.

Morton Horwitz observed, "If there is a single, overriding, and repetitive theme running through Holmes's writing, it is the necessity and desirability of establishing objective rules of law, that is, general rules that do not take the peculiar mental or moral state of individuals into account." Morton J. Horwitz, *The Transformation of American Law, 1870–1960: The Crisis of Legal Orthodoxy* 110 (Oxford Univ Press, 1992). Horwitz nevertheless maintained that a "revolutionary change . . . occur[ed] in Holmes' thought shortly before the turn of the century," id at 138, that "Holmes gradually abandoned objectivism," id at 139, and that "[b]y 1894 [Holmes] was willing to accept the uncertainty inherent in all inquiries into subjective states of mind in order to preserve the integrity of common law adjudication." Id.

The evidence offered by Horwitz of a "revolutionary change" in Holmes's position is thin. It consists of an article that Holmes published in 1894, *Privilege, Malice and Intent,* 8 Harv L Rev 1 (1894), reprinted in 3 *Collected Works* at 371. In that article, Holmes recognized that a defendant's bad motives might defeat a claim of

privilege. The same article, however, claimed the triumph of "a general theory"—
the principle of objective liability that Holmes had developed in *The Common Law*
and his opinions for the Supreme Judicial Court of Massachusetts. Holmes wrote:

> The law of torts as now administered has worked itself into substantial agreement
> with a general theory. I should sum up the first part of the theory in a few words,
> as follows. . . . The standard applied is external, and the words malice, intent and
> negligence, as used in this connection, refer to an external standard. If the manifest
> probability of harm is very great, and the harm follows, we say that it is done mali-
> ciously or intentionally; if not so great, but still considerable, we say that the harm
> is done negligently; if there is no apparent danger, we call it mischance.

Id. Before "pass[ing] to the inquiry, whether privilege, sometimes at least, is not
dependent upon the motives with which the act complained of is done," id at 5,
Holmes noted again, "I assume that we have got past the question which is answered by the test of the external standard." Id at 2.

Holmes's 1894 article recognized that once objective standards had established a tort defendant's *prima facie* liability, proof of intention might be relevant.
Impermissible motives could sometimes defeat a claim of privilege. A defendant's
subjective mental state therefore might matter, but only as an exception to an exception.

This position did not depart notably from Holmes's earlier stance. *The Common
Law* had recognized the persistence of subjective standards in many pockets of the
law and indeed had suggested that subjective malice might defeat a claim of privilege. Holmes noted, for example, that "malevolence" might make a teacher's dismissal by a school board actionable. He wrote:

> Policy, it might be said, forbids going behind their judgment, but actual evil mo-
> tives coupled with the absence of grounds withdraw this protection, because pol-
> icy, although it does not require them to take the risk of being right, does require
> that they should judge honestly on the merits.
>
> Other isolated instances like this last might, perhaps, be found in different parts
> of the law, in which actual malevolence would affect a man's liability for his
> conduct.

Holmes, *The Common Law* at 143.

Decades after the 1894 publication, Holmes continued to praise objective
standards. In 1913, for example, he declared in a Supreme Court opinion that at
common law "a man might have to answer with his life for consequences . . . he
neither intended nor foresaw," adding that "the law is full of instances where a
man's fate depends on his estimating rightly, that is as the jury subsequently estimates it, some matter of degree. If his judgment is wrong, not only may he incur
a fine or . . . imprisonment . . .; he may incur the penalty of death." *Nash v United
States,* 229 US 373, 377 (1913). See also *Abrams v United States,* 250 US 616,
626–27 (1919) (Holmes dissenting) ("A man may have to pay damages, may be
sent to prison, at common law might be hanged, if at the time of his act he knew
facts from which common experience showed that the consequences would follow, whether he individually could foresee them or not.").

John Goldberg appropriately concludes:

> [Horwitz's] entire account is premised on the notion that Holmes ultimately recognized the futility of the objective fault theory of liability which formed the preoccupation of his pre-skeptical common law days. Yet Holmes continued to endorse and advocate this theory in *The Path of the Law* and later essays, not to mention subsequent judicial decisions.

John C. P. Goldberg, *Style and Skepticism in* The Path of the Law, 63 Brook L Rev 225, 271 (1997).

197. Holmes, *The Common Law* at 50.

198. Max Radin, *Legal Realism,* 31 Colum L Rev 824, 826 (1931).

199. Id.

200. See Joseph Hutchinson, *The Judgment Intuitive: The Function of the "Hunch" in Judicial Decision,* 14 Cornell L Q 274 (1929). Although Judge Hutchinson's article presented a careful, cautious, and qualified description of the role of the "hunch" in his own decision making, Jerome Frank and others neglected the care, caution, and qualifications. When Karl Llewellyn invented the realist movement, he included Hutchinson on his quasi-official list of twenty realists. Apart from Jerome Frank who was practicing law at the time, Hutchinson was the only nonacademic so honored. See Karl Llewellyn, *Some Realism about Realism,* 44 Harv L Rev 1222, 1226 n18 (1931).

201. See, for example, Herman Oliphant, *Address as President, Association of American Law Schools,* Dec 29, 1927, in *1927 Handbook and Proceedings of the Association of American Law Schools* 61 (praising, of all things, the fourteenth-century English writ system for its lack of generalization and declaring, "No new era of sound scholarship can have for its principal business the further logical elaboration of present abstractions.").

202. See, for example, Jerome Frank, *Law and the Modern Mind* at 19, 210–18 (describing legal rules as the product of fetishism and father fixation and declaring that they had replaced religion as an outlet for the emotional cravings of childhood); Fred Rodell, *Woe Unto You, Lawyers!* (Reynal & Hitchcock, 2d ed 1957 (1939)) (describing law as "mumbojumbo," "streamlined voodoo," "chromium-plated theology," a "high-class racket," and "the killy-loo bird of the sciences.").

203. Karl N. Llewellyn, *Legal Illusion,* 31 Colum L Rev 82, 84 (1931).

204. Karl N. Llewellyn, *Holmes,* 35 Colum L Rev 485, 487 (1935).

205. Frank, *Law and the Modern Mind* at 253.

206. Id at 239. See also Fred Rodell, *Justice Holmes and His Hecklers,* 60 Yale L J 620 (1951) ("one of the finest minds and greatest spirits that American civilization has produced").

207. This irony seems worthy of a detective novel in which the previously unsuspected and seemingly heroic police chief proves on the last page to be the long-sought serial killer—or worthy of an even more ironic novel in which the police chief gets away with it.

208. See Simpson, *Book Review* at 2033 ("I cannot see why the discovery . . . of the single principle of civil liability . . . could be received with anything other than delight by someone like Dean Langdell.").

209. I use the word *factfinder* to describe the agency making the determinations that Holmes's analysis requires. This usage is generally accurate, but in some cases, judges might make some of these determinations as a matter of law.

210. See Holmes, *The Common Law* at 54, 91, 95, 152.

211. Id at 91–94. Holmes did recognize that the law of criminal attempts punished conduct that had not produced a harmful result. He tried to show that this body of law was consistent with his general theory, claiming that, contrary to common understanding, criminal intent was not required for some attempts. When courts did consider intent, moreover, they did so merely to assess the likelihood of harm. See id at 65–72. Oddly, Holmes not only recognized the courts' use of a subjective standard but also recognized that their use of this standard advanced the external preventive purposes that he attributed to the criminal law. Although Holmes's effort to minimize the role of subjective intent led him to mangle the law of attempts, his discussion seemed in the end, not to support his general thesis, but to contradict it.

212. See id at 54 ("[T]here must be actual present knowledge of the present facts which make an act dangerous."); id at 55, 133.

213. See, for example, id at 147 ("[The known circumstances] must be such as would have led a prudent man to perceive danger. . . .").

214. See id at 109. But see id ("Insanity is a more difficult matter. . . .").

215. See, for example, id at 161 ("[T]he philosophical analysis of every wrong begins by determining what the defendant has actually chosen, that is to say, what his voluntary act or conduct has been, and what consequences he has actually contemplated as flowing from them, and then goes on to determine what dangers attended either the conduct under the known circumstances, or its contemplated consequence under the contemplated circumstances.").

216. See, for example, id at 144–45, 156 ("The law allows some harms to be intentionally inflicted, and *a fortiori* some risks to be intentionally run.").

217. Rosenberg, *The Hidden Holmes* at 5–8.

218. David A. Hollinger, *The "Tough-Minded" Justice Holmes, Jewish Intellectuals, and the Making of an American Icon,* in *The Legacy of Oliver Wendell Holmes, Jr.* at 216, 219.

219. See, for example, G. Edward White, *Tort Law in America* 12–19 (Oxford Univ Press, 1980).

220. For a classic exposition of this concept of negligence, see *Carroll Towing Co v United States,* 159 F2d 169 (2d Cir 1947) (L. Hand, J). An influential article in 1915 by Henry T. Terry, *Negligence,* 29 Harv L Rev 40 (1915), effectively developed "the Hand formula." Nothing resembling this cost-benefit formula for assessing tort liability appears in *The Common Law.*

221. See Virginia E. Nolan and Edmund Ursin, *Understanding Enterprise Liability* (Temple Univ Press, 1995); George L. Priest, *The Invention of Enterprise Liability: A Critical History of the Intellectual Foundations of Modern Tort Law,* 14 J Leg Stud 461 (1985).

222. Rosenberg, *The Hidden Holmes* at 8–10, 160–69.

223. Holmes, *The Common Law* at 150.

224. Id.

225. Id at 158. See also id at 112 (suggesting that the traditional "vague test of the care exercised by a prudent man" should be replaced by "a precise one of specific acts and omissions"); id ("[N]egligence . . . mean[s] . . . a failure to act as a prudent man of average intelligence would have done.").

226. Id at 110.

227. Id at 51 ("The reconciliation of the doctrine that liability is founded on blameworthiness with the existence of liability where the party is not to blame . . . is found in the conception of the average man, the man or ordinary intelligence and reasonable prudence. Liability is said to arise out of such conduct as would be blameworthy in him."); id at 76 ("what would be blameworthy in [the prudent man]"); id at 103 ("The law considers . . . what would be blameworthy in the average man, the man of ordinary intelligence and prudence, and determines liability by that."); id at 111 (the test of liability is the "culpability or innocence" of the "average prudent man"); id at 162 (the test is "whether [the defendant's] conduct would have been wrong in the fair average member of the community, whom he is expected to equal at his peril").

228. Id at 147.

229. For David Rosenberg's tortured effort to extricate Holmes from this charge of confusion, see Rosenberg, *The Hidden Holmes* at 110–14. Rosenberg argues that Holmes recognized the error of equating foresight with blameworthiness about halfway through his torts lectures. He then shifted ground by substituting the word *wrongful* for the word *blameworthy.* (Strangely, however, Holmes did not bother to correct his equation of foresight and blameworthiness when he prepared his lectures for publication.)

   Rosenberg's central thesis—that Holmes endorsed foresight-based strict liability and that most modern torts scholars have not realized it—is correct, and his book displays impressive knowledge. Nevertheless, much of his Holmes-as-hero scholarship seems to me not only unconvincing but farfetched. Not since Delphi has anyone gone as far as Rosenberg in projecting untold wisdom onto meaningless phrases.

230. Holmes, *The Common Law* at 147–49, 162.

231. 82 Eng Rep 539 (KB 1647).

232. Holmes, *The Common Law* at 162.

233. Id; see also id at 148.

234. Id at 162.

235. Id at 149.

236. Id at 162. See also id at 149 ("[T]he degree of danger attending given conduct under certain known circumstances is sufficient to throw the risk upon the party pursuing it.").

237. Of course Holmes did intend his general principle as an alternative to a *subjective* negligence standard like John Austin's.

   Rosenberg does not mention Holmes's refusal to endorse the result in *Gilbert*—a refusal that poses substantial difficulties for Rosenberg's claim that Holmes not only favored foresight-based strict liability but also deliberately chose this standard in preference to an objective negligence standard.

238. One should not suppose that Holmes imported much cost-benefit analysis into his theory of liability at the final stage of inquiry—whether the defendant was privileged to inflict a harm that earlier stages of analysis made him presumptively liable for inflicting. Holmes contemplated only the application of a reasonably small number of recognized legal privileges, and almost all of these privileges were categorical. For example, a lawyer could defame someone whenever it was necessary to do so in presenting an argument in court. A privilege did not permit a person to take a slight chance of harm unless it also permitted her to inflict the harm intentionally or with certainty. Both in practice and as Holmes envisioned it, the law of privileges did not give courts and juries a significant opportunity to weigh the likelihood and magnitude of harm against the likelihood and magnitude of gain. But see Holmes, *Privilege, Malice and Intent,* 8 Harv L Rev at 120 (indicating Holmes's general approval of cost-benefit analysis in determining *whether* to afford a privilege).

239. 254 US 415 (1920).

240. Id at 417.

241. Id at 419 (Clarke joined by Day and Pitney dissenting).

242. Id at 418 (Holmes).

243. LR 3 HL 330 (1868); see also *Fletcher v Rylands,* LR 1 Ex 265 (1866).

244. Holmes, *The Common Law* at 157.

245. 151 Mass 359 (1890).

246. 151 Mass at 362.

247. *Burt v Advertiser Newspaper Co,* 154 Mass 238, 247 (1891).

248. Kelley, *Holmes on the Supreme Judicial Court* at 333–35.

249. In addition to the *Burt* and *Fessenden* rulings cited above, see *Clifford v Atlantic Cotton Mills,* 146 Mass 47 (1888); *Tasker v Stanley,* 153 Mass 148 (1891); *Hayes v Inhabitants of Hyde Park,* 153 Mass 514 (1891); *Graves v Johnson,* 256 Mass 211 (1892).

   In *Murray v Boston Ice Co,* 180 Mass 165 (1901), Holmes acknowledged that the *negligent* conduct of a wrongdoer other than the defendant would not shield the defendant from liability, but he intimated disapproval of the precedents that dictated this conclusion: "If there were no decisions upon the matter, the ruling requested for the defendant would have to be considered from a different point of view. . . ." 180 Mass at 167. Although Holmes recognized that prior decisions limited his limitation, Patrick Kelley says of the opinion in *Murray:* "[T]he theorist seems grumpy and querulous, upset that the law doesn't coincide with his elegant theory, even though this theory was neither elegant, coherent, nor descriptive." Kelley, *Holmes on the Supreme Judicial Court* at 340.

250. Holmes to Pollock, Mar 22, 1891, in 1 *Holmes–Pollock Letters* at 31; Holmes to Pollock, June 7, 1891, in id at 87.

251. Holmes, *Privilege, Malice, and Intent,* 8 Harv L Rev 1 (1894).

252. Rosenberg, *The Hidden Holmes* at 109. Holmes offered this explanation of the trespass to land cases:

> A man who walks knows that he is moving over the surface of the earth, he knows that he is surrounded by private estates which he has no right to enter, and he knows that his motion, unless guided, will carry him into one of those estates. He is thus warned, and the burden of his conduct is thrown upon himself.

Holmes, *The Common Law* at 153; see also id at 152–53 ("When a man does the series of acts called walking, it is assumed for all purposes of responsibility that he knows the earth is under his feet. . . . With that knowledge, he acts at his peril in certain respects. If he crosses his neighbor's boundary, he is a trespasser."). Holmes offered this explanation of a prominent bolting-horse case:

> Hard spurring is just so much more likely to lead to harm than merely riding a horse in the street, that the court thought that the defendant would be bound to look out for the consequences of the one, while it would not hold him liable for those resulting merely from the other; because the possibility of being run away with when riding quietly, though familiar, is comparatively slight.

Id at 94.

253. Patrick J. Kelley, *A Critical Analysis of Holmes's Theory of Torts,* 61 Wash U L Q 681, 687 (1983).

254. Holmes, *The Common Law* at 55.

255. Id at 147.

256. Id at 75.

257. Id at 162.

258. Id at 161.

259. See id at 147 ("[The circumstances] must be such as would have led a prudent man to perceive danger, although not necessarily to foresee the specific harm. But this is a vague test."); id at 159 ("The question in each case is whether the actual choice, or, in other words, the actually contemplated result, was near enough to the remoter result complained of to throw the peril of it upon the actor.").

260. 132 Eng Rep at 474–75.

261. Holmes, *The Common Law* at 108.

262. See Simpson, *Book Review* at 2029–30. As Holmes recognized elsewhere, however, cause-based strict liability is a senseless standard unless it employs a nar-

rower concept of causation than but-for cause. See Holmes, *The Common Law* at 91–93. When an injury occurs, innumerable innocent acts often can be identified as but-for causes. For example, no embezzlement from a bank would have occurred unless the embezzler's mother had given him birth, unless his teacher had taught him how to read and write, and unless an officer of the bank had given him a job. A but-for standard of causation, unmodified by any concept of "direct" causation, "proximate" causation, intervening causation, or the like, would permit the bank to recover its loss from the mother, the schoolteacher, or the bank officer.

A foresight standard seems to narrow the field of liability. It appears to carry its own principle of causation. Nevertheless, because foresight standards like Holmes's do not specify very clearly what must be foreseen and with how much certainty, they leave almost everything open. Mothers, teachers, and bank officers, for example, can foresee with a high degree of certainty that the benefits they bestow upon children, pupils, and employees will sometimes produce injury (along, one hopes, with much good). They can foresee a smaller but perhaps still substantial risk that their actions will aid one or more people to become a criminal. A mother or teacher may even perceive a small risk that she will enable one or more people to become a bank embezzler, a smaller risk that she will help someone to steal from a particular bank, and only the tiniest risk that she will help anyone steal $235,448 by submitting fraudulent charges to the trust account of Greg van Meveren. The more broadly "the injury" that an average man must foresee is defined, the more foreseeable this injury becomes. Perhaps the need to narrow a sweeping concept of causation justified Holmes's rejection of cause-based strict liability, but his argument supplied no reason for selecting the "average man" rather than the "expert" as the measure of appropriate foresight.

263. Holmes, *The Common Law* at 50.

264. Holmes also wrote that "to punish what would not be blameworthy in an average member of the community would be to enforce a standard which was indefensible theoretically, and which practically was too high for that community." Id at 76. Holmes never explained what was indefensible theoretically about doing to the average member of the community what Holmes proposed to do to the below-average member. His only argument was about how much the community would bear, and that argument was about politics, not principle.

265. Id at 51.

266. Id at 96.

267. Id. Compare the German law articulated in The Case of the Gable Wall (Giebelmauer), 56 RGSt 343, 349 (1922) ("A harm caused by defendants can be said to be caused by negligence only when it is established that they disregarded the care which they were obliged to exercise and of which they were capable under the circumstances and according to their personal knowledge and abilities."). See Simpson, *Book Review* at 2029–30 (declaring Holmes's analogies inapt because falling on someone in a fit involves no voluntary action while compelling someone

to insure her neighbor against lightning is an arbitrary wealth transfer unrelated to any receipt of benefits produced by the harmful action).

268. See Gordon, *Holmes's* Common Law *as Social and Legal Science* at 720.

269. See Marc Galanter, *Why the "Haves" Come Out Ahead: Speculation on the Limits of Legal Change,* 9 Law & Soc Rev 95 (1974).

270. Grant Gilmore, *The Death of Contract* (Ohio State Univ Press, 1974).

271. See chapter 3 at 31–32.

272. Gilmore, *The Death of Contract* at 6.

273. See James R. Gordley, *Book Review,* 89 Harv L Rev 452, 453 (1975); Ralph James Mooney, *Book Review,* 55 Or L Rev 155, 164–67 (1976); Richard A. Epstein, *Book Review,* 20 Am J Legal Hist 68, 69 (1976); Morton J. Horwitz, *Book Review,* 42 U Chi L Rev 787, 794 (1975).

274. Gilmore, *The Death of Contract* at 15.

275. See, for example, id at 48.

276. Id at 22–23 (quoting Holmes, *The Common Law* at 292).

277. Id at 22. Gilmore also wrote, "Holmesian consideration theory had, as Holmes perfectly well knew, not so much as a leg to stand on if the matter is taken historically. Going back into the past, there was an infinite number of cases which had imposed liability, in the name of consideration, where nothing like Holmes's 'reciprocal conventional inducement' was anywhere in sight." Id at 70.

278. Gordley, *Book Review* at 463–64. See Sir Frederick Pollock, *Principles of Contract* 164–74 (Stevens and Sons, 10th ed 1936).

279. Gordley, *Book Review* at 458–59.

280. Gilmore's work may merit criticism on grounds other than those noted in text. *The Death of Contract* repeatedly described the first *Restatement of Contracts* as "schizophrenic" because it endorsed both bargained-for consideration and foreseeable reliance as reasons for enforcing promises. Gilmore, *The Death of Contract* at 66–67. Gilmore declared, "The one thing that is clear is that these two contradictory propositions cannot live comfortably together: in the end one must swallow the other up." Id at 68. Recognizing both principles, he said, had resulted in "an uneasy and, it might be argued, intellectually indefensible stand-off." Id at 109. Although the *Restatement*'s recognition of two bases of promissory liability was the result of compromise, the reconciliation was not at all contradictory. A regime that enforces promises when they have induced reliance and also, in the absence of reliance, when they are supported by bargained-for consideration identifies most of the promises that merit enforcement. Courts have employed the two-pronged *Restatement* analysis with considerable success for more than half a century.

   Gilmore objected that "Holmesians" often read cases as supporting the requirement of bargained-for consideration although the judges who decided these cases had not endorsed this requirement. See id at 27–37. Gilmore seemed not to realize that reading cases for propositions unrecognized by the judges who decided them was the central mission of historicist scholarship. Some scholars even proposed disregarding opinions and limiting the doctrine of *stare decisis* to the results of cases. One, Christopher Gustavus Tiedeman, took this position to the point of arguing that judicial opinions should not be published. Instead, every state should create a scientific commission to prepare commentaries on that state's law and then update them in the light of each year's new rulings. See Christopher Gustavus Tiedeman, *The Doctrine of Stare Decisis,* 3 U L Rev 11, 25–26 (1896). See also Siegel, *Joel Bishop's Orthodoxy* at 245–48 (quoting Joel Bishop, 1 *New Commentaries on the Criminal Law* xxii (1892)). Gilmore's criticism of the use of precedent by Holmes and other turn-of-the-century scholars was equally a criticism of historicism itself. This criticism evidenced the same general unawareness of historicism that led Gilmore to misrepresent Langdell's jurisprudence and to express his bafflement at Holmes's use of historical methodology. See note 171.

281. Holmes, *The Common Law* at 289–90.

282. Id at 293–94.

283. After "a generation or more of needless litigation," Gilmore observed, requirements contracts were "granted political asylum within the domain of contract." Gilmore, *The Death of Contract* at 37.

284. See Holmes, *The Common Law* at 293 ("A consideration may be given and accepted . . . solely for the purpose of making a promise binding.").

285. See Horwitz, *Book Review* at 795. For an argument in favor of restoring pre-Holmesian decisions that love and affection can be sufficient consideration for a promise, see Mark K. Moller, Comment, *Sympathy, Community, and Promising: Adam Smith's Case for Reviving Moral Consideration,* 66 U Chi L Rev 213 (1999).

286. Robert W. Gordon, *Book Review,* 1974 Wis L Rev 1216, 1231.

287. See Gilmore, *The Death of Contract* at 62–65.

288. Holmes, *The Common Law* at 324.

289. See Oliver Wendell Holmes, *The Common Law* 230 (Mark DeWolfe Howe ed) (Harvard Univ Press 1963) (reproducing the annotation).

290. Gilmore, *The Death of Contract* at 47.

291. Id at 23.

292. Id at 48.

293. 2 Hurl and C 906, 159 Eng Rep 375 (Ex 1864).

294. But see A. W. Brian Simpson, *Leading Cases in the Common Law* 139 (Clarendon, 1995) (questioning this inference).

295. Holmes, *The Common Law* at 309.

296. Gilmore, *The Death of Contract* at 45.

297. See text at 84.

298. See text at 85. Five great paragraphs are, to be sure, five more than most of us will produce. I do not mean to disparage them but only to keep them in perspective. I

hope that they will continue to inspire lawyers and law students throughout this new century as they did throughout the last.

299. See Paul A. Samuelson, *Consumption Theory in Terms of Revealed Preference,* 15 Economica (n.s.) 243 (1948).

300. Mark Tushnet, *The Logic of Experience: Oliver Wendell Holmes on the Supreme Judicial Court,* 63 Va L Rev 975, 980 (1977).

301. Id at 1023. See also Gordon, *Holmes'* Common Law *as Social and Legal Science* at 731–33.

302. Kelley, *Holmes on the Supreme Judicial Court* at 352.

303. See, for example, Kenneth J. Vandevelde, *A History of Prima Facie Tort: The Origins of a General Theory of Intentional Tort,* 19 Hofstra L Rev 447, 457 (1990) ("It was Holmes who provided tort law with its modern theoretical structure.").

304. White, *Justice Oliver Wendell Holmes* at 264–65.

305. 254 US 415 (1920).

306. See text at 117–18.

307. 258 US 268 (1922).

308. 258 US at 278 (Clarke dissenting).

309. 258 US at 275.

310. 258 US at 276–77.

311. Holmes to Sir Frederick Pollock, Mar 29, 1922, in 2 *Holmes–Pollock Letters* at 92.

312. Holmes, *The Common Law* at 230. See also Holmes, *Law in Science and Science in Law* at 454–55, reprinted in 3 *Collected Works* at 414 ("Other cases of what I have called inflated and unreal explanations, which collapse at the touch of history, are the liability of a master for the torts of his servant in the course of his employment . . . which thus far never, in my opinion, has been put upon a rational footing.").

313. 175 Mass 510, 56 NE 698 (1900).

314. 175 Mass at 512, 56 NE at 698.

315. 175 Mass 150, 55 NE 891 (1900).

316. 150 Mass 362, 23 NE 100 (1889).

317. 177 Mass 128, 58 NE 182 (1900).

318. 177 Mass at 129, 58 NE at 183.

319. 177 Mass 144, 58 NE 585 (1900).

320. 173 Mass 217, 53 NE 401 (1899).

321. 177 Mass 176, 58 NE 639 (1900).

322. See text at 128.

323. 169 Mass 347, 47 NE 1012 (1897).

324. 170 Mass 596, 49 NE 1010 (1898).

325. 170 Mass at 601, 49 NE at 1011.

326. 139 Mass 238, 1 NE 548 (1885).

327. 138 Mass 14 (1884).

328. 138 Mass at 14.

329. Holmes, *The Common Law* at 124.

330. 275 US 66 (1927).

331. 275 US at 69–70.

332. *Pokora v Wabash Ry,* 292 US 98, 106 (1934).

333. See Tushnet, *The Logic of Experience* at 978, 1001.

334. Atiyah, *The Legacy of Holmes through English Eyes* at 359. See also Kelley, *Holmes on the Supreme Judicial Court* at 342–43 ("Holmes applied the contributory negligence and assumption of risk doctrines . . . at least as stringently as most other late 19th century judges.").

Chapter Seven

1. Sanford Levinson, *Strolling down the Path of the Law (and toward Critical Legal Studies?): The Jurisprudence of Richard Posner,* 91 Colum L Rev 1221, 1228 (1991).

2. Oliver Wendell Holmes, *The Path of the Law,* 10 Harv L Rev 457 (1897), reprinted in 3 *The Collected Works of Justice Holmes: Completed Public Writings and Selected Judicial Opinions of Oliver Wendell Holmes* 391 (Sheldon M. Novick ed) (Univ of Chicago Press, 1995) (hereinafter cited as *Collected Works*).

3. Morton J. Horwitz, *The Transformation of American Law 1870–1960: The Crisis of Legal Orthodoxy* 142 (Oxford Univ Press, 1992).

4. Phillip E. Johnson, *Reason in the Balance: The Case against Naturalism in Science, Law, and Education* 140 (Intervarsity, 1995).

5. Richard A. Posner, *Introduction* to *The Essential Holmes: Selections from the Letters, Speeches, Judicial Opinions, and Other Writings of Oliver Wendell Holmes, Jr.* at x (Richard A. Posner ed) (Univ of Chicago Press, 1990).

6. Saul Touster, *Holmes a Hundred Years Ago: The Common Law and Legal Theory,* 10 Hofstra L Rev 673, 685, 692 (1982).

7. Holmes, *The Path of the Law,* 10 Harv L Rev at 461, reprinted in 3 *Collected Works* at 393.

8. Id at 459, reprinted in 3 *Collected Works* at 392.

9. Id at 464, reprinted in 3 *Collected Works* at 396.

10. Id at 462, reprinted in 3 *Collected Works* at 394.

11. Many scholars who call themselves positivists would not accept Holmes's version of the doctrine. See H. L. A. Hart, *The Concept of Law* 39 (Oxford Univ Press, 1961); Hans Kelsen, *General Theory of Law and the State* 167–68 (Anders Wedberg transl) (Russell & Russell, 1961); Joseph Raz, *The Authority of Law* 37, 38–39 (Clarendon, 1979).

12. See, for example, William W. Fisher III, *Interpreting Holmes,* 110 Harv L Rev 1010, 1111 (1997).

13. Thomas C. Grey, *Plotting the Path of the Law,* 63 Brook L Rev 19, 28 (1997).

14. Id at 29.

15. Richard D. Parker, *The Mind of Darkness,* 110 Harv L Rev 1033 (1997).

16. See, for example, Richard A. Posner, *Foreword: Holmes,* 63 Brook L Rev 7, 16 (1997).

17. See Holmes, *The Path of the Law,* 10 Harv L Rev at 478, reprinted in 3 *Collected Works* at 406.

18. See Fisher, *Interpreting Holmes,* 110 Harv L Rev at 1010; Robert W. Gordon, *The Path of the Lawyer,* 110 Harv L Rev 1013, 1016 (1997); Martha Minow, *The Path as Prologue,* 110 Harv L Rev 1023, 1024 (1997); Sheldon M. Novick, *Holmes' Path, Holmes' Goal,* 110 Harv L Rev 1028, 1030 (1997); Parker, *The Mind of Darkness,* 110 Harv L Rev at 1037; G. Edward White, *Investing in Holmes at the Millennium,* 110 Harv L Rev 1049, 1052–53 (1997). See also David J. Seipp, *Holmes's Path,* 77 BU L Rev 515, 523 (1997); Catharine Pierce Wells, *Old-Fashioned Postmodernism and the Legal Theories of Oliver Wendell Holmes, Jr.,* 63 Brook L Rev 59, 61 (1997).

19. Holmes, *The Path of the Law,* 10 Harv L Rev at 466, reprinted in 3 *Collected Works* at 397.

20. Holmes to Morris Cohen, Jan 30, 1921, in Felix S. Cohen, *The Holmes–Cohen Correspondence,* 9 J Hist Ideas 3, 27 (1948).

21. Holmes to James Bryce, Sept 17, 1919, quoted in Mark DeWolfe Howe, *Justice Oliver Wendell Holmes: The Proving Years* 46 n41 (Harvard Univ Press, 1963).

22. David Luban, *The Bad Man and the Good Lawyer: A Centennial Essay on Holmes's* The Path of the Law, 72 NYU L Rev 1547, 1558 (1997).

23. As noted in chapter 1, the reference is to Thrasymachus, who contended in a dialogue with Socrates, "Justice is nothing else than the interest of the stronger." *Plato's The Republic* 19 (Benjamin Jowett transl) (Collier, rev ed 1901).

24. Gordon, *The Path of the Lawyer,* 110 Harv L Rev at 1015.

25. Id (citing Holmes, *The Path of the Law,* 10 Harv L Rev at 459, reprinted in 3 *Collected Works* at 392, and Oliver Wendell Holmes, *The Common Law* 5 (Mark DeWolfe Howe ed) (Harvard Univ Press, Belknap Press, 1963)).

26. Holmes, *The Path of the Law,* 10 Harv L Rev at 460, reprinted in 3 *Collected Works* at 393.

27. Id, reprinted in 3 *Collected Works* at 393.

28. Robert W. Gordon, *Introduction: Holmes's Shadow* in *The Legacy of Oliver Wendell Holmes, Jr.* 1 (Robert W. Gordon ed) (Stanford Univ Press 1992).

29. Robert W. Gordon, *Law as a Vocation: Holmes on the Lawyer's Path,* in *"The Path of the Law" and Its Influence: The Legacy of Oliver Wendell Holmes* (Steven J. Burton ed) (Cambridge Univ Press, forthcoming).

30. Grey, *Plotting the Path of the Law,* 63 Brook L Rev at 32 (quoting Holmes to Laski, Mar 4, 1920, in 1 *The Holmes–Laski Letters: The Correspondence of Mr. Justice Holmes and Harold J. Laski, 1916–1935* at 248, 249 (Mark DeWolfe Howe ed) (Harvard Univ Press, 1955)).

31. Id at 32 n54 (quoting Holmes, *The Path of the Law,* 10 Harv L Rev at 392, reprinted in 3 *Collected Works* at 392).

32. Thomas C. Grey, *Holmes and Legal Pragmatism,* 41 Stan L Rev 787, 851 (1989).

33. Luban, *The Bad Man and the Good Lawyer,* 72 NYU L Rev at 1582.

34. Id at 1561.

35. Id at 1548–49 (quoting Oliver Wendell Holmes, *Edward Avery and Erastus Worthington,* May 2, 1898, in *The Occasional Speeches of Justice Oliver Wendell Holmes* 102, 104 (Mark DeWolfe Howe ed) (Harvard Univ Press, 1962)).

36. Id.

37. Wells, *Old-Fashioned Postmodernism,* 63 Brook L Rev at 83.

38. Oliver Wendell Holmes, Jr., *The Gas Stokers' Strike,* 7 Am L Rev 582 (1873), reprinted in 3 *Collected Works* at 323, 325. See also Oliver Wendell Holmes, Jr., *The Common Law* 44 (Dover, 1991 (1881)) ("It seems clear that the *ultima ratio* . . . is force, and that at the bottom of all private relations, however tempered by sympathy and all the social feelings is a justifiable self-preference."); Oliver Wendell Holmes, *Speech at a Dinner Given to Chief Justice Holmes by the Bar Association of Boston on March 7, 1900,* in 3 *Collected Works* at 498, 499 ("I think 'Whatsoever thy hand findeth to do, do it with thy might,' infinitely more important than the vain attempt to love thy neighbor as thyself."); Francis B. Biddle, *Justice Holmes, Natural Law, and the Supreme Court* 7 (Macmillan, 1961) (reporting Holmes's declaration that "lov[ing] thy neighbor as thyself [is] the test of the meddling missionary"); Holmes to Lewis Einstein, Dec 19, 1910, in *The Holmes–Einstein Letters: Correspondence of Mr. Justice Holmes and Lewis Einstein* 57, 59 (James Bishop Peabody ed) (St. Martin's, 1964) ("[T]he condition of others . . . is certainly beyond our power. Whence the futility of the commandment to love one's brother as oneself.").

39. David Dolinko, *Alschuler's "Path,"* 49 Fla L Rev 421, 423–24 (1997).

40. Id at 427.

41. An equally apt comparison might be between Holmes and classical natural lawyers like Thomas Aquinas. For such a comparison, see James Gordley, *When Paths Diverge: A Response to Albert Alschuler on Oliver Wendell Holmes,* 49 Fla L Rev 441 (1997).

42. See chapter 2 at 17–19.

43. Holmes, *The Path of the Law,* 10 Harv L Rev at 457, reprinted in 3 *Collected Works* at 391.

44. Richard Posner contends that this "circularity" objection has force only for the judges of a jurisdiction's highest court; other judges can resolve questions of law by predicting what the judges of a higher court will do. Richard A. Posner, *The Problems of Jurisprudence* 224 (Harvard Univ Press, 1990).

   None of the opinions by Judge Posner that I have read, however, has noted which justices of the Supreme Court are likely to cast swing votes on an issue and then offered an assessment of how John Paul Stevens or Sandra Day O'Connor is likely to vote in fact. If Judge Posner had taken this predictive tack, I would have been less happy about paying part of his salary than I have been. For further discussion of the objection that Holmes's definition is useless to a judge, see text at 143–44.

45. Judges in some sorts of cases do consider how other judges would resolve legal issues. A federal judge in a diversity case, for example, is expected to decide substantive state law issues as state court judges would decide them.

46. Henry M. Hart, Jr., *Holmes' Positivism—An Addendum,* 64 Harv L Rev 929, 932 (1951).

47. Id. Some recent writing on client counseling has gone beyond Hart and has challenged even the assumption that a lawyer's principal goal should be to advance her client's interests. See, for example, David Wilkins, *Legal Realism for Lawyers,* 104 Harv L Rev 469, 470 (1990); William H. Simon, *Ethical Discretion in Lawyering,* 101 Harv L Rev 1083 (1988).

    When lawyers predict judicial rulings, they frequently view law, not as what they predict, but as one *predictor* of what the courts will do. Law, moreover, is not the only predictor. "Don't chew gum when we go to court," a lawyer may tell a client, fearing that gum-chewing, like prior decisions, will predict what a judge will do.

48. That is, unless the dissenting judges are "predicting" either a change of heart on the part of the majority or a reversal of its ruling by an outside agency. See Ronald Dworkin, *Taking Rights Seriously* 211–12 (Harvard Univ Press, 1977); Robert S. Summers, *Judge Posner's Jurisprudence,* 89 Mich L Rev 1302, 1304–05 (1991) (observing that Holmes-like definitions of law leave no room for the common practice of criticizing judicial behavior for its departure from law).

49. See Hart, *The Concept of Law* at 40. See also H. L. A. Hart, *Scandinavian Realism,* 1959 Cambridge L J 233, 237 (A declaration that "[t]his is a valid rule of law" is a statement of recognition, not of prediction.); Ronald Dworkin, *The Model of Rules,* 35 U Chi L Rev 14 (1967).

50. See text at 143.

51. See H. L. A. Hart, *Positivism and the Separation of Law and Morals,* 71 Harv L Rev 593, 603 (1958) ("Law surely is not the gunman situation writ large."); Dworkin, *Taking Rights Seriously* at 19 ("We make an important distinction between law and even the general orders of a gangster.").

52. In 1934, following the "Roehm purge" in which a number of Nazis opposed to Adolf Hitler were killed, Hitler announced that during the time of the purge "the supreme court of the German people . . . consisted of myself." See Lon L. Fuller, *Positivism and Fidelity to Law—A Reply to Professor Hart,* 71 Harv L Rev 630, 650 (1958) (citing NY Times, July 14, 1934, p 5, col 2 (late city ed)).

53. Lawyers have advanced a variety of process-focused concepts of law. Daniel Webster, for example, thought it a matter of definition that law would hear before it condemned, proceed upon inquiry, and render judgment only after trial. See *Trustees of Dartmouth College v Woodward,* 17 US (4 Wheat) 518, 581 (1819) (argument of D. Webster for plaintiffs in error, Mar 10, 1818), reprinted in Daniel Webster, 5 *The Works of Daniel Webster* 487–88 (Little, Brown, 1851). Lon Fuller maintained that a system of law must respect a number of principles designed to ensure a fair opportunity to comply with its rules. See Lon L. Fuller, *The Morality*

of Law 33–94 (Yale Univ Press, rev ed 1969) (described in text at 151–54). Webster, Fuller, and others have identified some of the circumstances that bear on the recognition of law, but I believe that the process of law recognition is too complex to reduce to a definition or a formula. See text at 161–72.

54. Positivists before and after Holmes—John Austin and H. L. A. Hart in particular—have denied that normative analysis is needed. They have contended that a sociological concept (a socially identified "sovereign" or a socially identified "rule of recognition") can do the work that Holmes failed to do. See, for example, John Austin, *The Province of Jurisprudence Determined* 13, 133 (H. L. A. Hart ed) (Noonday, 4th ed 1954); Hart, *The Concept of Law* at 89–93. For an indication of why these scholars' brands of positivism are no more satisfactory than Holmes's, see Philip Soper, *A Theory of Law* 26–34 (Harvard Univ Press, 1984).

Joseph Raz, a positivist, writes, "A jurisprudential theory is acceptable only if its tests for identifying the content of the law and determining its existence depend exclusively on facts of human behavior capable of being described in value-neutral terms, and applied without resort to moral argument." Raz, *The Authority of Law* at 39–40. This view leads Raz to such conclusions as that there is no *prima facie* obligation to obey the law and that the principal defining characteristic of law is a claim by public officials (even an insincere claim) that their directives are morally entitled to obedience. See note 137.

55. Colo Rev Stat § 18-6-501 (West 1990).

56. Sixty is the real speed limit for people not suspected of selling drugs, that is. See *Whren v United States,* 517 US 806 (1996).

57. Roscoe Pound, *Law in Books and Law in Action,* 44 Am L Rev 12 (1910).

58. Pronouncing even consistently unenforced law a nullity, however, goes too far. The Colorado statute concerning adultery may not have affected the incidence of this behavior, but some people do drive at fifty-five miles per hour. I have passed them on the highway myself.

Of course neither Pound nor Holmes invented the distinction between theory and practice; each simply emphasized this distinction in an arresting way.

59. See Kelsen, *General Theory of Law and the State* at 167–68.

60. Holmes, *The Path of the Law,* 10 Harv L Rev at 459, reprinted in 3 *Collected Works* at 392.

61. Holmes, *Article Review,* 6 Am L Rev 723, 724 (1872), reprinted in 1 *Collected Works* at 294, 295.

62. Robert Brauneis suggested that "Holmes implicitly accepted a definition of law as coercion that was regularized—in other words, that was applied in a way that could be described by rules—over a jurisdiction." Robert Brauneis, *"The Foundation of Our 'Regulatory Takings' Jurisprudence": The Myth and Meaning of Justice Holmes's Opinion in* Pennsylvania Coal Co. v. Mahon, 106 Yale L J 613, 633 (1996). Brauneis observed that the idea "that only coercion . . . regularized across a juris-

diction could and should count as law" assumes "that law has at least a minimum of moral content [and] is decidedly un-Holmesian." Id at 635 n96. He added, "Holmes never explained how to reconcile his predictive theory . . . with his practical treatment of law as uniform over a jurisdiction." Id at 634–35. Brauneis hypothesized that Holmes might have asserted that particularistic influences and personal idiosyncrasies are empirically unimportant so that judges do in fact "apply precedent and statutes in a reasonably uniform manner." Id at 635.

63. Luban, *The Bad Man and the Good Lawyer,* 72 NYU L Rev at 1571.

64. Posner, *The Problems of Jurisprudence* at 223.

65. Karl Llewellyn, *A Realistic Jurisprudence—The Next Step,* 30 Colum L Rev 431, 456 (1930).

66. Gray, a member of the Harvard Law School faculty, was also a founder of one of Boston's most prominent law firms, Ropes and Gray. In 1866, Gray and his partner, John Ropes, invited Holmes to contribute to a new law journal that they would edit, the *American Law Review.* Their invitation marked the beginning of Holmes's career as a legal scholar. Holmes became co-editor of the *American Law Review* in 1870. G. Edward White, *Justice Oliver Wendell Holmes: Law and the Inner Self* 95, 103, 113–14 (Oxford Univ Press, 1993). When, in 1905, Justice Holmes reluctantly agreed to hire a law secretary each year, Gray selected Holmes's secretaries. See Sheldon M. Novick, *Honorable Justice: The Life of Oliver Wendell Holmes* 275, 282 (1989). Following Gray's death in 1915, Felix Frankfurter assumed this responsibility. White, *Justice Oliver Wendell Holmes* at 313.

67. John Austin, 1 *Lectures on Jurisprudence* 178 (Robert Campbell ed) (Murray, 5th ed 1885). According to Austin, a command required a threat of sanction, and a sovereign was a person or group that was habitually obeyed without habitually obeying anyone or anything else. Austin, *The Province of Jurisprudence Determined* at 13–15, 193–94.

68. Indeed, Holmes regarded Austin's definition as both too broad and too narrow. It was too narrow because it failed to include customary international law. Holmes maintained that courts enforce the provisions of customary international law despite the fact that these provisions do not embody the commands of an identifiable sovereign. Oliver Wendell Holmes, *Codes and the Arrangement of the Law,* 5 Am L Rev 1, 4–5 (1870), reprinted in 1 *Collected Works* at 212, 215. But see *The Western Maid,* 257 US 419, 432 (1922) (Holmes) ("When a case is said to be governed by foreign law or by general maritime law that is only a short way of saying that for this purpose the sovereign power takes up a rule suggested from without and makes it part of its own rules.").

69. Holmes, *Codes and the Arrangement of the Law,* 5 Am L Rev at 5, reprinted in 1 *Collected Works* at 215. See also Oliver Wendell Holmes, Jr., *Article Review,* 6 Am L Rev 723, 724 (1872), reprinted in 1 *Collected Works* at 294, 295 ("A precedent may not be followed; a statute may be emptied of its contents by construction. . . . [I]t is not the will of the sovereign that makes lawyers' law, even when

that is its source, but what a body of subjects, namely, the judges, by whom it is enforced *say* is his will.").

70. John Chipman Gray, *Some Definitions and Questions in Jurisprudence,* 6 Harv L Rev 21, 25 (1892). See also id at 24 ("The power . . . of a man to have the aid of the courts in carrying out his wishes on any subject constitutes a legal right of that man, and the sum of such powers constitutes his legal rights."). Gray later restated his thesis by declaring "that rules for conduct which the courts do not apply are not law; that the fact that the courts apply rules is what makes them law; that there is no mysterious entity 'the law' apart from these rules; and that the judges are rather the creators than the discoverers of law." John Chipman Gray, *The Nature and Sources of Law* 116 (Columbia Univ Press, 1909). Compare C. C. Langdell, *Classification of Rights and Wrongs* (Part 2), 13 Harv L Rev 659, 673 (1900) (declaring it "impossible that there should be any other actual rights than such as are created by the State"); C. C. Langdell, *Dominant Opinions in England during the Nineteenth Century in Relation to Legislation as Illustrated by English Legislation, or the Absence of It, during That Period,* 13 Harv L Rev 151, 151 (1900) (the word *law* as used by attorneys commonly "means law as administered by courts of justice in suits between litigating parties").

71. Robert Gordon has argued that Holmes's claim concerning the legal profession's narrow focus on courts was untrue even when Holmes made it. See Robert W. Gordon, *Holmes'* Common Law *as Social and Legal Science,* 10 Hofstra L Rev 719, 734–35 n112 (1982).

72. Grey, *Holmes and Legal Pragmatism,* 41 Stan L Rev at 828.

73. *American Banana Co v United Fruit Co,* 213 US 347, 356 (1909).

74. Oliver Wendell Holmes, *Natural Law,* 32 Harv L Rev 40, 42 (1918), reprinted in 3 *Collected Works* at 445, 447.

75. Oliver Wendell Holmes, *Speech Prepared for Delivery at a Banquet for Admiral Dewey, Oct 14, 1899* in 3 *Collected Works* at 523, 523–24.

76. Holmes to Harold J. Laski, Sept 7, 1916, in 1 *Holmes–Laski Letters* at 16.

77. If Holmes initially meant his definition of law as a description of the concerns of lawyers rather than as a more ambitious statement of what law is and how it works, he probably had forgotten this intention by the time of *The Path of the Law,* as he certainly did later. The opening lines of Holmes's essay support Grey's thesis: "When we study law we are not studying a mystery but a well known profession. We are studying what we shall want in order to appear before judges, or to advise people in such a way as to keep them out of court." Holmes, *The Path of the Law,* 10 Harv L Rev at 457, reprinted in 3 *Collected Works* at 391. The remainder of Holmes's essay, however—including his articulation of the alternative theory of contract and his proposal to banish moral terminology from the law—reveals that he was attempting to develop "a conceptual truth about the nature of law."

78. Rudolf von Jhering, *Law as a Means to an End* 33 (Isaac Husik transl) (Boston Book, 1913) (originally published in two volumes as *Der Zweck im Recht,* 1877 and 1883). Jhering articulated an evolutionary and Darwinian view of law much like that of

Holmes, who read Jhering's work while writing *The Common Law*. Mathias Reimann calls it remarkable that Holmes failed to acknowledge the similarity of the two men's ideas. Mathias W. Reimann, *Holmes's* Common Law *and German Legal Science*, in *The Legacy of Oliver Wendell Holmes, Jr.* at 72, 101–05. Holmes, however, was "notorious for not giving credit to his intellectual forbears and for being petty in his insistence on the primacy of his own contributions." Touster, *Holmes a Hundred Years Ago*, 10 Hofstra L Rev at 687. See White, *Justice Oliver Wendell Holmes* at 113 ("Holmes was loath to acknowledge influences on and antecedents of his work.").

79. Holmes, *The Path of the Law*, 10 Harv L Rev at 42–43, reprinted in 3 *Collected Works* at 393.

80. See text at 132 (quoting Richard Posner).

81. 5 US (1 Cranch) 137, 177 (1803).

82. In Alexander Hamilton's classic language, "The judiciary, from the nature of its functions, will always be the least dangerous [branch of government]. . . . [It] has no influence over either the sword or the purse; no direction either of the strength or of the wealth of the society; and can take no active resolution whatever. It may truly be said to have neither FORCE nor WILL, but merely judgment; and must ultimately depend upon the aid of the executive arm even for the efficacy of its judgments." *The Federalist No. 78* at 489, 490 (Hamilton) (Benjamin Fletcher Wright ed) (Harvard Univ Press, 1966).

83. 476 US 79 (1986).

84. 476 US at 97.

85. Id.

86. See *United States v Cartlidge*, 808 F2d 1064, 1071 (5th Cir 1987) (holding this explanation adequate).

87. See *United States v Mathews*, 803 F2d 325, 331–32 (7th Cir 1986) (holding this explanation adequate), *rev'd on other grounds*, 485 US 58 (1988).

88. For a description of other ways to evade *Batson*, see Albert W. Alschuler, *The Supreme Court and the Jury: Voir Dire, Peremptory Challenges and the Review of Jury Verdicts*, 56 U Chi L Rev 153, 163–211 (1989).

89. Montesquieu, *The Spirit of the Laws* (Anne M. Cobler, Basia Carolyn Miller, and Harold Samuel Stone transl) (Cambridge Univ Press, 1989).

90. I suspect that the O. J. Simpson case, which indicated that race sometimes can be a powerful predictor of jurors' views, and the Supreme Court's near evisceration of *Batson* in *Purkett v Elem*, 514 US 765 (1995) (allowing a judge to accept the explanation "mustaches and . . . beards look suspicious to me"), have made trial lawyers less willing to take *Batson* seriously than they were in the years immediately following the decision. See Lawrence Schiller and James Willwerth, *American Tragedy: The Uncensored Story of the Simpson Defense* 193–94, 258–60 (Random, 1996) (describing Johnnie Cochran's race-focused jury selection in the O. J. Simpson criminal trial).

91. H. L. A. Hart wrote of Holmes's "bad man" view:

> Why should not law be equally if not more concerned with the "puzzled man" or "ignorant man" who is willing to do what is required, if only he can be told what it is? Or with the "man who wishes to arrange his affairs" if only he can be told how to do it? It is of course very important, if we are to understand the law, to see how the courts administer it when they come to apply its sanctions. But this should not lead us to think that all there is to understand is what happens in courts.

Hart, *The Concept of Law* at 39.

In *Sherman v Community Consolidated School Dist,* 980 F2d 437 (7th Cir 1992), Richard Sherman, an elementary school student, and his father challenged an Illinois statute that declared, "The Pledge of Allegiance shall be recited each school day by pupils in [public] elementary educational institutions." The defendants argued that Illinois had not made recitation of the pledge compulsory; they noted that the statute provided no penalty for noncompliance. Judge Easterbrook's opinion for the Seventh Circuit replied:

> Many people obey laws just because they represent the will of the majority expressed through democratic forms. . . . They revere law for the sake of civility, harmony, and consideration of others. . . . How ironic if Richard Sherman's first experience with law were to teach him that the legal sanction expresses the full meaning of a rule. Then the lesson of the Pledge of Allegiance would be cynicism rather than patriotism. Looking at the law through the lens of penalties is useful for many purposes, but not when the task is to teach civic virtue.

980 F2d at 442.

Commenting on an earlier version of this chapter, David Dolinko wrote that it was unfair "to insinuate that Holmes actually wanted people in general to view law as a 'bad man' would." Dolinko, *Alschuler's "Path,"* 49 Fla L Rev at 429. Viewing law as a bad man would, however, is just what Holmes proposed: "If you want to know the law and nothing else, you must look at it as a bad man. . . ." Holmes, *The Path of the Law,* 10 Harv L Rev at 459, reprinted in 3 *Collected Works* at 372. To be sure, Holmes did not contend that anyone should *be* a bad man or should *act* as a bad man would. Once people internalize the "bad man" perspective, however, the assumption that easily evaded law is *not* law becomes routine. Because that is what Holmes's definition says, it encourages the view that taking advantage of loopholes is unproblematic. I do not contend that Holmes or anyone else *wanted* people to behave in this fashion. Virtuous people do many things that the law— the *real* law—does not require.

To put the matter another way, although Holmes did not offer his definition of law for the purpose of telling his audience how to behave, one who internalizes this definition may not make the nice distinction between law as coercive power and law as a source of social obligation. She may instead assume that the two are coextensive.

92. Holmes, *The Path of the Law,* 10 Harv L Rev at 459, 3 *Collected Works* at 392.

93. See John Locke, *Second Treatise of Government,* in *Two Treatises of Government* 370–71 (Cambridge Univ Press, 1960).

94. See Albert W. Alschuler, *Rediscovering Blackstone,* 145 U Pa L Rev 1, 24–27 (1996).

95. Locke, *Second Treatise of Government* at 396.

96. Id.

97. William Blackstone, 1 *Commentaries* * 41.

98. Id. Blackstone advanced this argument to explain why divine revelation as well as natural law was needed. People who do not take their guidance from Scripture, however, may take it from Locke's known and indifferent judge. Following the *Batson* decision, some prosecutors in Chicago did.

99. Holmes, *The Path of the Law,* 10 Harv L Rev at 459 (emphasis added), reprinted in 3 *Collected Works* at 392.

100. See Lawrence G. Becker, *Reciprocity* 260–62 (Routledge & Kegan Paul, 1986); Herbert Morris, *Persons and Punishment,* in Herbert Morris, *On Guilt and Innocence: Essays in Legal Philosophy and Moral Psychology* 31 (Univ of California Press, 1976); Harold G. Grasmick and Donald E. Green, *Legal Punishment, Social Disapproval and Internalization as Inhibitors of Illegal Behavior,* 71 J Crim L & Crim 325, 334 (1980) (reporting a positive correlation between one's disposition to obey the law and the belief that respected peers obey it); Peter H. Huang and Ho-Mou Wu, *More Order without More Law: A Theory of Social Norms and Organizational Cultures,* 10 J Econ Org 390 (1994) (observing that although most "[e]conomic analysis of corruption postulates that rational actors compare the benefits and expected costs to behaving corruptly," the perceived likelihood of corrupt behavior by others influences their conduct as well); Dan M. Kahan, *Social Influence, Social Meaning, and Deterrence,* 83 Va L Rev 349, 354 (1997) ("[A] person's beliefs about whether other persons in her situation are paying their taxes plays a much more significant role in her decision to comply than does the burden of the tax or her perception of the expected punishment."); J. C. Baldry, *Tax Evasion Is Not a Gamble: A Report on Two Experiments,* 22 Economics Letters 333 (1986) (presenting empirical evidence that one's willingness to evade taxes depends on moral considerations independent of expected economic return); Frank A. Cowell, *Cheating the Government: The Economics of Evasion* 108 (MIT Press, 1990) ("[A] person's propensity to dodge taxes seems to be strongly affected by the number of other people who are already doing the same.").

101. The concept of "return-for-giving" differs from tit-for-tat exchange in a marketplace. Most notably, the psychological measure of equivalence may be effort as much as (or more than) wealth.

   Biologists have discovered in other species patterns of behavior that resemble our own. See Robert L. Trivers, *The Evolution of Reciprocal Altruism,* 46 Q Rev Biology 35 (1971). Vampire bats, for example, regurgitate blood to share with others, but they apparently decline to feed previous recipients that have failed to reciprocate. See Gerald S. Wilkinson, *Reciprocal Food Sharing in the Vampire Bat,* Nature, Mar 1984, at 181, 182–83. Our sense of justice may have something in common with the bat's.

102. Game theorists will recognize elements of "the prisoner's dilemma." As the next paragraph emphasizes, however, some of Adam's motivations lie outside the game.

103. A sense of reciprocity of a different sort may influence Adam's decision not to take spaces reserved for the handicapped, for Adam can envision himself as a handicapped person in need of one of those spaces. Empathy and "the vaguer sanctions of conscience" may themselves draw upon psychological concepts of reciprocity.

104. Holmes, *The Path of the Law*, 10 Harv L Rev at 459, reprinted in 3 *Collected Works* at 392.

105. Id, reprinted in 3 *Collected Works* at 392.

106. See, for example, Austin, *The Province of Jurisprudence Determined* at 184 n; Hart, *Positivism and the Separation of Law and Morals*, 71 Harv L Rev at 593, 593–94, 599, 601 (1958); Kelsen, *General Theory of Law and the State* at 15. Compare Jules L. Coleman, *Negative and Positive Positivism*, 11 J Legal Stud 139, 140 (1982) ("Positivism denies what natural law theory asserts: namely, a necessary connection between law and morality.").

107. See, for example, Lon L. Fuller, *Human Purpose and Natural Law*, 3 Nat L F 68, 75 (1958); John T. Noonan, *Book Review*, 7 Nat L F 169, 172 (1962). See generally Lon L. Fuller, *The Law in Quest of Itself* 1–42 (Foundation, 1940).

108. Augustine, *On Free Choice of the Will [De Libro Arbitrio]* 8 (Thomas Williams transl) (Hackett, 1993).

109. Few if any natural lawyers have contended, however, that people are never obliged to obey a law that is in any respect unjust. See, for example, the discussion of Aquinas's position in Norman Kretzmann, *Lex Injusta Non Ext Lex: Laws on Trial in Aquinas' Court of Conscience*, 33 Am J Juris 99 (1988).

110. Holmes, *The Path of the Law*, 10 Harv L Rev at 459, reprinted in 3 *Collected Works* at 392. See Hart, *The Concept of Law* at 7–8.

111. Hart, *Positivism and the Separation of Law and Morals*, 71 Harv L Rev at 615. The quoted language appears in response to one criticism of positivism. Hart's response to most other criticisms, however, was in substance the same.

112. Lon L. Fuller, *Positivism and Fidelity to Law—A Reply to Professor Hart*, 71 Harv L Rev 630 (1958). Remarkably, Fuller began his paper by praising Hart for clarifying the issue. Id at 630–33.

113. See Fuller, *The Morality of Law* at 97. See also Adolph Reinach, *The Apriori Foundations of the Civil Law* 7 (John F. Crosby transl) (1934) ("The structure of positive law can only become intelligible through the structure of the non-positive sphere of law.").

114. See Fuller, *Positivism and Fidelity to Law*, 71 Harv L Rev at 652.

115. That the Führer's order was retroactive makes this case easy. (Almost every legal system, however, including our own, does treat some retroactive pronouncements as "law.") One can imagine substantially more difficult questions of law

identification: The defendant's act contravened a published statute, but the Führer had secretly authorized and commanded this act in advance. Or a new rule authorizing the defendant's act had openly amended prior law, but the defendant was unaware of the new rule. Or the published "law" upon which the defendant relied was vague and open-ended, although unquestionably valid from the perspective of the German government. For example: "Every citizen is obliged to cooperate in eradicating the enemies of National Socialism." Or, "The will of the Führer is the law of the Volk." Or, "Once: no punishment without law! Now: no crime without punishment!" Or, "That person will be punished who commits an act which the law declares to be punishable or which deserves punishment according to the fundamental principle of a penal statute and the healthy sentiment of the Volk." See Markus D. Dubber, *The German Jury and the Metaphysical Volk: From Romantic Idealism to Nazi Ideology,* 43 Am J Comp L 227, 262–66 (1995) (quoting Nazi statutes, administrative guidelines, and unofficial mottoes).

116. Fuller, *The Morality of Law* at 33–94. Fuller did not maintain that every departure from the listed principles rendered a government lawless, only that sufficiently serious deficiencies in one or more categories would do so. My own view is that the characteristics listed by Fuller bear on the recognition of law but that they are not definitive. See text at 161–72.

To some degree, Fuller's views echoed Blackstone's. Differentiating between natural law and positive or "municipal" law, Blackstone defined municipal law as "a rule of civil conduct prescribed by the supreme power in a state." William Blackstone, 1 *Commentaries* * 46 (emphasis eliminated). He declared that to be a "rule," a directive must be general. "[A] particular act of the legislature to confiscate the goods of Titius . . . does not enter into the idea of municipal law." Id at * 44. In addition, a rule could not be simply "advice or counsel." It must bind "the unwilling." Id. The rule also must be "notified to the people who are to obey." Id at * 45. "Lastly, acts of parliament that are impossible to be performed are of no validity. . . ." Id at * 91.

117. H. L. A. Hart, *Book Review,* 78 Harv L Rev 1281, 1286 (1965); *accord,* Martin P Golding, *Philosophy of Law* 49 (Prentice-Hall, 1975); David Lyons, *Ethics and the Rule of Law* 77 (Cambridge Univ Press, 1984); Dolinko, *Alschuler's "Path,"* 49 Fla L Rev at 435–37.

118. James Herget, *American Jurisprudence 1870–1970: A History* 256 (Rice Univ Press, 1990).

119. US Const, art I, § 8, cls 12, 13, 14.

120. Dolinko, *Alschuler's Path,* 49 Fla L Rev at 429.

121. Id.

122. Id at 437.

123. See, for example, Posner, *The Problems of Jurisprudence* at 42; Peter Westen, *The Empty Idea of Equality,* 95 Harv L Rev 537 (1982).

124. Blackstone wrote, "Penal statutes must be construed strictly. Thus a statute . . . having enacted that those who are convicted of stealing horses should not have

the benefit of clergy [and so should be subject to execution], the judges conceived that this did not extend to him who should steal but *one horse*." William Blackstone, 1 *Commentaries* * 88. Consider, however, the case of "laying hands on a priest" noted in the next paragraph in text.

125. A philosopher might criticize my use of concepts like "literal meaning" and "words that are not there." What makes some meanings "literal" and others "figurative" is unclear; all meanings conveyed by symbols are in some sense figurative. When words convey a meaning that also can be expressed in other words, moreover, those other words always *are* there or, if one prefers, always are not. My language does adequately indicate the implicit normativity of most descriptions of positive law, and that is its only purpose.

126. The jurist and historian Samuel von Pufendorf published his *De Jure Naturae et Gentium* in 1672, a century before Blackstone published his *Commentaries*.

127. William Blackstone, 1 *Commentaries* * 59, 60 (spelling and punctuation modernized).

128. Id at * 61 (spelling and punctuation modernized).

129. Id (spelling and punctuation modernized).

130. See Richard Craswell, *Do Trade Customs Exist,* in *The Jurisprudential Foundations of Corporate and Commercial Law* (Jody S. Kraus and Steven Walt eds) (Cambridge Univ Press, 2000) ("appeals to custom in commercial law often turn out to be appeals to a kind of 'moral reflection'"); Nelson Goodman, *Fact, Fiction, and Forecast* 72–83 (Harvard Univ Press, 4th ed 1983) (asking how human beings recognize "law-like statements").

131. Jeremy Bentham scornfully attributed this fuzzy-mindedness to Blackstone. See Jeremy Bentham, *A Fragment on Government,* in 1 *Works* 221, 287 (John Bowring ed) (William Tait, 1843) (cl IV, 19th para). He also wrote, "[I]n the eyes of the lawyers—not to speak of their dupes—that is to say, as yet, the generality of non-lawyers—the *is* and *ought to be* were one and indivisible." Bentham, *A Commentary on Humphreys' Real Property Code,* in 5 *Works* at 389. John Austin also spoke of "the prevailing tendency to confound what is with what ought to be law." He declared that this "abuse of language is not merely puerile, it is mischievous." Austin, *The Province of Jurisprudence Determined* at 184–85. See also Karl Llewellyn, *Some Realism about Realism—Responding to Dean Pound,* 44 Harv L Rev 1222, 1237 (1931).

132. See *Trimble v Seattle,* 231 US 683, 688 (1914) (Holmes) ("Words express whatever meaning convention has attached to them."). *Accord,* Stanley Fish, *Is There a Text in This Class?* (Harvard Univ Press, 1980).

133. John Noonan, *Persons and Masks of the Law* ix (Farrar, Straus & Giroux, 1976).

134. See Fuller, *Positivism and Fidelity to Law,* 71 Harv L Rev at 632 ("There is . . . no frustration greater than to be confronted by a theory which purports merely to describe, when it not only plainly prescribes, but owes its special prescriptive powers precisely to the fact that it disclaims prescriptive intentions."); id at 656

("[W]e have an amoral datum called law, which has the peculiar quality of creating a moral duty to obey it.").

135. John Austin at least hinted that the purpose of his definition of law was to address the normative question of obligation. Austin criticized Blackstone's declarations that the laws of God were superior in obligation to other laws and that human laws were invalid if contrary to them. He wrote, "[T]he meaning of this passage of Blackstone, if it has a meaning, seems . . . to be this: that no human law which conflicts with the Divine law is obligatory or binding; in other words, that no human law which conflicts with the Divine law *is a law*. . . ." John Austin, *The Province of Jurisprudence Determined* 185 (Weidenfeld & Nicolson, 1954). From Austin's perspective, then, the point of calling a directive "law" was apparently to establish that this directive was "obligatory or binding." Why Austin, who did not in fact believe that all positive law was to be obeyed and who was a religious man himself, quarreled with Blackstone concerning the resolution of this issue is unclear. When the commands of God direct one thing and the commands of the king and parliament another, Whom to obey does not seem a disputable issue.

Although Austin apparently concluded that his positivist definition identified obligatory commands, both Hans Kelsen and H. L. A. Hart rested their criticism of Austin on his failure to address the question of obligation. See Hans Kelsen, *An Introduction to the Problems of Legal Theory* 43 (§ 24) (translation of the first edition of *Reine Rechtsleher* or *Pure Theory of Law* by Bonnie and Stanley Paulson) (Clarendon, 1992) ("[T]he Pure Theory of Law launches its critique of the received academic opinion by bringing the concept of obligation emphatically to the fore."); Hart, *The Concept of Law* at 6 ("The most prominent general feature of law . . . is that its existence means that certain kinds of human conduct are no longer optional, but in *some* sense obligatory.").

Hart observed that commands backed by force do not obligate; they merely oblige. Hart's own positivist concept of law deemphasized force, emphasizing instead the acceptance of law-identifying rules ("rules of recognition") by government officials. See Hart, *The Concept of Law* at 89–93, 97–107. As Philip Soper and others have demonstrated, one can no more get an "ought" from Hart's "is" than from Austin's, and Kelsen's positivist concept of law is even more clearly a nonstarter. See Philip Soper, *A Theory of Law* 26–34 (Harvard Univ Press, 1984).

136. Soper, *A Theory of Law* at 8.

137. See Raz, *The Authority of Law* at 233–61; Alan Simmons, *Moral Principles and Political Obligations* (Princeton Univ Press, 1979); Robert Paul Wolff, *In Defense of Anarchism* (Harper & Row, 1970); M. B. E. Smith, *Is There a Prima Facie Obligation to Obey the Law?*, 82 Yale L J 950 (1973). Some of these writers offer idiosyncratic concepts of law before concluding that there is no obligation to obey. Raz, for example, asserts that the principal defining characteristic of a legal system is a *claim* by public officials (even an insincere claim) that their directives are morally entitled to obedience. See Raz, *The Authority of Law* at 236–37. The modern positivists who deny a general presumptive obligation to obey the law do recognize obligations to obey particular laws.

138. See Soper, *A Theory of Law* at 9 ("If law is only force, one does not need pages of discussion about the nature and extent of the obligation to comply: there is none."); Luban, *The Bad Man and the Good Lawyer,* 72 NYU L Rev at 1571 ("Holmes doubted that we have any moral obligation to obey the law, but that is only because he doubted that we have any moral obligations."). Although some writers have claimed that there is no link between "legal positivism" and "logical positivism," see Posner, *The Problems of Jurisprudence* at 20 n31, the sense that Holmes and the logical positivists shared of the emptiness of moral discourse apparently led Holmes to his power-focused concept of law. See, for example, A. J. Ayer, *Logical Positivism* 21–23 (Free Press, 1959).

139. See Holmes to Alice Stopford Green, Feb 7, 1909, quoted in Sheldon M. Novick, *Justice Holmes's Philosophy,* 70 Wash U L Q 703, 721 (1992). Although Holmes romanticized a soldier's duty to obey orders, he did so only because the soldier's unquestioning obedience could manifest a commitment to invest his otherwise empty life with meaning. For Holmes, duty did not reflect any genuine obligation to others or any external moral constraint. See Oliver Wendell Holmes, *The Soldier's Faith: An Address Delivered on Memorial Day at a Meeting Called by the Graduating Class of Harvard University,* May 30, 1895, in 3 *Collected Works* at 486, 487.

140. Noting that the question, "What is law?" is too general, Philip Soper focused on the normative question, "What is law that it obligates?" Soper, *A Theory of Law* at 1–7. Commenting on Soper's work, Steven Burton observed that one also might ask: "What is law that it is prudent to obey it?" "What is law that it will be effective?" "What is law that it is justiciable?" "What is law that a student should learn it?" As Burton noted, the answers to these questions might not identify the same phenomenon. Steven J. Burton, *Review Essay: Law, Obligation, and a Good Faith Claim of Justice,* 73 Cal L Rev 1956, 1979–80 (1985). Holmes's definition probably works best as an answer to the question, "What is law that a lawyer should describe it to a client?" Indeed, Holmes initially posed something like this narrow question but then apparently lost sight of it. See text at 143–44. Even from the perspective of a practicing lawyer, however, Holmes's definition of law seems incomplete. See text at 140. And Holmes's definition does not quite capture the perspective of a bad man either. See text at 142, 144–45.

141. See Johnson, *Reason in the Balance* at 152 ("Holmes had it backwards. The primary focus of the lawmaker's interest is not the bad person but the good ones who want to do the right thing.").

142. The purpose of begging the right question is simply to focus attention in the right place. In that sense, a circle can be virtuous.

143. Hart, *The Concept of Law* at 28, 95.

144. See Dolinko, *Alschuler's "Path,"* 49 Fla L Rev at 431.

145. Note that even the least controversial elements of a conventional definition of law incorporate normative judgments—establishing, for example, a presumptive hierarchy of settlements in which the government's commands outrank those of

one's parents. Even my plainly question-begging definition of law may not beg enough questions.

146. See, for example, Austin, *The Province of Jurisprudence Determined* at 159, 161, 260; Hart, *The Concept of Law* at 205–07 ("[T]he certification of something as legally valid is not conclusive of the question of obedience[. H]owever great the aura of majesty or authority which the official system may have, its demands must in the end be submitted to a moral scrutiny."); Kelsen, *General Theory of Law and the State* at 374. Efforts to define law become both easier and less helpful when scholars can defer difficult issues to a second, unaddressed stage of inquiry: "Yes, I called that command a law, but I never said that anyone was required to obey it." Definitions of law that address the question of obedience, but only in part, are likely to have a rootless quality.

147. See Abe Fortas, *Concerning Dissent and Civil Disobedience* (New American Library, 1968); Mortimer Kadish and Sanford Kadish, *Discretion to Disobey: A Study of Lawful Departures from Legal Rules* 174 (Stanford Univ Press, 1973); Kent Greenawalt, *Promise, Benefit, and Need: Ties That Bind Us to the Law,* 18 Ga L Rev 727, 729–30 (1984).

148. The suggestion, again, is that, at least in the discourse of many legal theorists, law *means* "settlements entitled to respect."

149. See Soper, *A Theory of Law* at 8–9 (recognizing the artificiality of the customary bifurcation of questions of law recognition and political obligation but apparently leaving intact the customary bifurcation of questions of law recognition and civil disobedience).

150. See *Created Equal? The Complete Lincoln–Douglas Debates of 1858* at 304 (Paul M. Angle ed) (Univ of Chicago Press, 1958).

151. Id.

152. For Lincoln, the relevant normative-interpretive convention was simply that the law in action should, if possible, correspond to the law on the books. But see Frank H. Easterbrook, *Statutes' Domains,* 50 U Chi L Rev 542, 543 (1983) (arguing against the judicial implication of remedies on the ground that largely toothless laws may be the products of political compromise); Frank H. Easterbrook, *Foreword: The Court and the Economic System,* 98 Harv L Rev 4, 42 (1984) (same).

153. But see Soper, *A Theory of Law* at 121 ("[G]alley slaves . . . still face prima facie obligations as long as their positions are the result of an honestly held theory of justice."). For a response to Soper, see David Luban, *Conscientious Lawyers for Conscientious Lawbreakers,* 52 U Pitt L Rev 793, 806–09 (1991).

154. Only six states allowed free blacks to vote at the time of the Civil War. See *Oregon v Mitchell,* 400 US 112, 156 (1970) (Harlan, concurring in part and dissenting in part).

155. Even if female and unable to vote, moreover, a dissenter not in bondage might have written *Uncle Tom's Cabin.*

156. William Lloyd Garrison contended prior to the Civil War that no one was obliged to obey this "covenant with death and an agreement with hell." Staughton Lynd, *Class Conflict, Slavery and the United States Constitution* 154 (Bobbs-Merrill, 1967); see *Faneuil Hall Mass Meeting on the Fugitive Slave Bill,* Emancipator and Republican, Oct 17, 1850 ("the citizens of Boston in Faneuil Hall assembled, law or no law, constitution or no constitution, pledge themselves to protect at all hazards fugitive slaves who have taken shelter in their city").

Commenting on a draft of this chapter, Frank H. Easterbrook questioned William Lloyd Garrison's judgment:

> The point is not simply that the Union could not have been formed without the Clause—and that the fate of slaves would have been worse had the South become a separate nation. It is that, . . . at the margin, non-enforcement of the Clause after the formation of the Union could have made slaves worse off. If escaping slaves are not returned, then owners will take measures to prevent escape. There will be additional manacles, taller fences, meaner guards, and so on. . . . Returning an escaped slave is a terrible thing, but an approach to law that ignores the consequences of *not* returning slaves is a terrible thing too.

Letter from Frank H. Easterbrook to author, Feb 7, 1993.

My own view is that Easterbrook's argument in favor of returning slaves to their owners would have merited consideration in the antebellum period, but not so much consideration that someone might have accepted it. I hope that Judge Easterbrook, transported by a time machine to Portsmouth, Ohio in 1850, would not in fact have sent Eliza back to Legree.

Assessing long-range consequences is problematic. It often may be appropriate to do what appears to be "the right thing" in the situation at hand and to hope that one's decency will not backfire. Almost any well-intentioned choice *can* backfire, but one who takes literally the physician's (and the conservative's) admonition to "do no harm" rarely can act at all. One often must proceed in the face of uncertainty.

157. This choice would have denied the fugitive slave clause even the power to keep decent people out of office. If the officials' disregard of their oaths (and of the Constitution) suggested a breach of faith with people who had agreed to this document only on the condition that it contain a fugitive slave clause (or with their successors-in-interest), a reasonable official might not have considered that ethical difficulty decisive. Even apart from the conundrums posed by the efforts of one generation to bind successor generations, freeing slaves by snookering slaveholders is not evil.

The issue might be given a contemporary cast (as when Shakespeare is played in modern dress). To some extent, slaveholders resemble terrorists holding hostages, and the relevant "rules" might be similar to those governing hostage negotiations in an international community without (much) positive law. For example, a group of political terrorists claiming to be the rightful government of Dystopia might accept a treaty and promise their participation in a number of worthwhile international ventures. In return, the treaty might confirm the terrorists' right to hold hostages and to capture new ones until the year 2008. (Compare US Const, art I, § 9, cl 1.) The treaty could also require various officials to take oaths to support it. Could a negotiator named Rambo properly agree to the treaty, take the required oath, accept benefits under the treaty, and still act to free the hostages if he discovered an escape route? Would it matter whether Rambo had never intended to honor his oath or instead had taken the oath in good faith and then decided that his pledge was wrong? Should Rambo have refused to take the oath, thereby ensuring that he would be discharged from his position and unable to free the hostages?

If you believe that this sort of question can be profitably discussed, you may accept the concept of "natural law" whether you know it or not. The question (again) takes as its initial assumption an international community without positive law—that is, a state of nature. Then it adds rules that purport to be positive law and asks whether, and to what extent, Rambo (or anyone else) should regard these rules as binding. Discussion of the issue thus presupposes concepts of right and wrong that exist independently of positive law and of the customs of particular communities.

158. A president's duty is sometimes to disobey legislation that she considers unconstitutional—refusing, for example, to appoint the members of an unconstitutional commission. A person hired to type the president's or the commission's papers, however, does not have the same duty to judge the commission's constitutionality.

A government typist does have a duty—a legally enforceable as well as a moral duty—to resign or otherwise to withhold assistance if asked to type a paper facilitating flagrantly unconstitutional action (for example, a false application for a warrant to support a search whose purpose would be to harass and embarrass a political opponent). A president and a government typist are both obliged to respect the Constitution, but their obligations to judge independently the constitutionality of their actions are not precisely the same.

159. This wide-ranging chapter (it's about Holmes, remember) will not range widely enough to assess the circumstances that make some governments legitimate and others illegitimate. The chapter will, however, say enough to indicate that the issue of governmental legitimacy, like the issue of law-recognition, is a matter of more-or-less rather than yes-or-no.

160. That probably no more than 20 percent of the adult population was eligible to vote on the question merely puts this achievement in perspective. See Thurgood Marshall, *Commentary: Reflections on the Bicentennial of the United States Constitution,* 101 Harv L Rev 1, 2 (1987).

161. Surely the fugitive slave clause did not "bind" slaves. Did the clause bind freedmen whose families remained in slavery? Or freedmen whose *people* remained in slavery? Did it bind unenfranchised white women? Was the clause truly "law" for anyone?

162. 358 US 1 (1958).

163. 5 US (1 Cranch) 137, 177 (1803).

164. *Cooper,* 358 US at 18.

165. See Edwin Meese III, *The Law of the Constitution,* 61 Tul L Rev 979, 986 (1987); Sanford Levinson, *Could Meese Be Right This Time?* 61 Tul L Rev 1071, 1078 (1987).

166. But see *Weinberg v Salfi,* 422 US 749, 765 (1975) (declaring in dictum that "the constitutionality of a statutory requirement [is] a matter which is beyond [the president's] jurisdiction to determine").

167. Letter from Jefferson to Adams, Sept 11, 1804, in 8 *The Writings of Thomas Jefferson* 310, 311 (Paul Leicester Ford ed) (Putnam's, 1897) In 1819, Jefferson reiterated this position: "Each of the three departments has equally the right to decide for itself what is its duty under the constitution, without any regard to what the others may have decided for themselves under a similar question." Letter from Jefferson to Spencer Roane, Sept 6, 1819, in 12 *The Writings of Thomas Jefferson* 139 (Paul Leicester Ford ed) (Putnam's, 1905).

168. Andrew Jackson, *Veto Message, July 10, 1832,* in 3 *Messages and Papers of the Presidents* 1139, 1145 (James Richardson ed) (Bureau of National Literature, 1911). Jackson added, "The opinion of the judges has no more authority over Congress than the opinion of Congress has over the judges, and on that point the President is independent of both." Id.

169. Government typists do not take oaths to support the Constitution, but they are bound by the Constitution nevertheless. One wonders to what extent Jefferson and Jackson would have had White House clerks observe the Constitution, not as it was understood by others, but as they understood it themselves. See note 158.

170. *Cooper,* 358 US at 4.

171. 347 US 483 (1954).

172. President Jackson's veto of the bank bill did not pose a risk of this sort of disruption, and one might reasonably distinguish a refusal to acquiesce in a ruling upholding a governmental action from a refusal to accept a judicial determination of unconstitutionality. Jackson might have vetoed the bank bill simply because he did not like it, and his "extra" assertion of a view of the Constitution different from the Supreme Court's did no harm. In that respect, Jackson's declaration of independence from the federal judiciary differed from that of Governor Orval Faubus of Arkansas. See Frank H. Easterbrook, *Presidential Review,* 40 Case W Res L Rev 905, 909–10 (1989–90).

173. In 1956, 101 congressmen from the states of the old Confederacy (including all Southern senators except Lyndon Johnson, Estes Kefauver, and Albert Gore) signed "The Southern Manifesto." This manifesto declared that the decision in *Brown* was "unwarranted" and "a clear abuse of judicial power." *Brown* had substituted the justices' "personal political and social ideas for the established law of the land." The manifesto pledged "to use all lawful means to bring about a reversal of this decision which is contrary to the Constitution." See Richard Kluger, *Simple Justice: The History of* Brown v. Board of Education *and Black America's Struggle for Equality* 752 (Vintage, 1977).

174. See, for example, Gerald Rosenberg, *The Hollow Hope: Can Courts Bring About Social Change?* 55 (Univ of Chicago Press, 1991).

175. Some have suggested that America would have reached a stable, satisfactory resolution of the abortion issue a decade or two ago had the Supreme Court not "constitutionalized" this issue in *Roe v Wade,* 410 US 113 (1973). That is my sense of the situation. Prior to the decision in *Roe,* I was a reporter to the State Bar Committee on the Revision of the Texas Penal Code. Although Texas had substantial Catholic and Protestant populations opposed to abortion, our reporters' proposal for a permissive "therapeutic abortion" statute modeled after one already enacted in Colorado had encountered little opposition. Once our proposal had made its way through the State Bar Committee (a committee that the reporters had found recalcitrant on other issues), I was reasonably confident that the proposal would be enacted. Following a federal district court's invalidation of the Texas abortion statute in *Roe,* the committee and the Board of Directors of the Texas State Bar in fact substituted a still more permissive measure.

The weekend before Roe's counsel, Sara Weddington, argued her case before the Supreme Court, I impersonated a judge at a moot court session in which Weddington tested her argument. Following this exercise, there was a discussion of strategy and then, following Weddington's departure, a more general discussion of *Roe* among the University of Texas Law School faculty members present. All of us agreed that although Weddington had argued her case ably, she had no chance of victory in the Supreme Court. Every one of us would have bet the farm on it. Now, after a quarter century of the bitter division wrought by *Roe,* I wish that we had been right. Nations that have increased the availability of abortion through legislation have avoided our wrenching, hate-generating conflict. See generally Mary Ann Glendon, *Abortion and Divorce in Western Law* (Harvard Univ Press, 1987).

176. 60 US (19 How) 393 (1857).

177. See *Created Equal?* at 36.

178. Chief Justice Roger B. Taney, who had manumitted his own slaves decades before the decision in *Dred Scott,* wrote for the Court:

> [Blacks were] beings of an inferior order, and altogether unfit to associate with the white race, either in social or political relations; and so far inferior that they had no rights which the white man was bound to respect. . . . The unhappy black race . . . were never thought or spoken of except as property.

60 US (19 How) at 407, 410.

179. Resistance to permitting an expansion of slavery in the federal territories was the principal issue in both Lincoln's 1858 senatorial campaign and his presidential campaign two years later.

180. *Created Equal?* at 36–37.

181. Kluger, *Simple Justice* at 696.

182. Martin Luther King, Jr., *Letter from Birmingham City Jail,* in *A Testament of Hope: The Essential Writings of Martin Luther King, Jr.* 289, 294 (James Melvin Washington ed) (Harper San Francisco, 1986). King wrote this letter in response to eight white clergymen who called his demonstrations "unwise and untimely" and urged him

to end them. King drafted the letter partly on the edges of the Birmingham newspaper in which the clergymen's statement was published and partly on paper that his lawyer smuggled into jail. See David B. Oppenheimer, *Martin's March,* ABA J, June 1994, at 54.

183. See, for example, Fortas, *Concerning Dissent and Disobedience* at 30, 34, 37.

184. See id at 16, 31, 32.

185. See Sarah Bradford, *Harriet Tubman, The Moses of Her People* 33 (G. P. Lockwood, 1961).

186. Contrary to the apparent assumptions of those who consider only open, nonviolent disobedience appropriate, the goal of disobedience may not be to prick the community's conscience. Its object may be to free slaves or to keep cattle cars from rolling to the death camps.

187. See William L. Shirer, *The Rise and Fall of the Third Reich* 1050–54 (Simon & Schuster, 1960).

188. See Letter from Thomas Jefferson to William Stephens Smith, in 5 *The Writings of Thomas Jefferson* at 362 (Paul Leicester Ford ed) (Putnam's, 1904) ("The tree of liberty must be refreshed from time to time with the blood of patriots and tyrants."); Malcolm X, *The Black Revolution,* in *Malcolm X Speaks* 45, 49 (George Breitman ed) (Grove, 1966) ("If George Washington didn't get independence for this country nonviolently, and if Patrick Henry didn't come up with a nonviolent statement, and you taught me to look upon them as patriots and heroes, then it's time for you to realize that I have studied your books well.").

189. Qualities like baldness do not become undefinable simply because they may be matters of more-or-less, but these qualities can be conveyed by describing one or a few variables. The process of law recognition is not like that. The influential variables are too numerous and complex to fit within any manageable definition.

190. Ronald Dworkin, *Taking Rights Seriously* at 106.

191. Luban draws upon H. L. A. Hart's and John Rawls's "fair play" theories of obligation. See H. L. A. Hart, *Are There Any Natural Rights?,* 64 Phil Rev 175, 185 (1955); John Rawls, *Legal Obligation and the Duty of Fair Play,* in *Law and Philosophy* 3, 9 (Sidney Hook ed) (NYU Press, 1964) ("If one thinks of the constitution as a fundamental part of the scheme of social cooperation, then one can say that if the constitution is just, and if one has accepted the benefits of its working and intends to continue doing so, and if the rule enacted is within certain limits, then one has an obligation, based on the principle of fair play, to obey it when it comes one's turn.").

192. Luban includes small-scale cooperative schemes that are not regarded as creating legal obligations—projects like forming an orderly line at a bus stop. To transform Luban's checklist into a rough definition of law, one must limit it to cooperative schemes of a particular kind—"societal settlements," perhaps, or if that formulation is too inclusive, "governmentally prescribed societal settlements."

193. Luban initially offered his views of legal obligation in David Luban, *Lawyers and Justice* 31–49 (Princeton Univ Press, 1988). He has defended and refined these

views in Luban, *Freedom and Constraint in Legal Ethics: Some Mid-Course Corrections to Lawyers and Justice,* 49 Md L Rev 424, 454–62 (1990), and Luban, *Conscientious Lawyers for Conscientious Lawbreakers,* 52 U Pitt L Rev at 803–09.

194. Luban in fact endorses neither of these approaches. He declares that "even though we must not simply lump all laws together by asking about our obligation to obey 'the law' (meaning every law), we *should* assess the fairness of each law against the background of other laws as well as on its own terms." Luban, *Freedom and Constraint in Legal Ethics,* 49 Md L Rev at 457. Lincoln would have approved (and so do I), but this approach moves beyond the checklist.

195. I assume that inflicting physical injury would be appropriate if it were necessary to rescue a person who had been kidnapped by another person acting *without* color of law.

196. If someone were to ask why the public's rough understanding should motivate her at all, the answer might begin with the concepts of generality and reciprocity emphasized by Dworkin and Luban. As classic social contract theorists recognized, the alternative to law is a world in which each individual resolves disputed issues for herself, one in which social life is impossible. And once someone recognizes the need for law, the question becomes one of identifying it. Can she (or anyone else) know this social institution when she sees it? A person may not have a neat answer to this question, but the success of the public in identifying law most of the time is an evident fact. A rough, shared understanding of the concept of law should at least cast the burden of justifying dissent onto the dissenter. When a sociologist or a legal theorist can identify more precisely the circumstances that produce the general recognition of law, so much the better. But that is where things get sticky.

197. Abraham Lincoln, *First Inaugural Address, Mar 4, 1861, in 8 Messages and Papers of the Presidents* 3210 (James Richardson ed) (Bureau of National Literature, 1911).

198. Compare Martin Luther, 31 *Luther's Works* 44 (Harold J. Grimm ed) (Muhlenbert, 1958) ("I shall set down the following two propositions concerning the freedom and bondage of the spirit: A Christian is a perfectly free lord of all, subject to none. A Christian is a perfectly dutiful servant of all, subject to all."); Duncan Kennedy, *The Structure of Blackstone's Commentaries,* 28 Buff L Rev 205, 211–12 (1979) (describing as "the fundamental contradiction" the tension between the need to give power to other people and the need not to give them too much).

199. Perhaps our admiration for Lincoln would be even greater if he had resisted the fugitive slave clause as he did *Dred Scott.* We might never have heard of Lincoln, however, if he had taken this step and disqualified himself from holding political office.

200. Abraham Lincoln, *The Perpetuation of Our Political Institutions: Address Before the Young Men's Lyceum of Springfield, Illinois,* Jan 27, 1838, in *Abraham Lincoln: His Speeches and Writings* 76, 81 (Roy P. Basler ed) (World Publishing, 1946).

201. *Created Equal?* at 311. Just as fire was the most frequent and prominent metaphor in Holmes's writings, light was the most frequent and prominent in Lincoln's.

202. See David Herbert Donald, *Lincoln* 283 (Simon & Schuster, 1995); Robert Johannsen, *Stephen A. Douglas* 843 (Oxford Univ Press, 1973).

203. Johannsen, *Stephen A. Douglas* at 844–45.

204. Id at 859.

205. Id at 820.

206. Id at 866–67.

207. Id at 845, 869.

208. See Damon Wells, *Stephen Douglas: The Last Years 1857–1861* at 289 (Univ of Texas Press, 1971); Johannsen, *Stephen A. Douglas* at 872. Although the language quoted in the text is chiseled into Douglas's sarcophagus, the Johannsen biography quotes slightly different language, and Wells doubts that Douglas in fact uttered his famous last words. Wells notes, however, that Douglas had used similar language in his address to the Illinois General Assembly a few weeks before his death. Wells, *Stephen Douglas* at 289.

209. Holmes, *The Path of the Law,* 10 Harv L Rev at 460, reprinted in 3 *Collected Works* at 392–93.

210. See id at 461–62, reprinted in 3 *Collected Works* at 392–93.

211. Id at 462, reprinted in 3 *Collected Works* at 394.

212. Id, reprinted in 3 *Collected Works* at 394.

213. Compare Kelsen, *General Theory of Law and the State* at 167–68 ("The existence of a duty is the legal necessity, not the factual probability, of a sanction.").

214. Blackstone articulated an alternative theory of *mala prohibita* offenses a century before Holmes voiced "the alternative theory of contracts." Blackstone wrote that "in regard to . . . such offenses as are *mala in se* . . . we are bound in conscience. . . ." Nevertheless, we are not "bound in conscience" when laws "enjoin only positive duties, and forbid only such things as are not *mala in se* but *mala prohibita*":

> [I]n these cases the alternative is offered to every man: "Either abstain from this or submit to such a penalty," and his conscience will be clear whichever side of the alternative he thinks proper to embrace. Thus, by statutes for preserving the game, a penalty is announced against every unqualified person that kills a hare. Now these prohibitory laws do not make the transgression a moral offense or sin: the only obligation in conscience is to submit to the penalty if levied.

William Blackstone, 1 *Commentaries* * 57–58 (spelling and punctuation modernized). Blackstone's theory may understate the obligation that people should recognize to obey regulatory legislation; at least Blackstone's 225-year-old views are too Holmesian for me. The most noteworthy aspect of Blackstone's statement, however, may be its recognition that an "alternative" theory appropriately characterizes some obligations while the language of duty appropriately characterizes others.

215. Holmes, *The Path of the Law,* 10 Harv L Rev at 461, reprinted in 3 *Collected Works* at 393.

216. Id, reprinted in 3 *Collected Works* at 394.

217. Holmes's offhand reference to *wrongful* conversions of property amidst his criticism of the use of moral terminology in law is ironic. This reference suggests the magnitude of the task of self-censorship that Holmes proposed.

218. See, for example, Holmes, *The Common Law* at 148.

219. Holmes, *The Path of the Law,* 10 Harv L Rev at 462, reprinted in 3 *Collected Works* at 394.

220. Oliver Wendell Holmes, Jr., *Article Review,* 6 Am L Rev 723 (1872), reprinted in 1 *Collected Works* at 294, 296 (reviewing Frederick Pollock, *Law and Command,* 1 Law Mag & Rev 189 (1872)).

221. Holmes, *The Path of the Law,* 10 Harv L Rev at 462, reprinted in 3 *Collected Works* at 394.

222. Id at 461, reprinted in 3 *Collected Works* at 394.

223. See text at 143–44.

224. Holmes, *The Path of the Law,* 10 Harv L Rev at 459, reprinted in 3 *Collected Works* at 392.

225. Holmes, *The Common Law* at 38.

226. See Richard A. Posner, *An Economic Theory of the Criminal Law,* 85 Colum L Rev 1193, 1203–04 (1985).

227. See id.

228. An economically minded scholar might respond that imprisonment is a very costly sanction. Society can inflict the same disutility on a wrongdoer through imprisonment as through an award of damages, but not at the same price. Perhaps, just perhaps, the line between criminal and civil responsibility marks the point at which the high price of imprisonment becomes justified. This response seems implausible. Defective products, negligently labeled foods and drugs, and other "mass torts" can inflict more harm than the most tireless shoplifter, robber, or murderer could inflict in a lifetime.

229. Compare Stephen J. Schulhofer, *Criminal Justice Discretion as a Regulatory System,* 17 J Legal Stud 43, 48 n8 (1988).

230. For more detailed and scholarly arguments against viewing the criminal law as simply a system of pricing, see John C. Coffee, *Does "Unlawful" Mean "Criminal"? Reflections on the Disappearing Tort/Crime Distinction in American Law,* 71 BU L Rev 193 (1991); Kenneth Dau-Schmidt, *An Economic Analysis of the Criminal Law as a Preference-Shaping Possibility,* 1990 Duke L J 1; Louis Michael Seidman, *Soldiers, Martyrs, and Criminals: Utilitarian Theory and the Problem of Crime Control,* 94 Yale L J 315 (1984); Schulhofer, *Criminal Justice as a Regulatory System,* 17 J Legal Stud 43. See generally Henry M. Hart, *The Aims of the Criminal Law,* 23 Law and Contemp Probs 401 (1958).

231. Even as an economic matter, however, the scholars are probably wrong. When economists call something efficient, one must ask (as the economists recognize),

"Compared to what?" Although breach sometimes may seem efficient when compared to performance, that comparison is often inapt.

An alternative to both performance and breach is rescission by mutual consent. When a contracting party sees an opportunity to profit from the non-completion of a contract, she should be able to negotiate with the other contracting party for rescission, and an inability to secure rescission probably would indicate the "Kaldor-Hicks inefficiency" of her default. In other words, the non-performing party probably would not profit *enough* from her nonperformance to be able to compensate the other party for his losses (as those losses are valued subjectively by the other party).

The existence of the contractual relationship suggests that the "transaction costs" incurred in negotiating a mutually satisfactory solution would be low, and the costs of using a third party to ascertain damages often would drive the "process costs" of breach well above the "transaction costs" of negotiating rescission. Breach, moreover, produces "error costs" in the assessment of damages that could be avoided by permitting the injured party to value his own losses through negotiation. In other words, unilateral breach bypasses the use of a market-like mechanism for determining both whether abandonment of the contract would be wealth-maximizing and how the surplus generated by this abandonment should be divided. See Alan Schwartz, *The Case for Specific Performance,* 89 Yale L J 271 (1979); Thomas S. Ulen, *The Efficiency of Specific Performance: Toward a Unified Theory of Contract Remedies,* 83 Mich L Rev 341 (1984); David Friedman, *The Efficient Breach Fallacy,* 18 J Legal Stud 1 (1989); Ian Macneil, *Efficient Breach of Contract: Circles in the Sky,* 68 Va L Rev 947 (1982). But see Richard A. Posner, *Economic Analysis of Law* §§ 4.9, 4.12 (Little, Brown, 4th ed 1992); Richard A. Posner, *The Strangest Attack Yet on Law and Economics,* 20 Hofstra L Rev 933 (1992).

Punishing breach of contract even by death or imprisonment probably would not lead to the inefficient performance of contracts very often. When performance would be inefficient, contracting parties usually could arrange to share whatever benefits either one might gain from revising or rescinding their earlier agreement. My purpose in emphasizing the option of negotiated rescission, however, is not to propose the enforcement of contracts through capital punishment, to urge more frequent use of specific performance, or to propose any other alteration in the law of contract remedies. (The death penalty would in fact lead to the inefficient performance of contracts—not to mention death—often enough to make the idea a very poor one.) My goal is simply to explore the narrow issue that Holmes raised, the desirability of using moralistic language to characterize contractual undertakings.

This issue may seem more symbolic than consequential. At least the consequences of its resolution may lie more in shaping people's attitudes than in influencing the rate of contractual default in the short run. Even in the short run, however, the traditional use of moralistic terminology adds some weight to the side of the scale opposed to default. I see no reason to doubt that this tilt is desirable and efficient. The words to which Holmes objected encourage contracting parties to seek a mutually beneficial accommodation with one another rather than resort to unilateral breach at the first scent of profit.

232. To be sure, even when breach appears efficient, a contracting party could appropriately adhere to the contract if she would gain enough personal satisfaction from keeping her promise to be worth the lost profits.

233. The following observations of James Gustafson apply to at least some contractual defaults:

> The experience of betrayal of trust is, perhaps, one of the most bitter of human life. . . . Something about human relations that cannot be fully encompassed in a rule is violated in broken trust—whether promise-keeping, expectations that the other will tell one the truth, [or] reliance on institutions to meet their commitments and fulfill their functions. . . . Betrayal and deception are the sins against trust, and elaborate indeed are the cultural and social devices that have been developed to guard against them: vows, contracts, promises, surveillance procedures, laws, and regulations.

James M. Gustafson, 1 *Ethics from a Theocentric Perspective* 303 (Univ of Chicago Press, 1981).

234. As I have suggested in note 231, although this moralistic position is often rejected by law and economic scholars, it might in fact promote efficiency. A positive correlation between conventional morality and efficiency should come as no surprise.

235. Frederick Pollock, *Principles of Contract Law* xix (Stevens and Sons, 3d ed 1881). Pollock and Holmes disputed the alternative theory of contracts in their lengthy correspondence. See Pollock to Holmes, July 3, 1874, in 1 *The Holmes–Pollock Letters: The Correspondence of Mr. Justice Holmes and Sir Frederick Pollock, 1874–1932* at 3 (Mark DeWolfe Howe ed) (Harvard Univ Press, 1941); Holmes to Pollock, Mar 25, 1883, in 1 id at 21; Pollock to Holmes, Sept 17, 1897, in 1 id at 79–80; Holmes to Pollock, Mar 12, 1911, in 1 id at 177. For scholarly support of Pollock's position, see Charles Fried, *Contract as Promise* (Harvard Univ Press, 1981).

236. In this case, delivery of the coat to Trump without the purchaser's consent would maximize social utility only as a matter of economic definition. The case for breach might be stronger if Trump had told the tailor that he planned to give the coat to a homeless person whom he had just seen shivering outside the tailor's shop.

237. Karl Llewellyn, *A Realistic Jurisprudence—The Next Step,* 30 Colum L Rev 431, 437 (1930).

238. Id at 434.

239. Id at 437.

240. See, for example, Albert W. Alschuler, *Mediation with a Mugger: The Shortage of Adjudicative Services and the Need for a Two-Tier Trial System in Civil Cases,* 99 Harv L Rev 1808 (1986) (describing America's cost-ineffective legal system).

241. Most notably, our law does not permit an award of punitive damages for breach of contract and infrequently orders specific performance of a contract.

242. Compare Holmes, *The Path of the Law,* 10 Harv L Rev at 462, reprinted in 3 *Collected Works* at 394. Law and economics scholars especially should embrace traditional moral terminology. The common law's use of this language provides further support for the economists' thesis that the common law is efficient.

243. Oliver Wendell Holmes, *The Profession of Law,* in 3 *Collected Works* at 471, 473.

244. See text at 132.

245. Id.

Chapter Eight

1. Catherine Drinker Bowen, *The Yankee from Olympus* 408 (Atlantic/Little, Brown, 1944).

2. Liva Baker, *The Justice from Beacon Hill: The Life and Times of Oliver Wendell Holmes* 4 (HarperCollins, 1991).

3. Described as beautiful even by people disenchanted with him. See G. Edward White, *Justice Oliver Wendell Holmes: Law and the Inner Self* 92 (Oxford Univ Press, 1993).

4. A similar phenomenon in the 1980s and 1990s led observers to treat as liberal heroes such unlikely figures as Justice Ruth Bader Ginsburg and Justice John Paul Stevens. Although the Court on which Holmes served gave progressives little to cheer, this Court was no more monolithic than the Supreme Court today. During Holmes's thirty years on the Court, there was only a five-year gap between the death of one undoubted liberal hero, John Marshall Harlan (who was on the Court when Holmes arrived), and the appointment of another, Louis D. Brandeis (who was on the Court when Holmes departed). Throughout this five-year gap, a jurist who could fairly be described as a moderate-to-liberal hero, Charles Evans Hughes, was among Holmes's colleagues. It is difficult to think of a Supreme Court justice today who could be regarded as the heir of Hughes, Harlan, or Brandeis.

5. See Baker, *The Justice from Beacon Hill* at 17–18.

6. See Grant Gilmore, *The Ages of American Law* 48–49 (Yale Univ Press, 1977) (quoted in chapter 3 at 31–32).

7. White, *Justice Oliver Wendell Holmes* at 355–56.

8. Id at 408–09.

9. Id at 357–58 (footnotes omitted).

10. Sanford Levinson, *Fan Letters,* 75 Texas L Rev 1471, 1475, 1476, 1479 (1997). Levinson also uses the words *superficial, sycophantic,* and *fawning* to describe Frankfurter. Id at 1474, 1480.

11. The editors of the Holmes–Frankfurter correspondence comment, "Here began a relentless campaign to lionize Holmes. . . ." Robert M. Mennel and Christine M. Compson, *Introduction* to *Holmes and Frankfurter: Their Correspondence, 1912–*

1934 at xi, xvii (Robert M. Mennel and Christine M. Compson eds) (Univ Press of New England, 1996).

12. Felix Frankfurter, *The Constitutional Opinions of Justice Holmes,* 29 Harv L Rev 683 (1916). As G. Edward White describes Frankfurter's article, it "primarily consisted of a number of long quotations from Holmes' opinions, interspersed with commentary that often bordered on the vapid." White, *Justice Oliver Wendell Holmes* at 361. Upon receiving the symposium issue, Holmes wrote Frankfurter, "I can't tell you how touched and charmed I am. Very few things in life have given me so much pleasure." Id at 363. In the correspondence between Holmes and Frankfurter and between Holmes and Laski, each correspondent studiously avoids any significant expression of hostility or criticism while showering the other with praise. See Mennel and Compston, *Introduction* to *Holmes and Frankfurter* at xlii (observing that Holmes and Frankfurter became close partly because of "their mutual need for admiration").

13. Felix Frankfurter, *Twenty Years of Mr. Justice Holmes's Constitutional Opinions,* 36 Harv L Rev 909 (1923).

14. See Baker, *The Justice from Beacon Hill* at 564.

15. Id at 590. As early as 1916, Holmes wrote a correspondent, "Do you see the *New Republic?* . . . [T]he young men who write in it are, some of them, friends of mine, which doesn't prevent an occasional, flattering reference to this old man. . . . I fear they would be empty names to you. Frankfurter (Professor at Harvard Law School), Walter Lippman, Croly, Laski, etc." Holmes to Lewis Einstein, Aug 12, 1916, in *The Holmes–Einstein Letters: Correspondence of Mr. Justice Holmes and Lewis Einstein 1903–1935* at 135, 136 (James Bishop Peabody ed) (St. Martin's, 1964). Holmes wrote another correspondent that Laski, Frankfurter, "and the *New Republic* lot . . . make much of your venerable uncle and not only so, but by bringing an atmosphere of intellectual freedom in which one can breathe, make life to him a good deal more pleasant." Holmes to Sir Frederick Pollock, Feb 18, 1917, in 1 *The Holmes–Pollock Letters: The Correspondence of Mr. Justice Holmes and Sir Frederick Pollock 1874–1932* at 243, 243–44 (Harvard Univ Press, 1942). Holmes's declarations to Frankfurter of how much pleasure their relationship brought him are quoted in chapter 5 at 242–43 n204.

16. *Mr. Justice Holmes* (Felix Frankfurter ed) (Coward-McCaun, 1931).

17. See Felix Frankfurter, *Mr. Justice Holmes,* 48 Harv L Rev 1279 (1935); Felix Frankfurter, *Oliver Wendell Holmes, Jr.,* in 2 *Dictionary of American Biography* (supp I) 417 (Scribner's, 1944); Felix Frankfurter, *Foreword,* to 1 *The Holmes–Laski Letters: The Correspondence of Mr. Justice Holmes and Harold J. Laski, 1916–1935* at xiii (Mark De-Wolfe Howe ed) (Harvard Univ Press, 1953); Felix Frankfurter, *Mr. Justice Holmes and the Supreme Court* (Harvard Univ Press, Belknap Press, 2d ed 1965).

18. See Jeffrey O'Connell and Thomas E. O'Connell, *Book Review,* 55 Md L Rev 1384, 1394 n51 (1996) (reviewing Isaac Kramnick and Barry Sheerman, *Harold Laski: A Life on the Left* (Penguin, 1993) and Michael Newman, *Harold Laski: A Political Biography* (Macmillan, 1993)).

19. Laski to Holmes, July 7, 1916, quoted in Baker, *The Justice from Beacon Hill* at 488.

20. Id.

21. Oliver Wendell Holmes, Jr., *Collected Legal Papers* (Harcourt, Brace, 1920). See Baker, *The Justice from Beacon Hill* at 551; White, *Justice Oliver Wendell Holmes* at 365–66.

22. Sheldon M. Novick, *Editorial Principles,* in 1 *The Collected Works of Justice Holmes: Complete Public Writings and Selected Judicial Opinions of Oliver Wendell Holmes* xxi, xxiv (Sheldon M. Novick ed) (Univ of Chicago Press, 1995).

23. 160 Harper's Magazine 415 (1930).

24. 40 Yale L J 683 (1931).

25. Baker, *The Justice from Beacon Hill* at 9. See White, *Justice Oliver Wendell Holmes* at 378 ("In their haste to make Holmes into a figure of legend his enthusiasts . . . showed an inclination to distort his views."); G. Edward White, *Holmes's "Life Plan": Confronting, Ambition, Passion, and Powerlessness,* 65 NYU L Rev 1409, 1460 (1990) 1460 ("[A] group of early twentieth-century reformist intellectuals, the most prominent of whom was Felix Frankfurter, . . . can fairly be described as Holmes's mythmakers."); Mennel and Compston, *Introduction* to *Holmes and Frankfurter* at xvii ("That Holmes's actual decisions were inconsistent [with Frankfurter's portrayal of them] did not disturb Frankfurter in the least.").

26. See I. Scott Messinger, *The Judge as Mentor: Oliver Wendell Holmes, Jr., and His Law Clerks,* 11 Yale J Law and Humanities 119 (1999).

27. Id at 126.

28. See id at 124 n15 (quoting Alger Hiss, *Recollections of a Life* 40 (Holt, Seaver Books, 1988)).

29. Id at 135 n65 (quoting W. Barton Leach, *Recollections of a Holmes Secretary* (unpublished 1940)).

30. Id at 139 n83 (quoting Leach, *Recollections of a Holmes Secretary*).

31. Id at 133 (describing the unpublished diary of Chaucey Belknap).

32. Id at 139. Messinger comments that Holmes "enjoyed being the object of hero worship" and that his clerks served a "companionate function." Id at 125.

33. Frankfurter to Holmes, Jan 14, 1916, in *Holmes and Frankfurter* at 42.

34. Holmes to Frankfurter, Dec 19, 1915, in id at 42.

35. Holmes to Frankfurter, Jan 6, 1925, in id at 178.

36. Messinger, *The Judge as Mentor,* 11 Yale J Law and Humanities at 145 n104 (citing Harry C. Shriver, *What Justice Holmes Wrote and What Has Been Written about Him: A Bibliography 1866–1976* (Fox Hills, 1978) and adding that the figure noted in text may well be too low).

37. Morton White, *The Revolt against Formalism in American Social Thought of the Twentieth Century,* 8 J Hist of Ideas 131 (1947) (also published as chapter 2 of White's *Social Thought in America* (Viking, 1949)).

38. See Holmes to Morris Cohen, Feb 5, 1919, quoted in Sheldon M. Novick, *Honorable Justice: The Life of Oliver Wendell Holmes* 412 n11 (Little, Brown, 1989).

Chapter Nine

1. See Robert Samuel Summers, *Instrumentalism and American Legal Theory* 32 (Cornell Univ Press, 1982) (for pragmatists, "something is true if it proves to be useful in the appropriate human activity in the long run.").

2. Albert Borgmann, *Crossing the Postmodern Divide* 6 (Univ of Chicago Press, 1992).

3. See Jeremy Waldron, *Minority Cultures and the Cosmopolitan Alternatives,* 25 Mich J L Reform 751, 764–65 (1992).

4. Borgmann, *Crossing the Postmodern Divide* at 10.

5. See id at 8.

6. Robert D. Putnam, *Have We Become a Generation of Loners?,* Arizona Republic, Jan 16, 1996, at B5.

7. See the discussion of Adam's reasons for obeying and disobeying parking regulations in chapter 7 at 149–50.

8. The Council on Civil Society, *A Call to Civil Society: Why Democracy Needs Moral Truths* 3 (Institute for American Values, 1998) (report of a group of scholars and community leaders chaired by Jean Bethke Elshtain).

9. See Gregg Easterbrook, *Nabobs of Negativism: American Optimism Is the Last Refuge of Rubes and Babbitts, Say the Influential Pessimists, But Can a Society without Hope Still Try to Improve Itself?,* Los Angeles Times, May 12, 1996, at M1. In addition, the danger of global nuclear warfare has lessened since the days of Nikita Khrushchev.

10. See Putnam, *Have We Become a Generation of Loners?,* Arizona Republic, Jan 16, 1996, at B5 ("In the 1950s 75 percent [of Americans] said they 'trusted the government in Washington to do what is right most of the time,' but that barometer of civic health has plummeted steadily for three decades and now stands at barely 20 percent.").

11. See Robert Hughes, *The Culture of Complaint* 50 (Warner Books, 1993) ("To divide a polity you must have scapegoats and hate objects—human caricatures that dramatize the difference between Them and Us.").

12. See International Monetary Fund, *Balance of Payments Statistics Yearbook, Part 2: World and Regional Tables* at table A-2 (vol 48) (1997).

13. Borgmann, *Crossing the Postmodern Divide* at 44.

14. Sometimes, however, it is clever, sophisticated, chic, and dissociative. A prominent work included in a 1995 exhibit at the Museum of Contemporary Art in Chicago consisted of a dead lamb floating in a container of formaldehyde. The work was titled "Away From the Flock." Its creator described it as "quite an optimistic piece." An essay in the exhibit's catalogue said that this work revealed "the melancholy results of prescience, the decay that follows birth, violence after order, the particular leitmotif of what D. H. Lawrence called 'this essentially tragic age.'" The *Chicago Tribune* called the exhibit humdrum and visually conservative.

Alan G. Arthur, *Nothing's Shocking: Biggest Surprise of MCA Show Is That It's Humdrum,* Chicago Tribune, Jan 29, 1995, at § 13, p 20. In June 1998, a "seminal" work by Bruce Nauman consisting of a tape recorder enclosed in a concrete block and emitting a woman's continuous screams fetched $288,000 at a New York City auction. See David Ebony, *Christie's: Auction House of Kunsthalle? Exhibition of Works from the Herbig Collection at Christie's Auction House,* Art in America, May 1998, at 31.

15. For extreme examples, see MTV, *South Park, Beavis and Butthead,* rap lyrics, slasher films, Howard Stern, and Jerry Springer.

16. Marc Mauer, *Race to Incarcerate* 19 (The Sentencing Project, 1999).

17. Id.

18. See Fox Butterfield, *1 in 3 Young Black Men Is Caught Up in the Criminal Justice System,* NY Times, Oct 8, 1995, at § 4, p 2.

19. U.S. Bureau of the Census, U.S. Dep't of Commerce, March Current Population Survey at table H-2, at <http://www.census.gov/hhes/income/histinc/h02.html> (revised Oct 1, 1999).

20. Borgmann, *Crossing the Postmodern Divide* at 10.

21. See Victor Fuchs and Diane Reklis, *America's Children: Economic Perspectives and Policy Options,* 255 Science 41, 41–42 (Jan 3, 1992).

22. Karen Brandon, *Teen Girls Wising Up on Having Children,* Chicago Tribune, May 3, 1999, at § 1, p. 1. See *The Alan Guttmacher Institute, Teenage Pregnancy: Overall Trends and State by State Information,* at table 1 (April 1999) (at <http://www.agi-usa.org/pubs/teen_preg_states.html>).

23. See Brandon, *Teen Girls Wising Up on Having Children,* Chicago Tribune, May 3, 1999, at 1.

24. Bureau of the Census, U.S. Dep't of Commerce, *Statistical Abstract of the United States 1998* at 81 (1998).

25. Roger Worthington, *Adding Father to the Family,* Chicago Tribune, Feb 14, 1994, at § 1, p 1. Approximately 240,00 American children lived with a single, never-married parent in 1963; 3.7 million did in 1983; and 6.3 million—27 percent of all children—did in 1993. Births to unmarried women increased more than 70 percent between 1983 and 1993. In two-parent households, the median income is $43,578. In one-parent households following divorce, it is $17,014. In the one-parent households of never-married parents, it is $9,272. *The Coming Apart of America,* Chicago Tribune, July 23, 1994, at § 1, p. 18.

26. See Fuchs and Reklis, *America's Children,* 255 Science at 42–43.

27. See Fox Butterfield, *Homicides Plunge 11 Percent in U.S., F.B.I. Report Says,* NY Times, June 2, 1997, at A1 (quoting James Alan Fox). See also Fox Butterfield, *After a Decade, Juvenile Crime Begins to Drop,* NY Times, Aug 9, 1996, at A1 ("[T]he homicide rate for young people aged 10 to 17 rose to 14.5 per 100,000 in 1993, up from 5.4 per 100,000 in 1984. Then in 1994 it dropped to 13.2 per 100,000 and in 1995 to 11.2 per 100,000.").

28. See *School Officials, Police Grapple with Shootings,* Raleigh News and Observer, June 10, 1998, at A7; Richard A. Serrano, *Tragedy in Colorado,* Los Angeles Times, Apr 23, 1999, at A1; Edith Stanley and J. R. Moehringer, *Six Students Shot in Georgia,* Los Angeles Times, May 21, 1999, at A1.

29. Lloyd D. Johnston, Jerold G. Bachman, and Patrick M. O'Malley, *Monitoring the Future: Questionnaire Responses from the Nation's High School Seniors* 26 (Univ of Michigan, 1996).

30. U.S. Dep't of Health and Human Resources, *Trends in the Well-Being of America's Children and Youth: 1998* at table PF 2.3 (1999).

31. Id at 171, table HC 2.6.

32. Kay Redfield Jamison, *Night Falls Fast: Understanding Suicide* 21–22 (Knopf, 1999).

33. Greg Kot, *Porno for Pyros' Act a Fizzled Freak Show,* Chicago Tribune, June 14, 1993, at § 1, p 16.

34. Although what I call the "new epistemology" is associated primarily with post–World War II writers in philosophy and other fields, one might call Albert Einstein its father. For his pre–World War II articulation of important aspects of this new understanding, see Albert Einstein, *Physics and Reality,* 221 J of the Franklin Institute 349, 349–354 (1936) (noting that by developing concepts and examining the relationships among them, "we are able to orient ourselves in the labyrinth of sense impressions," defining "comprehensibility" as "the production of some sort of order among sense impressions," and describing our ability to make sense impressions comprehensible as a "miracle.").

35. I do not suggest that these terms are synonyms—only that they describe aspects of the same reasoning process. I recognize that the writings of some early pragmatists contributed to the epistemology I describe. What the pragmatists failed to see is that the perception of patterns in our sensory experience is not simply a matter of convention, consensus, personal preference, or adaptive success. The patterns that people discern are partly the product of the world around them.

36. Michael Moore, *Moral Reality,* 1982 Wis L Rev 1061, 1112–13.

37. Nelson Goodman, *Fact, Fiction and Forecast* 64 (Harvard Univ Press, 4th ed 1983). See also W. V. Quine, *From a Logical Point of View* (Harvard Univ Press, 1953); Gilbert Harman, *Thought* (Princeton Univ Press, 1973); John Rawls, *A Theory of Justice* 20–21 (Harvard Univ Press, Belknap Press, 1971); Michael Moore, *Moral Reality Revisited,* 90 Mich L Rev 2424 (1992).

38. Howard Margolis, *Thinking and Cognition: A Theory of Judgment* 73 (Univ of Chicago Press, 1987).

39. See Michael Polanyi, *Personal Knowledge: Towards a Post-Critical Philosophy* 69–131 (Univ of Chicago Press, 2d ed 1962).

40. See Martha Nussbaum, *Love's Knowledge: Essays on Philosophy and Literature* 40–42 (Oxford Univ Press, 1990) (rejecting the view that emotions are "blind animal reactions . . . in their nature unmixed with thought, undiscriminating and impervious to reasoning" and describing emotions as "intelligent parts of our ethical agency"); Ronald de Sousa, *The Rationality of Emotions,* in *Explaining Emotions*

(Amelie Oksenberg Rorty ed) (Univ of California Press, 1980); Lynne N. Henderson, *Legality and Empathy,* 85 Mich L Rev 1574 (1987).

41. A natural (but not inevitable) implication of pragmatism's forward-looking approach to truth is that the more constructions of reality we have, the more likely one or another of them is to "work." Pragmatism encourages the sense that every person (or every culture) is free to make up her own reality—indeed, that she has no alternative.

42. Einstein is quoted in Burton G. Malkiel, *A Random Walk down Wall Street* 210 (Norton, 4th ed 1985). The legal realist Jerome Frank complained, "Einstein—as a philosopher, not a scientist—longs for a tidy universe, a sort of old maid's paradise, with everything in place and a complete inventory of the world's contents." Jerome Frank, *Courts on Trial: Myth and Reality in American Jurisprudence* 361 (Princeton Univ Press, 1973 (1949)).

43. See Oliver Wendell Holmes, *Address of Chief Justice Holmes at the Dedication of the Northwestern University Law School Building, Chicago,* Oct 20, 1902, in 3 *Collected Works of Justice Holmes: Complete Public Writings and Selected Judicial Opinions of Oliver Wendell Holmes* 529, 530 (Sheldon M. Novick ed) (Univ of Chicago Press, 1995) (hereinafter cited as *Collected Works*).

44. Oliver Wendell Holmes, *Natural Law,* 32 Harv L Rev 40, 40–41 (1918), reprinted in 3 *Collected Works* at 445, 446.

45. See Laurence H. Tribe, *Channeling Technology through Law* (National Science Foundation, 1973); Laurence H. Tribe, *Ways Not to Think about Plastic Trees: New Foundations for Environmental Law,* 83 Yale L J 1315 (1974).

46. Harman, *Thought* at 164.

47. Id.

48. Holmes, *Natural Law* at 42–43, reprinted in 3 *Collected Works* at 447.

49. Bernard Williams, *Ethics and the Limits of Philosophy* 26 (Harvard Univ Press, 1985).

50. I do not mean that there is nothing one can say to someone who is incapable of distinguishing a moral objection to slavery from a fondness for apples. There is in fact a lot to say. See generally, for example, Moore, *Moral Reality.* My point (and Williams's) is simply that one should not accept the allocation of burdens implicit in the skeptic's "sez who?"

51. Now that Holmes's skeptical views have become conventional, the pleasure that he could take in being irascible and iconoclastic has faded and disappeared. This satisfaction was not one that he could transmit to his heirs.

Index

Dailey, Anne, 207n. 65
damages, 177–79
Darwin, Charles, 49, 226n. 84
Darwinism: epoch of moral realism
    ended by, 9; and historicism, 87;
    and the marketplace of ideas, 79,
    81; pragmatists influenced by,
    2–3. *See also* social Darwinism
Day, William R., 127
Debs, Eugene V., 72, 73, 238n. 157
Debs v United States (1919), 71–74, 76,
    77, 78, 238n. 148
defamation, law of, 69–70, 119
Delgado, Richard, 244n. 224
desires, 3, 5, 9
Dewey, John, 24, 183, 195n. 8, 206n.
    62
Dicey, Albert V., 106, 225n. 81
Dickinson, John, 94–95
Dietrich v Northampton (1884), 130
Director of Public Prosecutions v Smith
    (1961), 111
disobedience, nonviolent, 167, 191,
    294n. 186
dissenting opinions, 140
Dolinko, David, 138, 155–56, 282n. 91
Domat, Jean, 9
double jeopardy clause, 81–82
Douglas, Stephen A., 163, 166, 171–
    72, 296n. 208
Dred Scott v Sanford (1857), 166, 170,
    171, 293n. 178
Du Bois, W. E. B., 45, 223n. 45
Ducat v Chicago (1870), 227n. 2
Dunn v United States (1932), 82
Duns Scotus, John, 9
duty, 172–79
Dworkin, Andrea, 244n. 224
Dworkin, Ronald, 94, 168, 169, 295n.
    196

Easterbrook, Frank H., 259n. 52, 290n.
    156
economics: desires treated as exoge-
    nous, 3; law and economics move-
    ment, 3–4, 103, 176–77, 179;
    legislation viewed skeptically in,

6–7; public choice theory, 7; on
    revealed preferences, 125; as un-
    able to justify the minimal values
    it retains, 5
efficiency, 153
efficient breach, 177, 297n. 231, 299n.
    232
Eighth Amendment, 64, 233n. 77
Einstein, Albert, 191, 306n. 42
Einstein, Lewis, 32, 78
electronic surveillance, 83
Ellis, Havelock, 29
Elmer v Fessenden (1890), 119
Elshtain, Jean Bethke, 225n. 71
Emerson, Ralph Waldo, 41
enterprise liability, 115, 120
epistemology: moderate credulity, 194;
    the new epistemology, 12–13,
    190–94, 305nn. 34, 35. *See also*
    truth
Epstein, Richard A., 232n. 59
equality: conflicting claims of, 156;
    Holmes on, 26; in utilitarianism,
    5. *See also* racial equality
Erie RR Co v Tompkins (1938), 68
Espionage Act of 1917, 71–74
ethical skepticism. *See* moral skepticism
etiquette, 161
eugenics: *Buck v Bell,* 28, 65–67, 213n.
    159, 242n. 199; Holmes support-
    ing, 11, 16, 22, 27–29; positive
    and negative eugenics, 28
exclusionary rule, 82
existentialism, 19, 207nn. 69, 70,
    214n. 171
Exodus, Book of, 109
expression, freedom of. *See* freedom of
    expression

Fall v Eastin (1909), 228n. 13
Farrell, Perry, 189
Federalist Papers, 95
Feldman, Stephen M., 253n. 95, 255n.
    105, 259n. 154
feminist jurisprudence, 7, 8
Field, David Dudley, 90
fines, 177